Dafydd
Elis-Thomas

Dafydd Elis-Thomas

Nation Builder

Aled Eirug

UNIVERSITY OF WALES PRESS
2025

© Aled Eirug, 2025

Reprinted 2025

All rights reserved. No part of this book may be reproduced in any material form (including photocopying or storing it in any medium by electronic means and whether or not transiently or incidentally to some other use of this publication) without the written permission of the copyright owner except in accordance with the provisions of the Copyright, Designs and Patents Act 1988. Applications for the copyright owner's written permission to reproduce any part of this publication should be addressed to the University of Wales Press, University Registry, King Edward VII Avenue, Cardiff CF10 3NS.

www.uwp.co.uk

British Library Cataloguing-in-Publication Data
A catalogue record for this book is available from the British Library.

ISBN   978-1-83772-228-0
eISBN   978-1-83772-229-7

The right of Aled Eirug to be identified as author of this work has been asserted in accordance with sections 77 and 79 of the Copyright, Designs and Patents Act 1988.

For GPSR enquiries please contact:
Easy Access System Europe Oü, 16879218. Mustamäe tee 50, 10621, Tallinn, Estonia. gpsr.requests@easproject.com

Typeset by Marie Doherty
Printed and bound by CPI Group (UK) Ltd, Croydon, CR0 4YY

*This book is dedicated to the memory of
Dafydd Elis-Thomas, a great friend and life-force.*

*It is also dedicated to Alexandra, Holly,
Bençe, Max, Tane and Beca and our next
generation of 'nation-builders'!*

Contents

	Preface	ix
	List of Abbreviations	xiii
	List of Images	xv
1	The Golden Child	1
2	University Days	23
3	'A priest who has lost his faith'	53
4	The Aftermath of the 1979 Devolution Referendum – Heading Left	91
5	Taking the Ermine – for the Language	161
6	The Birth of the National Assembly for Wales	193
7	Dissent, Departure and Ministerial Office	253
	Postscript	303
	Notes	313
	Index	337

Preface

Lord Dafydd Elis-Thomas of Nant Conwy was one of the most controversial and magnetic Welsh public figures of the last fifty years. His political career spanned from joining Plaid Cymru in 1962, becoming the United Kingdom's youngest MP in 1974 at the age of 27, until May 2021 when he finally retired after twenty-two years of service as a member of the Senedd, the legislative parliament for Wales.

This biography is based on his own recollections given in a series of interviews with the author, and augmented by the perspectives of over seventy of his contemporaries. These interviews have been supplemented by material from archives, newspapers, biographies and memoirs, that shed light on his political journey.

He was branded a 'maverick' and a 'Merioneth Marxist', whose views upset many within his own party. He was labelled an 'intellectual acrobat and political chameleon', whose wit could sometimes outweigh his caution. He was branded a 'terrorist' for his interventions in Northern Ireland, and labelled a 'traitor' for opposing Sinn Féin's visit to language groups in Wales. And he courted controversy when, as a Plaid Cymru elected representative and party president, he publicly spurned the term 'nationalist'.

His fondness for smart dressing and his unashamed love of good wine and food grated with many of Plaid Cymru's more ascetic supporters. He was despised by many nationalists for his decision to join the House of Lords, changing his name to Baron Elis-Thomas of Nant Conwy. Many republicans reviled him for his respect for the monarchy. As the first Presiding Officer of the National Assembly for Wales, he stamped his authority on the institution and faced down attempts to bully and undermine him and the institution. In his relationship with the elected Assembly Members, he was charming, tolerant and compassionate, but could also be waspish and impatient.

The changes to his own name reflects the evolution of his political identity. This is an unorthodox biography, informed by a close friendship and a critical appreciation of the subject, but in the full understanding that Dafydd Êl would exercise no influence in the choice of interviewees, and of the judgements made by the author, and would not read the book until it was published. His untimely death on 7 February 2025 regrettably meant he would never read it.

I first met Dafydd Elis Thomas in 1975, when he was a charismatic and energetic young MP, and I was active in the Welsh language society, Cymdeithas yr Iaith Gymraeg, campaigning against the crisis in rural housing in Wales, and its impact on the Welsh language. He was already a well-known media figure who could as easily discuss postmodern concrete poetry as the future of the Cambrian Coast railway line. He inspired a younger generation in Wales to believe that political action could effect change, and as a Plaid MP in the 1970s and 1980s he supported Welsh language activists and could be relied upon to advocate causes such as the peace, feminist and anti-apartheid movements. He disavowed the description of him as a nationalist, and his political hinterland extended beyond his rugged and beautiful constituency to encompass an international perspective on human rights and assert Wales's place in Europe and the wider world.

He became the leader of the new Left in Wales, making Plaid an exciting and appealing political party to a younger generation, and pioneering his party's links with other political groups, for instance during the miners' strike.

Inevitably, his impatience with those who failed to understand his direction of travel, created frustrations for his party, but his presidency gave it momentum and, for good or ill, his leadership as chair of the Welsh Language Board removed the Welsh language out of the political arena to a large extent.

From 1974 onwards, he was a constant influence on the shape of Welsh politics, promoting devolution and enabling the 1997 referendum to be won.

As the first Presiding Officer of the National Assembly for Wales, he helped stabilise the new institution and, together with Rhodri Morgan, embedded devolution in its first tentative decade. His career was often marked by controversy, and certainly pursued power, but it was in order to improve the lives of the people he represented faithfully and passionately for five decades. This is what makes his story remarkable, just as his political life has proved to be unpredictable.

I am grateful to Dafydd for his trust in me as author, and for being so candid and open in conversation, which, I hope, captures the political essence of a remarkable individual. I am grateful to those kind archivists and librarians who have made the research for this book so much easier, including National Library of Wales staff, especially Iwan ap Dafydd for help with photographs, the Meirionnydd Archives and the Cardiff Cathays archives library. I am indebted to Peredur Lynch and the staff of Bangor University for their ready assistance in tracing Dafydd's academic career, and his role as the University's Chancellor. I am grateful to the staff of the University of Wales Press, its commissioning editor Llion Wigley, and its editor Dafydd Jones, for their continued support. I am especially grateful to those who have read and given detailed notes on various chapters, my friends Martin Shipton, Mark Palmer, Rhys Evans and Professor Sir Deian Hopkin – all mistakes are my own! I am, of course, particularly grateful to the many interviewees who gave their time and shared their insight, opinions and experience of Dafydd Elis's political contribution.

Lastly, I pay tribute and thanks to the one person who has made this publication possible – my wife Maggie, whose endless patience, love and understanding gave me the opportunity to complete this fascinating journey.

List of Abbreviations

DET   Dafydd Elis-Thomas

NLW   National Library of Wales

NA   National Archives

Dafydd Elis-Thomas's names and title

Lord Dafydd Elis-Thomas has several different iterations of his name.

He was born Dafydd Ellis Thomas, but changed his name to Dafydd Elis Thomas as a college student in the mid-1960s. His most radical change of name came when he was appointed a member of the House of Lords in September 1992, and became Lord Dafydd Elis-Thomas. For the sake of clarity, I have used the name he would have used himself in these different periods of his life, hoping that it will not confuse the reader.

List of Images

1. Dafydd's parents' wedding, 1944.
2. 'The golden child'.
3. Dafydd with his sister Elin Mair, 1960.
4. The winners of the Urdd public speaking competition at Llanrwst Grammar School, 1964.
5. Protesting against the Tryweryn dam, 1965. © Reach.
6. The lone protester, 1967.
7. Dafydd's wedding to Elen, 1970.
8. First elected as MP, 1974.
9. With Gwynfor Evans and Dafydd Wigley outside Parliament, 1974. © Aled Betts.
10. The 'President's committee', 1975. © Plaid Cymru.
11. Street politics, with the anti-apartheid campaign, 1982.
12. Dafydd and Elen's three sons, Rolant, Cai and Meilyr, 1981.
13. With Marjorie Thompson, 1992.
14. Dafydd's wedding to Mair, 1993.
15. Protesting against MoD proposals at RAF Brawdy, 1990.
16. With Cenwyn Edwards at HTV, 1988. © ITV Wales.
17. Dafydd at the Plaid Cymru conference in Porthmadog, 1991.
18. The Parliamentary handover, 1992. © Plaid Cymru.
19. As chairman of the Welsh Language Board, 1994.
20. With Sir Anthony Hopkins, 1998.
21. Celebrating the devolution referendum result, 1997.
22. With Edwina Hart, and the plan for the National Assembly building.
23. Honorary doctorate graduates at Bangor University, 2009. © Bangor University.
24. The opening of the National Assembly building, 2006.
25. With King Charles III.
26. The funeral procession before the Senedd, 2025. © Matthew Horwood.
27. The congregation at Llandaff Cathedral, 2025. © Matthew Horwood.

1

THE GOLDEN CHILD

Dafydd Ellis Thomas was born on 18 October 1946. His parents were William Ellis Thomas (W.E.), a minister of religion in the Presbyterian church of Seion, in the market town of Llanrwst, in the Conwy Valley, and Hannah Eirlys Thomas, formerly a teacher, from Newcastle Emlyn, in Carmarthenshire. His sister Elin was born on 27 April 1950, and this home proved a hothouse of cultural activity, with the children expected to participate in the extensive activity of the church. The lynchpin of this family was W.E.'s sister, Annie, who lived with them as a housekeeper and was a key influence on the two children, while Eirlys focused on her considerable social and pastoral duties.

Hannah Eirlys was born on 2 March 1916, one of two daughters of a prosperous builder, David Richard James and his wife Mary Jane, from Newcastle Emlyn. David Richard was Liberal in politics, a leading deacon in Bethel Presbyterian chapel, and a successful businessman while also a militant pacifist, and would undoubtedly have been involved in the League of Nations Union and its popular peace petition in 1924 that was signed by almost 400,000 Welsh women. Dafydd recalled being told of him walking two miles up the hill of Pant-y-Bwlch above the town, on every Remembrance Sunday morning, where he could avoid the pomp of the militarism that marked the local remembrance service.[1]

Mary had been a teacher in Maesteg, and her influence was reflected in her daughters' careers. Her elder daughter, Mary Gwenfil, trained at Swansea Teacher Training college, and then taught in Newcastle Emlyn primary school. She was unmarried, and lived in the family home, and unusually for women in this post-war period, became a deacon in Bethel Presbyterian chapel in Newcastle Emlyn.

Mary's other daughter, Eirlys, at the beginning of the Second World War, trained for a year at Swansea's Teacher Training College, before becoming an 'uncertificated' teacher in the elementary school in Llanbadarn Fynydd in Radnorshire. She subsequently moved to the village of Carrog near Corwen in east Merioneth near the border with Denbighshire, where she taught at the local county primary school. Her headmaster was W. D. Williams, a well-known poet and light entertainer, one of the stars of Welsh language radio on the BBC in the late 1930s. She became the accompanist to Williams's concert party of talented singers and harpists, which included Revd W. E. Thomas, the local minister.

In Newcastle Emlyn, David Richard's cousin Tom, had also profited from his involvement in housing developments, in Swansea's Sketty area, while the third brother David, worked in the busy docks area of the town in shipping companies' finance. Tom also had two daughters, Sarah Ann (known as Sal), who became a teacher and headmistress of Coed-y-bryn primary school, and Hannah Ellen, (known as Nel), who acted as housekeeper and gardener at *Talfan*, their substantial home on the Carmarthen road leading out of Newcastle Emlyn.

From his earliest years, Dafydd visited and stayed with his relatives in Newcastle Emlyn during the summer months, and after his sister was born in 1950, even attended Coed-y-bryn school for a few weeks. Both Sal and Nel, his 'aunts' as he called them, became Dafydd's benefactors and supporters, ensuring that as a pupil and student, he was well dressed and supplied with books.

Dafydd's father, William Ellis Thomas, was born on 5 August 1903, in Blaenau Ffestiniog, the younger of two children, his sister Annie Ellis Thomas born seven years previously. He was brought up in the Presbyterian tradition, at the Rhiw and Maenofferen chapels in Blaenau Ffestiniog, and later in Ebeneser, Tumble in Carmarthenshire.

His father Ellis had been born in Llanuwchllyn, before moving to Blaenau Ffestiniog in the 1880s. W.E.'s parents' antecedents could be traced to well-known Presbyterian preachers, including Revd J. R. Jones, Llanuwchllyn, and Revd Thomas Williams, Gwalchmai, Anglesey. Ellis was one of three sons working as slate rockmen, responsible for exploding slate from the rock face in the Oakeley quarry in Blaenau Ffestiniog. This was one of the most dangerous jobs in the industry, that involved breaking blocks of slate off the quarry face by means of a pick or crowbar, then drilling and shot firing, and assisting in the trimming of these large blocks into suitable size for transport to the mills.[2]

Ellis married his wife Ellen in 1895. Her father, William Williams, had been born in 1848, and had moved from Anglesey to the slate mines in Blaenau Ffestiniog in the 1860s, and had four children – Ellen the eldest, Mary, Elizabeth and Peter.

On the first night of January 1874, he was home with his wife, eldest child, Ellen, and a couple of lodgers. At midnight that evening, the Llyn Ffridd-y-Bwlch reservoir above their home broke its banks, and water cascaded down the valley into their village of Talweunydd:

> W. Williams understood the danger when the house filled halfway with water, and the furniture knocked into each other. With no hesitation, he pushed himself out through a small window at the side of his room, with a small daughter, Elen (sic) under his arm and pulling his wife through in the same way. The lodgers woke when they heard this commotion, and they made their way out through the roof, and they all manage to escape with their lives. Two children drowned at the next-door house as a result of this terrible incident.[3]

William's wife died in 1882, leaving him to raise four children singlehandedly, two of whom, Elizabeth and Peter, died in their teenage years. Ellen acted as her father's housekeeper until 1895, at the age of 22, she married Ellis Thomas.

Throughout his working life in Blaenau Ffestiniog, Ellis Thomas remained a rockman, Their daughter Annie Ellis was born in 1897, and William Ellis was born in 1903.

At the age of 36, Ellis Thomas had worked in the Oakeley quarry for over twenty years, but the slate industry in Blaenau Ffestiniog was hit by recession in 1908. That year he responded to a job advert in the Presbyterian magazine, *Y Goleuad*, seeking skilled young men to join the coal industry to sink the Great Mountain colliery in the anthracite coalfield, at Tumble in the Gwendraeth Valley, in Carmarthenshire. There he became a 'dangerman', using his experience to handle explosives. He also moved politically, having been a Liberal in north Wales, he joined the Independent Labour Party and, at the same time, befriended a fellow miner, the future union leader and Member of Parliament, S. O. Davies.

Davies's role as a checkweigher was a 'position of immense responsibility and trust' in which he ensured that miners were not cheated of payment for the amount of coal they had dug.[4] He became an industrial agitator, and after completing a degree in the social sciences in 1913, chose to return to his role at the colliery. There, he became one of the most prominent voices in south Wales opposed to the First World War. Both Ellis and William attended S.O.'s evening classes on economics and social sciences, sponsored by the Independent Labour Party, before S.O. left in November 1918 to become the miners' agent for the Dowlais district of the South Wales Miners' Federation. He would later become Member of Parliament for Merthyr Tydfil, from June 1934 until his death in February 1972.[5] His radical influence on the young William Ellis was long lasting and reflected Tumble's wider political culture.

The village's socialist and radical tradition was not limited to the workplace. It gained a reputation as a centre of anti-war opposition,[6] and later in the 1920s, Tom Nefyn Williams, the local Presbyterian minister of Ebeneser church,[7] split his denomination by preaching socialism from the pulpit, and campaigning against the slum housing owned by the local coal company. He was subsequently dismissed as a heretic, and his church dissolved.

At the age of eleven, in 1914, William Ellis was granted a prestigious scholarship to attend Llanelli Technical school (the forerunner of the town's grammar school), where he became a keen rugby player, described as tall with a 'solid body'. As a teenager, he grew up when views on the Great War were violently polarised in the area, and surprisingly, given his academic ability, at the age of 16, and without informing his family, he approached the local Great Mountain colliery to request a post as a trainee manager. At that point, in what must have been a major family row, his father insisted on returning to his job as a rockman in Blaenau Ffestiniog, taking his wife and daughter with him, and leaving William to lodge with a local colliery examiner's family. Although thwarted in his attempt to leave school, and in spite of what must have been a difficult separation from his family, he remained in education and succeeded in passing his final 'A' level examinations before entering Bangor University in the autumn of 1921, to study Welsh.

Bangor was then a small college of 672 students, mostly from Wales, many of whom were demobbed soldiers. The most flourishing student societies were the Welsh Society (*Y Cymric*) and the Literary and Debating Society (the *Lit and Deb*). Politically, the student body tended to be Welsh nationalist in inclination. In 1920, Moses Griffith had won the election standing as a Welsh Nationalist, even before the creation of Plaid Cymru five years later. Griffith's son Geraint, would later become Dafydd Ellis's university tutor. In the Welsh department, W.E. was lectured by the famed grammarian Sir John Morris Jones, in English as was the common practice, and by the renowned Professor Ifor Williams, a quarryman's son who laid the foundations for the study of Old Welsh, particularly the study of early poetry dating back to the sixth century. The brilliant Professor J. E. Lloyd, who wrote the first serious early history of Wales, lectured on Welsh history, and the painfully shy Principal, Harry Reichel, would invite senior students to breakfast with him, a 'difficult experience for both parties'. One of the most significant appointments in W.E.'s time in Bangor was that of the brilliant young poet R. Williams Parry as a lecturer in the Welsh department. One of W.E.'s contemporaries described the charismatic impact of his arrival during W.E.'s first year,

> Standing on Friday afternoon in the corridor by the Welsh room. "Here he comes", said W. E. Thomas by my side, and our eyes must have looked like organ stops. We followed him into the class and listened to him lecturing on lyrical poetry . . . this lecture stayed indelibly in my mind.[8]

In common with most other male students, W.E. lodged in the town, and paid about ten shillings a week for a shared bedsit, with another room for study, with a fire and lighted lamps. The landlady would cook and keep count of the food she had bought. He graduated in Welsh in the summer of 1924. Money was scarce, and W.E. was one of those students who took advantage of a grant of £25 per annum to train to be a teacher.

The students created their own entertainment, and in the morning breaks between lectures, one of their number, W. D. Williams, would lead students in singing a selection of Welsh language songs. W.E. played a full part in *Y Cymric*, and in 1925, took the role of the judge in a mock-trial of the famed poet Dafydd ap Gwilym, judging him to be fickle, unfaithful and flighty in his love relations, and sentencing him to marry his love, Dyddgu, pledging to do so with an oath of faithfulness.[9]

The College's Welsh language drama society was established during W.E.'s second year, at the beginning of 1923. W.E., with the College's future legendary drama lecturer, John Gwilym Jones, took part in their second production, *Gwyntoedd Croesion* (Cross Winds) by J. O. Francis.

He became an enthusiastic and respected actor, and in 1924 gave an acclaimed performance in the drama *Y Ddraenen Wen* (The Hawthorn), by the Llanrwst playwright R. G. Berry. In 1926, the highlight of his dramatic career was his role as Torvald in Ibsen's *Doll's House* produced by the College's Welsh language drama society, where he was given high praise for his performance.[10]

He also performed in a Welsh language version of *Outward Bound* by Sutton Vane at the Holyhead National Eisteddfod, and was one of the lead actors in Ibsen's *The Pretenders*, produced by the Russian Theodore Komisarjevsky, an exiled theatre director from the October communist revolution.

He had worked as an opera director at Covent Garden, and with actors' companies featuring some of the greatest talent of the age, including John Gielgud, Charles Laughton and Peggy Ashcroft. But he was drawn to north Wales by Lord Howard de Walden, who had taken the revolutionary step of creating a Welsh language theatre company named after his home, *Garthewin*, a historic house dating back to the early seventeenth century, near Conwy.

In October 1924, during W.E.'s fourth year in college, his father suffered a terrible accident at the Oakeley quarry. As he pushed a loaded tram weighing about three tons, it overturned, and fell on his legs. He fractured his right thigh, and was taken to Oakeley hospital, where his leg was amputated. Family lore states that in losing his leg, he lost his heart – *colli coes, colli calon*.[11] He was said to have been heartbroken, and this permanently affected his health. As a result of the accident, he received immediate compensation from his employer, Oakeley Quarry, at a rate of £5.18.4 a month, the equivalent of approximately £450 a month at current value, but these payments ceased in December 1927.[12] Ellis and Elen subsequently moved out from their home to establish a small grocer's shop at Glan-y-Pwll Crossing, in Blaenau Ffestiniog.

W.E. had graduated in Welsh in June 1924, and then spent another two years studying for a teaching certificate, but which he abandoned in the summer of 1926. He then started a three year BD theological course in the Presbyterian college in Aberystwyth, but abandoned it due to nervous exhaustion, probably exacerbated by his mother's sudden death after many years of illness, on 6 March 1927. Within thirteen months, on 24 May 1928, his father also died, at the age of 56, leaving both W.E. and his sister Annie stricken and bereft.

But the family's succession of tragedies continued two weeks later, when on 7 June 1928, their grandfather William Williams died at the age of 81, at the home of his daughter Mary, in Llanrug near Caernarfon. Within the week, she also died suddenly at the age of 48. In the space of three weeks, Annie and W.E. had lost their father, grandfather and aunt.[13]

One can only surmise at the impact these traumatic events had on the two children, and at this point, W.E. withdrew from his theological course. However, he transferred his diploma studies in order to qualify for the ministry, at Bala Presbyterian theological college, where he finally qualified as a minister of religion.

In 1930, he was ordained at his first church in the villages of Carrog and Glynceiriog, in the Edeyrnion area of eastern Merioneth and south Denbighshire, accompanied by his sister Annie, who became his housekeeper. Here he renewed his friendship with the local headmaster of the primary school, W. D. Williams and continued his love of performing, in drama and concert parties. It was here also that he met his future wife, Eirlys. He wrote sketches for the group, acted as the compere in its performances, and took part in the broadcast performances of the group for BBC radio's light variety Welsh language programmes from the BBC's Bangor studio.[14]

W. D. Williams was the driving force behind the formation of the concert party in Carrog, with W. E. Thomas chairing its first meeting. In Williams's account of the creation of the group W.E. was given special praise:

> He had written an amusing sketch for us – *Y Côr Mawr* (the Big Choir) – and we regarded him as one of us, and after the first night, took him with us to act as our compère ... the first performance was in a small chapel, the stage was rather cramped, with no curtain, but we managed well ... the programme included a total of twenty items, including *A Blackout – the grand new London Production*, by W. E. Thomas.

As they gained in popularity, W.E. also wrote farces and performed with the group in broadcasts.[15]

In 1940, he moved as minister to the Presbyterian church in the village of Tal-y-Bont in the Conwy valley, a small village located in an agricultural area near Dolgarrog aluminium works, where his zeal and passion quickly revived a dying congregation. Both he and his sister Annie moved to the manse in the village, but he maintained his links with Carrog, and W. D. Williams's concert party, as well as the local teacher, Eirlys James.

Eirlys and William Ellis were married on 12 April 1944 at Bethel Presbyterian chapel in Newcastle Emlyn. This 'popular and attractive' wedding saw Eirlys 'given away' by her uncle Tom Davies, from Swansea, and officiated over by the bridegroom's cousin, Revd Huw Llewelyn Williams. Following the service, the reception for about fifty people was held at the Cawdor Hotel and included deacons representing the bridegroom's church in Tal-y-bont. The honeymoon was spent in Porthcawl, and the newspaper report was keen to add that 'both parties are very popular in their respective districts and are in receipt of numerous and costly gifts'.[16]

In Spring 1946, accompanied by Annie as housekeeper, they moved six miles distant to Llanrwst for W.E. to become minister of Seion, a 'large and prosperous chapel' of over six hundred members, with three satellite Sunday schools scattered across the town. Within weeks, Eirlys returned home to Newcastle Emlyn for her last weeks of confinement while awaiting the birth of Dafydd Ellis, born on 18 October 1946 in the Priory Hospital in Carmarthen. But for much of his early life, Dafydd recalls that he was cared for by his aunt Annie, 'the person who mainly brought me up'.[17] The mainstay of the family, she was housekeeper and cook, also looking after their daughter Elin, born on 27 April 1950, and enabling Eirlys to have a greater pastoral and social role as the minister's wife. Annie was extraordinarily dedicated to the children, and while her shyness meant she had difficulty with social interaction, they came to understand that she had apparently lost a boyfriend during the First World War and had never fully recovered from that emotional trauma.

Seion chapel represented the established middle class of the town and was considered a cut above the other chapels in the Conwy Valley, certainly in the self-regard of the chapel's deacons. They were mostly middle-class professionals and conservative, often freemasons, and included members of some of the town's older families. During W.E.'s period as its pastor, the deacons included both of the town's headteachers and two solicitors, and their middle-class composition contrasted with the mainly working-class character of the majority of the chapel's congregation. By contrast the Congregationalist and Wesleyan chapels were rather less hierarchical and led by two national figures in Welsh language culture. They were Revd Gwilym Tilsley, the Wesleyan minister of Horeb, and Revd Idwal Jones, the Congregationalist minister of Tabernacl, who became W.E.'s closest friends. The three were united by a love of Welsh literature, active in the Welsh language culture of the town, and were all pioneering modernisers. W.E. used new recording technology in various imaginative ways, and he was fascinated by the potential of technology to reach a wider congregation. He had been inspired by his earlier experience of performing light entertainment at the BBC in Bangor, and one of Dafydd's earliest memories was of his father taking the revolutionary step of using a tape-recording machine to bring his sermons and interviews to those members who were too ill to attend chapel. He also recalls the excitement of visiting a radio studio specially built in Llanrwst for coverage of the National Eisteddfod in 1951, funded by that year's landmark Festival of Britain.[18]

W.E.'s friend Idwal Jones introduced a generation of Welsh speaking children to adventure thrillers through his spirited radio series *SOS Galw Gari Tryfan*, while Gwilym Tilsley's literary talent led him to being chaired twice for poems in tribute to the workman, in the 1950 National Eisteddfod in praise of the coal miner and in 1957 with a poem about the life of the slate quarryman. He eventually became Archdruid in 1969-72.

In keeping with their concerns for the spiritual welfare of their flock, these three sparkling cultural leaders shared a profound respect for the common man and had little regard for those of their members who viewed religiosity as a path to higher social status. The young Dafydd was not allowed to forget his father's working-class and political roots: 'he would always tell me that we belonged to the other side of the railway tunnel that separated industrial Blaenau Ffestiniog from the market town of Llanrwst, and that I should never forget it.'[19]

Ann Ffrancon, as a young member of Seion recalls her abhorrence of the social superiority that the chapel's leaders displayed:

> I never felt happy there. It was *Capel Mawr* – the big chapel – in the real sense that the deacons in the *sedd fawr* were mainly people who had advantages and privilege. It was a throwback to another time – lawyers, the headmaster of the grammar school, bankers, landowners. The 'big people' wanted to be seen. And those ordinary working class people who slogged their guts out for the chapel didn't get recognised and be promoted to be

deacons. The *bobl mawr* – the posh people – were good at praying publicly and the chapel was marked by a lot of snobbishness and fur coats. I felt uncomfortable there.[20]

She recalls that at home in the manse, Aunt Annie was the one who 'would do the hard work, so that if you visited for tea, for example, she would have baked the cakes, made *bara brith* and Welsh cakes, prepared cheese and jam, and also washed the family's clothes', while Eirlys would have been visiting members of the congregation, or organising the numerous chapel events.

Ann Ffrancon felt that Annie was 'taken for granted':

She was a backroom figure. I remember she would join Eirlys and the children at chapel in the morning service, but immediately after the hymn was sung before the sermon, she would slip out to complete preparations for the family's Sunday lunch. Mrs Thomas, of course, would stay until the end of the service and would return with the children. Annie did the hard work but without the perks.

Ann was Elin's closest friend, but saw that as children, both Dafydd and Elin could be short tempered and stubborn with their parents. Ann Ffrancon describes Eirlys as 'quite severe' and having a 'stormy temperament', who was very conscious of her status within the chapel.[21]

Dafydd spent his summer holidays in Newcastle Emlyn every year until his late teens, and this close link was maintained until the 1980s. His father would preach at Bethel Methodist church in the town throughout the summer, and these holidays would commence with lengthy train journeys of over ten hours, from Llanrwst to Aberystwyth, then Pencader, and finally the branch line to Newcastle Emlyn. W.E.'s constant fear was that he would have to undertake the arduous journey back again, if he was called back to Llanrwst in the case of an unexpected funeral.

The family stayed with Eirlys's sister, Gwenfil, and at the age of four, while Dafydd's mother was expecting Elin, he attended the local school of Coed-y-Bryn, where Aunt Sarah was head teacher, an 'experienced and competent teacher, producing a stimulating atmosphere, and who created habits of 'neatness, thoroughness and accuracy', according to school inspectors.[22]

Until the early 1960s, Dafydd continued to take part in Newcastle Emlyn's social life, including otter hunting, then a hugely popular pastime in rural west Wales, in which he won a badge for his enthusiasm for the hunt. The leader of the hunt was the prosperous local landowner, Ponsonby Lewes, who would dispatch his pack of specially bred otter hounds along the Teifi river towards Llechryd. Newcastle Emlyn became as familiar as Llanrwst for the young boy, and he gained an intimate impression of the social and cultural values of Welsh-speaking rural Carmarthenshire.

From their arrival in Llanrwst, both Eirlys and W.E. committed themselves to developing the social activity of the chapel, and she used her experience as a teacher to invigorate the social and performative life of the chapel.

They created a volume and intensity of cultural events that was truly impressive, ranging from the weekly prayer meetings, recitation competitions, the Band of Hope, and the annual celebration of Flowering Sunday, which included a cemetery decorating tradition, and which involved over a hundred of the chapel's children, together with those from the chapel's satellite branches, who would collectively lead a service in Seion. [23]

W.E. sustained his interest in drama throughout his life. He had been a skilled actor with great presence, and he created religious pageants to celebrate the lives of William Salesbury and Bishop Morgan and their contribution to the translation of the Bible into Welsh, and in 1969, created a production celebrating 200 years of the Methodist cause in Llanrwst. He 'anchored' his widespread cultural activity in the youth movement Urdd Gobaith Cymru (the Welsh League of Youth) and its fusion of Welsh patriotism and Christian duty. Eirlys also showed a flair for directing and producing large scale events. The chapel had an excellent reputation for its music, with a talented choir and a renowned organ designed at the beginning of the century by its own organist, Matthews Williams, regarded as one of the best in Wales, who was followed by an equally gifted organist and choirmaster, Arthur Vaughan Williams.

In the early 1960s, as a young trainee minister in the Conwy valley, Dafydd Andrew Jones was mentored by W.E. He recalls him as both approachable and wise, 'a clear and logical preacher', and a 'cheerful and entertaining character'.[24]

He was highly thought of within the denomination, and frequently preached at the Presbyterian's *Sasiwn Fawr*, its governing body for Wales.

In the Presbyterian churches' local quarterly meetings, and as minister of the most substantial chapel in the Conwy valley, he was known as an arbitrator and conciliator, and was often tasked with dealing with conflict between churches or individuals, working closely with one of his deacons, another Blaenau Ffestiniog man, Robert Jones, the imposing and respected figure who became headmaster of Llanrwst grammar school.

Myrddin ap Dafydd's parents ran a Welsh language bookshop in the town. He recalls W.E. as a gentle and humorous man, often stopping in the street to greet passersby with light conversation and leg pulling. One of Myrddin's tasks as a young boy was to fetch deliveries of various publishers' books from the Crosville bus depot in the town and carry them back in an old pram to his parents' bookshop. Myrddin recalls that W.E. immediately saw the humour of the situation:

> Oh, aren't these good little babies in the pram, Myrddin. What's his name? (and reading the label) 'Ah, his name is Hughes and Son. And Gomer is the name of the one next door . . . and Brython is the name of the one at the bottom of the pram!'

Myrddin recalls that 'more than likely he would be in the shop later that day to buy a couple of titles from each of the publishers. My parents thought the world of him.'[25]

Elen, Dafydd's first girlfriend, recalls her first impressions of W.E. as 'quiet, warm, he wore a round collar in the house. He was respectful, considerate, had a study with lots of books, and was conscientious in his pastoral care for his congregation.'[26] But the young Nesta Wyn Ellis growing up in the nineteen fifties, who would later become a well-known Liberal politician and author, shared Ann Ffrancon's disdain of the chapel's culture. Her father was a deacon in Seion, and active in the more working class Cae Person chapel, where her mother attended, before she 'got fed up' and defected to the Church in Wales:

> W. E. Thomas gave very stirring apocalyptic sermons. I remember him being tall and dark and rather strict. I remember I didn't think he had much of a sense of humour. but chapel was dreadful really. Dull. We got all dressed up on Sundays – we wore posies and big hats. it was very much a showy place. There were lots of middle-aged ladies who vied with each other.

But she valued the opportunities given to her to perform in chapel, under Eirlys's guidance:

> She (was) a middle aged woman, a bit hunched. She was the one who chose the plays to put on every year, and she always wanted me to play a leading role. I was a good actress. She kept out of the way, but she produced the plays. She was quite earnest – putting on these plays was no joke. She had to organise a bunch of amateurs, but she seemed to do it quite well. There were these plays and these *eisteddfodau*. She was very active – she organised the plays put on by the chapel in the big vestry, and every evening there was an event there. I was being steered to being a devout person at Sunday school. I remember the *eisteddfodau* and I did very well at recitation. She came to our house quite often because my father was a quite prominent person in the chapel. I had to be so serious as well.[27]

Dafydd and Elin were brought up in an intensely social and highly competitive home environment. They were coached remorselessly by their fiercely ambitious mother, who attempted to rule the children with iron discipline. Their regime, from an early age, included regular scripture exams, held at a chapel and county level, conducted for the children of the Conwy Valley, and both regularly won first prizes. They were highly competitive in the chapel's annual children's eisteddfodau and Urdd events, and on occasion, their mother was even known to submit entries in poetry and prose in Dafydd's name.[28]

The chapel's regular ambitious pageantries produced by W.E. and Eirlys, such as the celebration of William Salesbury's translation of the New Testament into Welsh, in December 1966, involved hundreds of children from the chapels scattered throughout the Conwy valley, and were logistical and creative triumphs. But Eirlys's pursuit of the best for both of her children translated into a strict home regime, that meant they could be locked in their rooms in order to finish their homework. Ann Ffrancon recalls that in her early teens, Elin was stopped from going to a dance at the Winter Gardens in Llandudno by her mother when she discovered the dress bought for the event and hidden in a washing pile. The father, according to Ann Ffrancon, was much more gentle, 'always very welcoming, and I was struck by how big a house it was, and the luxury of having a study with such a large library'. She recalls that he was 'a very able and dramatic orator and had an ability to charm an audience. This gift was also granted to Dafydd.'[29]

In primary school, Dafydd was in the same class as Emyr Williams (later the celebrated entertainer and actor Gari Williams), and another's minister's son, Gareth Tilsley, who recalls Dafydd even in primary school as a 'quite quiet boy, able, and who read Shakespeare through his mother's influence'. Gareth thought Dafydd's father more gracious and outgoing than Eirlys, and although his congregation may have wished to 'place him on a pedestal, there was nothing 'grand' about him'.[30]

Dafydd was a keen reader, and he would be allowed to smuggle schoolbooks into chapel services to keep him quiet. He recalls that:

> we weren't encouraged to play in public on Sundays outside, although we could play in the privacy of the house. My father was quite liberal in his theology and left-nationalist in his politics. He was always encouraging us to do things but not letting the more conservative chapel members know about it. That was certainly the case when I started reading books that were regarded as unacceptable ... *Lady Chatterley's Lover*, for example. That was very exciting. I used to take it out on the school playing fields, and read it, with a plain brown cover.[31]

Both Dafydd and Elin learnt to play the harp and piano, and performed in chapel events and local eisteddfodau. Dafydd's harp was bought for him by his aunt Gwenfil, and he recalls that he was taught the violin and the piano by the organist of Seion, Arthur Vaughan Williams – 'I was best on the harp. I took that more seriously and gave one or two public performances'[32] – but his reluctance to practise meant his ability took him no further than local eisteddfodau. The family's local status as public performers spread nationally when the BBC broadcast a radio programme featuring the family's various talents in a feature edition of *Teulu'r Aelwyd* in 1961.

Both parents unquestionably 'pushed' their children and were practised performers themselves. W.E. could often be playful, 'dear, spirited and caring,' but he could explode in frustration with his daughter, particularly whenever she chose to rebel. Ann Ffrancon recalls that 'I was best friends with Elin, and because we didn't have a television, I would go to watch Dickens series such as the *Old Curiosity Shop* at theirs, every Sunday afternoon at 4.30'. She recalls that conflict flared up easily in the home, particularly when Elin was required to take part in recitation competitions. She was also expected to take part in countless chapel devotional events, seasonal concerts, county exams, and to constantly practise on her instruments. There were exams upon exams, in addition to the schoolwork they were expected to prepare. This incessant pressure on both children would not cause Dafydd to complain, but Elin would sometimes refuse to cooperate. Ann Ffrancon recalls that on visits there, she was 'sent home many times when I had gone there for recitation practice, because Elin had argued and refused to take part'.

Elin was a livewire and more fun-loving than her more cerebral and academic elder brother. Ann Ffrancon recalls Elin's winning personality and that by her early teens she was 'mischievous and her parents had reached the end of their tether and were failing to keep control of her behaviour'. She relates that by the late 1960s, when W.E. came to their home to discuss with Ann's parents what could be done about Elin's behaviour, both girls sneaked out of the house through the parlour window and took off in Elin's car for a date with two boys, only returning a couple of hours later, without being detected. She could be headstrong – and not always totally virtuous.

By their early teens, both children had developed strong independent characters, but they were also privileged and given unique status within their chapel community. On Friday evenings, they would attend their harp lessons, when they would catch a train for the forty-minute journey to Blaenau Ffestiniog to be taught by an acclaimed harpist, Telynores Gwenllian Dwyryd. Their precedence was such that in their absence, any chapel activity for young people for that evening was invariably suspended. Ann Ffrancon recalls that 'Friday was sacred. Everything was fashioned to suit them. And Elin and Dafydd would not come to events in the chapel in which they were not included.'[33]

When Dafydd entered the gowned and venerable Llanrwst Grammar School in 1957, as a precocious, intelligent and lively child, his disciplined and literate home had prepared him for academic high achievement. The grammar school fashioned itself along traditional lines, and his subjects for 'O' levels included French, Greek and Latin. A visiting preacher was surprised to see Dafydd at the age of 14, during a service at Seion, have an open Bible before him, in order to follow his readings from the New

Testament. When he went to congratulate him on his diligence and devotion, he was amazed that the young scholar had been reading the Greek version of the text.[34]

His father nurtured in him a love of poetry and of Shakespeare, and his love of contemporary literature led him, at the age of 14, to dispatch his mother to the library in Colwyn Bay to borrow a copy of James Joyce's *Ulysses*, 'the most important book that I have read in my life'.

He also developed a great regard for theology and engaged in debate with his father, who introduced him to some of the great theologians and philosophers such as Martin Heidegger, Ludwig Wittgenstein and Søren Kierkegaard. The young budding intellectual and the collared vicar would compete to grab the quarterly copy of *Theology Today* when it was delivered through the post. Published by the Princeton Theological Seminary in the USA, it was aimed at an ecumenical readership of academics and religious leaders and attempted to show the relevancy of Protestantism to contemporary social and political problems. This sharpening of his theological and philosophical reasoning would stand him in good stead for his later public and political career.[35]

Selwyn Williams was two years above him in the school and remembers him as an ambitious pupil:

> Dafydd was 'driven' and Elin wasn't given the same support by her parents. Dafydd was very able and very competitive academically. He was one of a few to take the 'Use of English' exam, usually undertaken by those who wished to apply for Oxford or Cambridge.[36]

He was fortunate in being influenced by a number of inspirational teachers, including Gwilym O. Jones, the Welsh teacher, who coached him in his school debating skills. Gwilym Roberts taught woodwork and, more profitably in Dafydd's case, Welsh literature. The history teacher, Dewi Rees, from Cardiganshire would sometimes cancel the lesson and commence a challenging discussion on current affairs. He nurtured Dafydd's intellect and curiosity. When Elfyn Llwyd prepared for his 'A' levels in the late sixties, he recalls being given Dafydd's essays to be used as models for his history 'A' level exams. Although his scrawl was difficult to interpret, Dafydd's essays were thought to be brilliant models for those pupils who followed him.[37]

Gwyn Neale, the English teacher from south Wales, gave him, as Dafydd recalls, his 'lifelong love of the metaphysical poets and emphasised the Welsh links with poets such as Henry Vaughan and George Herbert'. He gave him the opportunity to act in plays such as Goldsmith's *She Stoops to Conquer* where he played the part of Mr. Hardcastle, and for a young schoolboy, was given the risqué opportunity of holding a clay pipe. The French teacher, Beryl Jones, from Porthmadog, delighted in introducing him to the dramatic works of Eugène Ionesco and Jean Paul Sartre, and involved him in organising a school visit to Paris.

His father took an intense interest in coaching him in debating skills throughout his teens, that would later stand him on good stead. On Saturday nights at home, W.E. would set him a debating question, and he would be expected to speak first in favour of a motion for five minutes, then against for another five. He became a well-known public speaker due to his success in bilingual school debating competitions in north Wales, and in early 1963, led his school team to victory in Urdd Gobaith Cymru's Welsh language national debating competition for secondary schools. The following year, he won the national prize as debater in the Urdd Eisteddfod competition and also won the individual debating prize for north Wales schools, which was broadcast on BBC radio. The active Urdd *Aelwyd* branch in the town brought grammar school and the secondary modern pupils together, and there, Dafydd was reunited with Emyr Williams. They wrote comedy sketches together and on one occasion, Emyr Williams acted the part of an interviewer, while Dafydd acted the part of the Labour leader Harold Wilson, mainly because he also owned one of Wilson's trademark Gannex coats.

In his lower sixth year, in 1963, he edited the school magazine, *The Grustensian*, in which he proposed the modernising of the school, but while welcoming the 'gurgle of cement-mixers', he also suggested judiciously that while the school's tradition dating back to 1610, should never be clung to too closely, 'neither should it be discarded completely'.

His most substantial contribution was a short story in Welsh on the emptiness of meaning – *Gwacter*. For a 15-year-old, it is an impressive attempt at creative writing, describing the emptiness of being, and enjoying the financial gains of materialism without the comfort of belief and faith: 'Confusion is everything. I came from emptiness, and I will return to emptiness. I am an empty spirit attempting to reach out to a Big Emptiness where there is no God.'[38]

In 1964, he contributed a meditative essay, describing the lonely author's room and his surroundings, together with two poems, *Sŵn y Gwynt* (Sound of the Wind), and *Y Chwilod* (The Bugs), a clever sonnet describing the impact of the Beatles on his teenage generation:

> 'Pedwarawd tenau, tal, trwysusau tyn,
> Yn twangio, twingio, twongio tair gitar
> Drydan, a drymio drwm. Eu symud syn
> Sy'n mesmereiddio miloedd, a'u cân groch
> Am garu, plesio, twistio i gyd i Ti,
> Am afael llaw, rhoi cusan ar Dy foch,
> Mewn ie ie ie o fyd sy'n ecstasi.
> Nhw yw Pibyddion mantell ddu eu hawr'

> 'A thin, tall foursome, with tight trousers,
> Twanging, Twinging, Twonging three electric guitars,
> and drumming drums. Their surprising movement
> Mesmerises thousands, with their raucous singing
> About loving, pleasing, twisting all for You,
> Holding hands, giving you a kiss on your cheek,
> In a yeah, yeah, yeah of a world that's ecstasy
> They are this hour's black cloaked Pipers.'[39]

His first engagement with politics arose through his father and their common interest in current affairs. Although W.E.'s role as pastor restrained him from being openly party political, Dafydd's earliest direct political memory was of his father's involvement in the Parliament for Wales campaign in 1953 and hearing some of the leading politicians of the time speaking at rallies in Llanrwst, including Lloyd George's daughter, Lady Megan Lloyd George, Liberal MP for Anglesey (1931–51), who later defected to the Labour party, and the Welsh Nationalist Party's general secretary, the indefatigable J. E. Jones. He recalls the sense of crisis surrounding the 1956 Suez emergency, and the nervousness of those local young men undertaking national service who were concerned that they might be called up to join the conflict.

Dafydd accompanied his father to the very well attended political meetings in the town, held usually in the school hall:

It was then the fashion to attend the political meetings of all parties, which is how I got to see Garner Evans. He was the local National Liberal Member for Denbigh between 1950 and 1959, and had an unconventional technique of drawing an audience. He would cheekily just take over a large stall selling crockery and sometimes break some plates, before then making spontaneous speeches. I recall Cledwyn (Hughes, Labour MP for Anglesey) coming to speak, and Glyn Tegai Hughes for the Liberals, standing in West Denbighshire.[40]

In 1959, at the age of 13, in his first election as a political candidate, Dafydd stood for Plaid Cymru in a mock election in Llanrwst Grammar School, and came a creditable third. But it was the impact of the atom bomb, and the growing anti-war movement led by the Campaign for Nuclear Disarmament (CND), that drew him most strongly into active politics. In October 1961, at the age of 15, he became chair of the Llanrwst branch of CND, and set about distributing leaflets around the town, organising a public meeting prior to a mass demonstration in Parliament, and wrote fruitlessly to the local Conservative MP for Denbigh, Geraint Morgan, to demand his support. His CND activism widened his political and social horizons, and he attended meetings along the north Wales coast in Colwyn Bay and Llandudno, as well as rallies at the university towns of Bangor and Aberystwyth, sometimes without his parents' knowledge:

> As long as I was keeping up with my school work, they didn't worry. I remember going to rallies in Bangor and around Aberystwyth, one of them certainly without telling my parents that I was going ... I was becoming an activist.

In a rally to thank CND's President, Bertrand Russell, and to pay tribute to his attempts to avert nuclear war during the Cuban missile crisis, he addressed a large crowd of CND supporters in Penrhyndeudraeth, on 10 November 1962, before they marched to Russell's Minffordd home.[41]

During the Llanelli Eisteddfod in August 1962, and in the week that Cymdeithas yr Iaith Gymraeg (the Welsh Language Society) was founded, he joined Plaid Cymru, 'the only party I have ever joined'.[42] The strongest political force within his school were the Young Conservatives, but he was recruited to Plaid Cymru by two older pupils, Brynmor Williams from Glan Conwy, who, Dafydd recalled, had a CND lapel badge with a green background, and David Jones, later a BBC sound engineer. He was also influenced by significant figures locally who were friends of his father. The first was the Plaid Cymru veteran Elwyn Roberts, a local deputy bank manager who had been a conscientious objector during the Second World War and who became the National Eisteddfod organiser in 1947, held in Llanrwst in 1951. In this capacity he became friends with W.E., who was a member of the Eisteddfod's literature and recitation committee. Roberts was then appointed as Plaid Cymru's Gwynedd organiser and head of finance, and from 1955, for two years, ran the campaign for a Parliament for Wales, succeeding in collecting a petition of over quarter of a million names. Another important influence on Dafydd was O. M. Roberts, a close friend of his father, a headteacher and councillor in Glan Conwy, and one of the organisers of the arson attack by members of Plaid Cymru on the Penyberth bombing school in 1936.[43]

Dafydd Ellis's reasoning for joining Plaid Cymru was that although he did not consider himself a conventional nationalist, he 'valued the culture and community and the idea of a Welsh nation having greater powers. We never talked about independence, never used the word. And I still find it very difficult to use it. I was very keen always because of my involvement with the Peace Movement, and my preference for cooperation rather than identity politics.'

An important influence on the schoolboy activist was the Council for Education and World Citizenship (CEWC), associated with the Temple of Peace in Cardiff, that promoted global citizenship in Wales. It organised conferences for sixth formers and Dafydd went to his first CEWC conference in Coleg Harlech, where he hugely impressed by the contribution of Goronwy Roberts, the Member of Parliament for Caernarvonshire, who had a deep interest in international affairs, and was 'a very dramatic speaker'. He became a friend of Goronwy Roberts's son David Grommis, and revelled in 'a whale of a time drinking in the pubs in Harlech'.[44]

In spite of his academic success at Llanrwst Grammar School, he disliked the school's ethos and its abiding ambition, championed by its headmaster, R. J. Parry, to ensure that its brightest students became Oxford or Cambridge bound. In January 1964, Dafydd in his last year in the sixth form, was pressed by his headmaster to maintain the school's ethos, and to apply for the Oxford scholarship. He firmly refused to do so, and with the full support of his father, applied for an open scholarship to Bangor University.

He had already investigated the possibility of entering there, and visited the college in 1963 to meet Derec Llwyd Morgan, a third-year student who was as passionate about contemporary Welsh literature. Morgan would leave for Oxford University the following year to commence his research, but in his room in Neuadd Reichel, he shared a bottle of Cinzano with the precocious school pupil, and discussed the comparative virtues of contemporary Welsh language poets. They were to become firm personal and intellectual friends, and this relationship affirmed Dafydd's desire to follow his father's academic footsteps. Llwyd Morgan recalls their common interest in contemporary poetry: 'I arranged for him to come over to my room in Reichel Hall and we talked for a long time. I championed Bobi Jones, he championed Euros Bowen. Not many other people would have taken an interest in it.' Their close friendship would lead to Derec becoming Dafydd's best man at his wedding in 1970, and dedicating his third volume of poetry to him.[45]

In applying for the open scholarship to Bangor, Dafydd had what he described as 'a very significant meeting in my life'[46] with Professor John Meurig Thomas, Professor of Chemistry at the university. He marked his three papers so highly that Dafydd Ellis was offered entry with the lowest required grades of two 'E's, and was also granted the James W. Lewis Scholarship, worth over £400 a year, together with permanent residence in students' hall for three years.

Whilst he performed well academically, and became increasingly engaged in active politics, he also shared the active social life of the older grammar school pupils and their drinking and smoking culture:

> We didn't drink alcohol in the house, but I had started drinking on school trips. I used to go to pubs in Llangernyw, Trefriw and the local area beyond Llanrwst, all sorts of places where I shouldn't have been, and to Betws-y-Coed. But I was caught once there in the Gwydir hotel by the landlady. I had been told in my 'A' level course in Welsh literature, that this was where Williams Parry went to drink, so a number of us went there. But I looked underage because I had a rather rosy complexion. We usually drank Guinness – black velvet – with lemon to sweeten it up.

Anyway, in the hotel, I was told immediately, that I was not going to be served, and 'Anyway' she said, 'I know your father'![47]

He had little trouble in qualifying for Bangor University. Although he had only been required to obtain two 'E's, he left school in the summer of 1964 with three straight 'A's, in English, History, and a distinction in Welsh, and entered the University in October 1964, three weeks short of his 18th birthday, where he elected to take Welsh, Philosophy and English in his first year. To add to his open scholarship, he also won the school scholarship of £100 to study at Bangor. For both his family and his school, Dafydd Ellis Thomas was truly the golden child.

2

University Days

When Dafydd Ellis Thomas entered Bangor College at the age of 17, in early October 1964, free tuition and grants that covered the cost of living, and his scholarships and free accommodation, meant that he was financially well off. He now had both the time and resources to devote himself to academic work and political activism.[1] He later recalled that this was 'a privileged period for me as a scholarship student, living like a lord, as it were, in Reichel Hall with full board, for three years. I put on weight in that period.'[2]

Dafydd Ellis was already well known in the College even before his arrival, due to his public profile as a schools debater, and his increasing political involvement in CND and Plaid Cymru. Gwynn Matthews, then a second-year student, recalled him there at a schools debating competition:

> In Neuadd Powis, I remember seeing this schoolboy who looked elderly, had a great voice, and somebody said he was awfully talented and that he was coming here. I think there were great expectations of him and he was aware of those expectations. They were a burden on him. I think he felt strained to some extent for a period, and perhaps it told on him – and one of the results was that he felt he had to make a conscious effort to be like everybody else.[3]

At the beginning of the 1964 academic year, the Welsh department's formidable scholar Enid Pierce Roberts, warned the year's women freshers, over tea, that they would be joined by only four men that year, including Dafydd. He was described as an 'extraordinarily clever young man', who had had three 'A's in his 'A' levels. She, and the department, seemed nervous about this 'bright young man for whom, we were told, we should better watch out!'[4]

Gwynn Matthews reflects that when Dafydd started in the College, 'he seemed to be already careworn' with expectation, yet he became quickly 'one of the crew, determined to join in, always very enthusiastic.'[5]

He had an immediate impact on his fellow students. Emyr Price recalled 'a short red-cheeked boy' with whom he became close friends and found him 'the most engaging company under the sun',[6] while Emlyn Davies was impressed by his debating abilities and thought his arguments were invariably head and shoulders above those of his competitors.[7] He was one of the few Welsh-speaking students to have the self-confidence to participate in the College's English-language debating society, the *Lit and Debs*, where he further developed his public speaking skills, and became a prominent and highly regarded member. Although only in his first year, Dafydd took part as one of the College's speakers in a debate to be broadcast by the BBC, but which was disrupted by student anarchists.

Dafydd immediately got involved in student politics, and also threw himself into the College's social and cultural life. He became a leading member of the college's Plaid Cymru branch, an active contributor to the *Cymric* Welsh society, of which he became President, and wrote both for the sophisticated literary magazine, *Ffenics* and the student newspaper, *Y Dyfodol* (The Future). He became a member of the Welsh language drama society, although failing to follow his father's distinguished dramatic career as a lead actor.

In the College, he was usually dressed smartly, often wearing his aunts' knitted jumpers, but also conscious of current fashion, fond of wearing smart brogues and large colourful kipper ties. In his first year, he used his scholarship money to buy a second-hand Morris Minor 1000 from his local garage in Llanrwst. Although he may have had little need of subventions from his 'aunts' in Newcastle Emlyn, yet with his local authority grants and annual scholarships, as his friend Emyr Price recalled, 'he was famous for buying grand expensive clothes with money given to him by two prosperous aunts.'[8]

His close friend Gwynn Matthews recalls that he was not the type to take part in light entertainment sketches, but he could be an effective and irreverent orator. There was a culture of heavy drinking in the College throughout the sixties, especially amongst the Welsh students in which Dafydd took part enthusiastically.[9] He could give an entertaining 'blue' speech, enjoyed an active life in the pubs of Upper Bangor, but was not a 'great drinker' and 'never made a show of himself'. Gwynn Matthews describes him as a highly respected figure amongst contemporaries, and who, he thought, found release from academic life in the pub. However, Matthews felt that his academic and political ambition meant that he never fully 'let go'.[10]

He arrived as concern amongst many students grew about the growing Anglicisation of the university. The number of Welsh speaking students at Bangor University had been in decline since the mid-1950s. By the autumn of 1966, however, that percentage had declined to only 24 per cent of Bangor's students. Of the 540 students who entered Bangor in the autumn of 1964, only 90 came from Wales, and in the Welsh department, that year's intake of only twenty students included sixteen women and four men, including Dafydd.[11]

The writer and activist

This growing Anglicisation caused political tension and resentment amongst Welsh speaking students. The greatest political controversy in Wales at that time was the impending drowning of the rural community of Capel Celyn in the Tryweryn valley near Bala, and the building of the dam there in order to supply Liverpool and the Wirral with water for industry. There was also the aftershock of Saunders Lewis's radio lecture *Tynged yr Iaith* (the Fate of the Language) broadcast in November 1962 which, although aimed at revitalising Plaid Cymru, spawned the creation of another organisation, the militant language movement, Cymdeithas yr Iaith Gymraeg (Welsh Language Society), which shortly after, started civil disobedience campaigns in favour of official status for the Welsh language.

Saunders Lewis drew attention to the recently published census figures that showed a decrease in the number of Welsh speakers from 36 per cent in 1931 to 26 per cent in 1961. In his lecture, Lewis predicted the extinction of the Welsh language unless 'revolutionary methods' were used to defend it and advocated direct action and civil disobedience as the means to achieve official recognition for the language.[12]

Cymdeithas became increasingly influential amongst Welsh speaking students, particularly in Aberystwyth and Bangor. Their civil disobedience campaigns intensified in the autumn of 1965, with people refusing to license their vehicles until they could do so in Welsh, and in April

1966 its first member was sent to prison.¹³ In June 1963, Bangor students had submitted a memorandum and petition to the Council, demanding 'more Welshness in the life of the College'. For the students, the choice was straightforward: 'either honour the Welsh language or hold it in contempt'. In the same month, twenty-one members of the academic staff called on the College's Council to 'give the Welsh language the dignity it deserves'. In response, the council appointed a sub-committee which recommended a more bilingual approach such as official publications and College buildings, which was approved, but it was scarcely sufficient for those campaigning for more extensive reform.[14]

The 1960s was a period of student protest worldwide. However, despite the frenzied political atmosphere in the University, Dafydd Ellis committed himself to constitutional methods rather than civil disobedience and although he joined Cymdeithas yr Iaith Gymraeg for a short time, he directed his energy to mainstream student politics and Plaid Cymru rather than Cymdeithas. In this period, he also made the political choice to change his middle name from 'Ellis' to the more Welsh 'Elis'. Dafydd Elis recalled making a very conscious decision not to take part in law breaking:

> I did join Cymdeithas yr Iaith briefly. I might have been a member for a year or so and went to some protests. Did I realise what I was doing? I tried to help occupy post offices in Aberystwyth, and there were other protests in Dolgellau and Machynlleth in 1965. But I wasn't comfortable with that sort of form of activity. I was more interested in representational politics, in convincing people.[15]

Dafydd Iwan, the iconic leader of Cymdeithas yr Iaith Gymraeg throughout its first decade, recalls seeing Dafydd Elis scurrying past, during a protest rally in Bangor:

> I remember one particular occasion of being in a Cymdeithas protest in Bangor in the sixties, of going with a crowd to protest . . . outside the BBC and passing Dafydd El in his college scarf and his briefcase, walking towards us and going the other way. It was obvious he wasn't going to join us then. I didn't see him in Cymdeithas, and to some extent he was opposed to what we did.[16]

One of his closest friends in Bangor, Cenwyn Edwards, thought that his upbringing explained Dafydd's reluctance to engage in law-breaking: 'he wasn't a part of Cymdeithas's extremism. There was also an element in him that was the son of the manse, although he wouldn't have acknowledged that himself.'[17]

He was already well known within Plaid Cymru, where he had started to address the party's national conferences, including a rally against unemployment in Aberystwyth:

> My father played a trick on me. He said, 'Oh, you're going to Aberystwyth, are you?' I said, 'Yes, I've got a lift or I might go by bus'. He came there and sat in the audience – he didn't have to, did he? All that was a very valuable experience, obviously, because I got to know [prominent Plaid Cymru] people – Chris Rees was very active then, a very good thinker and strategist; J. E. Jones was there. Also, Harri Webb was very prominent.[18] In this period I made the decision that I wouldn't continue to be active in Cymdeithas and get myself arrested and stuff like that. It occurred to me that a combination of success in public speaking competitions, being able to be on the executive of the party, being involved with the youth section and be able to campaign in elections, was what I could do.[19]

Opposition to the drowning of Tryweryn and the later protests at the investiture of the Prince of Wales in 1969, gave a political focus to the distinctive Welsh language popular culture of the mid-sixties. Welsh language pop music flourished, and its protest songs included political lyrics such as Dafydd Iwan's *Carlo*, ridiculing Prince Charles, while Huw Jones's *Dŵr* ('Water') protested against the drowning of Welsh valleys such as Tryweryn and Clywedog. The anarchic Welsh language magazine *Lol* (literally, 'Nonsense') set out to prick the pomposity of the Welsh language establishment, with its mixture of satire and, shockingly, nude photographs of young women. From 1964 onwards, the rite of passage for many Welsh speaking students was the language protest or march, which encouraged bold rebelliousness, a readiness to challenge authority, and an initiation into lawbreaking.

One of his closest friend in University, Emyr Price, became a student at the College in 1962, and although he had not previously considered himself a nationalist, felt that the experience of being part of a linguistic minority made him feel 'almost divorced from Wales's allegedly most Welsh College'. The overbearing English colonial style of Principal Charles Evans's sclerotic administration converted Price into a socialist supporter of Plaid Cymru. He asserted that being in Bangor 'during this difficult time would make anyone re-think their stance on the language and Welshness'.[20]

Dafydd studied Philosophy, History and Welsh in his first year, but given his acknowledged academic brilliance, remarkably, he totally failed Philosophy, due, as his report concluded bluntly, to 'no work' in his first two terms. He had been taken ill with flu at the end of the first term, but he had also failed utterly to grasp the Logic paper. This angered his father, who tutored his son at home that summer, and he subsequently passed his re-sit, before going on to study Welsh in his second year.[21] That autumn, the immediate impression he made on his first girlfriend, Elen Williams, a newly arrived student, was that he was 'full of confidence. He was very sure of himself, and very clever.' She was a bright student from a working-class family brought up in Dolgellau, and came to Bangor in October 1965 to study Music. One of the first occasions she remembers him was his passionate appeal to the members of the Plaid's College branch to attempt to disrupt the opening of the Tryweryn dam, in October 1965.[22]

He had accompanied his father to the deconsecration of the Presbyterian chapel in Tryweryn, in September 1963,[23] and he joined the protest against the opening of the dam, on 21 October 1965. Two busloads of protestors from Bangor and Aberystwyth Colleges joined the demonstrators in an attempt to disrupt proceedings, and Dafydd played an active part. The protest was largely non-violent, although stones were thrown at the Liverpool delegation, and the event also witnessed the first appearance of the uniformed paramilitary Free Wales Army. The Plaid Cymru President, Gwynfor Evans attempted unsuccessfully to pacify the crowd,[24] but retired to witness the event from the side of the hill looking down on the valley, as had the party's general secretary, Elwyn Roberts. He was a close friend of his namesake, Elwyn Roberts, also from Abergynolwyn, the Chief Constable of Meirionnydd. Dafydd Elis recalled that they had come to an agreement that nobody would be arrested if the proceedings were not disrupted:

Of course there was a serious attempt at disruption. I think the PA system was taken down, sort of pulled out. The ceremony didn't happen properly as they expected to be able to do it. The Chief Constable apparently told Elwyn Roberts; 'I kept my side of the bargain, didn't I?'[25]

Emyr Price recalled Dafydd as the brightest student of his generation. He achieved academic success 'without doing a stroke of work', and his main ambition was 'to be a politician'. He was an 'intellectual butterfly through political and intellectual circles throughout his subsequent career' and 'a skilled and original writer'.[26] Dafydd Elis became editor of the University Welsh language newspaper, *Y Dyfodol*, in 1965-6, succeeded a year later by Price, and then by his other close friend, Cenwyn Edwards.

Dafydd's concerns as editor reflected those of his fellow Welsh speaking students, and his last editorial, in March 1966, focused on Welsh language protests and the first imprisonment of a language activist, Geraint Jones, for refusing to fill official forms in English. He called on readers to follow his example and refuse to pay their car tax unless they were in Welsh.

His front page feature in March 1966, was a wittily written insider story on the illegal 'pirate' radio station, *Radio Bronco*, set up by Bangor students to raise money for their Rag Week. With a short range of five miles, its radio waves interrupted the playing of *God Save the Queen* on the BBC and TWW, the commercial television company. This stunt involved a radio transmitter, borrowed from Plaid Cymru and broadcast from the garden of Dafydd's hall of residence, for four nights and undetected by the Post Office (who regulated television transmission at the time). The article did not name those students involved, but craftily identified each student by their home town or village. Thus 'Llanrwst' (Dafydd Elis Thomas) was both author and one of the broadcasters. The radio was transported from Plaid Cymru by 'Llanber' (Emlyn Davies, from Llanberis), and 'Edern' (Glyn Williams). With the help of Rhosgadfan (Norman Williams), Llangennech (Cenwyn Edwards), Wyddgrug (Gwilym Hughes) and others, the aerial was placed in the garden of Reichel Hall. In the meantime, 'Cwmstrallyn' (Emyr Price) sat in Reichel's common room, monitoring the television to check reception.

This stunt attracted huge publicity with the *Daily Express, Daily Mirror, Western Mail*, the BBC and TWW all giving it widespread coverage. By its last night of transmission, the Post Office had dispatched two detection vans from Chester to investigate and track down the culprits. That evening, the students played a game of cat and mouse, following the vans, and then moving the radio transmitter to different locations. The following morning, the intrepid editor had the temerity to interview a Post Office representative, and described the exchange:

> At the main GPO building in Bangor, I asked an engineer whether a radio had been operating in Bangor. 'No', he said, "That's illegal.' When the correspondent referred to the van outside, the engineer lost his temper. 'Yes', he said, 'It's true. They broadcast at midnight after TWW shuts down. But we have nothing to do with it. It's Chester that you need.'
>
> Our correspondent insisted on seeing someone in authority. Mr Welsh, a pleasant Englishman, who is the Chief Engineer for the GPO in Bangor, led your correspondent to his office on the second floor, where the man who had been driving the van the previous evening was sat, with a tired look about him. 'You have caught us in our lair', said Mr Welsh. 'You understand', he said, 'that we can't say anything to the press.' Your correspondent explained that he wasn't from the press, but the College. 'The enemy', said the van man, and grimaced. He went to his wallet and took out every quotation and every picture which had appeared in every paper about the radio. 'No, I don't think I know them', said the correspondent.
>
> 'They are breaking the law and they are a nuisance to us. We have got to stop this' said the van man sullenly. The correspondent sympathised. 'Have you caught them yet?' 'No', said the van man bitterly, 'but we will.'[27]

No-one was ever detained, but this journalistic endeavour reflected Dafydd's wit and roguishness. Student politics figured heavily in his writing, and he railed against the rapid expansion of the College, and its ambitious target to attract an additional five thousand students by 1978. He warned that the College's policy would change Bangor's character:

This isn't sentimental nonsense about the working class's (werin) scarce pennies ... Bangor has always had a Welsh character. If this massive expansion takes place, it will be erased. We are told that the college is expanding its horizons. People say that the university is supposed to be an international institution. If it was a truly broad and international institution, I would not complain. But it is an English institution.[28]

Under Price's editorship, he started a series of satirical articles *O'r Gazelle i'r Bel Fiw*. The Gazelle pub in Anglesey had the best view of the Menai Straits, and the Belle Vue was a hierarchical hostelry in Upper Bangor where its landlord only allowed entry to postgraduate students if accompanied by an academic member of staff. One article purported to be the diary of a disgruntled card-playing student, another featured a satirical and mendacious view of the requirements for success in a candidate for the union Presidency (when his own friend Gwynn Matthews was competing successfully for the role), emphasising the need to be two-faced, cynical and image-conscious.[29]

In Price's view, Dafydd's writing showed 'real character', and in his judgement, never wrote anything better.[30] In October 1966, in a bold intervention in the sometimes tense relationship between Welsh speaking students in Aberystwyth and Bangor, the three friends, Dafydd, Emyr Price and Cenwyn Edwards, publicly criticised Aberystwyth for pursuing the aim of establishing a hall of residence solely for Welsh speaking male students. In doing so, they reflected their political philosophy of engagement with their fellow English and non-Welsh speaking students, rather than by creating a Welsh medium hostel as a bulwark against English influences:

> It was not 'through retreating and surrendering, and not through shrinking thought and community, but through living together openly' that the language would be protected, and they cited their success in student politics in Bangor, stating that 'although we fight against the increasing overflow of students from England, we do so in an open and unmalicious manner. The result here is that the few Welsh here can put their stamp clearly on the activities of the Students' Union'. In warning against student expansion and the threat to the University of Wales's character, they emphasised

that 'the Welsh language and Welsh life in the colleges must be central, rather than totally vacating the stage ... We in Bangor have learnt that it is not through preaching national obsessions in student newspapers, or retreating in monk-like purity to a Welsh language hostel we should do, but by insisting on our rights in Senate and council and common room, that Welsh language life in the University of Wales is maintained and expanded.'[31]

The trenchant tone of this letter reflected their distinctive approach to language politics in Bangor. As the College historian later commented, 'there do not appear to have been in the 1960s the sharp clashes in Bangor which characterised university-student relations elsewhere', notably Aberystwyth.[32]

However, a year later, Dafydd Elis had changed his mind, due to the perceived threat of increased recruitment from England. He used his platform in *Y Dyfodol* to congratulate Aberystwyth University on its decision to create a Welsh medium hall of residence, but stated this should only be the first step – 'the next step is to establish a Welsh medium college to teach a limited a number of subjects through the medium of Welsh alongside one of our present Colleges. This is the method of dealing with minority languages in Europe.'[33] Bangor College's first Welsh medium mixed hall of residence, Neuadd Syr John Morris Jones, was only opened in 1974, and also reflected a more liberal age – women had only previously been allowed in men's rooms in Reichel Hall on a Sunday evening.

In the Welsh language literary magazine, *Ffenics*, he composed learned and thoughtful articles on creating a new literary aesthetic,[34] wrote substantial book reviews such as his lengthy review of the newly published Penguin Book of Welsh Verse,[35] and wrestled with the moral crisis of Christianity.[36] All were remarkably mature discussions of theology and literature, including a post-modernist interpretation of medieval poetry that would presage his doctorate. He was considered a serious and exceptionally talented student, but he was often satirised kindly by his friends – *Y Dyfodol* suggested that his interest in the moral issue of the 'emptiness of meaning' might lead 'the arch-theologian Dafydd Ellis Thomas' to pursue the ministry of one of Bangor's most popular chapels amongst students, Twrgwyn Calvinist Methodist church, conveniently situated next door to the *Belle Vue*.[37]

As an articulate student activist, Dafydd naturally appealed to television producers eager to reflect the concerns of youth in their programmes. Programme producers such as the news editor of HTV's daily news magazine *Y Dydd*, Owen Roberts, had already controversially given a platform to Dafydd Iwan's satirical political songs, and encouraged other youthful voices.

From his second year onwards, Dafydd made frequent appearances on television, often accompanied by either Emyr Price or Cenwyn Edwards, driving to Cardiff to take part in live current affairs debates in order to reflect the views of the youth of the day. The media would often use *Y Dyfodol*'s serving and past editors to reflect the perspective of young people on politics, so, as Cenwyn Edwards recalls, 'Emyr, Dafydd and I would often go to Cardiff to record programmes like HTV's *Y Dydd* and *'04.05 ac ati'*, and discuss current affairs for young people'.[38] For instance, both Emyr and Dafydd went to Cardiff to appear on a current affairs programme to cross-examine Elystan Morgan, who had left Plaid Cymru for the Labour Party. As an enthusiastic Plaid member, Dafydd attacked Morgan, while Price was more conciliatory. They took part in other news programmes such as the BBC's *Heddiw* magazine programme recorded in Manchester, but a sad memory for them was Emyr Price and Dafydd's journey to Cardiff to take part in a BBC programme. On their journey down, they were told to take an alternative route to Cardiff around Merthyr Tydfil – it was the day of the Aberfan disaster, and that evening their appearance was inevitably cancelled.[39] Dafydd was now becoming a recognised public figure in Welsh speaking Wales, as he also become a regular panellist on heavyweight literary and philosophical programmes such as *Dan Sylw* with his friend Derec Llwyd Morgan, involving frequent discussions on literature, which attracted the scabrous magazine *Lol* to satirise his modish bouffant hair and wide kipper ties.

Student Politics

Dafydd Elis threw himself into student politics, and the experience of Welsh-speaking students being in a minority gave him valuable lessons in the art of creating political coalitions. Throughout his period in Bangor, the influential minority of Welsh speaking students retained political control over the students' union, under the leadership of a series of able Presidents such as Euryn Ogwen, a future television executive who helped nurture his broadcasting career, Iwan Humphreys, and Gwynn Matthews. He was elected deputy secretary of the students' representative council for the academic year 1965-6, and recalled succeeding in bringing order to a students' general meeting at which militant anarchists sought to disrupt proceedings:

> Those experiences were part of a greater training. I certainly learnt how to establish a constituency. So, I lived at Reichel Hall, which meant I got Reichel support which was close to the Plas Gwyn hall. I used to go there canvassing and then there were smaller residences so we would go there and campaign. But then I had some very good friends who were in agricultural sciences, and in other parts of the university. I would go and talk to these people because we had got to show them that the Student's Representatives are for everyone ... I learned the importance of the power of the Athletic Unions in terms of political pressure ... that was a very important learning experience that you had to cultivate support. Being available to be a spokesperson for different groups was something which I learnt very much at that time.
>
> It was coalition politics. We always used to get the votes of the overseas students, all the Iraqis because we bonded with them, we involved them, including the agriculture students, and the forestry people, we just mobilised them.[40]

Student politics in Bangor was inevitably embroiled in the debate over the Welshness of the College. In a presentation to the Bangor's Senate in 1966, two senior academics, the historian J. Gwynn Williams and Welsh scholar Melville Richards argued that for the first time, Bangor should develop Welsh medium provision. They expressed concern at Bangor being 'the least '"Welsh" of all the Welsh colleges and the most cosmopolitan', and that a Welsh medium programme might help to redress the balance.[41]

In May 1966, Dafydd was again elected on to the students' representative council (SRC). In an analysis of the candidates, the university's English language student newspaper *Forecast*, described Dafydd as 'a leading member of the UCNW Welsh community, editor of *Dyfodol* and President-elect of *Y Cymric*. Likely to do a solid job on SRC.'[42]

In November 1966, he became a member of the sub-committee to review the use of Welsh in the students' union and joined a student review group to consider the impact of student expansion on the social and academic nature of the College. Dafydd encouraged his friend Gwynn Matthews, who was then completing his teachers' training course, to stand for the presidency in the summer of 1966, which he won, and Dafydd became one of his closest allies. He also joined the Central Students Representative Council of the old federal University of Wales, and with Matthews,[43] took the radical step of disaffiliating Bangor's student union from the National Union of Students, buying in services such as travel and insurance, from Ireland's student body. Matthews became President of the National Council of students within the University of Wales, and Dafydd actively supported him, driving him on his visits, and campaigning with him in colleges across Wales.[44]

But his active social life, and his roles as editor of *Y Dyfodol*, student politician and media pundit, also extracted a price. For Bangor students, their second year in college was seen as a time for enjoyment rather than academic discipline. Dafydd was one of seven out of ten second year students in the Welsh department who failed that year's exams, achieving an average of only 36.5 marks for that year. By the following year however he had recovered his enthusiasm for academic life, and in June 1967, achieved a celebrated first-class honours degree in Welsh, with an average of 75 per cent, and joined his closest friends, Cenwyn Edwards and Emyr Price, in undertaking a Masters degree. At his degree ceremony that summer, he famously conducted a one-man 'sit-down' demonstration, in protest at the quality of Welsh used in the ceremony, and the playing of the national anthem, *God Save the Queen*. The local paper reported the comments of the 'lone protester':

> 'I will always do this when I am in Wales because I do not acknowledge the Queen of England as queen of my country'. Mr Thomas, who is a member of Plaid Cymru and the Welsh Language Society, said he was also making a protest against the way in which no effort was made at the ceremony to speak Welsh correctly. This is typical of the attitude in this University College towards the Welsh language. It was as if an attempt was being made to make a joke of the language. The incident took place after the playing of *Hen Wlad Fy Nhadau*.[45]

He was granted a full scholarship for his Masters and began his study of Welsh medieval elegiac poetry. In leaving Reichel Hall, his home for three years, he was ambitious for smart new accommodation befitting the trio's status as mature research students. They initially approached the Archdruid of Wales, A. E. 'Cynan' Jones, who owned a flat for rent in Menai Bridge overlooking the Straits, but which unfortunately had already been let. By luck they found two other flats in the palatial setting of Plas Rhianfa, set on the Menai Straits, and facing Bangor across the water. This was a Grade two listed chateau built in 1849–51, inspired by the chateaux of the Loire, and now converted into a number of apartments. Emyr Price and a fellow student lodged in the smaller top flat and Dafydd and Cenwyn shared the more sumptuous bottom floor flat, whose garden ran down to the water's edge.

A condition of their tenancy was that parties should not be hosted in the building. But at the end of the Annual Inter-college Eisteddfod in Bangor on the last day of February 1968, which had attracted hundreds of students from across Wales, Dafydd's excitement got the better of him, and in the Menai Vaults in Upper Bangor, he recklessly invited everyone to come back to their apartment to continue their celebrations. Those hundreds who turned up made for a memorable evening, spilling over the lawns leading down to the sea front, while dozens slept over. The following morning, the building's strict Scottish manager gave them notice to quit with immediate effect. The mortified tenants decided to appeal, and both Cenwyn and Dafydd, now wearing their best Sunday suits, figuratively threw themselves on the mercy of the owner, a local solicitor. Dafydd conducted the negotiation, and after fifteen minutes, over sherry, mentioned he was a prospective parliamentary candidate for Plaid Cymru, declared there had been no intention of holding such an unruly event, and apologised convincingly. The landlord was swayed and rescinded the decision to evict them.[46]

Meanwhile, he was establishing his academic career. Gaining a first class degree in July 1967 had confirmed his reputation as one of the brightest students of his generation in Bangor. He was seen as a young academic with great potential, and he quickly converted his Masters into a doctorate under the tutelage of one of his academic heroes, Professor Geraint Gruffydd:

> He was my counsel, a first time teacher at Bangor, and he persuaded me to do an MA. I was told that I had had the best first

in Welsh in Bangor since 1962. The added attraction was, of course, that I then got full funding for two years for the MA, with payment for accommodation. Praise and love poetry had already been 'done'. He wanted me to do the late-medieval early Renaissance period because he wanted me to have the experience of reading text. But he also knew that I was very interested as he was, in comparative literature ... there was the convention of addressing the dead person in the first person, as if that person was still alive. And, of course, the whole point of this convention is that the dead person cannot reply ... I read three thousand of the original penned manuscripts. It was a very important experience and it was at this point I converted from an MA into a PhD.[47]

These poems were written by *cywyddwyr*, a term derived from the most popular metre of the time, the *cywydd*, which consists of rhyming couplets with cynghanedd. These were the poets of the gentry in late medieval and early modern Wales, between the 1300s and the early 1600s. Many were highly trained professionals, though there was also a large amateur and semi-professional element. The literary students of these *cywyddau* based their studies on pure textual analysis, but Dafydd Elis's academic approach was more intellectually daring and aimed to assess and critique these elegies from a Marxist and an early post-modernist viewpoint, analysing the relationship between death and life. This pioneering approach marked his work as original and groundbreaking. His friend, Derec Llwyd Morgan, considered him to be:

> One of the best literary critics I know – he was literate and cultured and had original things to say about Welsh language poetry. He was a literary theoretician, and had a very different view to more conservative critics, and that is why his opinion was so valuable. He would have been an excellent University lecturer.[48]

His research work on elegiac poetry led him to work in the National Library of Wales, after being appointed by the Board of Celtic Studies in 1970, to index the *cywyddau* manuscripts, a laborious task that he intensely disliked. He found it 'the worst work that you could be doing, for years and years. I was in the library with my pencils and I was looking at manuscripts because none of this was online.'[49]

Plaid Cymru's electoral prospects had seemed moribund until the Carmarthen by-election in July 1966, when Gwynfor Evans, one of Dafydd's heroes at the time, won the party's first parliamentary seat and propelled the party into public recognition, where 'Welsh nationalism had come of age, and Gwynfor was its icon'.[50] In the year after the by-election, the party doubled its membership and predicted that it could win eight seats at the next General Election. In 1967, amongst local concerns at rising unemployment, Plaid won 39.9 per cent of the vote at a by-election in Rhondda West, reducing the Labour majority from 17,000 to just over 2,000. The following year, in Caerphilly, it reduced a Labour majority from over 21,000 to 1,874, and as the historian Martin Johnes suggests, 'suddenly, the Labour hegemony in Wales seemed under real threat'.[51]

Becoming a Plaid Cymru candidate

In his time in Bangor University, Dafydd had become the main conduit between its nationalist students and Plaid Cymru's general secretary, Elwyn Roberts, who worked from its national headquarters in Bangor. Dafydd was one of the few students to have a car, and in addition to ferrying fellow students to work for the party, was an active volunteer in the Plaid Cymru office. During the 1966 General Election, he proved his first experience of political and public humiliation. Jim Griffiths MP for Llanelli, the first Secretary of State for Wales, had come to speak in a Labour rally at a local school, near Bangor railway station, as Dafydd recalls:

> I had the temerity to heckle Jim Griffiths because he spoke mainly in English. I said (in Welsh) thank you for at least listening to a few words of Welsh from the Secretary of State for Wales. So, I had the best put down I have ever had in my whole life. He said, 'Don't you talk to me about Welsh, boy. There is more Welsh spoken in Llanelli than the whole of Wales put together.' Imagine I said something so silly. But that's what happened in political meetings in those days. People did heckle.[52]

But his intervention had impressed Griffiths, who, after the meeting, turned to one of his local aides, Wyn Thomas, and said that the young man should be in the Labour party.[53]

UNIVERSITY DAYS

But although he had an enthusiasm and aptitude for politics, Dafydd's ambition was to become an university lecturer in Welsh literature, and even though Gwynfor Evans's success was fresh in the mind, a career in politics for a Plaid Cymru member in the 1960s was extremely unlikely. However, working for the party took up an increasing amount of his time, and Gwynn Matthews recalls his growing involvement in the party:

> Dafydd had Elwyn Roberts's ear. He placed great trust in Dafydd, so that Dafydd was the link with Blaid centrally. Elwyn was a big influence on both Dafydd and me. His dedication to high standards was an example to all.[54]

In the summer of 1967, at the party's summer school in Dolgellau, Dafydd Elis was elected national chair of Plaid Cymru's youth branch and joined the party's monthly national executive:

> The key thing for me was that I had representation. I was treated as an equal. Had there been votes, although I don't think it tended to work like that, I would have been able to vote, representing the youth section. There was also a full-time youth organiser, who was Dyfrig Thomas from Llanelli – there was a (political) machine and could operate effectively. For that, I'm very grateful for the support I had more widely ... and that's where Dafydd Orwig comes in, because he was the organiser *par excellence*, him and Elwyn Roberts. They were absolutely determined to be organised. Dafydd Orwig had a mantra which was *Rhaid trefnu buddugoliaeth delfrydau*, that is, that it is fruitless having ideas, if they're not organised and you don't have the means to deliver.[55]

In 1967, fortified by the success of the Carmarthen by-election, Plaid Cymru decided to fight every parliamentary seat for the first time. Its General Secretary, Elwyn Roberts, asked Gwynn Matthews and Dafydd to fight two seats in the following general election, in Conway[56] and Denbigh, but left the final decision where they should stand to them. The choice was obvious, as Dafydd's hometown of Llanrwst was in the Conway constituency, but the final decision would need to be made by the local constituency. Before the critical selection meeting, he phoned his father for advice and expressed his fear that he was only a young and inexperienced student. His father's retort was that 'if people think you are good enough, if people ask you to do something, you have got to do it'. In 1967, at the remarkably young age of 21, he was selected as Plaid Cymru's prospective parliamentary candidate for the Conway constituency. He believes that his selection was orchestrated by Dafydd Orwig, a teacher and a pioneer of the party in the Ogwen Valley:

> It was a brilliant constituency to start in for me, because its where I had been brought up, where I had been a student. I knew the area, the characters and the people in the party, and I still had my family home there. There was a lot of opportunity for networking within those areas. I had a base at the eastern end in the Conwy valley in Llanrwst, and I'd also spend a lot of my time when I was growing up, going to Colwyn Bay or Llandudno, where there were a lot of musical performances and theatre.
>
> I knew the whole of the area very well and that's why I think we did so well in the 1970 General Election, because there was a base and there was a network. There is no other route, you can't just be parachuted in. We had a very strong organisation, and strong support from active people, independent councillors, as well as some Plaid councillors. There were Labour supporters who thought that there should be a change. Realising that that was possible was a very important lesson. Voting for Plaid was not about voting for independence for Wales tomorrow, it was about the beginning of a process for the people of Wales having their say ... In a sense, what we were trying to do was to say that we were a political party ... but that we were also the most effective pressure group for what you want in your community, whether it's economic, cultural, or agricultural policy. It was all about keeping up the pressure for Wales.[57]

Dafydd Elis's selection for the Conway seat in 1967 was greeted with enthusiasm locally. New party branches were created in his first year, and there was energetic fundraising, with a barbecue in the Ogwen valley for example, attracting 750 people. He was supported by his fellow Bangor students, and Conway's branch had 200 members by 1968, most joining the previous year. The party newspaper celebrated his impact, explaining that he kept himself in the news politically and socially in the local press, and that photographs of his visits to places such as Penrhyn Quarry and Dolgarrog Aluminium Works appeared constantly.[58] He was helped by the high profile of two of the other candidates who were well known television personalities – the Conservative Wyn Roberts, a former Head of Programmes for TWW, who had been a popular reporter on the company's Welsh news, and Ednyfed Hudson Davies, another well-known broadcaster, and the sitting Labour candidate, who had unexpectedly won the seat in 1966. Dafydd became good friends with both, and his relationship with Roberts would be significant in later years.

However, before the General Election, together with Gwynn Matthews, he campaigned in the 1968 Caerphilly by-election and absorbed the party's election tactics. One of Plaid's staff, the poet Gerallt Llwyd Owen, raised money for the campaign through Welsh language pop concerts – *Pinaclau Pop*. But it was a shock for both to realise that nobody spoke Welsh in the campaign's main office in Bargoed and that its candidate Phil Williams had prohibited north-Walians from speaking publicly in the campaign. As Dafydd recalls, 'we weren't to pronounce Gelligaer and Tirphil in too Welsh a manner!'[59]

His political campaigning and greater media profile took up much of his free time until the General Election held in June 1970. From May 1967 onwards, Plaid Cymru's greatest challenge had been to counter the political effect of the contentious Investiture of Charles, the eldest son of the Queen, as the Prince of Wales, to be held in July 1969 in Caernarfon Castle, and the following two years saw a succession of protest rallies and demonstrations to protest against what was seen as a political stunt, a colonial imposition and a waste of public money.[60] However, opinion was split in Wales, and Plaid Cymru was officially circumspect in its attitude, 'fearing alienating its youthful supporters by endorsing the event or the wider population by opposing it. In the end its official line was to ignore the investiture as much as possible.'[61]

The chair of Plaid's youth wing contested the party's lead however, and in May 1968, railed fiercely against the Investiture in its combative newspaper, *I'r Gad* ('To Battle'):

> Unfortunately for them, the English politicians have miscalculated the Cymru of 1969. We have voted for freedom at Caerfyrddin and Rhondda, and are not turning back. Some of us have been in English prisons because we are determined that

our national language will never die, and we will not give in. We
don't want the medieval hangover of a prince, we don't want the
meaningless, powerless symbol of a dying Empire. What we want
is the real institution of a modern nation, a Parliament. We want
a Parliament, not a Prince. *Senedd nid Tywysog*. And that is what
we are determined to get. So if you don't want to make a fool of
yourself in the greatest farce of modern Welsh history, don't come
to Caernarfon in '69 but go back to Cambridge, Charlie Boy.
Wales has her own leaders and her own destiny now.[62]

His rancorous opposition, however, did not prevent him from accepting a private invitation to meet Prince Charles while he was a student at Aberystwyth University, in the company of four other students, at the behest of Tedi Millward, a prominent nationalist and Prince Charles's Welsh language tutor. Dafydd stated clearly his distaste at having an English Prince of Wales foisted upon the nation, and the Prince, in turn, listened politely.[63]

But his life was shaken to its core on 24 May 1969, by the death of his beloved father. His sister Elin was away in college at the time, and his mother had been taken to hospital in Liverpool with a blood condition. Dafydd was at home when his father suffered an aneurysm, and accompanied him in the ambulance to Colwyn Bay hospital, where he died within days. Dafydd was in shock – 'it really hit me.'[64] His mother was too ill to attend the funeral and she remained in hospital for a few weeks. On her return, she had to be constantly administered courses of injections which failed to stem her ill-health related to the blood-condition, for the rest of her days.

A congregation of 800 attended the memorial service, and a series of seven speakers from the Presbyterian denomination, including a representative of the General Assembly of the Presbyterian Church of Wales, paid warm tributes to the passing of a popular and well-respected minister. 'He had something to say to everybody in Llanrwst', said Robert Jones, the secretary of Seion in his funeral oration, 'and he was the same with everybody, whether he met them fishing on the riverbank or in a church service, in their homes or working on local committees. He was a man of high principles and a man who won others to respect those principles.'[65]

One of W.E.'s responsibilities for the church in the Conwy Valley had been to mentor trainee ministers. One of his mentees, Revd Dafydd

Andrew Jones, recalls the main street of Llanrwst lined by local people, unrelated to the chapel, paying homage to W.E. and his contribution to the town, as the cortege passed. Only six weeks before the controversial Investiture, which he had opposed vehemently in his role as chair of Plaid Cymru's youth movement, the young Dafydd now had to set aside his political concerns to console his ill mother, young sister, and distressed aunt.[66] His parents had already arranged to move from their home in Llanrwst into an old manse two miles away in the village of Trefriw, on W.E.'s retirement, and now Eirlys and Annie suffered this tragic bereavement in totally unexpected circumstances. Over the following weeks, Dafydd helped them move into their new home where they quickly became members of the local Presbyterian chapel ministered by Dafydd Andrew Jones, and Eirlys became a particularly active member of the congregation.

Weeks later, on the first of July, the controversial Investiture of the Prince of Wales was held, but Dafydd Elis may well have felt that politics provided little consolation for his personal loss, and in common with his party, did not attempt a public protest:

> I had no intention of watching the investiture that day. I was working in the Plaid Cymru office in Bangor, which was a silly thing to do really because I was within five miles of the event, but I wasn't stopped or anything, it was business as usual. I thought the most sensible thing to do was to go to work. Many in the nationalist movement were tense . . . I did feel tense at the possibility of an attack on the event . . . which would have been political terrorism . . . And if you mess about with that, that has always had a negative political effect, in Wales, anyway.[67]

Within the family, the loss of W.E. broke Annie's heart. Her minister, Dafydd Andrew Jones believes that Annie did not possess the mental reserves to avoid crippling depression, recalling that she cried constantly for her brother, and that her previous emotional problems overwhelmed her:

> She had been obedient to her brother and sister-in-law, long suffering, never answering back, and acted as a surrogate mother, much loved, to Elin, and her brother Dafydd, but her brother's death broke her.[68]

Within the year, Annie spent a number of periods in the gloomy mental hospital in Denbigh, receiving treatment for depression, and finally died there, ostensibly of heart disease, in January 1974.

Elin's friend, Ann Ffrancon, recalls that Elin had 'gone wild' and become less disciplined even before losing her father, and although she had tried to concentrate on her college work at Bangor University College, where she had started in October 1968, she found it difficult to adjust to life during her holidays at their new home in Trefriw.[69] Revd Dafydd Andrew Jones, recalls 'that things were not well between the mother and Elin (even) before W.E.'s death'. Two years later, after she had finished her college course, Elin became a teacher in Llanfyllin, and the relationship with her mother remained fractious.[70]

W.E.'s death was naturally traumatic for his son. His father had provided him with an unshakeable confidence in his own abilities, skills of argument and oratory, and a profound respect for formal religion and public service. His father's heart problems encouraged Dafydd to exercise, and he took up running obsessively. After Cenwyn Edwards had joined HTV's news department, he recalls organising a television interview with Dafydd Elis in Rhydymain, six miles outside Dolgellau, where Dafydd had run twelve miles there and back from his home. He maintained a disciplined regime of daily running throughout his life, until his mid-seventies.[71]

His performance as Plaid Cymru's candidate in the June 1970 General Election in Conway was a great improvement on his party's performance in 1966, almost doubling the Plaid vote.

Conway	June 1970	
Wyn Roberts (Conservative)	16,927	42.4%
Ednyfed Hudson Davies (Labour)	16,024	40.2%
Dafydd Elis Thomas (Plaid Cymru)	4,311	10.8%
Elfyn Morris (Liberal)	2,626	6.6%[72]

He took most of his new voters from Labour, which effectively resulted in Labour's Ednyfed Hudson Davies losing his seat. His friend Gwynn Matthews also did well in Denbigh, succeeding in almost doubling the party's vote there, from 2,695 in 1966 to 5,254 in 1970.[73] Amongst those who also did well was Dafydd Wigley in Merioneth where he doubled the Plaid vote to 5,425, with 24.3 per cent of the vote.[74]

Overall, the party's performance showed an increase in its national vote from 61,071 in 1966 to 175,016 in 1970, and its voting share almost trebled from 4.3 per cent to 11.5 per cent. But in spite of some isolated improvements in performance, it was largely a disappointing election, mainly because Gwynfor Evans lost his Carmarthen seat, and 25 of their 36 candidates lost their deposits.[75]

Dafydd's relationship with his first girlfriend, Elen Williams from Dolgellau, had sustained, and after studying music in Bangor, she moved to train as a social worker in Cardiff University. After completing her year's course, she moved to live with Dafydd, who by this time lived in Llanarth, near Aberaeron, and they married in July 1970. Elen worked in the children's services unit in Cardiganshire Social Services, based in Aberaeron, while Dafydd Elis studied for his doctorate at the National Library of Wales. In November 1970, an invitation came from the Warden of Coleg Harlech, asking him to appear for an interview as a Welsh language lecturer.

Coleg Harlech was a notable hotbed of former union activists, militant socialists and Labour-leaning academic staff and students, and its appeal to the politically astute young academic seemed obvious. He was quickly appointed as a lecturer in Welsh language and literature,[76] and within two weeks of his appointment, in November 1970, at the ripe age of 24, he was teaching adults three times his age.[77] Dafydd moved to Dolgellau to live in a spare room in Elen's mother's house, and Elen joined him shortly, and within a few months started work in the social services department in Dolgellau. Dafydd continued to make regular appearances on the media, discussing politics as well as taking part in cultural and literary programmes, and appeared regularly as an interviewer on HTV Wales's *Cymru Heddiw* (Wales Today) series in the late 1960s.

As they settled in Dolgellau, he had already decided that after the 1970 Election he would not wish to contest Conway again, and was contemplating standing in the more promising seat of Caernarfon, partly because of his links with the adjacent Bangor University.[78] He formally turned down the candidacy for Conway in May 1972,[79] and recalls that this decision was made 'reluctantly' but eased by a 'major difference of opinion between myself and the Plaid Cymru executive committee in Conwy'.[80] This arose because of Dafydd Elis's support for the creation of a hydro-electric scheme in the Conway Valley and the *Daily Post* reported his response to his party's executive committee's opposition to the plan:

I have always strongly supported the scheme and in my view there can be no compromise where work for the unemployed people of Wales is at stake. I pointed out to the committee that I wanted to be free to press the Government to go ahead with this scheme.

Dafydd Elis was subsequently talked of as the candidate for Arfon, Plaid's most winnable seat, at the forthcoming General Election.[81] At the same time, the candidate for Merioneth, Dafydd Wigley, who had performed well there in the 1970 General Election, now found that his family circumstances made it unwise to stand again in that seat, as he recalls:

The background was complicated. One of the factors were Rio Tinto Zinc's (RTZ) plans to mine for copper in the Mawddach estuary area and I found myself in a difficult position. I had based my 1970 campaign on the importance of getting work for the area. My father-in-law was acting as a land and housing agent in Dolgellau and working on matters to do with RTZ.[82]

Dafydd Elis had been as uncompromising as Wigley in his support for RTZ's exploratory drilling, and in July 1971, as Plaid's director of policy, had publicly hailed the Secretary of State for Wales's decision to allow RTZ to drill in the Mawddach Estuary and the Coed y Brenin area as a victory for the people of Merioneth 'over a county council who took no notice of public opinion and over 80 per cent of the outside objectors at the public inquiry . . . It would be a crime to leave viable mineral resources in the ground undeveloped in Merioneth, with such a high rate of unemployment.'[83]

This was one of the most controversial political issues in mid Wales in the early seventies, and whilst he took a very clear stance in favour of RTZ, Dafydd Wigley was fatally compromised locally, since his father-in-law, Emrys Bennett Owen, acted as the land agent for Rio Tinto Zinc. Both Dafydds attended a protest meeting in Cwm Hermon in the summer of 1972, and it became utterly obvious from the strong anti-RTZ emotions on display that Wigley's family links made his political position untenable. Under the circumstances, Wigley announced his resignation to the Merioneth constituency party, and urged that Dafydd Elis should succeed him as the prospective Plaid candidate. Both he and Dafydd Wigley had already agreed privately that he should stand in Caernarfon and Dafydd Elis in Merioneth. The leaders of the local party in the Caernarfon constituency, such as the wealthy businessman Dilan Morgan Edwards, and the influential constituency agent, Wmffra Roberts, aided by the retirement of their previous candidate, Robyn Lewis, also pressed Wigley to stand in the constituency.[84]

Dafydd Elis recalls that this secret pact was revealed by the *Crossbencher* political gossip column in the *Sunday Express*, who had been tipped off about this example of political 'musical chairs', probably by the self-interested observer of nationalist politics, the Labour Member of Parliament for Merioneth, Will Edwards. Dafydd Elis recalls that the news came as a shock to many:

> Something appeared in the political gossip column *Crossbencher* in the Sunday Express saying, 'Who do these people think they are? Do they think that the electorate will be conned by these people swapping seats?' I honestly don't remember the detail of how this came about, but I'm sure that the shadow of Elwyn Roberts was there, and the central office of the party were supportive, because they could see it made sense. Wigley had done very well in coming second in Meirionnydd. Obviously, his family connections were with Arfon.[85]

Both Dafydds got on well. Although very different characters as reflected in their backgrounds – Wigley a privately-educated finance director in manufacturing, and Dafydd Elis, the grammar school literary academic – they had collaborated as ambitious young candidates during the 1970 election and shared a mutual respect, even though their differing political perspectives would only later develop into open disagreement. Wigley's 1970 campaign had stimulated the development of an effective electoral organisation in the Merioneth constituency, and a full time organiser, Elfed Roberts, had been appointed, as well as a full time agent, and their members included an enthusiastic and committed crowd of young people such as Llew Huxley and John Rogers, who led the successful campaign to save the Cambrian Coast railway in 1972–73. While the Caernarfon seat was considered to be Plaid's most winnable seat, Wigley genuinely believed that there was a real possibility of Dafydd Elis winning Merioneth.[86]

In the meantime, Dafydd Elis had strengthened his roots in the Merioneth constituency. Living in Dolgellau and working in Coleg Harlech, he lectured for the Workers' Education Association throughout the county, with his connections spreading throughout the constituency, His father's family had originated in Llanuwchllyn, and had moved to the constituency's largest town, Blaenau Ffestiniog, where Elen was now becoming a well-known and respected social worker.

Dafydd Elis was selected formally as Merioneth's Plaid Cymru candidate in the summer of 1972. He had already become active in the trade union movement locally, and in the county's trades' council in particular, where he formed important friendships with local union leaders such as John Cooke, the influential regional convener of the Transport and General Workers' Union (TGWU). The trade union movement locally refused to fund the local Labour candidate, although they could not fund Dafydd Elis directly, even though he was a member of the Transport and General. While most of the Coleg Harlech staff had decided to remain with the Association of University Teachers, Dafydd was amongst a few who were more radical and joined the clerical section of the TGWU.

He also nurtured a warm relationship with the powerful farming unions locally:

> I'd always been living close to traditional hill farming, stock farming, sheep farming. As soon as I got to live in Dolgellau, I lived just outside the town, I rented from a local farmer, and part of the deal was ... I remember him saying to me, 'You realise, you have obligations to your landlord'. I said, 'Oh, what does this mean now?' He said, 'Only during the annual gathering'. I was like an unpaid, bloody sheepdog running around Cader Idris ... You cannot represent these people without being part of the life. You can't just do politics. Politics is based on networks. I remember sitting down in the office of *Cymdeithas Meirionnydd*, the co-operative society for farming and for local businesses such as creameries. Their director and chief executive, H. R. Jones was very active in Eisteddfod circles ... and then became a county councillor. I remember him telling me who was related to whom in different parts of the county, and the importance of treating Corwen and Edeirnion in the east of Meirionnydd, very differently from the way I would treat

Blaenau Ffestiniog. Dolgellau was easier because I was living there, and teaching and working there, and I knew a lot of people along the coast. I'd been doing my WEA classes in Aberystwyth and extra mural classes in Bangor, so I had a network of people that I knew. It was the same message, that you've got to be a proper part of the community before you can pretend you should be representing them.[87]

The drowning of Tryweryn became a totemic issue for Plaid Cymru from the 1960s onwards, and the party focused on it as an example of Wales's helplessness against the demands of London Government. But the issue was much more nuanced locally and divided opinion, because many tenant farmers had gratefully accepted Liverpool Corporation's compensation payments for removing them from Cwm Celyn. Dafydd recalls the support of one of the most influential councillors in the Bala area, the surveyor and auctioneer Tom Jones, of Llanuwchllyn who also led the popular *Godre'r Aran* choir, advising him how to deal with this particularly thorny question:

> I was in the *Cymdeithas Meirion* (the local farmers' cooperative society) company office. He came in, put £60 on the table, which was a hell of a lot of money in those days. He said, 'Pass this onto the treasury. Don't mention the drowning of Tryweryn.' I replied that I hadn't planned to do that . . . I remembered during the opening of the dam, that Tom Jones had driven in as quickly as he could, without running over any of the protesters, to go to the opening ceremony, because he'd been representing the interests of lots of tenant farmers . . . Some people had taken the money and agreed to move, and others had been bought up. That's lived with me.

In retrospect, he believed that Plaid Cymru's opposition to the drowning of Tryweryn had become self-indulgent:

> There's no point wandering around the place as if the bad old days were still with us. I think it's almost an illness, a particular condition of how a certain kind of nationalist who if he doesn't have a grievance, doesn't feel happy.[88]

He later wrote about the 'myth of Tryweryn' and Tom Jones's warning:

> I was given a serious piece of advice by a very senior member of the party in the constituency which I have followed ... It was the local equivalent of 'don't mention the war'. Never raise the issue of Celyn (Tryweryn). At the time I did not quite understand why. As a pale schoolboy I had attended the dissolution service at the chapel with my father, who had preached there many times, and later I joined other students from Bangor University to disrupt the official opening ceremony. My attitude towards the acts of violence on the construction site had been ambivalent. But neither could I sign up to 'Remembering Tryweryn'. The advice I was given was that Celyn had been seriously divisive within the local community, turning neighbour against neighbour and family against family.
>
> After 1974, I decided I had been right to take that advice. Within less than ten years of the opening of the enforced lake an elected representative of the party that had most strongly opposed the project now represented that site in the UK Parliament. This, and the subsequent creation of a Welsh National Water Development Authority, with the devolution of legislative power some twenty years later, meant that such an environment, social and cultural act of submersion could never happen again.[89]

But the fate of Tryweryn had fired up young nationalists in particular and was a motivating factor for the masses of young canvassers in the forthcoming election. In the summer of 1973, Dafydd and Elen bought their first house, *Fron Wnion*, a bungalow on the road towards Cader Idris, and Elen became pregnant with their first child. Dafydd continued to campaign enthusiastically, and took advantage of the party's effective organisation throughout the constituency. The stage was set for the next General Election. It is therefore remarkable that in the autumn of 1973, he decided to apply for a post as a lecturer in drama in Bangor College. This strongly suggests that at this point he was not convinced that he would succeed as a parliamentary candidate.

The party had also thought as much, and whilst Merioneth was a target seat, 'the reality was that Arfon was the only seat that Plaid realistically expected to win in 1974'.[90]

The job vacancy in Bangor University's drama department had arisen following Emyr Humphreys's departure to become a full-time writer. Drama was located within the English department, but the vacancy was for a Welsh medium lecturer. Dafydd Elis was one of six candidates, and in October 1973, three were interviewed on the short list.

He made an immediate impact in his interview, dressed flamboyantly with his trademark kipper tie. Already well known as a frequent broadcaster on literary topics, Meirion Edwards, one of the interviewing panel, recalls that 'he was the obvious choice; he was very broad in his range of interests and culture. He was very enthusiastic, had an extensive knowledge of drama, although that hadn't been the subject of his degree, and his youth made him a promising recruit.'[91]

He started as a lecturer in his alma mater in January 1974, and gave a few lectures. He then became ill with flu for a few days, and after the announcement of the 1974 General Election, did not return. Meirion Edwards recalls that:

> I don't think he had expected to be elected – he was only with us for between four and six weeks before disappearing. In those days, you were allowed to take time off for campaigning if you were a candidate. And that was the story of Dafydd Elis and his link with the drama department![92]

After barely a month of employment by the College, the election was called for 28 February 1974. Dafydd immediately claimed his holiday entitlement to a month's annual leave and launched his campaign.

3

'A PRIEST WHO HAS LOST HIS FAITH'

Plaid Cymru's campaigns in the Merioneth and Caernarfon constituencies during the February 1974 General Election were marked by a high degree of professionalism and enthusiasm. The two Plaid candidates represented a new generation who were, according to one of their close colleagues, a 'different breed'. Dafydd Wigley and Dafydd Elis Thomas were 'political to their fingertips' and shared a renewed desire for political power and electoral success.[1]

From 1967 onwards, Plaid had set its sights on both Caernarfon and Merioneth as realistic target seats for the party. The Merioneth party's membership reportedly increased from only forty in October 1966, to a thousand by July 1967.[2] Before 1970, even those Merioneth Labour party members who despised nationalists, had admired Wigley for his determined effort to embed Plaid Cymru in the constituency, particularly in working class Labour strongholds such as the constituency's biggest town of Blaenau Ffestiniog.[3]

By the 1970 Election, Plaid could boast a team of 400 canvassers throughout the constituency, who worked energetically up until election day.[4] The party moved beyond its heartland support from traditional cultural nationalists, and attracted a new generation of young people, impatient for change, so that the character of the local constituency party was transformed. Capitalising on the services of a dedicated agent and a full-time organiser for the duration of the campaign, more homes than ever before were canvassed, and the party produced locally focused publications on subjects such as farming and rural depopulation.[5]

By the February 1974 election, Dafydd Elis Thomas represented a younger, more dynamic party, making up in energy, enthusiasm and engagement, what Plaid Cymru lacked in financial clout.[6] He inherited a strong local organisation from Dafydd Wigley, who had crucially succeeded in coming second in the 1970 General Election, overtaking the Liberal candidate and doubling its share of the vote, making Plaid the challenger to Labour.[7]

Combating Labour

William Edwards, the sitting MP, was a generous man even to his political opponents, and he and Dafydd Elis agreed on much politically, with the exception of their contrasting views on membership of the European community, which Dafydd opposed, and Will Edwards enthusiastically championed. Dafydd Elis recalls Edwards generously giving him a lift home from London in 1973, after a cross-party demonstration there to save the Cambrian Coast Railway line that ran through the constituency. This campaign was led by a number of Plaid's local members and exemplified the party's attempt to broaden its base in the constituency.[8]

Eleri, Will Edwards's wife, recalls her husband's difficulty in combating his Plaid opponents, who posed as a radical alternative to Labour. Both Wigley and Dafydd Elis could be 'more Labour than Labour. In Plaid Cymru, you could be whoever you wanted to be.'[9] From his nomination in 1972 onwards, Dafydd Elis established good relations with the trade unions locally, through his involvement in the local trades council and his engagement with the influential union, the Transport and General. In contrast, Will Edwards was at loggerheads with the union's organiser for mid Wales, John Cooke, notably over the union's tactics during a bitter pay dispute between council lorry drivers, who were TGWU members, and the County Surveyor who dealt with the dispute on behalf of Merioneth County Council.

In a letter written three months before the 1974 General Election, Cooke wrote to the Merioneth Labour party's long-standing secretary, the redoubtable Owen Edwards, and berated the local MP for his attitude towards the union's lorry drivers, and ominously suggested that 'other parties', by which he meant Plaid Cymru, had shown greater support. He described the Surveyor's conduct as 'diabolical':

> You will be aware that we have called for his resignation on these facts. We do not much appreciate statements from the press from Mr Will Edwards MP disassociating himself from the resignation

call, and setting out how good the Surveyor is. Many of our council workers are furious over this matter. They would go further and tar and feathers have been mentioned! Will's stab in the back will not be forgotten in a hurry. Meetings are being held all over the county and I suggest you try and educate your MP on how Trades Unions operate. On the one hand he had criticised us for not being involved and on the other hand, as soon as we get involved, he reacts like a startled elephant and runs for cover. I might add that other parties involved in the political scene in Merioneth are taking a far more helpful attitude. I will keep you informed.[10]

Cooke was close to Dafydd Elis, and had arranged for him to chair a meeting organised in order to broker an agreement between the TGWU lorry drivers and the council. His support was also invaluable in gaining credibility for Plaid Cymru with the largest employer in the constituency, the Trawsfynydd nuclear power station, that employed over 600 staff, as well as with the quarrymen in the remaining slate quarries in the Blaenau Ffestiniog area.

In his reply to Cooke, Will Edwards argued that his support for the plight of low paid workers in Merioneth went back 'quite a long way':

> I don't think that I have ever shirked a fight or an unpopular issue and I do believe that one can make a major mistake when one confuses issues with personalities. I do not believe that the tactic of head on collision is an alternative to consistent effort in negotiation, neither do I believe a personal vendetta is constructive.

But Edwards's unsent draft reply had been even more aggressive and decried Plaid Cymru's influence on TGWU members, 'a handful of Activists which you brought together in Dolgellau, many of whom belong to the Welsh Nationalist Party':

> I am also very sorry to see you confirm what I have long suspected, that your relationship with other parties in this County is very much closer than it is with Merioneth Labour party or with me ... Your constant undermining of my position I am accustomed to but your personalisation of a straightforward dispute with the County was unwise and damaging to your members.[11]

Although they were not aware of the date of the impending General Election, this level of disharmony within the labour movement in the county hardly assisted Will Edwards's forthcoming campaign. On 7 February 1974, the General Election was called by Ted Heath's Conservative Government for three weeks later, on 28 February. Edwards's wife Eleri recalls the election campaign as a nasty and bitter experience for him and the family, in which 'things got very personal. There were lots of young men disrupting our campaign, and for the first time that I could remember, Plaid stickers appeared on council lorries.'[12] A key component of Dafydd Elis's election strategy in Merioneth was to behave as if he was already the local Member. This fitted with his communitarian ethos, and entailed dealing with constituents' immediate concerns.[13] He won admirers in the rural parts of the constituency, and close links were formed with the local farming community, while his trade union activism and involvement in the local TGWU had a positive impact in urban centres such as Blaenau Ffestiniog.[14]

One of his supporters, and later leader of the party, Ieuan Wyn Jones, a 25 year-old solicitor based in Corwen, recalls that the party's campaigning methods involved carefully organised and thorough canvassing as well as the traditional evening meetings held throughout the campaign, in which 'it was an honour for me to speak in meetings and keep the audience there before the candidate arrived – four or five times a night.'[15] At the beginning of each of his hustings speeches, Dafydd Elis consciously appealed to the spirit of the county's most illustrious representative:

> What I tried to do was to speak like Thomas Edward Ellis, who is my political hero. I saw myself as a twentieth century version of *Cymru Fydd*, really. In that sense, I was picking up the two traditions, the Labour tradition of Meirionnydd, as well as the Liberal tradition. My first line in every speech was Ellis's mantra, *Mae'n amser i wrandaw ar lais Cymru* (It is time to listen to the voice of Wales).[16]

But from Dafydd Elis's standpoint, the election was remarkably illtimed. The two months before the Election had proved a turbulent time for him both in his career and within his immediate family. He had only recently started his new role as a lecturer in the English department in Bangor University, in December 1973. In January 1974, his beloved aunt

Annie, who had suffered from profound depression after her brother's death, sadly died of heart disease in Denbigh mental hospital at the age of 74. On 18 January, she was laid to rest with her parents in the family grave in Blaenau Ffestiniog.[17] Her minister recalled her 'as a very dear person, a rock who had kept the family going . . . a backbone to Mrs Thomas. She hadn't been herself after her brother's death.'[18]

Immediately after Annie's burial, Dafydd's sister, Elin, then 24, a Welsh teacher at Llanfyllin secondary school, wrote a short story based on the experience of a young girl entering a mental hospital, and was a moving tribute to Annie's life and sad death. This composition won the first Literary medal to be awarded at the Urdd Eisteddfod, in June 1974, and was highly commended by the two judges, Marian Eames and Bedwyr Lewis Jones. But her success caused a huge argument with her mother, who was appalled that she had made her aunt's condition public. Elin had refused to show her the winning entry, but when the Urdd authorities requested Elin to correct the proofs of her manuscript for it to be returned for publication, she failed to respond, and her essay was never published. Presumably, she did not do so under pressure from her mother, and her concern for the family's public reputation.[19,20]

On 21 January, only three days after Annie's funeral, Dafydd and Elen's first son, Rolant, was born. When the General Election was called for 28 February, Elen recalls thinking:

> What on earth have I done? I was 27, and the house was in turmoil, while I was learning to be a mother, and Dafydd learning to be a father, which had to be a secondary issue for him at the time. Every day, Dafydd was planning where to go to be taken by his driver. It was exciting but I wasn't prepared for such a major change in circumstances so soon after the birth of our first child. I didn't go out much to canvass. At the end of the campaign there was a chance he might win, but we thought it unlikely.

She recalls the final conversation they had on the evening of the count:

> By the end of the campaign both of us were totally exhausted – we went to bed to rest, early in the evening before we had to go down to the count. As we lay in bed together, I asked him, 'Do you think you're going to win?' He said 'I don't know,

I don't know.' I said, 'Well, I think that our marriage will have to be very strong to withstand this.' It was exciting, but it was not what I had planned, nor for him, with the baby at the same time.[21]

Dafydd Elis had been as dubious as Elen that he would win:

> Oh God, yes. It was horrendous. I'd been advised earlier ... it was a very long night ... When I would get to the count, which was then held in Neuadd Idris, the hall in the square in the centre of Dolgellau, there would be a bit of tension and excitement. One of my leading supporters, Gwenfron Hughes, a local councillor, a very clever, very attractive personality, wonderful person, said to me, 'It's very close. Keep your eyes on both piles over there. I think we might possibly have won.'[22]

The result in Merioneth gave the 27-year old Dafydd Elis a majority of 588 over Will Edwards, and immediately propelled him to public prominence:

Merioneth Result	February 1974	
Dafydd Elis Thomas, Plaid Cymru	7,823	34.6 per cent
William Edwards, Labour	7,235	32.0 per cent
Iolo A. Jones, Liberal	4,153	18.4 per cent
Roy Owen, Conservative	3,392	15.0 per cent[23]

After Ieuan Lloyd Jones, Merioneth's council's chief executive, had made the announcement in the hall, and those present sang *Hen Wlad fy Nhadau*, the announcement of the result was repeated outside in the main square in Dolgellau. Jones had a flashlight with him and as they walked down the steps, Dafydd Elis was approached by 'the fine figure of Inspector Taliesin Edwards of the Gwynedd Constabulary', who said 'don't look so depressed, because your mate is in with you. We've had the news from Caernarfon!' He was then driven to the BBC studios in Bangor, where he was congratulated by Plaid's *bête noire*, the Labour Shadow Secretary of State for Wales, George Thomas:

> It was the results programme, and I was asked, 'It's very close between the two main parties. Which side will you support?' I

said, 'Oh, if it's a choice between Labour and Conservative, I will support Labour.' George Thomas exclaimed, 'Well, did you hear what the boy said?' It was a unique situation to be in with the hung Parliament. It was a gift, really, which we had to pursue.[24]

Elen recalled the unexpected shock of the evening and the surprising result:

> My life had been quite sheltered in the previous months because of the baby. It was exciting, but I didn't know how to support Dafydd that night whilst at the same time care for a very young breast-fed baby not even six weeks old. I borrowed Dafydd's sister's coat to go to the count in order to look as respectable as I could. Suddenly I was in front of these people. I remember going down the steps for the announcement. The square was full with great excitement. After the result was announced, Dafydd had to go to a TV studio in Bangor and I went home. I thought – what has just happened? I didn't really understand what an MP did. We had to adapt very quickly to a new life – he from being a university lecturer and now the youngest MP. You didn't know what was going to happen next.[25]

The February 1974 Election produced a hung Parliament, with Labour forming the largest party with 301 seats, and the Conservatives with 297. The Labour Prime Minister found himself seventeen seats short of an overall majority. Plaid Cymru gained two seats but lost Gwynfor Evans's seat in Carmarthen by only three votes. In Caernarfon, Dafydd Wigley defeated the veteran Labour parliamentarian, Goronwy Roberts, who had held the seat since 1950. The Scottish Nationalists gained seven seats, based on the slogan 'It's Scotland's Oil'. This meant that the Labour Government was uncomfortably dependent on these nine seats together with the six won by the Liberals, and still two seats short of a full majority.

However, losing Dafydd Elis from academic life was the greatest concern of the venerable literary society, the Owain Cyfeiliog Society meeting in Corwen on the evening of this historic win. Here, the modernist Welsh language poet Euros Bowen greeted the winner with dismay. He believed that Dafydd had been the only literary critic who understood his poetry. His departure for the House of Commons, he declared, was 'a waste of time!'[26]

The Baby of the House

Elen recalls their young family's first journey to London, accompanying the fresh-faced young Member in their family car in order for him to swear his oath as a new Member in the House of Commons:

> I hadn't been on a motorway before, never mind going to London. We took Rolant in his cot in the back, and stayed with my cousin and his wife in Blackheath, then I went with Dafydd to the Commons. I remember meeting Dafydd Wigley and Elinor beforehand – they seemed more prepared than us. Dafydd drove (he hadn't driven in London before) and driving into the Palace of Westminster was a very strange experience. He introduced himself to the policeman at the gate and said 'I'm Thomas from Merioneth. Do you believe me?' (Because, I silently thought, he didn't quite believe it himself). In the civil way the police have in the Palace of Westminster, he said, 'Yes, sir. We've been expecting you.'[27]

Dafydd recalled that when he finally got in the chamber of the House of Commons, he asked one of the doorkeepers, where he should sit:

> All these characters are very experienced security people who had come from the Armed Forces, and in reply, he said 'Oh, I believe you should sit on the third bench below the gangway. Those are the rebel benches.' It was a shock to me to be there. It was a shock to my family, but the delightful part of it, of course, is that people in Meirionnydd were proud of what they'd done.[28]

The impetus for the political preoccupation with devolution in the 1974–9 Parliament grew from the growing nationalist movement in the late sixties. The creation of the Welsh Office in 1964 was followed by Gwynfor Evans's win in the Carmarthen by-election in July 1966, Winnie Ewing's win in Hamilton for the SNP in 1967, and shocks for the Labour Government following the impact of the nationalist parties in a series of by-elections in Glasgow Pollock (1967), Rhondda Fawr (1967) and Caerphilly (1968). This mounting evidence of support for nationalism led Harold Wilson, the then Prime Minister, to create a Royal Commission under Lord Crowther (subsequently called the Kilbrandon Commission following Crowther's death). The Commission was asked to inquire into the relationship between Parliament, central government and the nations and regions of the United Kingdom, and whether a change was needed in economic and constitutional arrangements. In the same month as the Report was published in October 1973, Margo Macdonald won the Govan by-election for the Scottish National Party, and that, with the campaign for 'Scotland's oil', added to the pressure to act on the Kilbrandon report in order to contain the Scottish nationalist movement. A majority of members of the Commission proposed legislative devolution for Wales, with a hundred-member unicameral assembly, elected by proportional representation. The report suggested 'Senate' as the title of the new institution, and it was also suggested that the office of Secretary of State for Wales should be abolished, and the number of Westminster MPs from Wales reduced.[29]

At the age of 27, Dafydd Elis was the youngest member of the House of Commons in February 1974, and as the 'baby of the House', drew immediate publicity. In his maiden speech, on 14 March, he consciously placed himself squarely in the lineage of Merioneth's parliamentary representatives as liberal radical devolutionists, and having paid tribute to his immediate predecessor Will Edwards, reminded his audience of the unique contribution of the Liberal Thomas Edward Elis, who had risen to the role of the Liberal Government's Chief Whip in the House of Commons:

> One of his early dreams was the creation of an independent Welsh party in the House which would press for an elected assembly for Wales, with legislative powers. That was eighty years before the Royal Commission on the Constitution was initiated. I am sure, therefore, that honourable Members will pardon the ironic chuckle that came from this bench when . . . we heard that the Government are to initiate discussions in Wales about constitutional changes. Devolution has been an issue in Welsh politics for eighty years. We believe that eighty years of discussion is more than adequate. That is why we want a firm commitment that the Government will introduce legislation on the lines of the Kilbrandon Commission majority report within the lifetime of this Parliament.

> The independent Welsh Party about which Tom Ellis dreamed now exists. At the moment it has a membership of only two, but wherever two hon. Members are gathered together there is a parliamentary party. Such a party must have its officers. After a lapse of 75 years, the tradition of a Chief Whip representing Merioneth has been revived.

He then gave the customary *tour d'horizon* of his constituency and focused on Blaenau Ffestiniog's need for greater industrial investment:

> The economic and social decline of Blaenau over the last thirty years must have few parallels throughout the United Kingdom. Its population has decreased by half in one generation. Blaenau urgently needs an influx of new manufacturing industry to give it a more secure economic base and to prevent the further drain of young lifeblood from the community. The people of Blaenau Ffestiniog and the other old industrial towns of Gwynedd welcome the commitment in the Gracious Speech to give high priority to the stimulation of regional development and employment.

He called for the establishment of a national economic development authority to put a growth centre strategy into effect, the monitoring and control of tourism, and measures to safeguard the future of agriculture and the medium sized family farm. He demanded measures similar to those used in Denmark, to end speculation by institutional investors in agricultural land, welcomed the Government's intention to seek a fundamental renegotiation of the terms of entry into the EEC, and called for hill farmers to continue to receive hill grants and subsidies.

Perhaps most significantly, he made it abundantly clear where his loyalties lay between supporting a minority Labour Government or the Conservative Opposition:

> There has been much speculation both inside and outside the Chamber about my party's attitude towards the Government and their legislative programme. If the Government bring forward radical measures in social and economic policy they will be assured of our support for those measures, but we expect

from the House and the Government a positive, unambiguous response to the constitutional aspirations of the Welsh people.³⁰

On his arrival in the Commons, Dafydd Elis was warmly welcomed by his predecessor, T. W. Jones (now Lord Maelor), the former Labour MP for Merioneth between 1950 and 1966. More surprisingly, he was also again warmly greeted by George Thomas, whose role as a Methodist lay preacher, and a full-time officer of the National Union of Teachers (NUT) before being elected as an MP in 1945, had brought him into contact with Gwenfil James, Dafydd Elis's aunt, who had been prominent in the NUT in Carmarthenshire. Thomas warmed to the new Member, and after being made Speaker of the House of Commons in 1976, on one occasion hosted Dafydd's mother and Gwenfil for tea in the Speaker's House. These unlikely friends were united again, when Dafydd Elis joined the House of Lords, and would share an office with the former Speaker.

His closest political colleague, apart from Dafydd Wigley, was Walter Harrison, the MP for Wakefield, the Labour party's Deputy Chief Whip. He already knew other Presbyterian sons of the manse amongst the Members of Parliament, including Cledwyn Hughes, the MP for Anglesey and an old family friend, and Wyn Roberts, who arguably owed his seat to Dafydd Elis's candidacy in Conway in 1970. He had excellent relationships with a number of other Welsh Labour MPs such as the erudite Michael Foot, MP for Ebbw Vale and Caerwyn Roderick, MP for Brecon and Radnor, a left-wing internationalist and supporter of devolution, together with the avuncular Liberal farmer Geraint Howells, MP for Ceredigion, another passionate devolutionist. But he had little in common with the mostly right of centre Welsh Labour MPs, and had greater affinity with a number of English Labour MPs on the left of the party. As Plaid's whip, he was constantly phoned on Sunday lunchtime by the famed political bruiser Bob Mellish, Labour's Chief Whip, or his deputy Walter Harrison, to check how he and his colleague intended to vote the following week. His reply was mostly in support of the Government.

While he got along well with most of the more anti-Labour Scottish Nationalist Party group, his greatest friendship was with the cerebral George Thompson, the MP for Galloway, whose Catholic faith, intellect and shared interest in theology made him an engaging companion, and after losing his seat in May 1979, would become a Roman Catholic priest.³¹

The General Election of October 1974

Given that the Labour Government was in a minority, it was inevitable that a second election would be called quickly but when it was held six months later, on 10 October, it only secured a precarious majority of three seats for Labour. Given the short space of time between elections, there was little change in Plaid's national policy position and its October manifesto followed the February election's theme of 'Rich Welsh or Poor British' with its emphasis on Wales's exploitation by the British state.[32]

Dafydd Elis compared his re-election campaign in October 1974 to being 'hauled in front of your bosses after a six month probation period'.[33] His energy and work rate in Parliament had been truly prestigious, and between March and October 1974, he gave eight Commons speeches, asked 300 Commons questions and answered over a thousand constituents' letters, dealing with subjects ranging from farming to silicosis, pensions, social security and devolution, as well as campaigning for the building of new factories locally, in keeping with his campaign slogan, 'On with the work'.[34]

The *Western Mail*'s constituency profile of the battle for Merioneth featured a complaining Wil Edwards, alleging that Dafydd Elis Thomas was going around 'presenting himself as some kind of political John Wayne'. He conceded that a third of the Merioneth vote was 'hard nationalist' but alleged that the rest 'is just exploited grievance grafted on'. For his part, Dafydd Elis asserted that 'more has been heard of Merioneth in the last six months than in the last six years. Their two biggest coups had been the saving of the Cambrian Coast railway line and winning special development area status for Gwynedd.'[35]

The Guardian reported a bitter battle for the seat, and reviewed the reasons for Edwards's initial defeat:

> Wil Edwards, a pro-Marketeer who stands well to Labour's Right and had been the Labour MP for Merioneth for eight years, fought a traditional type of campaign, but says he was defeated because Plaid Cymru 'grovelled about in political dustbins'. There is no doubt that the fight was a highly personalised one. Mr Edwards runs a busy law practice in Bala and was the professional adviser for the TV serial *The Carnforth Practice* ...

is uneasily aware material success is not always an achievement that commends itself to Welsh rural voters.[36]

Edwards's reputation for high living hindered his campaign. His opponents cast doubt on his character, focusing on his seemingly affluent lifestyle, the personalised number plates on his saloon car, and his verve and sense of mischief, which were easily misinterpreted by a socially conservative electorate.[37] In the short period between the two elections, Dafydd Elis's punishing schedule extended throughout Wales as Plaid Cymru attempted to galvanise the party beyond Merioneth. Within the constituency, he leveraged his experience of building coalitions:

> I knew there'd be another election later that year, so for months, I made sure that I went to as many places as I could. This is where I started my love affair with Trawsfynydd, because I'd been involved with the trades council and because I knew a lot of these people – a lot of the senior engineers actually lived in Dolgellau. I was welcomed there . . . I think I was a made an honorary member of the sports and social club. I made a commitment to them very early on, because obviously, they knew that I'd been in CND, that I supported not only the power station as it existed, but other employment in the area, including further development, as we had a combination between hydro-electric pump storage, and nuclear power. It was very important that I did that at the time. There were other major sites which were controversial, like the ICI explosives works in Penrhyndeudraeth, which was a very dangerous place for people to work. We got involved in trying to find replacements for employment there, where people could change jobs. Similarly, I strongly supported the Royal Aircraft Establishment in Llanbedr and its relationship with RAE Aberporth. I thought it was very important for me to appear to be a representative of anyone that wanted to be represented.[38]

In the October Election, in Merioneth, Dafydd Elis's success was emphatic, increasing his majority fourfold, from 589 to 2,592[39] and was 'the best vote I ever had, at forty-two per cent. The majority had become safe.'[40]

Merioneth General Election	October 1974	
Dafydd Elis Thomas, Plaid Cymru	9,543	42.0 per cent
William Edwards, Labour	6,951	30.9 per cent
Richard O. Jones, Liberal	3,454	15.4 per cent
Roy Owen, Conservative	2,509	11.2 per cent[41]

Dafydd Wigley also retained his seat, almost doubling his majority from 1,728 to 3,254.

Between the first and second election of 1974, both Dafydds had worked closely together. They split their Parliamentary work effectively and acknowledged their differing expertise. Wigley recalls a period of excellent cooperation between them: 'Dafydd Elis was obviously someone that Labour thought should be with them, and he became very friendly with their Whip, Walter Harrison. He could then find out what was going on.'

But he noted the difficulties of the weekly journey to Westminster for Dafydd Elis. While Wigley's direct train journey from Bangor to London took a comparatively stress-free four hours, Dafydd Elis's more difficult journey to Westminster involved either driving directly to London, or more frequently, driving the two hour journey to Crewe and then taking the three hour train journey to London. Wigley recalls that 'he had a hellish journey to get to London, sometimes through Crewe, sometimes through Bangor, or through Machynlleth. It was easy for me from Caernarfon compared to Dafydd Elis.'[42]

The commute to London would start on a Monday morning, returning, if and when the parliamentary timetable allowed it, on a Thursday evening. Fridays and Saturdays would be dedicated to constituency surgeries and only Sundays were regarded as 'personal' time, which even then would be frequently disrupted by regular phone calls from journalists or the Government's whip. A reflection of the pressure on him was that on a number of occasions, Dafydd Elis drove to Crewe, but could not face the journey to London, and returned immediately to Dolgellau, not wishing to be separated from his family. Both MPs were also expected to be prominent in Plaid's campaigns throughout Wales and they maintained a punishing schedule, in order, in Dafydd Wigley's words, 'to create an impression.'[43]

The October 1974 election also saw the return of Gwynfor Evans as member of Parliament for Carmarthen. The group of three were immediately significant because of the parliamentary arithmetic. The Labour

Government now only had a majority of three seats and the devolution question was high on the political agenda, as the Scottish National Party had gained eleven seats, and 30 per cent of the Scottish popular vote. By-elections and defections whittled away Labour's majority, and by 1977, the Government's wafer-thin majority had forced it to enter into deals with the Liberal party, the Ulster Unionists, the Scottish Nationalists and Plaid Cymru.

Gwynfor Evans, at 61, was twice the age of the two Dafydds. According to his biographer, 'the only apparent difference between him and Elis Thomas and Wigley was Elis Thomas's liking for socialising with members of the left of the Labour party in those days when the party was a socialist party.' In the evening, while the two Dafydds would spend time with other Members, Gwynfor Evans would retreat to his office to write letters.[44]

The two Dafydds had spent the previous eight months at Westminster free of the presence of their leader, 'a man of an authoritarian cast of mind and unyielding seriousness of purpose.'[45] They had colonised the Welsh table in the members' tearoom, and were made to feel particularly welcome by a number of MPs including Cledwyn Hughes. A fellow son of the manse, Cledwyn kept a fatherly eye on his young protégé, Dafydd Elis, and when he retired as a Member of Parliament in 1979, Dafydd's mother Eirlys thanked him for his care over her son:

> Mae Dafydd yn gweld eich colli'n fawr iawn. Diolch o galon i chwi am eich caredigrwydd a'ch gofal ohono, ac yntau yn llanc ifanc dibrofiad yn wynebu at San Steffan. Mae ei edmygedd ohonoch yn fawr iawn, ac roedd yn gwerthfawrogi eich cyngor a'ch arweiniad.[46]

> 'Dafydd misses you very much. Thanks from the bottom of my heart to you for your kindness and your care for him, with him such an inexperienced young man going to Westminster. His admiration of you is very great, and he appreciated your advice and guidance.'

Dafydd Wigley recalled at the time, that 'Labour eyed Dafydd Elis as someone who should be with them. Dafydd Elis had formed a very good relationship with the Chief Whip Bob Mellish and his deputy, Walter Harrison':

We were incredibly active and either Dafydd or myself would come top of the list for the most written questions asked in the House of Commons throughout our period up to 1979. Soon after the second election we looked at sharing a flat – that was pretty crucial in our relationship. I wasn't sensitive enough to Dafydd Elis's financial position – he couldn't afford to rent the flat, even jointly. I was lucky coming from my background in industry, although I was taking a cut of fifty per cent in my salary. But Dafydd hadn't had an opportunity or time to consolidate his finances.

After the October Election, Ednyfed Hudson Davies, the former MP for Conway who had lost his seat in the 1970 General Election, offered to rent his London flat to both Dafydds – but Dafydd Elis could not afford his half of the rent, and Dafydd Wigley could not afford it on his own. One of Dafydd Wigley's constituents, Brian Morgan Edwards, based in Pwllheli, was a colourful businessman who funded radical new Welsh language companies such as the Sain recording company, and helped establish Cymdeithas Tai Gwynedd, the first rural housing association in Wales. He came to Wigley's rescue and gave him a make-do bedroom in his office in Montague Square in central London for free (apparently contrary to the lease conditions of the flat). He stayed there until he bought a flat in London in 1978, with financial help from friends in the constituency. Wigley recalls that 'since I now had that option, I wasn't really in a hurry to share a flat with Gwynfor'.[47]

Dafydd Elis, however, found himself compelled to share a flat with Gwynfor for the following five years. This flat was also owned by Morgan Edwards and located conveniently near Sloane Square and within twenty minute of Parliament. This was an incongruous match, and in addition to their wildly different personalities, Dafydd Elis also privately viewed Gwynfor's leadership of the party as overly patrician and autocratic, and disagreed with his extreme pacifism and innate conservatism. Their lifestyle and political outlook could not have been more different, but Dafydd recalled taking Gwynfor to his first experience of a wine bar, and in spite of their political differences, they shared some common ground in their embrace of Nonconformist radicalism and the broader peace movement.[48]

Dafydd Wigley reflected that this arrangement 'didn't help our relationship'. Gwynfor and Wigley's more conservative traditional nationalism contrasted sharply with Dafydd Elis's increasing left wing radicalism.

Dafydd Wigley recognised that politically they represented different parts of the party's political spectrum. Dafydd El was very much on the loft of the party, and both worked closely with the party's enthusiastic researcher, Robert Griffiths, a bright economics graduate from Cardiff whose politics were socialist and republican. Wigley recalled: 'it was interesting the way Robert Griffiths worked with both of us. Robert aligned more with Dafydd Elis but he was good with me.'[49] Robert Griffiths recalled that:

> Dafydd Elis was always more to the left. I worked with the three MPs and got on with them all well. He was also the youngest and least conservative (small 'c') of the three. Perhaps I worked more with him because we had the same interests in economic planning, issues to do with public ownership and similar progressive issues, and we also had a common interest in foreign policy, in South Africa and apartheid and the anti-colonial wars in Angola and Mozambique. To me the three Members collaborated together very well. Sometimes there were differences of opinion but nothing serious.[50]

Interestingly, when challenged about his political differences with Dafydd Elis, Wigley found it difficult to describe his own politics and disavowed the description of 'right-wing' but rather claimed to be a left of centre social democrat. He also tended to dwell on the practical and operational, rather than the theoretical and philosophical. Both men disliked conflict and remarkably, only recalled one face-to-face, open argument and disagreement in the eighteen years they worked together as Members of Parliament. Their relationship was constantly mediated by their staff in London, Cardiff and the constituencies, and for most purposes, they operated independently of each other. The only real open row that Dafydd Wigley recalled was in the 1979–80 period, the details long forgotten, and any apparent disagreement resolved at the time with no open conflict.[51]

But Plaid Cymru's performance in the October 1974 election masked fundamental issues for the party, which were to emerge over the following four years. As Dafydd's close friend, Emyr Price, wrote at the time:

> Truly, even in those seats that were won, apart perhaps from Meirion, where Plaid has allied itself with the Labour movement,

especially in Blaenau Ffestiniog, Plaid had very little impact on the Labour vote. Is it not a short term policy, a policy that will in the long-term be counter-productive and unsuccessful, by depending on the dubious support, socially esoteric and in some cases reactionary sections of society, rather than appealing to the majority of the population – the mass of ordinary working people.[52]

In the independent socialist nationalist magazine, *Y Saeth*, Dafydd Elis wrote unequivocally in support of a left-wing strategy for Plaid Cymru:

It is not self-government for Wales we should be seeking but self-government for every individual and community in Wales . . . that system must be biased towards self-determination throughout that society and full participation in it. This mean workers' control at plant level; it means tenants' control of housing estates . . . The ideology here is radically different from that of Labourism or Conservatism, individualism or collectivism. Our starting point in Plaid Cymru as nationalists has been the historic distinctiveness of the people of Wales as a cultural group. But we must now move to stress the functional importance of Wales in organising a radically different system of social relationships.[53]

This call for a more socialist strategy for the party was quickly stamped upon by the party's President, Gwynfor Evans. He suggested that Plaid Cymru's mistake in the October 1974 election had been to attempt to be 'better socialists than the socialists'.[54] His brand of Christian utopianism and liberal pacifism, couched in the Welsh radical tradition, was fundamentally socially conservative, and revealed his profound distrust of the Labour party. It was nurtured by his bitter experience of their long-lasting contempt towards him on Carmarthenshire County Council, and made it difficult for him to share either Wigley or Elis-Thomas's greater pragmatism towards working with the Labour Government.

Dafydd Elis's public advocacy of a socialist policy for Plaid Cymru reflected his profound scepticism about the party's political direction. He voiced his private doubts about whether he even wished to consider himself a Welsh nationalist, in conversation with his close friend Gwynn

Matthews, soon after being elected in February 1974. While walking on the Denbigh Moors, Dafydd revealed a remarkable secret to Matthews:

> He told me that he didn't want to be in the mindset of nationalism. He needed to plough his own furrow. He said 'I'm not a nationalist anymore. I feel like a priest who has lost his faith. I'm in a position where I'm one of the pillars of the establishment, but I don't feel it.'

Gwynn Matthews was shocked by this revelation and recalls Dafydd as saying that 'there was so much to be done and that Plaid, at the time, was the totally necessary conduit for it. And this was not an encumbrance', but he said categorically that he was not a nationalist:

> I was such in shock when he shared this, that I didn't press him ... obviously he was a patriot. But in the period after the October 1974 Election, he wasn't happy with things. With Gwynfor and Wigley there (in Parliament), it was two against one and Dafydd Elis wasn't happy. The two Dafydds understood each other – both knew how far to push each other. When Gwynfor came, then Dafydd Elis pulled more and more towards the left.

Matthews recalls that from 1970 onwards in Plaid, the party had been charmed by the left-wing Phil Williams, the Aberystwyth-based astronomer, who had stood in the 1968 Caerphilly by-election, and who had created a conducive theoretical atmosphere that made Dafydd Elis comfortable. He recalls Wigley stating that 'we don't have to worry about Dafydd Elis. Although he's reading Italian Marxists, Phil Williams was keeping an eye on him. He's OK.'[55]

However, many in Plaid wished to reject the left versus right narrative within the party and Gwynfor Evans, for example, had his concern about the influence of the left underlined by the experience of opposing the European Referendum from a left-wing perspective. He thought it 'harmful' to be associated with the left, and in July 1975, wrote to emphasise his view that Welsh nationalism was most conducive to conservatism: 'although Plaid Cymru is the most radical party, the fundamental conservative element in the policy makes it the natural home for those conservative patriots who give their first loyalty to the nation'.[56]

The march of devolution

The Labour Government had entered the 1974 February election with no reference to the Commission's report in its manifesto, but subsequently a White Paper, outlining options for devolution, was published on 17 September 1974.[57] In the October 1974 General Election, the Welsh Labour manifesto committed itself to a directly elected Welsh Assembly with responsibility for 'a wide range of functions, for instance, housing, health, education, economic and environmental planning, and water, currently performed by central government and undemocratic nominated bodies... and... real powers in the field of economic and industrial development'.[58]

With the election of eleven SNP MPs and three Plaid MPs, and a Government majority of only three seats, devolution was thus cast in a central role in the Parliament. Plaid Cymru's hopes for the new Parliament were to ensure that devolution would be delivered for Wales. Dafydd Elis recalled that the group did not have a set strategy, and whilst they were concerned with Wales's economy and social policy, they believed that the key issue was to ensure that the devolution commitments that had been made should be enacted. Gwynfor in particular wanted parity with Scotland, the meaning of which was vague at this stage.

Dafydd Elis's personal political strategy was to ensure that the Plaid group was not responsible for the Labour minority government losing a vote of no confidence:

> That was my only strategic objective, actually. I wanted to make sure that we weren't responsible for the fall of the Government, because I do remember early on in 1974 we actually voted against the government's programme in the Queen's Speech, because it was very important to emphasise the need for devolution. I don't remember how I was persuaded to do that, but that was my failure to understand Parliamentary procedure early on, and I resisted doing that any time after.[59]

He continued to work closely with the Labour whips, especially Walter Harrison, who would phone him late every Sunday morning to ascertain whether the Plaid members would be voting with the Government the following week:

> It was basically, for me, to work with the Labour government, on a weekly basis, on specific votes, with government whips and to ensure that we didn't actually cause the Government to lose a crucial vote. Michael Foot was another important contact. He was the Leader of the House, and the person who responded to many of the important debates on behalf of the minority Government. I recollect having private meetings with his office and with himself when that was required. I think there were one or two formal meetings which involved the Plaid group. Obviously, Michael Foot understood UK politics, understood Welsh politics, understood where we were coming from, but also, understood where I was coming from.
>
> I wasn't quite a double agent, but it was pretty close, because I was representing the Leader of the House and the government whip's position to my colleagues, so Walter had the votes of my two colleagues, and some of my SNP colleagues. The SNP group, as I recollect in '74–9, was ideologically very marked in its divisions, in the sense that we weren't. Between the three of us, I would have put Dafydd Wigley down as a Social Democrat, and Gwynfor as a pacifist liberal, really. I thought I was Thomas Edward Ellis reincarnate!
>
> That's how we operated. With parliamentary votes, Walter would ask on the phone on a Sunday, 'How many of your boys are on this week?' The guy was a complete genius – a brilliant guy. The other figure was Bob Mellish, the Labour senior chief whip, and he was somebody for whom I had complete respect. I knew that, with these people, while there were no formal agreements, if we discussed something week by week or if there was something longer term, we would see how we would do that and what the legislation might be.
>
> It was a very positive working relationship ... What I was trying to do was to promote as much collaboration as I could, as much understanding as I could, but I don't think I used to report too much of this back to my constituency party.[60]

Since 1971, Plaid Cymru had a policy of opposing membership of the European Economic Community (EEC), arguing that Wales would be disadvantaged by being a member of an undemocratic and capitalistic club. For pacifists such as Gwynfor Evans, the EEC was a military bloc that threatened international stability.[61] Plaid Cymru's formal policy for Europe, advocated for the United Kingdom to join a similar body to the European Free Trade Area (EFTA). This policy was captured by the slogan, 'Yes to Europe, No to the Common Market'.

Rejecting membership in the upcoming referendum therefore became the party's policy in its annual conference in January 1975, and Dafydd Elis campaigned with, and spoke on the same platforms, as Labour luminaries such as Neil Kinnock and Michael Foot, while Dafydd Wigley opted to campaign against his own party's policy. Plaid Cymru's official view was that a No vote would emphasise Wales's independence of thought, but this view did not prevail in the poll held on 5 June 1975, Wales voting by a majority of two to one to stay in the European Economic Community. In retrospect, Dafydd Elis considered his opposition to membership of the EEC to have been his biggest political mistake:

> I was heavily influenced by the Welsh Trades Union Congress and by the trade unions at the time. All I could say when afterwards I met European colleagues from the Basque country, Catalonia and Galicia, was 'How could I be so stupid?' They were exasperated that anybody with my attitude could have voted No in 1975. In fairness to Wigley, he took a principled pro-European stance at that time, which I didn't . . . I'm not really keen to defend myself on any of that, it was wrong. I shouldn't have done what I did.[62]

Even during the campaign, Plaid leaders such as Ieuan Wyn Jones, the party's agriculture spokesman viewed the party's position as untenable:

> We drew up a policy document to say why Wales shouldn't be part of the European Union, and the more I looked at the policy, the more I thought our policy was silly. I thought it didn't bear scrutiny. It was Dafydd Elis himself who announced that the party would change its policy after the referendum.[63]

As the *Daily Post* pointed out in its analysis of the campaign, Plaid Cymru had misread the public mood, and the Yes majorities in both Wales and Scotland were a severe rebuff for the Nationalist opponents of the Market: 'both Plaid Cymru and the SNP saw the referendum as a fortuitous means of demonstrating that their countries wanted separatism. They too have been given their verdict.'[64] The following weekend, the leadership of Plaid Cymru met in Dolgellau to discuss the lessons of the vote, and within hours, decided to reverse their policy on Europe in order to support membership, and also change the party's constitutional aim so that instead of wishing for Commonwealth or 'dominion' status, they would seek full national status for Wales within Europe.[65]

In the meantime, the devolution project was already running into trouble by the summer of 1975. The Labour Cabinet was split on the matter, between devolution's supporters, led by Cledwyn Hughes, then the chairman of the Parliamentary Labour group, and its sceptics, led by Ted Short, the unenthusiastic Minister for Devolution. Ten out of the 23 Welsh Labour MPs opposed the Government's proposals,[66] and a survey in the *Daily Post* showed that the majority of electors in north Wales were against devolution.[67]

When the White Paper was published on 27 November 1975, recommending weaker powers for the Assembly than Plaid had envisaged, Dafydd Wigley was stranded on a visit to Paris. Gwynfor and Dafydd Elis had to respond to its content, while unable to talk to Wigley. In his absence, a statement was issued, welcoming the proposals. Wigley was livid and later wrote to Gwynfor saying that he would not contemplate standing for such a supine body as the proposed Assembly.[68] Others argued that supporters would not understand why the party was opposed to even this emasculated version of devolution. There was disagreement within the National Executive, where Phil Williams opposed any agreement with the Labour Government, later writing that Plaid's support for the proposals was a major error:

> May I be forgiven for pointing out the greatest mistake we made? Two and a half years ago, some of us tried to persuade Plaid Cymru of the trap that was being prepared for us on the Wales Bill. The trap was obvious but many refused to see it. They were seduced by a very attractive prospect, the promise of an easy road to self-government. Do you remember the argument? That

once the Assembly was set up, its weaknesses would be so serious that it would lead inevitably to conflict between a Welsh Labour Party and the Tories in London. The leadership of Plaid Cymru had persuaded themselves there was an easier road to self-government on the backs of the Labour party.[69]

Labour's White Paper was supported officially by Plaid Cymru, and Wigley kept his counsel, but the hostile response to the proposals by the SNP and its overwhelmingly negative response from Labour MPs made Dafydd Elis and Gwynfor Evans's position difficult to sustain. In its meeting of January 1976, the party's National Council now decided to oppose the White Paper. In February and March, more organisations in Wales came out against the devolution proposals. At the same time, the plans for a Welsh language television channel were thrown in doubt, when the Chancellor of the Exchequer announced the postponement of the creation of the Welsh language fourth channel because of economic pressures. Cymdeithas yr Iaith subsequently announced the recommencement of their lawbreaking campaign for the Welsh language channel.

The devolution process had slowed down markedly, but Harold Wilson's resignation as Prime Minister in March 1976 and the appointment of James Callaghan, the MP for Cardiff South-East, as his replacement, gave it fresh impetus, with the Leader of the House, Michael Foot, a committed devolutionist, given responsibility for taking the legislation through the House of Commons. In May 1976, Foot promised further powers for the Welsh Development Agency and threatened to nationalise ship repair companies, including Bristol Channel Ship Repairs, a Barry-based company. Gwynfor in particular was very keen to help its owner, Christopher Bailey, a friend, and opposed nationalisation of the company, but Dafydd Elis was far more reluctant to support this exemplar of free enterprise. He was out-voted by his two colleagues, and not for the first time, felt ignored by the president of the party.[70]

Three weeks previously, on 9 June 1976, the group had voted against the Government in a vote of confidence. There had been no danger of the Government losing, but the Plaid group was now being seen as a more serious and effective opposition party. The *Western Mail*'s veteran parliamentary correspondent, David Rosser, commented that after Plaid's successful intervention to save Bristol Channel Ship Repairs from nationalisation:

A new dimension is appearing at Westminster. The trio of Plaid Cymru MPs are emerging as a pocket power bloc with grim and purposeful determination ... Rightly and judiciously too, they are playing the artful dodger to Michael Foot and the Government's other managers to no mean effect.[71]

The devolution legislation contained in the Scotland and Wales Bill, unhelpfully (from a Welsh devolutionist perspective) tying both countries together in legislation, was eventually published on 29 November 1976 in the unpromising context of no Government majority and the worst economic crisis since the nineteen thirties. The Second Reading of the Bill only passed by the slim majority of 45 votes. Tellingly, on this most important piece of legislation in the 1974–9 Parliament, a number of the Welsh Labour MPs abstained, including Neil Kinnock, Leo Abse, Donald Anderson and Ifor Davies.

Foot was now forced to cave in to pressure from the opponents of devolution, for referenda to be held in Wales and Scotland in order to decide whether devolved assemblies should be granted.[72] In response to nationalist pressure, the Government attempted to re-introduce a guillotine on the Bill on 22 February 1977, but it was defeated, and the Bill had effectively fallen. All now seemed lost for devolution, and the Secretary of State for Wales, John Morris, who was responsible for the Welsh element of the legislation, was reported to be in resulting low spirits. Dafydd Elis went to see him to dissuade him from resigning, as John Morris later recalled:

> I contemplated momentarily the idea of resignation. It was a government defeat after all, not mine alone. I decided to soldier on. If I remained, I would be able to participate fully in salvaging the position. My resignation could be counter-productive to the cause which I had put so much effort. To my surprise, others thought I might go. Dafydd Elis Thomas MP, on behalf of himself at least, came and saw me in Gwydir House, the home of the Welsh Office in London, and tried to persuade me not to resign. It was thoughtful of him, but it was never on the cards. My job was to go on and win the next battle. I was not going to give up now.[73]

Two days later, and following this catastrophic failure, Plaid Cymru and the SNP proposed a vote of no confidence in the Government. However, while Gwynfor was absent due to illness, both Dafydds and the SNP were invited to meet Jim Callaghan, while Michael Foot wrote to Gwynfor separately to ask how they could progress the devolution process. Discussions continued with the Government throughout March 1977, even though Plaid Cymru's national executive called on their MPs to discontinue their discussions.[74] Two days before the vote of confidence, the three MPs stated publicly, and disingenuously in Dafydd Elis's case, that they would oppose the Government because the two parties 'were as bad as each other'.[75]

He had in fact already told Cledwyn Hughes that he would abstain 'if it went to the wire in the vote'. Hughes noted in his private diary that 'Dafydd Elis Thomas is particularly upset ... He has a better grasp of political realities than his two colleagues although he is the youngest of them.'[76] But on 23 March 1977, the Labour Government was saved by a pact with the Liberal party, and although the three Plaid MPs voted with the Conservatives in the vote of confidence, the outcome was foreseeable and the Government prevailed. In February, Dafydd Elis had already warned of Plaid Cymru's confusion in its devolution policy and the danger of 'blowing hot and cold' on the issue:

> This has confused the Press and ordinary members of the national movement. When the various devolution White Papers were published some Plaid Cymru leaders welcomed them as a great step forward, indeed, as an historical event. But within a couple of days other leaders were declaring that the Assembly was useless and suggested that no fervent nationalist should support the policy, let alone welcome it. The confusion penetrates the very root of Plaid Cymru's role as the national political movement. The party had made a fundamental mistake in presenting only its long-term aim of full self-government to the Kilbrandon Commission on the Constitution, instead of setting out a shorter-term evolutionary policy as well. People vote for representation and for government ... The main justification for a Welsh Assembly is that it gives Plaid Cymru a chance to rule Wales and to prove to the people of Wales that self-government is possible.[77]

This period of political chess damaged Gwynfor's reputation,[78] but the party's scepticism towards the Labour Government's intentions proved unfounded. At the end of March, Foot announced his intention to present two new separate Devolution Bills for Wales and Scotland, and the White Paper on devolution was published in July 1977.

A number of Plaid's leaders, such as Phil Williams and Dafydd Wigley, continued to warn of the danger of shifting too closely to the Labour party's official position, but Plaid itself was moving decidedly to the left. In the party's 1977 national conference, for instance, an unavowedly socialist motion calling for 'the social ownership of the instruments of production and distribution' was only defeated by the small margin of 108 votes to 82.[79]

The Scotland Bill was the first to be finally taken through the Commons and it became immediately clear that opposition to it was even better organised and more widespread than that which had faced the first Devolution Bill. The opposition to it reached its apex on Burns Night, 25 January 1978, when the Labour backbencher, George Cunningham, a Scot sitting for Islington South, won the amendment that a majority voting Yes in the referendum would have to constitute a least forty per cent of the Scottish electorate, without which the proposal would be withdrawn and the Act repealed. This had huge consequences for the vote in Scotland, for when the referendum was fought, the Yes side won by a small majority, but only constituted 32.9 per cent of the total electorate, and the vote was lost.

Dafydd Wigley recalls what he considered to be the naivety of the SNP MPs in failing to grasp the importance of the forty per cent clause:

> The point when I realised that we weren't getting anywhere with Labour was when they allowed the forty per cent threshold for the Scottish vote to go through. They should have imposed a three-line whip and Cunningham should have been thrown out of the party, and Scotland would have had its Parliament. The truth was, the SNP could have stopped that by running a filibuster on the previous motion to stop Cunningham from having time to take his amendment through. Maggie Bain[80] only spoke for 20 minutes – I couldn't believe that they hadn't done that with their eleven members, and I was pulling my hair out.[81]

The three Plaid MPs' support for the Welsh Devolution Bill was in sharp contrast to the attitude of many of the Welsh Labour MPs whose barely concealed antipathy and lack of enthusiasm were encouraged by the group of six Welsh Labour rebel MPs who agitated against the Bill. On 22 February 1978, the Government failed to impose a guillotine on discussion of the Bill on the floor of the House of Commons, by 312 to 283, and any devolution legislation seemed lost. The Bill had seen bitter arguments during the committee stages included a major row between Neil Kinnock and Dafydd Elis over Welsh language education in Ynys Môn, which would influence their relationship for the following five decades.

During the Bill's committee stage, Neil Kinnock accused Anglesey schools of victimising monoglot English speaking children, by stopping them from going to the lavatory unless they asked to do so in Welsh. These allegations were strongly refuted by Dafydd Elis, and Gwynedd County Council asked Kinnock to support his assertions. Kinnock had in fact been told the story in conversations with Glenys's sister-in-law, Barbara Parry, but failed to produce any documentary evidence at the time. While he later produced eighteen letters written by parents in support of his remarks, a Gwynedd Council inquiry found that all the letters had been written after he had initially made his allegations, while only four specifically referred to the incident mentioned by Kinnock, and of these, two were subsequently withdrawn.[82] Dafydd Elis recalled that he enjoyed his parliamentary jousts with Neil Kinnock and had a 'warm but strange relationship with him'.[83]

Both had campaigned together against membership of the European Union in 1975, but Kinnock's vituperative attacks against him and other Plaid members strained their previously good relationship. During his parliamentary speeches in the committee stage of the Devolution Bill, Kinnock accused Plaid Cymru members of being 'Nazis' because they had supported the burning of the bombing school at Penyberth in 1936.[84] The Labour left-wing firebrand also made a particularly feeble attempt to stain Dafydd Elis's reputation, in accusing him of being a Marxist:

> The umbrella of nationalism certainly shelters the Welsh nationalists from reality. But underneath that umbrella there is a division between the humanitarian capitalism of the hon. Member

for Carmarthen [Gwynfor Evans] – a Tory who in time of difficulty will fall back upon Keynesian propositions such as the Tennessee Valley Authority – and the Marxist from Merioneth, who will suggest the most profound social and economic changes in the name of Socialist Wales ... The Wales that the nationalists propose might be an independent Wales, a Socialist Wales, a Socialist nationalist Wales, but it will be a very poor Wales and an empty Wales.[85]

The Labour anti-devolution MPs kept up their attacks on the Bill as it completed its progress through the Commons by 25 April 1978, but because of the forty per cent threshold in which the referendum had also to gain a majority in Wales, in Wigley's words, 'it had been castrated',[86] and in any case, academics warned that the Devolution Act was:

A legal minefield, unstable and rich with possibilities of litigation. The proposed Welsh Assembly resembled a local authority in that it had executive powers only, could not pass any laws for Wales and had no power of general competence in any field.[87]

Whilst devolution had dominated the Parliamentary agenda between 1974 and 1979, and although Dafydd Elis had been assiduous in campaigning outside Parliament with a range of civil society organisations, including the peace movement and trades unions, it was only gradually that he gained the confidence to risk associating with Cymdeithas yr Iaith Gymraeg and its law-breaking campaigns. He supported the campaign against second homes, and their symbolic occupation by Cymdeithas in his constituency and other parts of Welsh speaking Wales, and he spoke frequently at Cymdeithas rallies in support of illegal, but strictly non-violent, direct action.[88] This became a source of tension with Gwynfor Evans's supporters in Carmarthenshire were afraid that lawbreaking would alienate his electors, and asked Dafydd Elis to rein in his public support for the Cymdeithas campaign against second homes and for a Welsh language television channel.

The most violent action taken by Cymdeithas following the recommencement of its broadcasting campaign in 1977, was the damaging of technical equipment and property to the value of £26,000 at the Blaenplwyf television mast outside Aberystwyth, in February 1977. Unusually, no Cymdeithas members took responsibility for their actions and the police arrested and charged two of its leading members, its chairman Rhodri Williams and one of its senior leaders, Wynfford James, on charges of conspiracy to cause criminal damage.

The subsequent case in Carmarthen became a *cause célèbre* for civil rights activists, with claims of jury rigging and accusations against the police for what was viewed as a political use of the conspiracy laws. This trial, in July 1978 drew huge attention, and the jury failed to reach a verdict, so the case was re-scheduled for later that year. The court's proceedings were disrupted constantly, and dozens arrested protesting during the trial. Although Dafydd Elis was warned by local Plaid staff in Carmarthen, such as Peter Hughes Griffiths, Gwynfor Evans's agent, to stay away, he insisted on speaking at a rally in support of the two defendants before their re-trial in November 1978.[89]

The summer parliamentary term came to an end in July 1978 with many doubting that the Government could hold on to office. But the political atmosphere changed in the following few weeks and gave Callaghan more confidence in being able to maintain his minority government. Gwynfor Evans had promised John Morris at the end of July that the Plaid group would continue to support the Government, and the Ulster Unionists had also indicated their support on condition that the number of MPs for the province was increased.[90]

Following the Liberals' withdrawal from its agreement with the Government, arguably the most crucial meeting in this period for Plaid Cymru was the private meeting between the Plaid triumvirate of MPs and Michael Foot during the National Eisteddfod in Cardiff in August 1978. It was held at the home of Caerwyn Roderick, Foot's parliamentary private secretary. Dafydd Wigley recalls that 'Michael Foot was there, looking embarrassed, apparently staring at his shoes, and he asked whether there was any possibility that the group might be prepared to consider supporting the Government over the coming winter?'

During that meeting the three Plaid MPs proposed that in exchange for key concessions they would commit not to bring the Government down and arranged a subsequent meeting to finalise terms. Rather quixotically, Gwynfor emphasised the importance of holding the devolution Referendum on St David's Day, but Dafydd Elis emphasised the need for hard discussions over the terms of the agreement.[91]

On the first of September, a further meeting was held between the two Dafydds and Cledwyn Hughes in the Anglesey Arms in Menai Bridge. Both had consulted with Gwynfor, and Wigley recalls that 'we gave our demands. Dafydd Elis was emotional, and he was very close friends with Cledwyn, much closer than I was. Dafydd's father had been very close to Cledwyn, which was very important.' They presented a six-point shopping list to be included in the Queen's Speech, which was to increase the budget of the Welsh Development Agency; to move on with the technical work in order to accelerate the creation of a Welsh language television channel; to provide more funding for the Welsh language in education; to introduce leasehold reform; to secure aid for family farms as small businesses, and lastly to create a silicosis compensation scheme for quarrymen.[92] The subsequent Queen's Speech included every one of their demands. The *Financial Times* noted its 'unprecedented Welsh proposals',[93] and the *Western Mail*'s veteran correspondent David Rosser, shared his astonishment that he hadn't seen such a thing in his thirty-two years of working in the House of Commons.[94]

Minutes after the Queen's Speech was delivered, Dafydd Wigley bumped into David Rose, the *Daily Post* lobby correspondent, who exclaimed, 'What did you think of that for a Welsh Queen's Speech!'. But Plaid's undoubted success in gaining these concessions failed to aid the success of the devolution campaign.

The 1979 Devolution Referendum

There were early signs before the campaign that the opposition to devolution was mustering. In December 1978, the 'Gang of Six' Welsh Labour MPs – Ioan Evans, Leo Abse, Neil Kinnock, Donald Anderson, Fred Evans and Ifor Davies – formally started its campaign against the Assembly. The Labour Government was increasingly unpopular as a public sector workers' strike made the political atmosphere toxic, and this period became known as the 'winter of discontent', which poisoned Labour's attempts to revive its fortunes after Callaghan's surprising decision not to go to the polls the previous autumn.[95]

This unpromising political backdrop to the referendum campaign would prove to be disastrous for supporters of devolution. In keeping with Gwynfor's wish, the referendum was held on St David's Day 1979, but there was little support for the type of administrative devolution on offer, and its protagonists focused on the principle of devolution rather than the details of the scheme. The chair of the Yes campaign was the former Labour MP for Cardiganshire, Elystan Morgan, who had been out of frontline politics for nine years. The lack of support given to the Yes campaign by the majority of Labour MPs or councillors left the impression that its real supporters were from Plaid Cymru, lending credence to the belief that this might be a first step towards independence for Wales.

The arguments of the opponents to devolution focused on four main themes – devolution as the start of a 'slippery slope' to separatism; the cost of the Assembly; the danger of over-government; and that the Welsh language would be imposed on the non-Welsh speakers. The polls had shown a dramatic decline in support for devolution in the preceding year. In truth, Labour failed to persuade people that devolution would deliver better government.[96] Opinion polls held afterwards revealed that respondents felt that it would be too costly (61 per cent), would create another layer of bureaucracy (43 per cent), and would lead to the break-up of the UK (40 per cent).[97]

The 'Yes' campaign comprised the Executive of the Welsh Labour party, the bulk of Welsh Labour MPs, Plaid Cymru, the Welsh Liberal Party, and the Wales TUC. The 'No' campaign was comprised of the Conservative Party in Wales, seven of the eight county councils in Wales (comprising many of Labour's influential leaders at a local level), the National Federation of the Self-Employed; NALGO, the local government trade union, the Country Landowners' Association, and the key group of six Labour MPs who had done so much to sabotage the devolution bill. During the campaign itself, while some local Labour parties were supportive in south-west Wales, most Labour Party members were either apathetic or actively opposed devolution, especially in north-east and south-east Wales. Those who worked most actively for the Yes campaign were largely Plaid members, even though many of its membership were ambivalent about the devolution proposals. A minority, represented by Wigley and Phil Williams, perceived the legislation as wholly inadequate to create a legislative Assembly. The larger faction, including Dafydd Elis, adopted a more pragmatic position, regarding it as a step in the right direction. He recalled collecting thousands of leaflets printed with the unlikely message stating 'Conservatives vote Yes!', with a picture of Edward Heath on its front, from the nationalist Whittington printers in

Neath, before driving them up to north Wales for invariably Plaid members, to distribute this literature.[98]

The referendum vote, announced on 2 March, showed a margin of four to one against devolution, 956,330 voting No, to 243,048 voting Yes, on a turnout of 58.3 per cent, and rejected by every part of the country. As the Secretary of State for Wales, John Morris acknowledged, this was the political equivalent of receiving 'an elephant on your doorstep'.[99]

A testimony to the strength of Plaid Cymru in Merioneth was that its voters' turnout of 70.6 per cent was the highest in Wales, providing evidence of Dafydd Elis and his efficient party machine's ability to stimulate public interest and involvement. However, while Gwynedd had the highest percentage in favour of devolution, it still had a No majority of 33 per cent. The historian John Davies noted that 'it is difficult to overstate the sense of hopelessness felt by the members of Plaid Cymru in the spring of 1979. It seemed as if the strategy of two decades – indeed the entire strategy of Welsh progressive patriotism since the Cymru Fydd era in the 1890s – had come to nought.'[100] The historian of Welsh radicalism Gwyn A. Williams went further, stating that the Welsh had 'written *finis* to nearly two hundred years of Welsh history'.[101]

In the days that followed the Referendum, disappointed campaigners turned on each other, Dafydd Elis Thomas criticised the naivety of those who believed that there was a short cut towards self-government, on the back of the Labour party. He also stated what he believed to be 'the unpalatable truth', that Plaid had exaggerated its parliamentary influence between 1974 and 1979.[102] The Secretary of State for Wales, John Morris, had expected the defeat, but was shocked by its enormity: 'the government's low esteem and the campaigning of the opposition, joined by our dissidents, defeated us and undoubtedly paved the way for a Conservative win at the general election'. He described it as a 'horrendous defeat, a knock-out blow ... It was undoubtedly the biggest disappointment of my life'. He believed that the 'No' side had played on the fear of social division:

> In South Wales the electorate had been persuaded that the Assembly would be run by bigoted Welsh speakers from the north and west. This was the kind of propaganda that Leo Abse would have trilled. In the north, too many of the electorate had been

persuaded that the Assembly would be run by the Glamorgan County Council 'Taffia' and the like. It was a 'no-win' situation.[103]

Dafydd Elis recalled that:

> It was a bloody awful campaign. Very badly run, and organised, and led. It's a very good example of a not properly informed electorate being asked a question which they don't understand. But it's more than that. Obviously, with a margin of four to one against, it's clear that the people of Wales didn't want it at the time.

He was very critical of the leadership of the devolution campaign:

> I shouldn't really be personal about Elystan Morgan but I found him very difficult as a figure because it seems to me that he was more a Gwynforite than Gwynfor. I used to love listening to him going on but the nationalism that he was describing would have sounded old fashioned to Thomas Edward Ellis, the way that it was put over.[104]

Elystan Morgan later wrote that he thought that winning the referendum had been 'Mission Impossible', and had initially doubted whether he should have undertaken this role. When Parliament decided that it was necessary to win forty per cent of all electors in Wales to the result 'I knew in my bones that this was totally impossible, even if we had a fair wind behind us. Under such circumstances, I felt that the most correct thing to do was to condemn the referendum as a fraud.'[105]

Every day during the campaign, the media and the Assembly's opponents focused on concerns over the cost of an Assembly in Cardiff. Prejudices about the language and domination by south Wales were amplified, and it became a referendum on Callaghan's increasingly unpopular Government. Dafydd Elis believed that the referendum campaign failed totally to persuade the Welsh public of the merits of devolution:

> What I argued after the referendum in 1979 was that if people are not engaged with the issues, and if . . . this debate is not shared extensively with the Welsh public or is endorsed by the political class or political parties in a wider way, it won't happen.

In a funny way, I don't remember being deeply depressed after the loss in the 1979 referendum. I tried to appear enthusiastic in public. I also feel I didn't do enough to argue for the principle of devolution.[106]

The response to the referendum votes by nationalists in Scotland and Wales was very different. In the House of Commons, the SNP decided to move a vote of no confidence in the Labour Government unless it revived its devolution proposals for a Scottish Parliament, and they did so under the impression that Plaid would follow their lead. But on 21 March, the story broke that Callaghan was preparing to meet one of Plaid's main demands and implement legislation giving compensation to at least 800 quarrymen who had suffered from pneumoconiosis.[107] The following evening, both the SNP and the Conservatives put down motions of no confidence in the Government, and the three Plaid members were required to decide which way to vote.

On Saturday 24 March, they met in Aberystwyth to decide on their approach, before the no confidence vote to be held the following Wednesday. Although they had originally arranged to meet in the Belle Vue hotel on the sea front, so many journalists had gathered there that they decided to re-convene in Pantycelyn Hall on the University campus. Wigley insisted that Dafydd Elis accompany him in the car and on the short journey, explained to him that Gwynfor wanted to vote with the Conservatives. Wigley recalled:

> This was possibly the meeting where we were closest together on a matter of substance. Gwynfor stated that he was afraid that in supporting the government he would lose his seat, which he did of course. That meeting was totally crucial – if it had gone another way, I don't know what would have happened to us. A split would have been irrevocable for Plaid. After many hours, we agreed not to vote to bring the Government down.[108]

The following Tuesday, Wigley met Michael Foot and revealed they would support the Government in the following day's no confidence vote. Dafydd Elis was delighted with his group's decision and the Government's concessions to them, and especially its support for those slate quarrymen suffering from *clefyd y llwch* (dust disease):

The pneumoconiosis legislation was to replicate what the miners had in the coal industry, and this was a campaign which Wigley and I had really strongly supported. Harold Walker was the minister that got it through in the end, but it was also about working very closely with the Transport and General Workers' Union. The argument was very clear, really. The pneumoconiosis compensation scheme for the National Union of Mineworkers (NUM) had been promoted by Tony Benn and was part of a deal between the NUM and the Labour government at the time.

It was all based on the fact that the coal industry was in public ownership, and therefore, that industrial diseases such as asbestosis, illnesses or serious terminal illnesses, could also come from similar experiences of working in a situation that was deeply unhealthy, with its effect on people's breathing ... There were similarities between the silicosis of people working in the slate industry and the asbestosis of people who worked with asbestos, and people who would have been covered by the original pneumoconiosis scheme. Working with the unions, we pushed the case for it. We had strong support from Labour colleagues who were directly affected, and Dafydd Wigley was very strong on the issue.

I do remember some particularly powerful discussions with the quarry workers, and working closely with Labour supporters in the North of England on that issue. I think the major beneficiaries from that scheme, because it had to be a UK scheme, were in fact those who had suffered from asbestos.[109]

Wigley recalled that it was obvious in early 1979 that the Referendum would be lost, but that the miners' compensation scheme was 'very important for me in Llanberis and for Dafydd Elis in Blaenau Ffestiniog, where he was even more involved than I was – he was actually on the campaign committee in Blaenau Ffestiniog and close to the unions involved.'[110]

The no confidence vote in the Government was held on 28 March, and lost by the Government by only one vote, by 311 to 310, triggering a General Election for 3 May 1979. Parliament was not dissolved immediately after the vote, and a couple of days' wash-up period was allowed for the completion of uncontroversial business, including the passing of legislation for the silicosis compensation scheme.

The resulting election was won handsomely by the Conservative Party under Margaret Thatcher's leadership and led to eighteen years of Conservative rule. After losing, James Callaghan remained Labour leader for another year before he was succeeded by Michael Foot. The Scottish National Party also suffered in the 1979 general election with its group reduced from eleven members to just two The incoming Conservative government repealed the Scotland Act and devolution legislation would not be re-presented until 1997 under Tony Blair's Government.

As Gwynfor Evans had prophesied, supporting the Labour Government proved disastrous for him in Carmarthen, and he lost the seat to the Labour candidate Dr Roger Thomas, with his vote declining from 23,325 in 1974 to 16,689 in 1979, losing most of his votes to the Conservatives. Plaid Cymru's national vote declined from 11 per cent to 8 per cent, and the only gleam of light in the party's performance was the safe retention of their parliamentary seats by the two Dafydds. In Caernarfon, Dafydd Wigley increased his share of the vote to a massive 49.7 per cent, with 17,420 votes. Dafydd Elis Thomas achieved 40.8 per cent in Merioneth, with a further increase of 1,300 in his vote, but a sign of the political weather was the performance of his runner up, an Eton-educated Tory and *Daily Telegraph* leader writer, Robert Harvey, who registered the highest vote for a Conservative in Merioneth since the 1910 General Election. He more than doubled their share of the vote, from 11.2 per cent to 23.6 per cent, reflecting the huge general swing of over 8 per cent to the Conservatives across Britain.

Merioneth		May 1979 General Election
Dafydd Elis Thomas, Plaid Cymru	9,275	40.8%
Robert Harvey, Conservative	5,365	23.6%
R. H. Jones, Labour	5,332	23.5%
J. H. Parsons, Liberal	2,752	12.1%[111]

In Caernarfon, Dafydd Wigley won even more comfortably with over half the vote, and a majority of 8,724:

Caernarfon	May 1979	
Dafydd Wigley, Plaid Cymru	17,420	49.7%
T. Merfyn Hughes, Labour	8,696	24.8%
James Paice, Conservative	6,968	19.9%
J. Trevor Edwards, Liberal	1,999	5.7%[112]

The General Election was a triumph for the Conservatives' leader, Margaret Thatcher, winning 339 seats, and she would remain in Government for eleven years, until November 1990, to be replaced by John Major.

The concessions won by the Plaid Cymru MPs added momentum to their election campaign in north-west Wales. Dafydd Elis recalled how securing the silicosis compensation had a huge impact in Gwynedd's slate quarrying areas:

> Wigley was brilliant at that time, but so too were the colleagues in the trade union movement. I do remember the election after the compensation scheme had gone through. I knocked on a door in Blaenau Ffestiniog and the woman answering the door looked at me, and said, 'What are you doing here? There are carpets all over this town to remember you by!'. I gave her a big hug. I didn't know what to do really.[113]

But for Plaid Cymru more generally, the election result was predictable and extremely disappointing. In their targeted south Wales Valleys seats, their vote slumped in Aberdare, for instance, from 21.3 per cent in 1974 to 9.8 per cent, and in Caerphilly, from 24.5 per cent to 14.9 per cent, with mostly the Conservatives replacing the party in second place. Wales elected the unprecedented number of eleven Conservative MPs, the largest number since October 1924, and again, Plaid Cymru faced a protracted period in the political wilderness.

Throughout the nineteen seventies, both Dafydd Wigley and Dafydd Elis Thomas had created the conditions for Caernarfon and Merioneth to become safe Plaid Cymru parliamentary seats by May 1979. But the impact of the 1979 devolution referendum ground the *raison d'être* of the party, of securing a Welsh Parliament or Assembly, to a shuddering halt.

4

The Aftermath of the 1979 Devolution Referendum – Heading Left

The period from the 1979 Referendum to the General Election in March 1992 was a momentous time for Dafydd Elis's personal and professional life, and a transformational time for Plaid Cymru. He was the central figure at the heart of the raging existential debate about the future direction of the party, becoming the figurehead of the left and winning the Presidency of the party. He reached out to the left in the labour and trade union, peace and women's movements, and created the unity of purpose that by the mid-nineties, led to the coalition of activists who would later work together to campaign for, and win Welsh democratic devolution. Much of the credit for the making of this broader alliance lay in his charismatic personality and passionate campaigning.

The disappointment of the 1979 Referendum loss depressed many in the national movement but fired Dafydd Elis up to force Plaid Cymru to confront its own contradictions. To what extent was it a cultural Welsh language movement rather than a political party? And where did its nationalism stand in the spectrum of socialism and conservatism? He attempted to convert Plaid into a more socialist and, he would argue, more mainstream political party, but was initially thwarted by Gwynfor Evans's unilateral decision in 1980 to undertake a hunger strike for a Welsh language channel. Plaid Cymru was bullied by this quixotic act into abandoning its search for an identity as a modern political party and reverted to the comfort blanket of its origins as a linguistic cultural movement.

Plaid Cymru's political despair in March 1979 was converted by an extreme section of the language movement into an arson campaign against second homes and estate agents by the end of the year. Dafydd Elis's attempt to make common cause with the anger of those steelworkers in Wales threatened by mass redundancies in late 1979 and early 1980, was undermined by Gwynfor Evans's hijacking of the political agenda, and the opportunity to fuse Welsh industrial and political discontent was lost until the miners' strike of 1984.

Dafydd Elis attempted to broaden the base of the party, and in the latter half of the eighties, hoped that Wales could become part of a wider European polity, less restricted by the British political context. But as the decade drew on, he also gradually shed some of the radical alliances that had led to him becoming Plaid Cymru's President, and fell out with Cymdeithas yr Iaith Gymraeg, the anti-nuclear lobby, and disappointed the women's section within the party. This decade was also a turbulent time for him personally. He separated formally from his wife Elen in 1988, and he lived from 1986 until the summer of 1992, with the American anti-nuclear activist, Marjorie Thompson, a lobbyist for the Royal College of Nursing, who became chair of the Campaign for Nuclear Disarmament. During the latter half of the eighties, he also became closer to the Conservative Ministers in the Welsh Office, and when he announced in 1990 that he would stand down in the next General Election, his path to securing further political influence was smoothed by his ability to work with his friend and colleague Wyn Roberts, yet another accomplished son of the manse.

After its disappointing General Election, and the disastrous Referendum result, Plaid Cymru's response was to create a Commission of Inquiry in June 1979 to review the party's performance. The five members of the Commission included those from the left of the party, Phil Williams, Owen John Thomas and Emrys Roberts and those from the centre-right, Eurfyl ap Gwilym and Dafydd Wigley.[1]

But the first substantial salvo to be fired in the debate on the future direction of the party came from the party's research officer, Robert Griffiths, and Gareth Miles, then the organiser of Undeb Cenedlaethol Athrawon Cymru (UCAC), the Welsh language teachers' union, a well-known language campaigner, brilliant satirist, novelist, dramatist and Marxist theoretician. In August 1979, at that year's National Eisteddfod in Caernarfon, they published a highly controversial pamphlet that criticised both 'bourgeois nationalism' and 'corporate Labourism', and advocated the creation of a Socialist Republican movement.[2] This was no new phenomenon – similar attempts could be traced back to Plaid's earlier history in the thirties, when a republican movement was formed within the party to challenge the leadership, but was eventually defeated. But this pamphlet 'shook the Gwynfor establishment to its core'.[3] The tone was uncompromisingly critical of Plaid's traditionalist leadership, stating that it was not surprising that a 'readiness to compromise, a lack of daring, a vacillation of intent and cowardice are the main characteristics of the party that a large number of its members, including its leaders, are petty bourgeoise, Non-conformists and pacifists.'[4]

The impact of this explosive pamphlet was compounded by its foreword, written by Dafydd Elis Thomas, who voiced his disillusionment with the party very clearly:

> This pamphlet challenges those Nationalists who consider that it is an all embracing philosophy. In the opinion of those Nationalists (still the largest section of Plaid Cymru), the Nation, as in the bourgeois image of God, is 'above' class conflict; they believe that they can fight for cultural policies, and for language groups that face extinction, without giving any consideration to the economic structure that exists. This version of history ignores the real history of conquered nations such as Wales and the historical links between the development of states such as Britain, its imperial role, and Capitalism. But this pamphlet also challenges those people on the Left who deny, in as unhistorical a way, the existence of the Welsh nation and cultural problems; socialists who espouse inhuman economics by pushing an abstract and non-historical 'working class' to some beautiful socialist dawn.

He called for a mass movement beyond Westminster to create social change and warned 'that there was no hope for Wales unless its people dedicate to undermine and overthrow the capitalist system in all its forms'.[5]

The party attempted to dampen down this nascent rebellion. That summer, Robert Griffiths was manoeuvred out of his role as the party's research officer when his post was re-located to London.[6] The political context was changing rapidly and the economic depression started to bite harder. In July the announcement was made to dismiss 6,500 steelworkers in the Shotton steelworks on Deeside and exploratory mining started in mid Wales to look for suitable sites for the burial of nuclear waste.

As unemployment figures in Wales was rising rapidly to over 100,000, the political temperature was also rising in Wales.

Even before the return of the new Parliament in May 1979, Elen and Dafydd had already decided to move the family to London the following year. Dafydd Elis had found the constant commuting to be a huge strain, and had pressed Elen for some time, to move to London. They had had two more boys – Meilyr Hywel, on 11 March 1976, and Cai Dafydd, on 5 April 1979, and Elen now also wished to undertake a two-year social work qualification in the University of London. Remarkably, in an indication of the sense of entitlement that the local constituency party felt it had over the family, Dafydd Elis's constituency agent, Elfed Roberts, insisted that Elen should present herself before them to justify whether they should be permitted to move home:

> The constituency party wanted to decide whether I was allowed to go to London. They believed that Dafydd had to have an address in the constituency, and this was seriously discussed. We kept the house in Dolgellau because I was doing a two year course and I had to promise that I would return. There was a feeling that they owned not only Dafydd but myself as well. It wasn't a nice experience, but I remember saying I would be back in two years, even though I wasn't sure if I would. I couldn't see us bringing up the children in London, and that's why I came back after two years. By moving to London, both Dafydd and I thought we would see each other more often, and that Dafydd could play a bigger part in the upbringing of the children.[7]

In the summer of 1980, they rented a flat in Willesden Green, in north London, and as Elen started her course, the two older boys, Meilyr and Rolant, enrolled at the small London Welsh school, and their father enjoyed having the family nearer him during the week in London. But his continuing peripatetic lifestyle, including commitments in the constituency, and the House of Commons's punishing schedule, meant that the pressures on him and the family remained. He also returned to part-time university teaching, re-establishing his academic credentials at the Institute of Education in Bedford Way in central London, and lecturing on the Welsh police's inspectors' development courses.

Living in north London also meant that he lived close to prominent figures in London's Labour left:

> My views at the time were very much influenced by my other intellectual life in London as a Member of Parliament and working alongside what was happening on the left . . . I lived in Brent in north London then, so I was part of discussions there. I talked a lot to the left in London and to Ken Livingstone,[8] who I knew quite well in those days. In fact, I voted for him in the Greater London Council elections. We had a few lovely discussions, because he was interested in where I was coming from, because we were influenced by the idea that state socialism is not what we wanted; community socialism is too small, doesn't work, and doesn't make sense – so what do we do? What does the left do, especially in local or regional government?

His engagement with London's Labour politicians convinced him that Plaid needed to be a broader based party:

> There were lots of people that I'd known in CND and the Green movement in those days who were very interested in supporting Plaid, but thought we were only about devolution or constitutional change in Wales. That was the key thing. It was about ensuring that broad-ranging movements could relate to us as a democratic, political elected party. I'd seen that in the Green movement in Germany. I thought Plaid could be that. That did happen marginally, but not seriously. The point for me was that in losing the referendum for devolution by four to one, what do we do next? We had to be a deeper, broader part of the political culture. We couldn't go on and on about what Wales needed being self-government, and that would solve everything, because that was the biggest lie at the heart of any autonomous nationalist politics: the idea that just getting greater autonomy solves the economic, social, environmental, political issues of the polity which it is alleged would benefit.[9]

The Parliament that Dafydd Elis returned to in May 1979 was very different to his previous sessions, with the Labour Government having survived a persistent existential threat for almost five years. With Thatcherism in the ascendancy and with a large Conservative majority, parliamentary votes were now foregone conclusions. In this less frenetic context, Dafydd Elis was able to pause and reflect that Plaid Cymru now had minimal influence on Government policy, but he found the Welsh Office Ministers helpful:

> I didn't know exactly where I would find myself with the Conservative incoming government, but I found Nicholas Edwards, Wyn Roberts and Michael Roberts to be three ministers with whom I could do business whenever they wanted some support or some understanding or discussions about anything to do with the issues I was concerned about.[10]

In the new Parliament, he became close to some of the new left-wing Labour MPs. He became friendly with Stuart Holland, the Labour MP for Vauxhall who had drafted the party's economic programme in the early seventies, and his proposals for regional development agencies and the Greater London Enterprise Agency had entered the party's February 1974 manifesto. But his ground-breaking Marxist analysis of regional policy in Britain made him an object of suspicion within his own party. Others included Reg Race, the MP for Wood Green, who would later create a left-wing group of MPs named 'Labour Party Socialists' with Jeremy Corbyn and Tony Benn.[11] Another important friend was David Lloyd, a Welsh journalist, who worked in the parliamentary lobby for the Communist Party's *Morning Star*, and was an important link between Dafydd Elis and the group of left-wing Labour MPs who would create the Labour Coordinating Committee, supporting Tony Benn for the deputy leadership campaign of the party in 1981.

In October 1979, a new system of select committees was put in place in order to scrutinise Government and these cross-party committees often became more effective than debates in the Commons chamber, dominated by a large Conservative majority. Dafydd Elis pointedly declined to join the generalist Welsh Affairs Select Committee under the chairmanship of Leo Abse, but with the support of his Labour colleagues, supplanted the Liberal nominee to the select committee on education, whose main role was to scrutinise the controversial Secretary of State for Education, Sir Keith Joseph:

That's where I began to be a proper parliamentarian. Labour nominated me instead of a Liberal, although usually, when there was minority party representation, it would usually be the Liberals and then Labour. That's where I learned what it was like to cross-examine people and ministers. I remember cross-examining Keith Joseph and civil servants, but Chris Price [the committee chair] was absolutely brilliant in supporting what I was trying to do. I never used that committee to drum home Plaid policies in any way, because that's not what it was about, but I did get the opportunity to spend a lot of time in further and higher education, and cultural institutions in England, and to understand the best way of asking questions. That's how I started my strong relationships with parliamentary clerks and the special advisers. That's where I learned what parliamentary scrutiny should be like.

I do remember a particular occasion when the committee had decided that we would organise a teaching seminar for the whole education sector. This included, obviously, the Department of Education and Science. I did have to laugh about it. The Permanent Secretary from the Department then turned up in person at this session because they were so worried about these new creatures of the select committees and that they would undermine the status of ministers and civil servants![12]

This experience was formative for him later when he came to develop the scrutiny role of the National Assembly for Wales. Because of his experience of adult education, he was encouraged by the chair, Chris Price,[13] the committee clerk Frank McShane, and a series of different academic advisers and encouraging colleagues, to lead in some of the committee's enquiries:

> That's when I became a parliamentarian. Because when you are just an opposition MP, even in a party group, you don't get that. Well, nobody had that experience, because we hadn't done it before in the UK system. When I came to try to establish the new devolution system in Wales, I was very keen that every elected member had that experience.

In that period on the education select committee, he dealt with a wide range of subjects with his Labour colleagues, and produced substantial minority reports, on subjects such as multicultural education, higher education funding and multi-lingualism in English schools.[14]

Hunger Strike – The Martyr's Crown

The fate of Welsh language broadcasting had been a controversial subject throughout the nineteen seventies. Dafydd Elis had been one of the most vocal supporters of a Welsh language channel, and had campaigned successfully to secure an increase in Welsh language children's programmes in 1977–8.

The Conservative manifesto in the 1979 election unequivocally committed the party to 'an increase in the amount of Welsh language broadcasting starting on the fourth channel as quickly as possible'. The Secretary of State for Wales, Nick Edwards, re-emphasised this commitment in a speech to the party's Welsh conference on 23 June 1979, that 'we have made clear our intention to press ahead with plans for Welsh language broadcasting on the fourth channel'.[15]

But in spite of this clear promise, immediate doubts were raised. On the day of Edwards's speech, Owen Edwards, the BBC's Director in Wales, stated that a new Welsh language television channel was probably unaffordable,[16] and Wales's commercial television company HTV, responded that Welsh language television programmes should be broadcast on two channels rather than one.[17]

On 12 September 1979, Willie Whitelaw, the Home Secretary, announced at the Royal Television Society conference in Cambridge that the Government was reneging on its commitment to establish a Welsh language fourth channel, but would increase the number of hours of Welsh language programming on the BBC and ITV, rather than replace Channel Four in Wales. The Government's mind had been changed mainly because the technical problems associated with creating a Welsh channel were deemed to be insuperable. But Whitelaw had also been intensely lobbied to change Government policy by influential HTV board members such as Lord Harlech and Sir Alun Talfan Davies. The regulatory body, the Independent Broadcasting Authority, was also persuaded to oppose the single channel solution, and Lady Plowden, its chair, was implacably opposed, stating that the idea was unrealistic.[18]

The Home Office ignored the Welsh Office's opposition to this U-turn, where the change in policy aroused total consternation. Bob Jones, the Blaenau Ffestiniog civil servant responsible for Welsh language policy, and a friend of Dafydd Elis, privately vented his rage:

> The Home Office have behaved disgracefully in this matter; for the Secretary of State {for Wales} to be presented with what is virtually a fait accompli is really quite intolerable and to argue that the Secretary of State has no statutory responsibility for broadcasting is no answer . . . These proposals, if accepted, and I would be surprised if they are not, will cause considerable embarrassment, not only to the Secretary of State . . . but also to the Government.[19]

A letter from his boss, the Secretary of State for Wales, Nick Edwards, to Willie Whitelaw, railed against this change in policy:

> It is not merely that what you now propose will create the most profound political problems in Wales, where as you know, this Government's commitment to the furtherance of the language is being questioned and a major political row is brewing . . . What I find unacceptable is that the recommendations in your paper should have emerged in the way that they did one week before they are due to be discussed by colleagues without any prior consultation whatever with me or with my Department.[20]

But Nick Edwards and his deputy, the Under-Secretary of State for Wales, Wyn Roberts, agreed not to dispute the policy further in view of the Home Office's obstinacy. Welsh nationalists and language activists saw this *volte face* as treachery, and rightly detected HTV's hand in the affair, confirming their suspicion that the company's commercial interests had seemingly killed the desire for a single Welsh language television channel. Since 1977, the relationship between Plaid Cymru and HTV Wales had been strained. Dafydd Elis had complained regularly about the company's ownership based in the West Country, and in July 1979, even demanded that it lose its ITV licence for Wales because of its 'media imperialism from across the Severn'.[21]

The day after Whitelaw's announcement, Gwynfor Evans declared that Plaid needed to go beyond 'conventional political methods' to challenge the Government's decision. Cymdeithas yr Iaith Gymraeg immediately promised more serious direct action,[22] and Dafydd Elis Thomas was amongst the first to commit to refuse to pay his TV licence, followed by Gwynfor Evans and Dafydd Wigley a few days later.

Plaid developed its licence fee non-payment campaign that autumn, while HTV produced five thousand copies of its own pamphlet, attractively written by the company's head of news and current affairs, Geraint Talfan Davies, Sir Alun Talfan's nephew. It attempted to justify the Government's U-turn, and, when attacked heavily by Dafydd Elis, he was criticised in turn by HTV's head of public affairs, David Meredith, for 'creating social division by locating all Welsh language programmes on one channel'.[23] The disparaging of HTV continued in Plaid Cymru's annual conference in October, when in a fit of pique, delegates voted to exclude two respected HTV journalists, Max Perkins and Gwilym Owen.[24] At the conference, Gwynfor Evans declared ominously that the issue of the Welsh language channel was as important as Tryweryn.[25]

On 11 December 1979, Dafydd Elis Thomas again called on language supporters not to pay their TV licence. At the same time, the crisis in the steel industry in Wales was becoming critical, and the British Steel Corporation announced that its workforce in Wales was to be halved to twenty thousand posts. BSC Shotton in Flintshire was threatened with closure, and either BSC Llanwern or BSC Port Talbot were now also faced with the halving of their capacity. Wales TUC's general secretary, George Wright, predicted that Wales was about to experience its worse economic depression since the thirties.[26] In the first major industrial dispute of the Thatcher era, the steel unions, representing forty thousand workers in Wales, went on strike from 2 January to 3 April 1980, ostensibly for an increase in pay but also to ensure greater job security. But their campaign was marred by deep divisions within the labour movement in Wales. Steelworkers had failed to support miners in a number of disputes over pit closures, and members of the National Union of Mineworkers still harboured resentment towards their lack of solidarity. Kim Howells, the research officer for the National Union of Mineworkers in south Wales, witnessed this lack of unity within the labour movement:

The only way we could get through this was to pull everybody together. But at exactly the same time, this sectarianism was reasserting itself, probably because the steelworkers union had had a gutsful. I remember being in a meeting with Bill Sirs, the general secretary of the Iron and Steel Trades Confederation (ISTC) in the TUC in Cardiff, who said in response to the suggestion that a day of solidarity be held for the steelworkers, that 'you all want to do this, you want to do that, until the last drop of steelworkers' blood'. In 1981, as some south Wales pits faced closure, the south Wales representative of the electricians' union, the AUEW, took a similar view and the NUM deputy secretary George Rees, responded, 'that you can stuff your solidarity up your arse'. There was tremendous unity on television, but the internecine union warfare was dreadful.

Howells, who would become one of the key organisers of the miners' strike in south Wales in 1984–5, had met Dafydd previously:

I met him first of all in about 1977. I had no idea who he was. We met through *Llafur* first.[27] I couldn't understand why there was a bit of reverence around for this kid. He was quite young, a good looking boy, I thought he was a footballer – he wasn't big enough to be a rugby player. I didn't know he was a MP. He was a very attractive personality. I remember consciously not asking him about politics, but we spoke about the north Wales quarrymen.

We kept in touch, and I think I wanted to keep in touch with him because he was never once doctrinaire, and I never felt that he was being self-righteous in any shape or form. We maintained links after that because, in 1980, when those strikes started to get serious, we started to lose jobs and the steel industry had a battering, I asked him 'what are Plaid Cymru going to do about Shotton and north-east Wales? Are you even interested?' He was always interested, but I doubted if the party was interested.[28]

In December 1979 the Wales TUC called for a Welsh general strike to take place on 21 January 1980 in protest against the proposed steel closures. In January 1980, Dafydd Elis met with the deputy general secretary of the Wales TUC, David Jenkins, to discuss the possibility of holding symbolic acts of civil disobedience in protest at steel closures, such as the blockading of the Severn Bridge, but no action was eventually taken. The Wales TUC resigned itself to only organising a one day stoppage and a Day of Action, in defence of all public sector jobs. Any hope for further action was dashed by the South Wales miners' refusal to strike in support of the steelworkers in February 1980.[29] The Shotton plant was finally closed in March 1980, with a loss of seven thousand jobs, and in the summer of 1980, 17,000 of the 24,000 remaining Welsh steel workers were put on short-time working. The Wales TUC's report to the European Commission in 1981, *Wales at the Abyss*, noted that the industry had lost 27 per cent of its workforce in eighteen months.[30]

The beginning of a concerted arson campaign against holiday homes further added to this febrile political atmosphere. On 13 December 1979, the first attacks on English-owned second homes occurred, at four houses in two locations, in Nefyn on the Llŷn peninsula and in the Pembrokeshire village of Llanrhian.

The ostensible purpose of the campaign, in the name of *Meibion Glyndŵr* (Sons of Glyndŵr) was to draw attention to the increased prevalence of second homes in Welsh-speaking areas in particular. Within four weeks, eight English-owned holiday cottages were destroyed. Over the course of the next fourteen years, during a campaign that had two distinct periods, over two hundred second homes were burnt down, and the campaign extended to placing explosive devices at estate agents' offices along the Welsh-English border.[31]

There were also attacks on other targets, including a construction business based in Stratford upon Avon, associated with the Prime Minister's husband, Denis Thatcher. This attack was triggered by a political storm following the revelation that he had written to the Secretary of State for Wales, lobbying on behalf of his company to expedite a planning application it had made for a holiday development near Harlech. Exposed by *The Times*, Dafydd Elis, as the local MP, pursued this scandal relentlessly.[32]

The police responded to the arson campaign by raiding the homes of nationalist sympathisers throughout Wales. In the early hours of Palm Sunday, 30 March 1980, 52 nationalists were arrested. In the police's so-called 'Operation Fire', they arrested members of the Welsh Socialist Republican Movement, including its chairman, secretary and treasurer.

These suspects were held for periods of between a few hours and three and a half days, before being released. No charges ensued, and the raid merely added to the siege mentality of many in the nationalist movement.

In a later inquiry, the evidence of those arrested showed that the police were primarily concerned with political intelligence gathering, and that while questions about criminal damage often opened the proceedings, they were quickly followed by more detailed information gathering on political activities and contacts. Dafydd Elis led the parliamentary protest against the police's conduct, questioning the Home Office, and pressing the police to account for their actions.[33]

The authorities' desperate search for the culprits radicalised Welsh nationalists. In January 1980, the Socialist Republican movement had formally been established after the publication of its manifesto. Although Dafydd Elis had written its introduction, he did not continue his involvement, although its members were not required to relinquish membership of Plaid or any other party. At its high point, the movement had a membership of around three hundred, organised into twelve clubs, and scattered mainly throughout the south Wales valleys.

In this fevered atmosphere, to reduce political tension around the language question, the Secretary of State for Wales, Nicholas Edwards, announced his department's greatest ever financial commitment hitherto to the Welsh language, on 14 April 1980, in a speech at Llanrwst. He committed the Government to supporting the Welsh language and granted the substantial sum of £1.5 million to Welsh medium education. This significant statement would eventually help to extract the language issue out of the political firing line and create a cross-party consensus in favour of supporting the Welsh language.[34]

But Plaid's President, Gwynfor Evans, was already preparing to launch his own personal political bombshell. Over Christmas 1979, he had decided to undertake a hunger strike until death for the Welsh language television channel, and before the last day of February had only shared his decision with his family, the party's general secretary, Dafydd Williams, and his constituency agent, Peter Hughes Griffiths. He then informed Dafydd Wigley in March, and swore him to secrecy. Gwynfor Evans only shared his intention with his fellow Plaid Cymru members in a meeting of the party's national executive on 3 May, when he declared his intention, in the last item on the agenda, under 'any other business'.[35]

Dafydd Elis's reaction was one of shock, horror and anger. What angered him most of all was that the timing of the hunger strike was an incredible diversion for Plaid Cymru as it attempted to oppose steelworks closures and rapidly increasing unemployment. He believed that Gwynfor's tactic was naïve and confusing and would return Plaid to its past cultural preoccupations. Privately, he believed that the Government's *volte face* had been reasonable and that broadcasting Welsh language programmes on the two channels would have been well funded: 'I didn't see Willie Whitelaw's statement as being all that disastrous at the time. The resources were going to be put in place.'

He also had a 'basic moral objection to a hunger strike as 'an instrument of politics'. However, throughout this saga, he remained silent as to his true views, although he personally challenged Gwynfor as to the morality of his actions, at a private meeting with him at his holiday home outside Dolgellau, but with no success.[36]

Following Gwynfor's announcement, when Dafydd Elis returned to Parliament the following week, he discussed the impending crisis with government ministers:

> I was actually on the committee of the 1981 Broadcasting Bill, then going through the House of Commons. I talked to Wyn Roberts, who was the Welsh Minister on the Bill, and I talked to one of my favourite civil servants, Dr Bob Jones of Blaenau Ffestiniog about this. I also had a private meeting in Westminster with Nick [Edwards], I spoke to parliamentary colleagues and I put down amendments of my own to the Broadcasting Bill.[37]

On 28 June 1980, the first of a series of mass rallies of hundreds of people in support of Gwynfor was held in Aberystwyth. In an informal meeting between Whitelaw, Nicholas Edwards, Wyn Roberts and the chairmen and directors of the BBC and the IBA, it became clear that Whitelaw was seriously worried about the impact that capitulating to Evans could have on the attitudes of Republican prisoners in Northern Ireland, who were considering whether to go on hunger strike in order to secure political status. The idea that emerged from this meeting was to offer to set up a committee to coordinate Welsh language programming across two channels, a proposal that was promptly refused by Gwynfor Evans.[38]

On 18 July 1980, demonstrators threw themselves in front of the Prime Minister's car when she visited Anglesey. More seriously, on the same day, an explosive device was discovered on the windowsill of the bedroom of Nicholas Edwards's young son at their home in Crickhowell, and made safe by a bomb disposal team. Dafydd Wigley was thrown out of the Welsh Grand Committee in the House of Commons, after he disrupted the meeting in order to protest against the Government's refusal to change its mind and set up a Welsh language channel, and Dafydd Elis met a number of times with Nicholas Edwards privately in order to ensure, in his words, that 'Plaid would not return to being a language party'.[39]

In the midst of this heated and increasingly emotional campaign, Gwynfor Evans announced in mid-August that he intended to remain as president of the party, thus avoiding the need for a distracting contest, but which only postponed the inevitable showdown between left and right within the party until the following year. The protest rallies continued and on 6 September, two thousand protestors marched through the centre of Cardiff to call for a Welsh language television channel. A senior Welsh Office civil servant warned Nicholas Edwards of the danger of the campaign being linked with industrial discontent, and spinning out of the government's control:

> Mr Evans and his friends are mounting a most effective campaign; there are signs that this will continue, and it shows every indication of being a skilfully orchestrated exercise. The Government, on the other hand, has had a poor press ... the tide of public opinion seems to be running against the Government on this issue ... it may be possible for the Government to win the day in Parliament and the country – but this will not stop Gwynfor from seeking the martyr's crown. And I find it difficult to predict whether it will be possible to isolate the major problems we face in other fields from his campaign on this emotive issue.[40]

Moderate opinion in Wales drove a deputation of the National Eisteddfod, consisting of Cledwyn Hughes, representing the University of Wales, Sir Goronwy Daniel, the former first Permanent Secretary of the Welsh Office, the Archbishop of Wales, G. O. Williams, and the National Eisteddfod's director, Emyr Jenkins, to meet Willie Whitelaw on the afternoon of 10 September. Hughes led the discussion and warned that if Gwynfor Evans died, 'the consequences would be incalculable ... One cannot separate the linguistic/cultural side from the economic situation.' His clinching argument to Whitelaw was that the channel could be put on probation for two years, and that the government could not therefore be accused of giving in to blackmail.[41]

The Government did not capitulate at once, but on 15 September, Edwards and Whitelaw agreed to surrender. After lunch together, they went to see the Prime Minister, and Whitelaw admitted to her that they had been taken aback by the response to the Gwynfor Evans's threat of a hunger strike. They advised the Prime Minister that in view of the 'likely consequences', they should change the Government's policy, and she quickly agreed.[42]

On the morning of 17 September, a number of newspapers announced that the Government had made a U-turn, and Gwynfor's proposed series of campaigning rallies turned instead into a celebratory procession. The concession had been won partly due to Gwynfor's seriousness of intent and his readiness to die for the cause, but also to the key intervention of the three-man deputation. That night's meeting in Crymych turned into a canonisation of its hero by the hundreds present, and the following celebratory meetings around Wales attracted large crowds.[43]

As Whitelaw had feared, this change in policy was noted by Irish Republican prisoners in Long Kesh, otherwise known as the H-blocks, and encouraged them to demand that the IRA's Army Council sanction a hunger strike, in protest at their lack of political status.[44] The lesson that the prisoners in Northern Ireland's notorious H-Blocks drew from Gwynfor's success in ensuring the Government's capitulation, 'seemed clear and the prisoners in the Kesh renewed their pressure on the Army Council'.[45] There was a long history of hunger strikes by Irish republicans dating back to the 1920s, and Gwynfor Evans's successful campaign suggested to them that the Thatcher Government might weaken in the face of such a threat.

This victory was a great one for Gwynfor Evans but had a negative or neutral impact on the public's perception of Plaid Cymru. It confirmed the prejudice that Plaid Cymru was the political arm of the language movement and Evans's hope that the campaign would give broader momentum to the resistance against growing unemployment and Thatcher's economic policies, proved fruitless.

Still on the committee of the Broadcasting Bill, Dafydd Elis recalled being approached by Wyn Roberts and being surprised by his proposal for a Welsh language broadcasting authority to run the new Welsh language channel:

> I thought it was over the top because I saw too many broadcasting organisations in Wales already. I asked in a discussion with Nick Edwards himself, 'Why do we need an authority?'. He said, 'Well, the officials think this is the only way we can do it.' I said, 'I will support it if this is the only way we can get ourselves out of this situation'.

But Dafydd Elis became increasingly alienated from Gwynfor because of his hunger strike campaign:

> Gwynfor was going around the country on a suicide mission, basically. He was holding all these public meetings and stirring people up. I really shouldn't say this, but I lost respect for him during that period. If he was younger, I would have said it was an attention seeking attitude. This was some of my difficulty in my relationship with him over the years. I never knew, really, where he was coming from, or where he was trying to go.
>
> I don't think Gwynfor thought about Plaid. He thought about some ageing histrionics he could make for himself... When you receive the opportunity from other citizens to be elected, which then gives you a higher public profile, you don't begin using that then to create mayhem, which could have happened.[46]

Dafydd Elis played a leading part in the formulation of the legislation to set up the new Welsh language channel, S4C, to be run by a broadcasting authority, but thought its constitutional position anomalous, and lacking democratic accountability:

> I suppose, on reflection, for a period, a separate authority made sense. The fact that you had an independent authority created a new Welsh institution, but the accountability lay with the UK Parliament. There still isn't any accountability to a Welsh Parliament.[47]

The Plaid Cymru Presidency

Plaid Cymru's campaign for the Welsh language channel drew it away from the desire of many of its members to pursue campaigns against rising unemployment and the threat of closure of the major Welsh steelworks. By October 1980, it was known that Gwynfor Evans would stand down the following year, and the developing argument between the two wings of the party started to take shape. Cynog Dafis expressed the feelings of many members in doubting whether Plaid could encompass such a wide range of philosophies, and that it 'had to abandon the idea that this umbrella body could include all those – from left and right – who wanted to "save" Wales. Because "saving Wales" is an empty concept.'[48]

The answer for Cynog Dafis was socialism, and when Dafydd Elis Thomas was elected vice-president of the party in October 1980, the stage was set for a major confrontation between the left and right of the party.

Gwynfor Evans had been president of the party since 1945, and his party management style was personalised, autocratic and secretive. The business of the party was often done informally, rather than through the party's national executive and National Council, and he depended on a tight-knit group of mostly friends and advisers, known as the 'President's committee', described by his biographer as a 'secretive body of faithful Gwynforites'.[49]

In 1977, when Phil Williams resigned from his role as vice-president of the party in protest at Plaid's support for the Labour devolution proposals, he highlighted the role of the 'President's committee' as a small clique that guided the party, even though it had no place in its constitution.[50] In June 1979, the party's National Council took the extraordinary step of demanding that the party deny the existence of this secretive president's committee.[51]

As president of the party, Gwynfor Evans dismissed socialism and considered that 'ideological arguments' were a 'false battle ... socialism was an unclear and misleading term, which created division'. He considered it to have little appeal to the *werin* (the ordinary people) and advocated following the so-called Welsh Nonconformist radical tradition typified by Michael D. Jones, who created a self-governing Welsh colony of Patagonia, in Argentina,[52] but who seemingly failed to consider the impact of colonisation on the indigenous population.

The report of the party's Commission of Inquiry, published in

January 1981, reflected its authors' desire to break out of Plaid's electoral fastnesses in north-west Wales and become an effective challenger to the Labour party, and across the south Wales valleys in particular. The report called on the party to reject the 'centralist approach' of a 'primitive form of socialism, reflecting the imperialist traditions of the countries where it is practised' and advocated that Plaid should espouse a 'decentralist, community-based form of socialism, not to be confused with the state centralism and British imperialism of the Labour Party'.[53]

This report was remarkable in that its balanced membership, including traditionalists such as Wigley and ap Gwilym, advocated a more left-wing ideology for the party, and was a blow to those Gwynforites who had wished to avoid the positioning of the party on the left-right axis. But rather than welcoming the report, Dafydd Elis and Emyr Williams, a Montgomeryshire left-wing political theorist and academic, lambasted it as an 'essentially conservative device to short-circuit deeper, more meaningful debate on its future'. The Commission was accused of 'nauseating paternalism' and of echoing the party's Nonconformist roots and its 'almost religious conception of the party's role in Welsh society'. Their response highlighted the Commission's failure to respond to the current economic crisis, and emphasised that what was needed was not 'converts to a cause' but 'comrades in a struggle':

> These are to be found for example, in the trade union movement, in the vitally located and deeply significant women's movement, in the ecological movement, in rank-and-file movements (even within the Labour party) and certainly within the international peace movement. They are to be found in direct individual issue pressure groups, who as they commit themselves to fighting more than one individual round of cuts, will be led increasingly to an analysis linking the question of economic policy with the question of the control of the economy. It is not a case of adopting positions which will 'appeal' to the Welsh working class. It is a case of positioning ourselves as a party at the service of that class. And, through that class, at the service of a new national and international economic and political order.[54]

This declaration of intent gave an ideological basis for the development of the left within Plaid over the following decade. However, Gwynfor Evans believed that 'Dafydd El and his personal campaign' against the party's 'tradition' cut across the 'central policy of the party'.[55]

The major political challenge for the UK Government in the Spring of 1981 was the hunger strike conducted by IRA prisoners in the H-Block prison complex, held as a protest against not being recognised as political prisoners. The hunger strike commenced on 1 March, and when Frank Maguire, the nationalist MP for Fermanagh and South Tyrone, died on 5 March, Bobby Sands, the IRA's commanding officer in the Maze prison was put forward as an 'anti-H-Blocks/Armagh Political Prisoner' candidate in the following by-election.

The latent political tension between Dafydd Elis and Wigley was dramatically heightened in April 1981, when following meetings that Dafydd Elis had with Sinn Féin republican representatives in London, he hosted a press conference in the House of Commons to support Sands's candidature, where he invited Marcella, Bobby Sands's sister, and his election agent, Owen Carron, to address the UK media. Together with ten other Republican prisoners, Sands had been on hunger strike since 1 March, and on 9 April he was elected as the MP for Fermanagh and South Tyrone, polling 30,492 votes, a majority of 1,446 over the Official Unionist candidate Harry West. He died 29 days later in the H-Block prison.

The cloak and dagger nature of Dafydd Elis's involvement with the Sands campaign was reflected in his first clandestine meeting with his republican contact, who introduced himself as 'Dave', a council worker with Lambeth council. They met in Roundwood Park, near Dafydd Elis's family flat in Willesden, north London, and spoke in an area in the centre of the park, surrounded by high privet hedges, where, as 'Dave' explained, it was more difficult to be spied upon. Dafydd Elis had not told Wigley of his initiative, and he was only informed in passing by his researcher, who was on his way to the Sands press conference. Wigley was horrified at this controversial intervention in Irish politics, and only three weeks before local elections were to be held in Wales. He reported a hostile response to Dafydd Elis's intervention amongst Plaid supporters, at the Urdd Eisteddfod in May and in an agricultural show that he visited, and it was this, as he admitted to Gwynfor later, that sparked his decision to stand for the Presidency of the party in the forthcoming 1981 annual conference in Carmarthen, with Gwynfor Evans's private support.[56] Plaid indeed performed badly in the local elections in May, and lost a third of its seats, but the most important factor was not Dafydd Elis's intervention, but the rise of the Social Democratic Party as a 'third force' in British politics, which for a short time at least, seemed not only to threaten Labour, but also Plaid Cymru in its heartland.

After Sands's death, in spite of the virulent criticism he received, Dafydd Elis continued his involvement with Sinn Féin, and he campaigned with Ken Livingstone and republican London Labour MPs such as Ernie Roberts and Frank Allaun, taking part in meetings in Westminster, a number of which were hosted by the Celtic Congress, to ensure that the voters of Fermanagh and South Tyrone were provided with parliamentary representation. In June 1981, the Government passed legislation to prohibit prisoners serving a sentence of over two years from being able to stand for Parliament, but Dafydd Elis, now with Wigley's support, and the Government's tacit encouragement, moved the writ for the Fermanagh and South Tyrone by-election in the House of Commons. This was held on 20 August and won by Sands's agent Owen Carron, standing as a 'Proxy Political Prisoner'.

Dafydd Elis's moving of the writ was a crucial intervention, that Sinn Féin's director of publicity at the time, Danny Morrison, views as the first significant step in beginning the process of slowly shifting the republican movement's strategy from the IRA's armed struggle to the political transformation reflected in the Good Friday agreement in 1998. Morrison considers that the election of hunger striker Bobby Sands to Westminster (and two others, Kieran Doherty and Paddy Agnew to the Irish Parliament), together with the moving of the by-election writ after Sands's death, were key moments for the Republican movement. He believes that it is doubtful whether Sinn Fein could have made its transition to embracing electoralism so smoothly, if the writ had not been moved:

> It's remarkable he did this. It changed everything. If he hadn't moved it I can't see how we could be in the same situation that we are today, with Michelle O'Neill the First Minister in the North, herself the daughter of a former IRA prisoner and in the South the largest party [Sinn Féin], with 33 per cent of the vote.[57]

Dafydd Elis's involvement in Irish politics had excited the ire of many and had divided Plaid Cymru, but his brave intervention proved to be of lasting significance. But by the summer of 1981, Dafydd Elis was scathing about the state of his own party:

It wasn't a proper political party. It was a sort of cultural society, but now I realise it wasn't even cultural – it was monocultural, because it was only targeting itself towards the 'Welshies' – a certain type of people who tend to a certain kind of view of Wales, and this is no good to anybody . . . I wanted to change it from a cultural nationalist ragbag and make it become a proper political party, as I had seen in the Basque country and Catalonia. That was my view.[58]

The showdown – the 1981 Carmarthen Plaid Cymru annual conference

In June 1981, Dafydd Elis formally established a left-wing organisation not only to further his ideas within Plaid Cymru but to organise his support in the campaign for the leadership of the party. It was partly inspired by the creation of the left-wing movement within the Scottish National Party, the 79 Group, which had given the party renewed impetus after the disastrous 1979 General Election. But little thought had been given to the structure or the name of this nascent organisation until the day before its launch meeting, when he and his researcher, while sitting on a bench in St James Park near the House of Commons, pondered what to call this new pressure group. A white National coach drove passed, inspiring the origin of its nomenclature 'National Left':

> I didn't want people to think this was a bunch of Trotskyists or a mini-version of the Labour party. It was something that was Welsh, which had aspirations for Wales, and clearly by saying 'National Left', it wasn't 'Nationalist Left'. What I wanted to do, mostly, was to reach out to people in Wales, of which I knew there were hundreds if not thousands of politically interested people who were not happy with a feeling that the Labour party was too unionist, that Plaid was too nationalist, and that there was nowhere they could go politically.[59]

The launch event was held on a balmy Friday night in the General and Municipal Workers Union's (GMWU) conference centre at their offices in the centre of Cardiff, on 27 June 1981, and a packed meeting of about 200 people heard addresses by Dafydd Elis Thomas, Phylip Rosser, a full-time official of the GMWU in Wales who had left the Labour party the previous year, and Steve Butler, representing the 79 Group, the left-wing group within the Scottish National Party. Dafydd Elis asserted that progressive politics in Wales had been frozen and called on Plaid Cymru to break out of this with 'a clear shift towards the left', which he defined as 'a programme of direct politics in which trade union and community action have the same value as electoral politics'.

He referred to the growth of the Bennite left in the Labour party,[60] and contended that 'the rank-and-file movement which is breaking through to make the Labour party more democratic in parts of England appears in Wales in the form of the National Left challenge'.[61]

The National Left was intended to include not only Plaid members, but also those of no party and who were sympathetic to devolution. The following day, about sixty National Left supporters met to discuss policy and strategy for the Plaid Cymru annual conference in October, and while the National Left was not formally constituted until November, its aim was to support Dafydd Elis's bid for the party's presidency. It included scores of young activists, amongst whom were a number of prominent academics such as Phil Cooke, Gareth Rees and Lynn Mainwaring, who developed fresh thinking on Welsh social and economic policy and served as an informal network for Dafydd Elis's left-wing supporters during the leadership campaign.

Its first formal meeting was held in Newtown, in mid Wales, on 29 November 1981, and its main philosophical driving force was Dr Emyr Wynn Williams, a bright academic from Aberhosan in Montgomeryshire, whose political analysis married Marxist theory with a historical understanding of Plaid Cymru's political roots. However, Dafydd Elis's main philosophical influence in this period was Raymond Williams, the novelist and literary theoretician, whom he first met in meetings of the Socialist Society in London:

> Raymond would be there, wearing the most wonderful rural tweed suits. These meetings were in the University of London in Bedford Way, where I did a bit of teaching on multicultural policy, bilingualism theory and so forth. The problem was that the people there were mainly from metropolitan England. Raymond then came and spoke at a Plaid Cymru summer school and he actually joined Plaid.[62]

Williams, a Cambridge University don, had been closely associated with the Labour party and British New Left politics. Late in life, he decided to join Plaid Cymru, seeing the party as the rightful inheritor of the Welsh radical tradition. The son of a railway signalman from the small agricultural village of Pandy, near the border between Wales and England, he argued that 'culturally I find more sense in a Welsh European identity than in the dominating English versions of sovereignty and tradition', and 'validated Dafydd Elis's belief that Europe offered a suitable context to Plaid's political strategies'.[63]

The battle between the left of Plaid Cymru, represented by Dafydd Elis, and the right (or the traditionalists, as they preferred to be called) by Dafydd Wigley, came to a head in the party's annual conference in October 1981 in Carmarthen, when they stood against each other for the presidency. On the eve of conference, in his last press conference as president, Gwynfor Evans desperately asserted his view, contrary to what he believed privately, that in fact, there was no difference between either candidate's politics.[64]

Both Dafydds had been both colleagues and rivals since they joined together as Plaid Members of Parliament in 1974. Within the party, Dafydd Wigley was considered as the leader of the 'traditionalists' against the moderniser, Dafydd Elis Thomas. Both were middle class, with Wigley, the son of a local government officer in north Wales, privately educated at Rydal public school in Colwyn Bay and then at Manchester University, a physicist by training who had worked as a cost accountant for a number of multinational companies, including Mars and Hoover. Dafydd Elis on the other hand, was an intellectual and academic, a grammar school boy and Bangor university graduate, steeped in Welsh literature, philosophy and cultural theory. Whilst tempting to interpret the political differences between them as one between left and right, Wigley would describe himself as a 'pragmatic radical', and less interested in political philosophy than its practice. Dafydd Elis on the other hand, would not have described himself as a Marxist, although he would have paid tribute to its key importance in analysing the nature of capitalist society. Rather, he laid emphasis on socialism, collaborating with other progressive movements such as the anti-apartheid and the Welsh language movements, making common cause with the peace and feminist movements, and positioning himself as the leader of a party 'in service of the Welsh working class'.[65]

Their rivalry was to bridge several decades but its major flashpoint came in Plaid's 1981 annual conference. The remarkable, and unlikely, decision that Plaid had become a 'decentralist socialist' party, took place at this annual conference with the passing of an amendment to its constitution which declared that the establishment of a decentralised socialist state was now to be one of the party's fundamental aims. This formulation caused considerable unease to a number of Plaid Cymru's members, among them Dafydd Wigley, who felt that it gave 'an Eastern European flavour to our aspirations as a party'.[66]

The fact that Gwynfor Evans had himself uncharacteristically voted for such a change to the party's aims apparently influenced a number of delegates to vote for the motion. This change of policy preceded the vote for the presidency, which was lost narrowly by Dafydd Elis by 212 votes to Wigley's 273. This narrow margin was attributed by the left to the arrival of a bus especially hired for Caernarfon delegates to travel to Carmarthen, solely to cast their vote in the presidential election, in spite of an attempt at sabotage by a local National Left member, who failed to deflate the bus's tyres before its departure.[67]

Whilst Wigley had won the vote, the left could argue it had won the philosophical argument. The new President was exasperated by some of what he viewed as 'the hard left's extremism: It was our failure ... to develop the ideology of our nationalism which allowed the ideology of the British Left to fill the vacuum ... Our analysis must grow from our experience here in Wales.'[68]

The socialist Phil Williams accused 'some members' of the National Left of being 'guilty of the most distressing form of laziness ... the taking of our ideological clothes off the peg from the pseudo-left of English politics'.[69] Gwynfor Evans's private view of this momentous annual conference was that while Wigley's victory had been 'very helpful', it was useful for the party that Dafydd Elis remained as vice-president. In a letter to his friend Leopold Kohr, he was critical of Dafydd Elis, and downplayed the significance of the party's adoption of socialism:

> Two motions were passed to include the word 'socialism' in our aims. One was to 'establish an independent socialist state'; the other spoke of 'decentralist socialism'. This will now have to be accepted. There was no change at all in our policies, which remain as they have been for a generation. Speaking on the last

afternoon Dafydd El said that with the change of wording in our aims our policies have been transformed. This is of course a nonsense. If they are socialist now, they were socialist one, ten, twenty and thirty years ago. The policies of the party remain unchanged. In the last month or two, Dafydd El has vigorously denied that he is a Marxist, and has spoken of 'community, decentralist socialism', which was what our Commission recommended. Anyway, we came out of the conference, where the spirit was very good, a united party.[70]

This rosy, if not nonsensical, version of the schism in the Carmarthen conference, does not adequately reflect the depth of the rift within the party. Ieuan Wyn Jones was the chair of the party at the time and supported Wigley for the leadership:

I had become distanced from Dafydd El, to be honest. The National Left had been established and I wasn't happy that a movement within a movement had been created. I felt that this would create a split. The argument was that this was needed to push the party to the left – I didn't have a problem with that, but I thought that a movement within a movement was unwise. I wasn't happy with what Dafydd El was advocating. So I couldn't support him. The reality was that the period 1980–2 was hellishly difficult. The failure of the referendum had put the party in a serious hole, many people didn't see the way forward, whether the constitutional path was the correct path – and a number of different factions were pushing the party in various directions. I don't think that people realised how difficult it was to keep the ship afloat, because you had the National Left, the republican movement, the Hydro group,[71] and this factioning didn't help. Like many others, I thought the most important thing was to keep the party going.[72]

Alun Davies, a young Plaid activist from Tredegar, who later became president of the National Union of Students in Wales, recalls Dafydd Elis's charismatic appeal in this period:

He was friendly, likeable, quietly impressive, I was inspired by him, everyone knew him, and he was easy with people. At the time, Plaid Cymru was a conservative party, and Dafydd Elis Thomas was a different figure to most Plaid leaders. Coming from the south Wales valleys, that's what I wanted to see.[73]

The growing influence of the National Left was not stemmed by Wigley's victory. The Falklands military campaign in April–June 1982 isolated Plaid as the only parliamentary party to oppose the war, and while it briefly united the party, the internecine battle between left and right continued. Dafydd Elis's affinity with Ken Livingstone, the leader of the GLC, sparked controversy in the party when he not only spoke in rallies in London to protest against the abolition of the GLC by the Conservative government, but revealed that he had also voted for Livingstone as the Labour candidate in his local council election in Brent. Alun Davies recalls him speaking with Ken Livingstone at a rally in defence of the GLC against Thatcher's attempt to abolish the council: 'He was an incredible figure, listening to him addressing a major left-wing conference and explaining why the fate of the GLC was so important to Wales.'[74]

A *Western Mail* report by its Westminster correspondent, David Hughes, echoed Dafydd Wigley's view, on the eve of the 1982 Plaid annual conference in Llandudno, that Dafydd Elis was too close to the London left. Hughes said that Dafydd Elis Thomas made little attempt to conceal the fact that he was in the wrong party, and suggested that:

> He would feel more at home on the Bennite fringes of the Labour party. This has been evident for some time at Westminster; what is raising Plaid eyebrows is that it is becoming increasingly evident in Wales. The MP is genuinely torn by the dilemma he finds himself in; his loyalty to Plaid Cymru is preventing him making a break for Labour.

He highlighted how the recent Gower by-election in September 1982 had shown how little Plaid's policy of 'decentralist socialism' had appealed to the electorate. There, Plaid's candidate had come fourth, with only a small increase of 1.5 per cent in their vote. But in fact, the main feature of the campaign was the impact of the Social Democratic Party, whose candidate Gwynoro Jones, won 25 per cent of the vote (an increase of 16 per cent from the General Election, coming second to the successful Labour candidate Gareth Wardell).[75]

Hughes however, stated that during the by-election, 'a new platform of decentralised socialism was wheeled out for the first time':

> Its impact on the voters had all the power of a lightly wielded feather duster. Plaid Cymru President Dafydd Wigley might be tempted to say "I told you so" if he wasn't so dejected about the whole business. He argued long and hard in the party's national executive that Gower should be fought on a less strident platform but was over-ruled by a left-wing majority on the executive. It would be no surprise if Mr Wigley's political instincts were allowed a freer rein in future.[76]

At the following annual conference, the National Left captured the majority of the National Executive seats in the party, but Plaid Cymru approached the 1983 General Election with little confidence, and their results were correspondingly disappointing. This was the high-water mark for the Conservatives, winning a massive majority of 188 over Labour, and in Wales, winning eleven seats and 32 per cent of the vote, the most in any election in Wales throughout the twentieth century. Although Plaid retained its two seats nationally, its total vote fell from 8.1 per cent to 7.8 per cent, and it found difficulty in meeting the challenge of the new alliance between the Social Democrats and the Liberals.[77] For Dafydd Elis, the lacklustre election campaign confirmed that Plaid Cymru needed to escape from the influence of Gwynfor and Wigley. In his own constituency, the boundaries of the Merioneth seat, re-named Meirionnydd Nant Conwy, had been expanded with an addition of five thousand additional voters from the Conwy Valley and his hometown of Llanrwst. He retained his seat by 2,643 votes, and 39.2 per cent of the poll.

National Left maintained its grip on the running of the party, not only through the elected positions it gained, but also in its political energy. The magazine *Radical Wales* was established by the party in October 1983 and edited by a group of mainly National Left supporters such as the brilliantly effervescent historian Gwyn Alf Williams.[78] Its crucial question for its readership in its first edition was: 'Is Plaid Cymru a political party or an extramural branch of Merched y Wawr and Côr Meibion Cwmsgwt?'[79] Their activism contrasted with the fate of the SNP's 79 Group, which was proscribed by the party in its annual conference in September 1982, although its members who were office holders, largely retained their roles within the party.[80]

Even after retiring as President, Gwynfor Evans was still influential within the party and was privately contemptuous of Dafydd Elis's delight in political theorising. He disliked what he considered to be his 'intellectualism', viewed him as undependable, faddish and maverick, and thought he craved public attention. He believed him to be inconsistent, and oddly, he attributed this facet to Dafydd Elis's 'allegedly complicated' relationship with his father.[81] He was mistaken, however, since an understanding of Dafydd's upbringing would suggest that his more difficult relationship was with his highly ambitious mother.

However, in the interest of party unity, Gwynfor did not voice these reservations publicly, but discretely attempted to influence individual members of the National Executive and the National Council. At a time when the arson campaign against second homes offered a nihilistic path for some Welsh nationalists, Plaid Cymru's move to the left was reflected in other elements of the national movement. Cymdeithas yr Iaith Gymraeg's manifesto was published in 1982 and committed to 'the principles of Welsh socialism' which meant community, rather than state ownership, encapsulated by the term *cymdeithasiaeth*, which translated as communitarianism. Dafydd Elis greeted it warmly as demonstrating 'the essential link between economy and culture, and sees language for what it is – a system of material social signifiers, rather than a 'precious phial'.'[82]

As Richard Wyn Jones suggests, Dafydd Elis attempted to make Plaid Cymru more relevant in the light of the unpopularity of the Conservative Government in Wales: 'by linking the campaign for linguistic and cultural survival, and national annihilation, against unemployment, and in favour of sexual and gender equality, Welsh nationalism appeared not only relevant but enlightened, progressive and internationalist.'[83]

But his involvement in left wing politics and his support for Irish republicanism, also made him a target for those in the police desperate to establish his link with the second home arson campaign. A case was eventually brought in Cardiff Crown Court, against members of the Welsh Socialist Republican Movement (WSRM) in September 1983, and rapidly deteriorated into farce. The defendants were accused of conspiracy to cause explosions, but the evidence revealed police corruption and the forging of evidence. The political motivation behind the prosecution case was dramatically exposed by the defendants' declarations, at an early bail hearing, that the police had pressured them to name Dafydd Elis as the mastermind in the conspiracy behind the terrorist campaign. In evidence, one of the defendants, Adrian Stone, revealed that he had been offered ten thousand pounds by police officers to implicate Dafydd Elis in the bombing campaign. He added that during questioning by the police, there were insistent suggestions that the MP knew of the bombings, and he was appalled when police called Elis Thomas a 'Mick lover' and a 'Red'. Another defendant, Nick Hodges, testified that 'the police tried to make a deal with me. They said things would go better with me if I would implicate, in a statement, Dafydd Elis Thomas, as the top man – the political brains, if you like – in the bombing campaign.'[84]

The conduct of the detectives involved in framing a number of the defendants, and in spuriously dragging a sitting MP into the conspiracy, undermined the credibility of the prosecution. While the court case destroyed the Welsh Republicans as an effective political movement, it also reflected the extent to which Dafydd Elis's readiness to challenge civil liberties breaches by Welsh police forces, had stung the leadership of South Wales Police's CID and Special Branch into action. By now, his stature as a socialist alternative voice was significant and enabled him to offer political hope to the left during what Gwyn Alf Williams called 'the 'plague years' of Thatcherism. The academic critic and language campaigner, Richard Wyn Jones, recalls his reputation at the time:

> His was the public voice and face of this ideology. He was an effective and charismatic propagandist: willing to argue the case even when it grated on the sensibilities of Plaid Cymru's traditional supporters or touched upon such taboo subjects as Northern Ireland during the republican prisoners' hunger strike. Indeed, and turning momentarily to his personality, Dafydd El seemed to personify that cosmopolitan Welshness which we were so eager to emulate; a Welshness which was equally comfortable in Notting Hill and Rhydymain. With Dafydd Elis Thomas, it was possible to mention Plaid Cymru in the same breath as CND and the GLC, and that without fear of embarrassment.[85]

His contempt for Plaid Cymru's traditionalist political legacy was visceral. In a review of Hywel Davies's history of the party, he made a full-frontal attack on three of the party's hallowed founders:

Put as bluntly as all released and spoken psychological truths must be put, these intellectual leaders were a bunch of ultra-reactionary 'fascist' sympathisers, as their contemporary critics alleged. Ambrose Bebb called for a Mussolini for Wales; J. E. Daniel described the Spanish Civil War as a battle between Communism and the 'European tradition'; *The Welsh Nationalist* [Plaid Cymru's official monthly publication] called Dr Salazar of Portugal 'one of the greatest statesmen of Europe'; Saunders Lewis told Plaid's 1939 summer school not to believe the anti-Hitler propaganda of the English media though Bebb by this time opposed the idea of 'Welsh neutrality' in the face of Nazism.[86]

He argued that these pioneers had proposed a Welsh social philosophy that was conservative and reactionary and called it Welsh (with a big W). Never again, he said, inevitably courting controversy, 'would he call himself a nationalist'.[87]

The opportunity for him to campaign again for the presidency of the party came about due to Dafydd Wigley and his wife, Elinor Bennett's particular family tragedy. Their first two sons, Alun and Geraint, had a congenital illness that meant that they would not survive into adulthood. Their health had markedly declined, and at the Annual Conference in October 1984 Wigley stood down from the presidency. His son, Alun, died in December 1984, followed by Geraint in March 1985.[88]

In the ensuing election, Ieuan Wyn Jones supported Dafydd Elis, reasoning that the President needed to be both an elected member and a professional politician. He recalls Dafydd's initial amazement at his decision – 'I remember meeting him in a car park somewhere and I told him I supported him – "Really?" he replied in disbelief.'[89]

At Plaid's Annual Conference in Lampeter that year, Dafydd Elis defeated Dafydd Iwan for the party's Presidency by the comparatively small margin of 1,570 to 1,382, a majority of only 188, reflecting a divided party. During the campaign, the National Left organised its supporters, many of whom included those from interest groups he had championed in the party, including the women's section, and those who had been active in the recent Greenham Common campaigns and the Campaign for Nuclear Disarmament. Dafydd Iwan attracted Wigley supporters, representing the traditional core of the party, and concerned with language issues primarily. Iwan recalls that:

I am not an ideological man although I count myself on the left
– and celebrate people like Allende in Chile, and Victor Jara, the
folk singer.[90] I didn't see the Wigley-Thomas issue as a left-right
split. Wigley was a safer pair of hands and followed a path that
I could understand. I was worried that Dafydd El every now
and then, weakened on the national question. It was as if he was
frightened of the implications of nationalism and I was worried
to where that would lead. I didn't see the purpose of Plaid Cymru
if you lost the clear national element.[91]

The chair of the Plaid youth movement at the time, Alun Davies, recalls that the Welsh speaking students in Aberystwyth University supported Dafydd Iwan because he was 'a linguistic comfort blanket'. Dafydd Elis Thomas on the other hand, pushed people to think and 'challenged the party, and people hated that. People were very self-righteous about the language, and they thought they had the right to lead Wales. Dafydd challenged that assumption.'[92]

On his election, Dafydd Elis immediately announced that his first priority would be to end Plaid Cymru being identified solely as a party of Welsh speakers. He pointed out the seriousness of the position for the party, and that in the 1983 General Election, its share of the vote had dropped to 5.6 per cent in the mainly English-speaking areas of Wales, whilst maintaining 36.5 per cent in the mainly Welsh-speaking areas of south-west and north-west Wales: 'We have become more than ever a party of only part of the Welsh nation.'[93]

The *Western Mail* observed that his small margin of victory over Dafydd Iwan 'shows the weakness of his position in pursuing radical initiatives ... The greatest joy came from the party's women's section, whose members unfurled their large trade-union style banner in the hall and cheered'. It reported that Dafydd Elis 'made it clear that he would not compromise his beliefs in order to gain greater support', and urged the party to work with other radical groups, such as the peace movement:

> We must remove all NATO bases from our soil and remove those low flying strike attack aircraft from our skies. As Britain lurches further and further to the right, only we in Wales can stop our own society from moving the same way. There is no alternative for us, and there is no alternative to us.[94]

The Guardian reported that Plaid Cymru had 'moved further to the left' with this election and had consolidated its position. Dafydd Elis's campaign manager, Syd Morgan, was elected chairman of the party, and the National Left again gained a majority of seats on the national executive, much to the disappointment of the Hydro group, who believed that the party should not be other than a nationalist party. Plaid Cymru officials played down the rift, and claimed that the right had over-reacted in proposing a motion, which was narrowly defeated, that each member should 'above all be a nationalist'. One constituency official tore up his membership card and Hydro claimed that another key motion had effectively denied non-socialists their right to be members of the party. Hydro's leader, Keith Bush, resigned from the party.[95]

The new President of the party was now in the vanguard of a refreshed brand of politics. Adam Price, the son of a mining family and a future leader of the party, believes that Dafydd Elis 'defined the politics of the 1980s as Gwynfor defined the politics of the 1950s'. He was elected President of his party at the height of the miners' strike and at a time when he, more than any other Plaid figure, had already been actively campaigning on behalf of the National Union of Mineworkers (NUM) against pit closures.[96]

The Miners' Strike

The bitter miners' strike lasted a year from 6 March 1984 to 3 March 1985, and proved a profoundly wounding experience for Welsh society. From the beginning of the dispute, the miners' leader Arthur Scargill's decision not to ballot his members for strike action, fatally wounded the unity of the NUM throughout the UK. The South Wales NUM region, under the leadership of Emlyn Williams, whilst disagreeing fundamentally with Scargill's strategy, nevertheless maintained that unity in south Wales until the strike's final weeks, when the trickle of returning miners turned into a flood.

The 1984–5 miners' strike was the most debilitating industrial dispute of the nineteen eighties, led to the destruction of the industry in Wales, and consigned the south Wales coalfield and areas of north-east Wales to disastrous economic and social dislocation. But this doomed enterprise also created alliances across Wales and brought a number of Plaid Cymru members together with members of the National Union of Mineworkers, miners' community support groups, and other activists from the feminist, gay and peace movements.[97]

Dafydd Elis immediately threw himself into the campaign against pit closures. Kim Howells was the NUM's research officer in south Wales, a leading strategist, and one of the main organisers of the strike in the region. He recalled Dafydd Elis as the strike's leading Plaid supporter. Hywel Francis, the son of the legendary NUM President, Dai Francis, and the prime organiser of the support groups for the striking miners and their families, at the time a member of the Communist party, was the main catalyst for mustering support for the strike from beyond the NUM. He worked with Dafydd Elis, and with key civil society organisations such as the ecumenical Council of Churches, and its director, John Morgan. Howells recalled that Dafydd Elis was carefully not to indulge in partisan politicking:

> Hywel tried to bring people together and the significance of the strike, of bringing movements together such as the church, vague lefties and support groups ... gave them a chance to express something they hadn't expressed through conventional politics. I think Dafydd understood that, which is why he never pushed a party political line. And we really disapproved when party political lines were pushed, whoever was doing it. We didn't want to have the strike as a slanging match, using the strike as a battlefield. I hadn't experienced anything like that before, when it came to engendering some sort of image of a society we might have a chance of creating. It was an important debating platform for a lot of people. It taught me about Wales. It was meeting people and understanding that if you use enough energy, and you care enough, that you can do things. A lot of people who were active [politically] then, remained active for a long time.

The striking miners and their families discovered that:

> We are part of a real nation which extends northwards beyond the coalfield, into the mountains of Powys, Dyfed and Gwynedd. For the first time since the industrial revolution in Wales, the two halves of the nation came together in mutual support. Pickets from the south travelled to the nuclear and hydro-electric

stations in the north. Support groups in the north brought food, money and clothes to the south. Friendships and alliances flourished – old differences of attitude and accent withered and out of it grew the most important formal political organisation to emerge during the course of the strike – the Wales Congress in Support of Mining Communities.[98]

Howells coordinated the south Wales NUM's picketing, and also organised accommodation for them, which brought him into contact with support groups throughout Wales:

> We started to tap into offers of help we had – for instance from Blaenau Ffestiniog, lefty teachers in Bangor as well as in England . . . what became our focal point were Trawsfynydd and Wylfa power stations. We tried to stop Traws and Wylfa . . . It was a way into the trade unions in both areas, which were very well organised in both power stations.
>
> However, our biggest problem was not so much finding places to stay but getting the pickets home! They 'bedded in' very well with the local communities. It was a real nightmare. Members of the Merthyr Vale lodge were the first ones to go to Blaenau Ffestiniog. We'd get calls from wives and girlfriends asking how they were – 'I haven't seen so and so for so many weeks – is he all right?' and 'when are they coming home?' We'd have to send people up or I would have to go myself, and say, 'Come on now!'
>
> I remember the first meeting in Blaenau Ffestiniog. It was early on in the strike, and we all met in the Queens Hotel. The meeting got more and more passionate, and at some point, three or four boys got up at the back of the pub and were so fired up that they marched outside to the street. We knew cops were there and this was 7.30 at night – they started insulting the two policemen. One of the picketers turned to me and said – 'It's a bit bloody mental up here, isn't it!'
>
> They gave us tremendous backing, and Dafydd was very supportive. Dafydd was much revered by the young left in north Wales. He wasn't so well known in south Wales in this period, but he was working flat out, playing a prominent role in Plaid Cymru and as an MP.[99]

Links were made throughout Wales and beyond, twinning towns such as Bangor and Llangefni in north Wales, with coalfield villages such as Pontyberem and Blaen-nant in the Neath Valley. Blaenau Ffestiniog was twinned with Gwaun-cae-Gurwen, hosted pickets from the local Abernant colliery, and distributed food parcels directly to individual families.[100]

By 1984, Elen Thomas and the family had returned to Dolgellau from London, and she recalls providing overnight accommodation to eight snoring miners at their home in Dolgellau, during their picketing of the nearby Trawsfynydd nuclear power station.[101]

For the youth of Plaid Cymru such as Adam Price, this period saw Dafydd Elis provide the national movement with a sense of purpose:

> I hated the politics of the 1980s. It was a struggle, and as the son of a miner, I took part in supporting the striking miners' campaigns in 1984–5. I collected food and raised money. It was a real struggle ... we marched ... we were fighting something more important that student politics. It was a period of excitement as well as social breakdown. Dafydd El represented that excitement ... he was an inspiration.[102]

Dafydd Elis became the public face of Plaid's support for the miners, doggedly fundraising, marching, protesting and addressing countless rallies and demonstrations. Emlyn Williams, the NUM's President for the south Wales area, paid tribute to his support:

> He's projecting himself during this strike. Never misses a march, always on a platform by me, always, if I go the House of Commons, [he's] prepared to show every avenue to get my case over. I know there are thousands in Plaid who are dedicated socialists.[103]

He also created new political alliances and common cause with the miners and their families and alliances began to be created with other groups of workers, such as those farmers protesting against the imposition of milk quotas who donated milk to the miners.[104]

The strike was the most significant political event of the 1980s in Wales and marked Dafydd Elis out as a charismatic left-wing politician, who attracted young supporters such as Adam Price and Alun Davies. Davies's enthusiasm for Dafydd Elis's leadership reflected his impact on so many people who may not have been natural Plaid sympathisers:

> I first met Dafydd during the miners' strike when he spoke with a vibrant urgency of a new radical vision, uniting rural and urban, Welsh- and non-Welsh speaking, north and south in creating a different sort of Wales. Together with Gwyn Alf Williams, he created the tune which helped to define Welsh radical politics in the 1980s and which led, after a long winding path, to devolution a decade or so later. It was a bold and inspiring vision. His was a vision of a Wales at peace with itself which was radical in itself. This was a time when the country was as divided as it ever has been in our history. We often forget that the period of the strike also witnessed the burning of holiday homes and the election of the biggest Conservative representation in the House of Commons since the popular vote.
>
> He led the party with a confidence and verve rarely seen in the more traditional parts of our country, who were shocked and horrified in equal measure. When he spoke up to champion equality campaigns and as an active supporter of Ken Livingstone's GLC, describing himself as a Labour voter, he challenged and terrified a party more used to the comfort blanket of Gwynfor Evans and reassuring rhetoric of Dafydd Wigley.[105]

The longer-term significance of the strike for both Dafydd Elis and Plaid Cymru was that the mutual trust built in the miners' strike would create the basis for the broad alliance required for the later campaign for devolution. One of the founders of the Wales Congress in Support of Mining Communities, Hywel Francis, asserted that the strike created an anti-Thatcherite resistance movement, building alliances and coordinating the activism of those who supported the miners. These included trade unions, religious leaders, the women's peace movement, gay rights activists, as well as Labour members and Plaid Cymru supporters.[106]

Undoubtedly, the creation of the Wales Congress in Support of Mining Communities was a precursor of the 'Yes for Wales' campaign for devolution in 1997, as Kim Howells recalled:

In setting up the Wales Congress, I worked very closely with Dafydd Elis Thomas. I didn't like his friends very much, but I always got on with Dafydd. I suspect because he was a socialist and a hustler. I took to him. It was a sort of spiritual thing rather than a political thing. I didn't meet anybody who was opposed to the Wales Congress apart from Tories obviously, who thought it was a kind of aberration, and some of the most unimaginative hatchet-faced Labour bureaucrats, apparatchiks, who just saw any kind of inclusive move as being a threat to their hegemony.[107]

In this spirit of unity, it seems that a temporary reconciliation between Gwynfor and Dafydd Elis occurred after Dafydd Elis had won the Plaid Presidency. Gwynfor was moved to write to him to express his admiration for his stand on the miners, and in a private note to himself, added that 'D. El coming to his senses – wonderful with the miners'.[108]

Dafydd Elis replied to Gwynfor's letter, expressing his impatience with what he saw as the desultory support given by Plaid members to the strike: 'as you know I have been churning recently – I feel that I need to say something because traditional supporters are abandoning us'.[109] He criticised his own party's officials and members for their abysmal lack of support for the miners' strike, and berated the party's *Welsh Nation* newspaper for giving prominence to a Wigley-inspired water rates campaign rather than the miners' battle.[110] The criticisms not only emanated from the new president, but also from the party's national executive, concerned about the 'lack of activity' over the strike by the party's central office in Cardiff.

In the party's youth magazine, *Penderyn*, Dafydd Elis was scathing of Plaid members and their lack of support for miners' demonstrations:

> At most rallies I've attended, the attendance is abysmal. I speak at two or three miners' support meetings every week. Support in the south-east is good but poor in Llanelli and the west, where the party has plenty of members. There is concern that so much attention is being given to the water rates issue which took page one lead in the last two issues of the *Welsh Nation*. This is 'old-style nationalism'.

He stated that 'the struggle of the mining communities is the national struggle today' and attributed Plaid's lack of action to its domination by the 'worst aspects of the Nonconformist tradition'. He criticised Nonconformist denominations for opening their vestries to the police while scarcely one chapel had arranged collections for the miners.[111]

Party officials were said to be 'saddened' by this attack, and the general secretary, Dafydd Williams, rejected the criticisms stating that the party's staff had been concentrating on the miners' dispute 'for some time'. But this response suggested that the new President had work to do to change the nature of the party.[112]

Welsh Labour Members of Parliament became increasingly sensitive to Dafydd Elis's growing profile. Ogmore's Labour MP Ray Powell, the secretary of the Welsh group of Labour members and its liaison with the National Union of Mineworkers, was moved to querulously defend his colleagues' record of support for the NUM:

> There is an element of sniping going on with left wing Plaid Cymru circles making much of the frequent appearances of their President Dafydd Elis Thomas at miners' rallies around the coalfield. But I have it on good authority that NUM vice-president Terry Thomas himself said he would like to see more Labour members on platforms in the new year ... When it was stated that Dafydd Elis Thomas had been to a number of miners' rallies it was pointed out that he was not under the control of the Whips ... While most of us attend meetings in other Members' constituencies by agreement, Dafydd Elis Thomas can please himself. We are not criticising Mr Elis Thomas but I think if you look back in retrospect since last March a number of Welsh Labour members have been attending rallies and meetings and our contributions have been quite formidable.[113]

While Gwynfor Evans complimented him for his leadership, he also belatedly, and rather disingenuously accepted some responsibility for Plaid's outdated image, accepting that 'we must get rid of the image, which I created unintentionally, of a Nonconformist rural nationalism, with its whole emphasis on the language. We are none the wiser of complaining that this image is a caricature. It exists and we must get rid of it.'[114]

But Gwynfor also warned him privately, of the major issue that would return to haunt Dafydd Elis for the rest of his presidency, namely the concern over the decline of the Welsh language in its heartlands, which threatened to drag the party back to its cultural and campaigning roots.[115]

At the end of the miners' strike, a sour assessment of Plaid Cymru's participation in the dispute, written by the *Guardian* journalist Tony Heath, based in Blaenau Ffestiniog, and who had been close to Dafydd Elis politically, doubted whether the party's support had created an impact:

> The fact is that the party's grassroots particularly in areas where it is numerically strong, failed to deliver. The party's President, Dafydd Elis Thomas MP and a handful of socialists, worked extremely hard on behalf of the miners during the twelve months. The bulk of the party was ineffective.[116]

The defeated miners' strike came to its sad end in March 1985, but the alliances created in that year, were to re-emerge as devolution neared in the late nineties. The significance of the strike for Plaid Cymru and organisations such as the Wales Congress in Support of Mining Communities and the local miners' support groups was to be long-lasting. Dafydd Elis celebrated a new-found social solidarity:

> We are, after all, all Welsh, all fighting for the community of communities, that is Wales; a revelation incarnated in the initiative of the South Wales NUM itself, giving a lead to the nation befitting the heirs to the Fed, in the most significant political development in recent Welsh history – the Wales Congress in Support of Mining Communities.[117]

But the strike, despite its heroic resistance to the destruction of the coalfield, was a failure. It had occurred in the context of the overall decline of the political left, which would continue throughout the 1980s. In Wales, Labour's vote for instance had declined from 61 per cent in 1966 to 38 per cent in 1983. In Britain, it had declined from 48 per cent in 1966 to 28 per cent in the same period. Reflecting on the lessons of the strike, in the autumn of 1985, Dafydd Elis wrote of the 'gamble' of creating the National Left in 1981, the danger if the public failed to understand 'an excessively abstract' strategy, and the confusion that could arise if Plaid Cymru lacked an identity distinct from that of the Labour party.

He recognised that while they may have gained more supporters, the party had not attracted more voters:

> Crossovers from Labour and those who have joined because of our party's policies on peace and women's issues probably number several hundred and their energy, radicalism and commitment have made a noticeable difference in branches in many parts of Wales, but have not been matched by crossover voters.[118]

Dafydd Elis now contended that the miners' strike, although it pointed out some of the potential for community self-help, in fact was the last great celebration of the working-class tradition of solidarity, and that 'it was particularly moving during that period that south Wales was able to stay together with relatively little dissension compared with elsewhere. The march back to Maerdy symbolised the end of a tradition.'[119]

However, a smaller dispute dominated Merioneth politics between September 1985 and October 1986, over the sacking of eighteen workers by the Ffestiniog slate company. The dispute was over a new bonus scheme that would have reduced wages substantially, by £28.50 a week. Dafydd Elis was one of the leaders of the campaign and railed against the company's treatment of its workers. Mass demonstrations were held with speakers from the labour movement and Labour MPs, and a support group was created for the strikers, which received food and money from those they had aided earlier in the miners' support groups in south Wales. The dispute led to the eventual sacking of the workers, who agreed to ex-gratia payments of two thousand pounds each, but Dafydd Elis's verdict on the dispute was to celebrate the community's fighting spirit:

> When employers treat their workforce as the equivalent of wage slaves, then they are denying their own humanity. We now have a government that wants to go back to Victorian values, and Victorian work habits. Although the last seven months of fighting have been sad and hard, there were also heroic aspects to the dispute. The quarrymen and their families showed unity, dignity and bravery. It was also shown that the links that grew in the miners' strike, between different parts of Wales, still thrived.[120]

As president of the party, Dafydd Elis deliberately prioritised his public campaigning over his parliamentary activity. Throughout the early eighties, he was a fearless pursuer of civil liberties, a keen campaigner against the Falklands War, and was one of the few MPs to support CND and the protests against the location of Cruise missiles on American bases such as Greenham Common. From May 1984, he employed a researcher, Tim Williams, a Labour party supporter, who ironically, would later become the most effective spokesman for the No campaign during the devolution referendum in 1997. He was attracted to work for Dafydd Elis by the 'project in his (Dafydd's) head – to nationalise the left and socialise the nationalists'. He felt that Dafydd Elis was pragmatic in his views on devolution and that he was 'the creator of a third force in Wales, of a socialised nationalism and a nationalised socialist movement'. For Williams, Dafydd's greatest attribute was his lack of political partisanship, as reflected in his own appointment, 'although I wasn't a pure nationalist ... we got on well – I was a Welsh patriotic member of the left and a member of the Labour party. Dafydd was playing 'the third way'. Williams's role was to liaise and excite interest in the party with the London and Welsh press:

> My job was to show we were progressive and interested in these agendas, that Plaid wasn't right wing. Dafydd Elis's intellect was the key and but for him, the opportunity would not have been taken. He created links with the progressive left in England, which contrasted with the more conservative Labour party in Wales. In the most intense years, between May 1984 and June 1985, I was a bit of a bridge with the Labour party in London, but Dafydd Elis also had his own links.[121]

One of those links was Marjorie Ellis Thompson, a young public affairs lobbyist for the Royal College of Nursing, and from 1984, the unpaid parliamentary officer for the Campaign for Nuclear Disarmament, closely allied with the London left. An American from St Louis, Missouri, her mother was a right-wing Republican, a former campaigner for Barry Goldwater, who helped run Ronald Reagan's campaign for the governorship of California. Her father was a three-star general in the US Navy, and her siblings were American intelligence officers.

Her friendship with Dafydd Elis started in January 1984, when he met her in the company of Joan Ruddock, the chair of CND, at the House of Commons. Within a year, it developed into a full relationship as his marriage to Elen broke down. Marjorie was certainly not the Plaid Cymru spouse from central casting – an American from a high Republican background, by April 1986, they were living together discreetly in a flat in north London.[122]

Their relationship lasted until the summer of 1992. While sometimes stormy, there is no doubt that this was one of the three most important relationships in Dafydd Elis's personal life. She recalls that they were 'intoxicated' with each other, and the affair became public in 1986:

> I hugely admired him . . . I revered him . . . he was an intellectual giant compared to figures like Wigley and Gwynfor. They gave the impression that they loved the language more than Dafydd did, which was ridiculous. It really hurt him, because they could not understand what he was trying to do. He was accused of selling out the party. I learned a lot from him.[123]

Tim Williams recalls that at the beginning of their affair, Dafydd Elis had 'a Nonconformist guilt' about their relationship:

> He was very uncomfortable, and I think he felt a bit of a moral problem. But it was also a part of his blossoming – he became more dapper, more sociable, sophisticated and svelte. Politically he was also trying to shock Wales – he was saying in a way 'come on then!'[124]

In the constituency, Marjorie stayed at Dafydd's rented home, Maes-y-Bryner, in Llanfachreth, near Dolgellau, owned by the largest local landowner, the Nannau Estate. The estate agent's description of the property, a long low stone-built country gentleman's residence, explains the appeal of his new rented home:

> This fine house provides a principal Residence for the Estate and occupies a magnificent site with wonderful south-westerly views beyond Dolgellau to Cader Idris in the distance.
> It is approached from the Llanfachreth Road two miles north of Dolgellau by a winding tarmacadam drive, with white painted

entrance gates, which passes beneath the George III Memorial Arch. The house, dating back to the nineteenth century, had four bedrooms, and three attractive grass parks.[125]

The long front room was adapted into a voluminous library of at least three thousand of his books, and photographs of him in a fashion magazine in this period portray him as a country squire, and there he hosted friends and weekend parties. He and Marjorie would host Dafydd's sons and their friends on the weekends, and in the summer, they would camp out on the front lawn and be treated to firework displays. A number of the children have a very clear recollection that food could be scarce, however, the only meal available on one occasion being Baxter's lobster bisque soup and oat biscuits.

In 1987, Marjorie started work as a parliamentary researcher for the MP for Cynon Valley, Ann Clwyd, then a shadow minister of education on Labour's front bench. Dafydd had recommended her, and Ann Clwyd later wrote in her autobiography that 'she was clearly a very bright and an able researcher, but she was American and unfamiliar with the UK education system'. Eventually she found out that she was Dafydd's girlfriend: 'after his divorce they lived openly together but I did feel miffed that he had not been upfront with me at the outset. Years later Dafydd apologised for not coming clean.'[126] However, Marjorie recalls that Clwyd had been 'totally aware', and that Dafydd had already told her of their relationship. Furthermore, she says that Ann Clwyd was an awful boss and had a poor reputation for retaining parliamentary staff for any length of time. Her ex-staff kept in touch with each other, and on yet another leaving do for one of her staff, they banded together to present the departing researcher with a drinking pewter mug inscribed with the moniker 'Congratulations from the victims of Ann Clwyd!'[127]

Marjorie accompanied Dafydd to public events such as eisteddfodau and Plaid Cymru conferences. By October 1988, the tabloid newspapers had belatedly caught up with their relationship. The scandal-mongering *News of the World* breathlessly reported the 'MP's bit of nukey with his CND beauty' and featured his love for the 'ban-the-bomb girl':

> A Leftie MP has blown up his marriage – for a beautiful ban-the-bomb campaigner. Fiery Welsh nationalist party president Dafydd Elis Thomas, 41, has fallen for gorgeous Greenham

Common girl Marjorie Thompson. The couple have set up a love nest just around the corner from the home he shares with his wife Elen.[128]

Marjorie was a key part of his life for six years, and an influential policy-maker in her own right, an effective lobbyist for the Royal College of Nursing, moving within left-wing social circles in London and beyond, and developing a growing profile as spokesperson for the anti-nuclear movement to the extent that in 1990, she became the chair of the Campaign for Nuclear Disarmament.[129]

Moving to the Centre?

Following the profound disappointment of the miners' brave but fruitless fight, the battle lines within Plaid Cymru between left and right were drawn up following a hotly contested by-election in Brecon and Radnor in July 1985. Plaid's dreadful result, where it only gained 435 votes, galvanised Dafydd Elis to change his approach. In *Radical Wales*, he and his parliamentary researcher, the educationalist David Reynolds, co-wrote a conciliatory article attempting to unite the party:

> Socialists must be nationalists – nationalists must also appreciate socialism. The green of nationalism, the red of socialism and the white of pacifism, belong together in our Welsh rainbow coalition.[130]

This re-positioning was accompanied by an attempt by Dafydd Wigley to flirt with the SDP Alliance. A week before the by-election polling day, Wigley had made 'a revealing gaffe' in which he endorsed the candidature of the winning Liberal-SDP candidate, Richard Livsey.[131] Following a suggestion that Plaid might not stand in the contest, he warned that if Plaid did not do so, local members would be likely to support Richard Livsey, the SDP candidate. Wigley explained that the party's poor performance was due to the constant row between left and right 'which affected our ability to campaign effectively and to present a consistent image.'[132] While Wigley's intervention helped ensure that Plaid Cymru fielded a candidate, his endorsement of Livsey, as the SDP leader David Steel later stated, enabled him to win the seat by the small margin of 559 votes.[133]

There was a belief at the time amongst members of the National Left that both Dafydd Williams, Plaid's general secretary, and Dafydd Wigley, had attempted to engineer a formal agreement with the Social Democratic Party before the by-election, an accusation denied by both.[134] But after the disappointment of the Brecon and Radnor result, Dafydd Elis now decided to reverse his previous emphasis on targeting the more Anglicised areas of Wales, to concentrate on those areas where Plaid Cymru could make most impact, by appealing to the Welsh speaking heartland seats of Ynys Môn and Ceredigion in particular.

Later that month, in a speech in Tal-y-bont, Ceredigion, Dafydd Elis admitted that the party had failed to ensure that Welsh issues were on the agenda during the Brecon and Radnor campaign, and the *Western Mail*'s informed reporter Clive Betts, a former editor of the party's newspaper, *Welsh Nation*, ruminated that this change of direction exposed the considerable fears among the leadership 'that recriminations in the aftermath of Brecon will only widen the existing tensions within the party between the Nationalist and Socialist wings and undermine their electoral credibility even further – with fatal results'.

Betts also reported that Dafydd Wigley had already indicated that he was:

> Prepared to put himself at the head of a backlash against the president's policies that could conceivably culminate in another damaging leadership contest only a year after the last one ... the lesson of the Brecon by-election was that the Liberal victory came from anti-Tory tactical voting – and it was that example which should spur Plaid in the drive to capture the targeted seats of Carmarthen and Ynys Môn.[135]

Over the following two years as President, Dafydd Elis attempted to pacify the right within the party, and his conference keynote speech in 1986, for instance, indicated a change in his tone, as the *Western Mail* succinctly phrased it, from 'left-wing guru to elder statesman', which reminded its listeners of Gwynfor Evans's traditionalist message:

> There was no mention of socialism or other potentially divisive concepts. Instead, members were invited to take pride in their country, despite the problems for which Mr Thomas

spelled out his answers . . . The factional divisions between left and right which bedevilled the party since 1980, were forgotten. He said 'There is no question that our progress there is very much related to what happens to the Labour party.' His wish was for a Labour government which would inevitably show within a year that it had no worthwhile answer to the Valleys' problems.[136]

However, Dafydd Elis continued to involve himself with the English left, and *The Guardian*'s increasingly catty correspondent, Tony Heath, reported his prominent involvement in a *Marxism Today* conference:

> Outside Wales, Thomas is at home taking part in *Marxism Today*'s recent Staying Alive weekend, joining Molesworth [CND] protestors and addressing Stoke-on-Trent Fabians. Cultural conservatives find these activities somewhat strange for the leader of Plaid Cymru. Welsh radicals however, applaud this reaching out to a wider audience. Thomas says, 'Neil Kinnock once called me the Merioneth Marxist. But he only did that to damage me politically.' Is he still a Marxist? 'No-one serious about left politics can afford to ignore Marx', he says. Guile, as well as language, seems to be a measure of Welshness.[137]

Within Plaid Cymru the most important policy development, which would have longer term implications for its political impact, was the work of its constitutional sub-committee, to formulate a policy for a devolved Welsh Senate. On the committee were Dafydd Elis (who rarely attended), his closest political ally, the National Left secretary, Emyr Wynn Williams, Dafydd Huws, Gwynfor Evans, and Phil Williams. The driving force was Emyr Williams, who became the report's main author. This document guided Plaid's political strategy from the 1989 European election campaign onwards into the nineteen nineties.[138]

By the autumn of 1986, Plaid Cymru was being overwhelmed by the increasing concern of its members about the fate of the language. The immigration of English newcomers into Welsh speaking rural Wales became a hot topic and Plaid found itself in increasing difficulties in attempting to deal with the sensitivities relating to accusations of racism against English people on the one hand, and the decline of

Welsh language communities on the other. The iconic Welsh language cultural figure, the former television producer and language campaigner, Meredydd Evans, made a speech at the National Eisteddfod in August 1986, in which he warned against the influx of English immigrants into Welsh speaking areas. He subsequently resigned his membership of Plaid Cymru, because he felt that Dafydd Elis in particular, did not take the issue seriously enough, and this increasingly caused a major rift amongst party activists.[139]

The Cyfamodwyr (Covenanters), a hard-line nationalist group, admirers of Meibion Glyndŵr and vocally anti-English, threatened to stand against Dafydd Elis in the next General Election in protest at what it considered his opposition to the second home arson campaign and his refusal to criticise English immigrants. Plaid Cymru was torn over how to respond to this knotty issue, which was to dog his Presidency for the next four years.

Gwynfor Evans castigated him privately for his reluctance to call himself a nationalist and condoned the aims of Meibion Glyndŵr, if not their methods:

> You say about the Welsh who are responsible, that they are 'racists concerned with the purity of the nation' or comparable to the National Front. May I disagree totally. Although I condemn their methods as I condemn every violence, I believe that their motives are the same as mine. What is there in Welsh nationalism that you refuse so utterly that you refuse to use the word?[140]

But Dafydd Elis was adamant that he should voice his opposition to the extreme nationalism of the second home arson campaign. He created a furore in his criticism of the poet R. S. Thomas who had expressed his support for the arsonists:

> I had a bit of a spat with my favourite English language poet of the twentieth century, R. S. Thomas, but he was complicated. It's the same issue about direct action, albeit nonviolent direct action in the case of Gwynfor. It's ... a more dangerous issue because property was destroyed and people could have been killed, which takes me right back to the 1969 Investiture when

people were killed, who had purported to be in favour of greater autonomy for Wales.

His abhorrence towards the second home arson campaign was absolute, and he dismissed the suggestion from Dafydd Iwan and Wigley, that the firebombing campaign was contrived by intelligence services to bring Plaid Cymru into disrepute:

> I don't believe it was agent provocateurs. I think that's rubbish. I believe it was totally misguided right-wing nationalists who enjoyed a bit of a thrill. That's my view. I admit to shopping a few people. If I got any hint that anybody of my constituents, or anybody that I knew in north Wales or the rest of Wales were involved in violent activity, then those names should be known to the police. The police's comparative failure to catch these people was because the community weren't prepared to work with the forces of law and order, which is a very serious problem in a democracy. I was desperate whenever I heard the news in the morning about the arson campaign ... and I thought, 'I don't want to be in politics in a country that thinks that this is the way to do anything.' I felt the same thing about violence in Ireland. Violence was and will hopefully never again be a way of doing politics by other means for some people in Ireland. I didn't want to see that happening in Wales ... There was no justification for it. My main concern was that somebody would be killed.[141]

In January 1987, his strongly held views on the use of violence to deal with the language issue caused a furious row within the nationalist movement. Cymdeithas yr Iaith had agreed to host a visit to Gwynedd by a deputation of language activists from the north of Ireland, including members of Sinn Féin. His decision to disassociate himself in such a public manner from the organisers of the visit alienated him from many Cymdeithas members and supporters.[142] The visit followed a reciprocal visit to Belfast, during which the Welsh delegation had met Gerry Adams, the Sinn Féin leader. In a remarkable *volte face*, given his former involvement with Irish politics, Dafydd Elis called on the Home Secretary, Douglas Hurd, to refuse entry to the group, claiming that the Irish connection would be used to smear the nationalist movement, and that 'such a visit would be an affront to people in this country whose relatives have been killed while serving with the forces in the province'. Mr Thomas's appeal to the Home Secretary was described as 'an authoritarian intervention worthy of Westminster governments' by Toni Schiavone, chairman of Cymdeithas – 'we are shocked. Political capital was being made out of the visit in an election year.'[143]

This dispute added to the growing belief of language campaigners that their former champion was rapidly becoming part of the establishment, and his vocal condemnation alienated some of Plaid Cymru's core supporters. But his strategy was to appeal to the broader electorate rather than to sectional campaigning groups such as Cymdeithas yr Iaith. Ieuan Wyn Jones recalls that as president, he emphasised Plaid Cymru's historic choice to be a political party rather than a campaigning movement, which inevitably led to political compromise and conflict with some of his most ardent supporters:

> Dafydd always said that in order to win, you had to build a coalition of supporters. Dafydd El understood this and to break through in other places, he was dexterous in adapting some of his political standpoints. He realised that we needed a broad base of support beyond the party, and that to win, we had to have some sort of coalition, attracting those who were not necessarily Plaid supporters.[144]

By mid-1987, the former language activist, Rhodri Williams had detected a political shift in Dafydd Elis's political strategy and a belief that extra-parliamentary protests and securing wide electoral support through appealing to different communities of interest had not worked. For Dafydd Elis, if one door had closed, then another had to be opened. He became increasingly keen to collaborate with the Conservative Government, where he felt he could influence policy. The young socialist, Carwyn Jones,[145] living in university in Aberystwyth amid the ardent nationalists of Pantycelyn Hall, recalls that from 1987 onwards, Dafydd Elis Thomas seemed to move to the centre ground of Welsh politics. Some of his former followers believed he had 'sold out', that he did not support independence and now seemed to support NATO rather than CND's opposition to such a military bloc.[146]

The May 1987 General Election saw little comparative improvement in Plaid's performance, with the party's share of the vote falling slightly from 7.8 per cent in 1983 to 7.3 in 1987. However, the notable exception was Ieuan Wyn Jones's success in gaining Ynys Môn, while Dafydd Elis increased his majority in Meirionnydd Nant Conwy. As President, he campaigned throughout Wales, and Wyn Jones believed that Dafydd Elis's success in building a coalition of different interest groups paid off in Ynys Môn, detecting that former Cledwyn Hughes Labour supporters moved over to Plaid in their hundreds. Before the campaign, a sign of Dafydd Elis's attempt to broaden the party's appeal was his success in persuading his former neighbouring MP, Geraint Morgan, who had held the Denbigh seat for the Conservatives from 1959 to 1983, to support Plaid Cymru in the 1987 election. Jones had been assisted in his campaign by the revelation that the sitting MP for the island, Keith Best, had made illegal multiple share applications for British Telecom shares, and had been forced to resign.[147]

For Ieuan Wyn Jones, Dafydd's more moderate tone was reflected in one of his election campaign meetings, in Holyhead, which he described as 'the nearest he had experienced to a revivalist meeting', with Dafydd Elis and the radical Gwyn Alf Williams as speakers:

> Gwyn Alf had been persuaded to tone down his left-wing rhetoric and greeted the conversion of the former Conservative MP Geraint Morgan to Plaid Cymru. The audience were eating out of his hands. As the old preachers would utter their amens, the audience were standing on their feet – the place was packed to capacity and fired up. He was the star of the night.[148]

Even Wigley believed that the campaign saw Plaid Cymru more unified than before. Much attention was paid to Plaid's formalised partnership with the SNP, the concept of Wales's place in Europe had started to formulate, and the party's proposals for a Welsh Senate had also started to take shape.[149] By the 1987 election, the Meirionnydd Nant Conwy constituency was unique in that it had the lowest population of any constituency in England or Wales, and also had the second highest proportion of Welsh speakers. Dafydd Elis increased his majority handsomely, yet again:

May 1987 General Election	Meirionnydd Nant Conwy	
Dafydd Elis Thomas, Plaid Cymru	10,392	40 per cent
Dennis Jones, Conservative	7,366	28.4 per cent
Hugh Roberts, Labour	4,397	16.9 per cent
David Roberts, Social Democratic Party	3,814	14.7 per cent
Majority:	3,026	11.7 per cent[150]

Back in Parliament, Dafydd Elis took advantage of Ieuan Wyn Jones's arrival to remove himself from his shared office with Wigley in the House of Commons's office block of Norman Shaw North (the former Scotland Yard), to the main side of the House. That summer, Dafydd Elis was lent Will Edwards's apartment in Marbella, in southern Spain, to complete his doctorate thesis on Welsh elegiac poetry, and with Gwerfyl Arthur's secretarial support,[151] managed at last to submit his manuscript to the University of Wales, with only minutes of his deadline to spare. Spoken into a Dictaphone, recorded on buses, trains, and whilst driving between his constituency and London, drafted during snatched hours between his constituency and political duties, its completion, twenty years after its commencement, was a minor miracle.[152]

His external examiner, Professor J. E. Caerwyn Williams, complimented his thesis for its originality and described it as 'new and revolutionary', while insisting that key changes should be made before it could be finally passed:

> The candidate's general viewpoint is that of the Marxist perspective, i.e., the standpoint of historical materialism, but it is obvious that he has read the works of literary critics who are not Marxists but who like himself, are keen to take advantage of the new methods of studying literature that are now possible. I cannot fail to be amazed at the reading range of the candidate and to admire his ability to follow some of the leading pioneers in the field, but this does not mean that there is no room for criticism. He leaves the impression, like a number of those he follows, that he is more interested in the theory and methodology of literary criticism than in literature, and eventually we find ourselves admiring the abilities of the critic rather than the abilities of the author whose works are being discussed.

It is difficult for me to think of any other Welsh person who takes an interest in Welsh literature at present, who could come to the subject of elegiac poetry with such a scholarly arsenal as the author, and it's difficult for me to imagine any other Welsh person discussing the subject with such originality.

Williams perceptively detected the methods used to complete the thesis, identified the candidate's dependence on key bookshops, notably the famed left-wing Collet's bookshop in Charing Cross Road, and recognised the chaotic nature of its drafting:

> I get the impression that he had spoken much of it onto tape and left a typist to type directly – that would explain the little mistakes and the various inconsistencies that he has been asked to remove – it appears to me that he is too ready to accept the standpoint of some Marxist literary critics – I must say that I have learnt a great deal from reading this essay and had much pleasure from doing so, and I am convinced that he fully deserves the PhD degree from the University of Wales.[153]

Plaid Cymru's annual conference in Bedwas in 1987 again sparked dissent within the party. A number of its more traditionalist members were alienated by Plaid's social liberalism and its support for gay rights, and after Dafydd Elis's organiser in Meirionnydd, Elfed Roberts threatened to resign from the party, an attempt to lower the age of consent from twenty-one to sixteen was narrowly rejected by the conference. The right in the party, led by representatives from Gwynedd, secured a majority on the national executive, and the President was now outmanoeuvred. At this conference, one of the architects of the National Left, Emyr Williams, saw the political writing on the wall for Dafydd Elis as the party's intellectual leader, believing that he had been captured by the right:

> He was cornered after the 1987 conference when Wigley and his friends ensured that no-one from the left was elected to the national executive and it meant that Dafydd El was isolated. I think that was an important turning point, and also that Wigley attempted to bring the party together with the Liberals. The thing

was hellish. There was evidence of that. I understand the discussions were started by Dafydd Huws, the party's chairman on election night in 1987, and it was obvious that Wigley had thought along those lines a year earlier, when he argued in a St David's Day speech for a cross-party campaign for self-government for Wales.[154]

Losing control of the party's executive seemed to embolden Dafydd Elis to make more controversial statements. In Spring 1988, he again caused political havoc within Plaid Cymru, when he compared the venerated poet R. S. Thomas to the French fascist leader Jean-Marie le Pen, because of his support of the arson campaign against second homes.[155] Whilst Gwynfor refused to criticise Dafydd Elis publicly,[156] this issue became a huge source of tension. In May 1988, R. S. Thomas spoke at the extremist Cyfamodwyr annual general meeting, and *The Guardian* reported that the greatest vitriol was deployed against Dafydd Elis 'whose attachment to Marxism is regarded as a betrayal of nationalist principles which has thinned the ranks'. Dafydd Elis, 'who has tried with only limited success to widen his party's appeal beyond the cultural redoubt of the North-West' dismissed the challenge as coming 'from a fringe organisation with few members and I don't regard it as part of the national movement'. *The Guardian* concluded that 'the continued arson campaign against holiday homes – more than 130 attacks have been carried out since December 1979 – is casting a malevolent shadow over today's proceedings'.[157]

Dafydd Elis's worry that Plaid would retreat into its cultural and linguistic concerns drew him to fundamentally challenge the party's cherished beliefs. He advised members to stop talking about the language dying and being swamped by English speaking immigrants: 'Welsh culture has to be seen to be self-confident enough to take on all-comers. The idea that we can be swamped has to be rejected.'[158]

That summer, he decided to stand for the North Wales regional seat in the 1989 European election. Ieuan Wyn Jones recalls a conversation with Dafydd Elis in 1988, who told him that the party needed to widen its appeal, and that because of his own status and reputation, he was most likely to win the seat and extend Plaid's electoral reach. In standing, he was faced with the challenge of appealing on the one hand to the traditional Conservative voters of rural north Wales and the traditionally conservative Liberals of Montgomeryshire, and on the other to the Labour voters of industrial Deeside. He was aware that he would need to change his political emphasis and in doing so, risk alienating some of his own left-wing supporters. After his selection as candidate, the *Western Mail* reported that he was to go for the 'middle ground':

> He said his aim is to win the votes of left-wing Tories and supporters of the former Alliance plus a few Labourites, to enable him to shoot from fourth in the poll and seize the seat from Tory Beata Brookes. This move, he calculates, will bring him the votes from Clwyd and Montgomery to add to the party's solid Gwynedd support.
>
> He admitted he did not know whether his bid for the middle ground would also lose him crucial support from left-wingers . . . 'My job is to win in the Euro-election a broad left of centre majority; we have to win Liberal, Labour and some wet-Tory support in order to rise from fourth position to unseat Beata Brookes, the Conservative, and come first. I am trying to start a debate on Plaid's position in the political spectrum. The argument about socialism in the party is won. We now have to create a broad-based consensus . . . Unfortunately there are people in the party who do not seem to understand the need for adaptation . . . a lot of people in Plaid do not have an understanding of most of Wales, of areas such as Montgomery and Clwyd. Do people want to win an election? Either we make substantial inroads in these areas, or we do not win the seat.'[159]

He showed increasing impatience with Plaid Cymru's more traditionalist members as the election came nearer. In the autumn of 1988, he launched an angry diatribe against the party's vice-president, Dafydd Iwan, after he was arrested for criminal damage for daubing a sign on the Welsh Office calling for a new Welsh Language Act. He called Dafydd Iwan an 'embarrassment':

> Plaid Cymru is a political party whose main activity is winning elections. There is of course room for all kinds of other campaigns in Wales to try and influence Government policy. But I believe it is a political mistake for elected national officers of a

political party to take part in any form of direct action, particularly during the run up to elections.¹⁶⁰

Dafydd Iwan had been a language campaigner since the 1960s and had been the party's previous candidate in 1984 for the North Wales Euro seat. A number of his supporters were now reluctant to campaign for Dafydd Elis, because members of the National Left had in turn refused to canvass for Iwan. In the 1988 Plaid annual conference, one of the party's most prominent members in north Wales, Eifion Lloyd Jones, defended Dafydd Elis's change in tone, and emphasised the importance of the party shifting to the centre ground of politics in order to win votes in north-east Wales:

> Dr Thomas has been criticised for weakening the party's traditional policies to appeal to voters from all parties. In order for our party to have power, it must gain new support. If necessary, its image has to be changed. I appeal for loyalty to Plaid Cymru and to its president.¹⁶¹

Plaid members had been invigorated by the SNP's success in gaining the Glasgow Govan seat in a by-election in November 1988, when the Labour majority of 19,509 was transformed into an SNP majority of 3,554 votes, by the former Labour MP Jim Sillars. Dafydd Elis Thomas campaigned there for a month, staying with party stalwart Mike Russell. A Parliamentary by-election in Pontypridd on 23 February 1989 also excited Plaid Cymru, who selected the National Left stalwart Syd Morgan as candidate and made a huge effort to win the seat. Dafydd Elis threw himself into the fractious battle, helping to unite the party, and although Labour won, as expected, with a large majority, the result saw a swing of 13 per cent from Labour to Plaid Cymru. The Labour candidate, the charismatic Kim Howells, won with 20,000 votes and a majority of 10,794 over Plaid Cymru.

Karl Davies, the party's researcher at the time, considered the Pontypridd by-election to have been the first time that Plaid had thrown off the shadow of the 1979 Referendum. These results gave grounds for optimism for the European election in June 1989, he believed. Dafydd Elis was now a convinced Europhile and saw winning the North Wales Euro seat as 'a crucial means of bypassing Plaid's difficulties in challenging at Westminster general elections; they were a way of breaking out of the morass of UK politics'.[162] As Dafydd Elis prepared for the European election, his close colleague, Emyr Wynn Williams, the organisational mainstay of the National Left, quietly left the party, concerned at Dafydd Elis's ready cooperation with Conservative ministers, and his shift to the right, politically:

> In February 1989, I decided to turn my back on the party because I could see that the tide was flowing so strongly against us. Peter Walker and Wyn in the Welsh Office were very important to Dafydd in this period, and I think that Dafydd saw a better way forward for himself through them than within the party. The steps that happened then, including securing the role of Welsh in the curriculum, and Dafydd's securing of a place in the House of Lords, the chairmanship of the Welsh Language Board, confirmed that. In a way it was a logical step to take.[163]

Tim Williams also detected a change in his thinking, following Labour's failure to win the 1987 General Election:

> He realised that before Blairism, there was no cut through. So he was partly pragmatic about the left-right issue then, and he was ideological about the long term . . . He was a radical reformist, a pragmatist – not cynical.[164]

The added appeal of Europe for Dafydd Elis was that it also offered a more conducive arena for Plaid Cymru to work hand in glove with other progressive regionalist and nationalist groups. Ieuan Wyn Jones's experience of standing in the European election in 1979 gave him a valuable perspective on the momentous size of the task ahead:

> The problem was that the constituency was so vast, and canvassing from Holyhead Island in the west, to Connah's Quay in the east, was a real challenge. I think Plaid thought that Dafydd Elis's name was enough. The political reality was that of the comparative popularity of the parties, where Conservatives were on a downward spiral and Labour on the up, Plaid was stuck in the middle.[165]

From early 1989, Dafydd Elis worked hard across the north Wales constituency to appeal to a broader spread of voters from across the parties. His message was moderate and conciliatory, and Karl Davies, as his agent, saw him present a centre-left persona in this election, rather than the more 'extreme left-winger' that he'd witnessed beforehand. At times, the campaign felt like a 'grand tour gourmet' on occasions for Karl Davies, where 'we succeeded to eat in most of the best of north Wales's restaurants at the time'. Karl Davies had worked closely as the party's researcher with Dafydd Elis in the House of Commons and recalls how Dafydd enjoyed 'the good things in life'.[166] Dafydd was accompanied on the intensive campaign trail by his now partner, Marjorie, who was not impressed by its organisation, and disparagingly thought that her mother could have run a better campaign. They attempted to set up a chain of local offices, but 'people didn't even have each other's telephone numbers. They weren't a campaigning political organisation. It was amazing that he did as well as he did.'[167]

However, his campaign for the North Wales Euro seat was one of his happiest ever election contests. The European context was clearly the place where he felt most at home, and his experience of the Basque country and Catalonia gave him an awareness of the importance of 'proper solidarity, a rejection of state nationalism. That's why I think the European context is so important'. He made allies with key north Wales Conservatives, including Geraint Morgan, the former MP for Denbigh, and Sir Anthony Meyer, the Conservative MP for Clwyd North-West, who had gained a reputation for independence of thought and for putting the interests of his constituency above his party. Later that year, he stood against Margaret Thatcher for the Conservative leadership, and locally opposed the closure of the Shotton steelworks. He was also tacitly supported by Geraint Howells, the Liberal MP for Ceredigion.

But two weeks before polling day, Ieuan Wyn Jones presented the results of an opinion poll held in north Wales, to Dafydd Elis's election team. This indicated that Dafydd Elis had very little chance of winning, and that the Labour candidate, Joe Wilson was the favourite. Dafydd Elis was upset, and angrily rejected this Cassandra-like projection but he believed that it then cast a shadow over the campaign for the last ten days.[168]

While he could count on support from key individuals from other parties, Dafydd Elis laboured under the disadvantage that some Plaid members refused to work for him in protest against the refusal of some of his left-wing supporters to work for Dafydd Iwan in the 1984 European election. The collapse of the Liberal party, the increasing strength of the Labour party at the expense of the Conservatives, and Plaid's failure to break into the Tories' heartland vote along the north Wales coast, all contributed to the highest European election turnout in Britain, but a disappointing result for Dafydd Elis. He almost doubled Plaid's vote but only managed to increase the party's vote share by 8 per cent, disappointingly only moving Plaid Cymru from fourth to third place:

North Wales European Election	June 1989		
Joe Wilson, Labour	83,638	33.1%	+8.1%
Beata Brookes, Conservative	79,178	31.3%	−0.3%
Dafydd Elis Thomas, Plaid Cymru	64,120	25.3%	+7.9%
Patrick Adams, Green Party	15,832	6.3%	new
R. L. Marshall, SLDP	10,056	4.0%	−22.0%
Turnout	252,824	46.8%	+4.4%[169]

His hard-fought campaign saw him win over fifty per cent of the vote in Môn, Arfon and Merioneth, and over 35 per cent in Montgomeryshire, Conwy and south-west Clwyd, where he succeeded in gaining a substantial proportion of Liberal votes. But in the traditionally Labour seats of Alun Deeside and Wrexham, the Plaid vote was decimated.[170] His disappointment was inevitable after he had expended such energy on the campaign. Wigley thought that the result had a profound effect on him, and noted his grumpier attitude towards the Labour party: 'I saw this as a reaction to the North Wales European election. Labour at times had played quite dirty, and support hadn't come over to Plaid from Labour voters as we had hoped for.' [171]

By the summer of 1989, both Dafydds were exhausted. Wigley and Dafydd Elis had become frustrated and tired after fifteen years in a demanding role that gave them little privacy, a commitment to spending time in London in an unpromising parliamentary setting, and with ceaseless constituency and party duties.

That summer, Dafydd Wigley allowed his name to be put forward by headhunters for three key roles, and in September, he received prestigious offers from each in quick succession, namely the roles of chief executive of Gwynedd County Council, the chief executive of the Welsh Development

Agency, and the chief executive of MENCAP, the charity for disabled people, based in London, that he had worked with closely after his sons' deaths. He visited Gwynfor Evans at his home in Pencarreg, in order to break the news that he was leaving politics. Gwynfor Evans made a tearful plea for him not to give up his role in the party. On his journey home, he called to see Dafydd Elis. In his frustration, he demanded to know what the president's political strategy was for the party:

> I received an interesting, and perhaps revelatory answer considering what happened afterwards – 'Quango Wales' was the answer. Since the Tories were creating dozens of them, this would be the new level of government in Wales, and from having them, taking them over and then pressing to democratise them. I was dubious that you could persuade the London Government to depart its policy from depending on nominated bodies, and more doubtful if they would appoint patriotic Welsh people to fill the quangos.[172]

This strategy drew on Raymond Williams's idea of 'the long march through the institutions',[173] to encourage the creation of more Welsh administrative institutions, while in parallel, to increase the pressure for their democratisation. This seemed to supersede Dafydd Elis's previous strategy of creating popular alliances with the environment, language, labour, peace and feminist movements. As Richard Wyn Jones points out, this strategy was an 'entirely individualistic one: a strategy in which only the elite could hope to play an active role'.[174] It suggests very strongly that Dafydd Elis, as exhausted as Wigley, and not able to envisage immediate success at the ballot box after fifteen years as a Member of Parliament, had reached the end of his political tether.

At the 1989 annual conference, Dafydd Wigley resigned as the party's election vice-president, and in its wake, a number of long-standing members resigned, including his agent, Elfed Roberts, following a motion to support the rights of gay and lesbian people. A member of his party in Meirionnydd Nant Conwy, Pedr ap Llwyd, wrote to Dafydd Elis to express his disappointment at Roberts's resignation:

> I had the honour of accompanying you to the Parliament for the first time in the seventies and seeing Elfed winning Meirionnydd

time after time after that for Plaid. I hope that you will do everything within your ability to keep Elfed and to ensure that we retain our hold on the constituency. It is time for you to realise, Dafydd, the danger of taking your support for granted ... Nationalism is at an ebb, and you are playing at things.[175]

Another bitter letter from another activist, Derfel Gruffydd complained about the party's support for gay rights:

Why, oh why, does Plaid Cymru appear to put more emphasis on the rights of homosexuals and lesbians than on education, the problems of immigration and self-government. The conduct of these people is disgusting and hateful to me, but it is a matter that is personal and confidential for them – as long as they don't declare it from the roofs of houses about their condition and affect other people. It appears that our Plaid has been succoured by them to sympathise with their lack of maturity, uncertainty and selfishness. They succeeded in getting Plaid to wave their banner without counting its cost. I appeal to you to use your powers as President to call a meeting of the National Executive immediately to try and steer the ship from the storm to the centre of the sea of Nationalism, Self-Government and self-respect.[176]

His scant reply defended 'social tolerance, especially in the case of minorities of all types'.[177] Dafydd Elis had sacrificed much to sustain his role as a Member of Parliament and leader of the party. His personal commitment to his constituency and his campaigning for the party had given him widespread recognition throughout Wales as one of its most able and challenging politicians, but it also led, as feared by Elen on the eve of his first victory as a candidate, to the end of his marriage. After the disappointment of his defeat in the 1989 European election, Marjorie feels he had what she considered to be a midlife crisis, and he became deeply religious. His chapel upbringing had been an important influence on him, and as a student, he had been a faithful chapelgoer at Twr-Gwyn Presbyterian chapel in upper Bangor. When he moved to Dolgellau, he remembers thinking initially whether he wished to 'throw this religion away?':

I decided not to, mainly because of my friendship with the local Congregationalist minister, Meurwyn Williams. We both shared a commitment to the social gospel and liberation theology, and an admiration for the experience of revolutionary Catholic priests in South America, who identified with the poor and oppressed rather than the state. In London I would go to Radnor Walk (the Welsh Congregationalist church in Chelsea). I read a lot of theology, not because it made me godlier, but it indicated how we could change society. I was inspired by Welsh theologians such as J. R. Jones and Dewi Z. Phillips and I read a lot of south American liberation theology. They simplified my understanding of religion, and it was an inspiration. I remember one Sunday morning in about 1986 or 1987, waking up in my flat in Notting Hill, and hearing church bells. I went to find them . . . and I found a high church Anglican church.

This inspired him to start worshipping regularly at the Church of Wales's St Mary's Church in the centre of Dolgellau, where he was baptised by the Bishop of Bangor, Cledan Mears:

I felt I had come home. I had been with the Presbyterians and the Congregationalists, but I came to appreciate the importance of the holy mass and the services based on the holy mass. It is a matter of choice, isn't it? Either choosing to listen a sermon 20 minutes in length and singing lots of hymns of dubious or unacceptable theological standpoints, or something more formal that is a form of renewal.

He also started attending Llanfachreth parish church, near his home in Maes-y-Bryner:

There was a welcoming congregation of around two dozen people. Elen and I had just separated and I felt a sense of forgiveness and understanding. My work on Welsh language elegiac poetry, which always had a religious element, gave me an understanding of the importance of the Catholic form of worship and the comfort it offers.[178]

He was also ready to return from his political career to academia. In January 1990, he unsuccessfully applied for two university roles, as a senior lecturer in Clark University in Massachusetts, and as Vice-Chancellor of the University of Wales, Lampeter. In his application to Clark University, he expressed his hope to 'combine my political experience with a place and a space where I would be able to develop theory and research in the whole question of cultural identity, related to the political and economic and communication structures of a wider world society'. He highlighted his role as an associate research fellow in the University of St Andrews working on post-nationalism and the impact of the break-up of the Soviet bloc, and ended his application with a heartfelt plea, that 'on a personal level, I would also welcome a career break from full-time politics in a setting where I could develop all aspects of my personal and social experience'.[179]

After Plaid's 1990 autumn annual conference, Dafydd Elis informed Ieuan Wyn Jones, as chair of the party, that he intended to stand down as president at the next conference and pressed him to stand as his replacement. He was implacably opposed to Wigley succeeding him, as Jones recalls:

> We had two or three meetings in which he tried to persuade me to stand. He told me how he felt and that he would only have one condition, that if there was to be a competition for the Presidency, 'you must stand'. I said I didn't think that was possible, because Wigley would stand and he would be elected because that was what the party wanted. Dafydd wasn't happy about that at all.[180]

In November 1990, at the age of only 33, Marjorie Thompson was elected chair of the Campaign for Nuclear Disarmament and became a recognised public figure across the UK. She came over as highly principled and extremely opinionated, and in her first television appearance on *Question Time*, *The Guardian* unkindly thought her 'an arrogant young woman', assessing that 'she not only failed to gauge the mood of the audience, she did not even try. The impression she gave was of a churlish high school girl lashing out unthinkingly.'[181] Inevitably searching for the 'Welsh' angle, the *Wales on Sunday* referred to the 'politics and passion of the young peace crusader' and the 'unlikely partner for Plaid President

Dafydd Elis Thomas'. Stating she was a 'lapsed member' of the Labour party, she described what drew her to Dafydd:

> My mother warned me about Welshmen, she said they were melancholic. I think Dafydd has a vision, he is a true European intellectual, and obviously what Dafydd campaigns for in Wales, I will support. [182]

In January 1991, Dafydd Elis finally announced publicly that he would be standing down as a Member of Parliament, emphasising it was very much a personal, not a political decision, and expressed his hope that he would continue to work politically through education and act perhaps like a 'cultural ambassador for Wales, if that does not sound too pompous'. He wished to relinquish his role as an MP because he didn't think the party wanted to go further. 'I wasn't convinced that I was the guy to do it, anyway. I left the Commons because I'd spent 18 years there and I thought, "I can't spend my whole life here. You can't go on doing something for ever."'[183]

Given his own misgivings about remaining in politics, Dafydd Wigley was not surprised by his decision and noted how honourably he behaved in holding on until the April 1992 election, avoiding a by-election and giving the opportunity for his nominated successor to have a period of apprenticeship in the constituency:

> Not everyone realises how generous and kind was Dafydd Elis Thomas's conduct in this regard. He did not know when the election would be, and it was impossible for him to take a new job until the Election had been held. This meant insecurity for him after the Election.[184]

However, Dafydd Elis was still determined to prevent Wigley succeeding him as president of the party, as Ieuan Wyn Jones recalls:

> He then said he would need to have a meeting with Wigley to discuss terms. By then he had already announced publicly that he was standing down as an MP, and practically this meant that it would have been very difficult for him to continue as president. The three of us had lunch at the Commons, where I said I

would not stand and that Wigley should stand on the basis that I was happy with the direction he would take the party. I do not remember the conditions we agreed, but I remember that the two Dafydds had been such front-runners (as presidents), that there was a feeling that they didn't carry people with them, and that they needed to be more inclusive and share responsibilities. I don't think there was a difference of views on fundamental principles, just in the way they acted as leaders. They are very strong, able characters, and somehow it was easier when there were three of us.[185]

The least charitable public response to his resignation within Plaid came from Phil Williams, the party's vice chair, who stated that Dafydd Elis's wish for Plaid to be an 'anti-nationalist party' had confused voters, and that he had been better suited to be an academic rather than a politician as 'his real joy is in stimulating thought'.[186] But the *Western Mail's* Westminster column reflected a warmer regard for him amongst his House of Commons colleagues:

> The departing MP is currently contemplating his future with the joy of a man released into the community after 17 years in a rather unpleasant institution ... The independently-thinking, free-thinking Dr Thomas will be missed by all those who value the ability to think and speak outside a party brief. His departure also leaves a large gap in another area. As a pioneer of designer nationalism, the Plaid leader has become something of a thinking man's fashion victim. Unlike half the Commons, his sartorial elegance has yet to fall victim to the men-in-suits syndrome. His demob-happiness is easily understandable. Who else has a demob suit designed by Giorgio Armani?[187]

Later that year, as he stood down from the Presidency of Plaid Cymru, he reflected on his own political contribution and claimed that the party's main success had been 'to get other parties – even perhaps the Conservatives – to accept the idea of a Welsh assembly to control the country's number of quangos as part of a federal Europe'. He said that he had decided on returning to academia and part-time politics because his disappointment with Westminster meant he could not face another twenty years of travelling through Wales to carry out the duties of an MP. When asked if he was a divisive person in Plaid, he said 'I have been an outreach person. I do not believe in running a party for the benefit of its membership. Parties exist to recruit and to create new ideas.' His re-definition of nationalism involved 'getting people to see themselves as Welsh-Europeans. This included the incomers, the ethnic minorities in the inner cities and realising that to be Welsh is a multilingual thing.'[188]

It may well have been a subliminal mark of his gradual disillusionment with his role as Plaid Cymru's President that he was over an hour late for his last televised speech in that role, at the party's 1991 annual conference in Porthmadog. He had been delayed by heavy traffic on his journey there from the Queen's opening of the Conwy road tunnels on the A55 North Wales expressway. But he had already alienated a number of the traditionalists in the party. The veteran O. M. Roberts, a close friend of his father, at the age of 88 wrote that:

> I have a high opinion of Dafydd Elis and admire his undoubted ability but in my opinion his Presidency was not a success... trying to make Plaid's policies acceptable to everyone and everything. That isn't the way. There is only one policy, which is first to be able to win the right to put socialist aims, or whatever they may be, in action; that is, self-government. Under Dafydd Elis's presidency, he was frivolous with this basic aim.[189]

However, this traditionalist view of Dafydd Elis's contribution as president fails to give regard to his success in building a cross-party consensus for Welsh devolution throughout the 1980s. He considered that his main achievement as president of the party was the creation of the National Left:

> It was something which was Welsh, which had aspirations for Wales, and clearly by saying 'National Left', it emphasised that it wasn't 'nationalist left'. That was very important to me. I believe the National Left led to... the success of the devolution agenda. It led to a mentality of understanding of how people needed to work together, and I imagine, of course, a direct line from National Left to a Plaid coalition government with Labour (in

2007). Because it goes to the heart of Welsh politics. I don't think what Wales needs is a nationalist organisation which is committed to something called an independent state, whatever a 'state' or 'independence' means in the twenty-first century. What Wales does need is to have our politicians and governments reflect what the Welsh people want at successive elections.

His continuing objection to using the term 'nationalism' alienated many members within the party and confused others:

> Over my life, I've been more and more convinced that nationalist ideology is the worst ideological, philosophical position on Earth, because it's based on the assertion that a state form, or an ethnicity or nationality of some kind is an appropriate way to develop an organisation or a viewpoint or a way of thinking that will inspire people to change. I think it's appalling, because nationalism belongs to the nineteenth century, and of course in the twentieth century in its fascist form, it caused disasters.
>
> My preferred politics is 'decentralist socialism' because 'it is not statist. It recognises the existence of states and governments, but values governance ... This links way back to Raymond Williams's work, and the importance of an educated and participating democracy. People have to know what's going on, and they have to be part of it.'[190]

He had indicated to a number of friends and colleagues who were Plaid activists that he might support them as his successor as Member of Parliament for Merioneth. But the person he most encouraged was Elfyn Llwyd, a solicitor who lived in Llanuwchllyn, and was a partner in the local law firm of Guthrie Jones, with offices in Bala, Barmouth and Dolgellau. Although not an active member of the party, he was well known and respected throughout the constituency and had helped Dafydd Elis in his case work. Six candidates put in for nomination, mainly experienced party workers and former parliamentary candidates, and he discreetly pressed local members to support Elfyn Llwyd. After his nomination as the next candidate, both worked together in the constituency, and Dafydd Elis shepherded him through the election campaign.

In the May 1992 election, Elfyn Llwyd won the seat with an increased Plaid majority:

Meirionnydd Nant Conwy	General Election April 1992
Elfyn Llwyd, Plaid Cymru	11,608
Gwyn Lewis, Conservative	6,995
Rhys Williams, Labour	4,978
Ruth Parry, Lib Dem	2,358
Plaid Cymru majority:	4,613[191]

Andrew Roth's aggregated parliamentary profile of Dafydd Elis Thomas at the end of his eighteen year career in the House of Commons captures much of his rare essence as a free-thinking and independent Member of Parliament. A range of comments from parliamentary sketchwriters collected by Roth, reflect a Member of Parliament who was 'personable ... and had a large capacity for political debate and a sense of humour' (*The Times*), 'surprisingly and refreshingly honest for an MP of his long standing' (*The Scotsman*), and referred to his sartorial elegance as 'a sharp dresser' and wearer of 'bookmaker's Regency suits' (*The Guardian*).

The Scotsman viewed him as an 'intellectual gadfly', in retreat into academia, abandoning his Parliamentary seat, but said he was popular with journalists because he was a free thinker and had a sense of mischief, a combination that 'ensures lively press conferences and interviews, often to the despair of his party'.[192]

On departing the House of Commons, he stated to the *Daily Post* that the institution was beyond reform and that Westminster 'is the most undemocratic tradition-bound, inefficient, anti-social legislature in the Western world'. He said that he would like it pulled down, or perhaps given to Granada as a set to film soap operas. He also revealed that he had stayed in Parliament three years longer than he had envisaged.[193]

His presidency laid the foundations for Plaid Cymru's future political breakthrough, particularly with the successful alliance with the Wales Green Party in 1992, and the working together of the broad left in Wales in future years, leading to devolution in 1999. The ideas and embryonic strategies for progress that he started were taken up by others subsequently and contributed in no small measure to the party's later successes.

One of his most important legacies was to open up Plaid Cymru to a wider audience than ever before. Much of the scepticism about the national movement's association with socialism was diluted through Thomas' emergence as one of the flagbearers of the left in Britain. His implacable opposition to the Falklands war, his dedicated support for the miners' strike, his commitment to the peace movement and his charismatic intellect made him a key voice in the British left during much of the 1980s. He made his party welcoming and more broadly based, appealing to those who might have doubted the party's relevance. As McAllister suggests:

> He may not have succeeded in bringing about the fundamental reinvention of Plaid Cymru that he desired, but his period as President at least forced the party itself, the other political parties and the media in Britain to reassess their views of Plaid Cymru. That in itself was no mean feat.[194]

His own assessment of his period as President of the party was that 'it made it possible to have Welsh devolution and then finally, to make it work with a better relationship between Plaid and Labour. That's the thing I've most enjoyed about looking back.' He was a pivotal figure in Plaid Cymru's post-war development, and his principal legacy as President was, for the first time, to clearly assert Plaid Cymru's identity as a credible left of centre political force.[195]

5

Taking the Ermine – for the Language

It was Lord Emlyn Hooson, previously the Liberal MP for Montgomeryshire, who made the first approach to Dafydd Elis Thomas to join the House of Lords, two months before the 1992 General Election held on 9 April. As former neighbouring MPs and with common interests in the mid Wales economy and culture, they counted themselves friends, and Hooson had also proved himself a pioneer devolutionist, unsuccessfully attempting to introduce a Home Rule for Wales Bill in 1967 in the House of Commons:

> Emlyn Hooson asked to meet me for lunch at the members' dining room of the House of Lords where, coming to the end of our meal, he said, 'Wouldn't you like to come here?' I said, 'I hadn't thought about this'. He said, 'I'd like you to think about it, and I think it'd be really good for Wales'. I was keen, but I didn't want to make any difficulty for Plaid in the Commons.

A few days later, and within weeks of the General Election, he was phoned by Wyn Roberts from his home: 'He did this classic Wyn thing. "We think," he said, "that you could help us a lot in the future if you went there (the House of Lords)". I said, "Here we go, there's obviously a campaign going on here".'[1]

No offer of a peerage could be made formally until after the General Election, and Labour, under the leadership of Neil Kinnock, had been fancied to win until the last few days of the campaign. But Dafydd Elis was given the definite understanding that if the Conservatives won, he would be invited to join the House of Lords. The reason given for this was that he would be expected to use his elevation to bolster his influence as chair of the proposed new body to be created to safeguard the Welsh language, the Welsh Language Board. After the Conservatives' victory, with a majority of 21, Wyn Roberts was re-appointed Minister of State in the Welsh Office, becoming the longest serving Minister in a single department for more than a hundred years.[2] He and the Secretary of State for Wales, David Hunt, quickly pressed the Prime Minister, John Major, to allow the peerage for Dafydd Elis, and immediately after the election, a letter arrived in his Dolgellau office from the Prime Minister's office, formally offering him the honour. Before sending his reply, he went for a meditative walk from the town towards the Cader Idris mountain that dominates the area – 'I went halfway up when I decided, Yes, I will do this'. In fact, he had no hesitancy in accepting the honour. As Wyn Roberts had reasoned, it gave him a platform to support the Government's Welsh language policy and gave the putative Welsh Language Board greater status in an UK context.

At this stage, only he and the relevant Government Ministers knew of the formal offer. He certainly had not discussed it either with his family or his Plaid Cymru colleagues: 'I couldn't because the party policy was not to go there. If I was going to do it, I was going to have to do it as a crossbencher.'[3]

On the Saturday morning after the election, the President of the party, Dafydd Wigley was gardening at home, and resting from a comparatively successful campaign which had increased the number of Plaid Cymru's seats from three to four, with the winning of Ceredigion. The phone rang, with a civil servant from No. 10 on the line, asking whether he would have any objection to Dafydd Elis Thomas being put forward as a peer? In order to circumvent his party's opposition to the second chamber, Wigley had already nominated an 'independent nationalist', and the name of Ioan Bowen Rees, the former chief executive of Gwynedd County Council, and former Plaid candidate, had been put forward to the Prime Minister's office.[4] He checked with the official to ascertain that it was Dafydd Elis Thomas, rather than Rees, who was being nominated.

Wigley writes in his memoirs that this was the first time that he knew that Dafydd Elis had formally been nominated, but he was not totally surprised since Emlyn Hooson had raised the possibility with him some weeks previously. He had not felt that Dafydd Elis, given his left-wing background, would be interested in going to the Lords, but it is significant that neither chose to discuss the issue beforehand. Wigley had no objection to Dafydd Elis's nomination, but he felt unable to reply at that stage, because of the need to consult with the other members of the four-strong Plaid group. They met the following day at the picturesque George III Hotel in Penmaenpool, overlooking the Mawddach estuary, near Dolgellau, to discuss their post-election strategy. The most immediate issue on their agenda was their attitude towards Dafydd Elis's intention to join the Lords.

Elfyn Llwyd suggested that they should go and see him to discuss the offer of a peerage and to confirm whether he wished to accept it. All four jumped into a car to go to Dafydd's home nearby, but when they got there, although the doors were open and books scattered on the floor of the library, there was no sign of the occupant. He was eventually tracked down by Elfyn Llwyd the following Wednesday evening and in their discussion, he confirmed his wish to take up the offer of a peerage.

His personal decision totally contradicted party policy, but the quartet did not wish for a confrontation with him, and took the pragmatic view that it would be advantageous for Plaid to have a member in the House of Lords, since some Welsh legislation was likely to be introduced there, including the proposed controversial Welsh Language Bill to establish the Welsh Language Board, as well as a Bill to re-organise Welsh local government. The response of the Plaid parliamentary group to his elevation was remarkably temperate, given the party's total opposition to membership of the House of Lords, but the MPs saw the obvious advantage of having a former Plaid MP in the House of Lords, even though he would have to sit as a non-aligned cross-bencher, given that there was no Plaid Cymru group there as such.

However, after the formal announcement of his elevation to the House of Lords on 5 June 1992, the group of Plaid Cymru MPs issued a press statement, distancing them from the appointment and reiterating the party's opposition to the House of Lords.[5] But the Plaid MPs' acquiescence led to bitter recrimination from elements within the party.[6] Plaid Cymru would not agree to formally nominate a representative to the House of Lords for another nineteen years, when Dafydd Wigley was made Baron Wigley of Caernarfon in January 2011, and was supported formally by Lord Dafydd Elis-Thomas.

The first public report of his elevation and its political fall-out had appeared in *The Times* a week previously, and was based on his partner Marjorie Thompson's tip off to the journalist:

The tranquillity of the Welsh valleys is about to be shattered by the appointment of the first Welsh nationalist in the House of Lords. Dafydd Elis Thomas, the former president of Plaid Cymru who stood down at the election after 18 years as an MP, is expected to receive a peerage in next month's honours list. Thomas is acutely aware that the award would divide the party, which is committed to the abolition of the House of Lords.

No other member of Plaid Cymru has ever accepted an honour for political service, but John Major is believed to have sanctioned the peerage after a recommendation from Dafydd Wigley, now the party's President. However, in response, Plaid's general secretary, Dafydd Williams, says; 'many members regard the House of Lords as a remote institution which is why we have never had a knight, never mind a peer. If an honour were to be bestowed on a member there would be a lively debate . . . There is no doubt that for some it would be beyond the pale.' There are those who believe Thomas's long-standing partner CND chairman Marjorie Thompson, is among that number.[7]

John Osmond, a former supporter and friend, railed against this decision, describing the 'widespread dismay, even anguish, in some nationalist circles at Dafydd Elis Thomas allowing his name to go through these mysterious channels whereby appointments such as his are made'. He reminded his audience of the:

> Left-wing radical who first entered the Houses of Parliament as a long-haired throwback to the 1960s in February 1974. Could it be that he was suffering withdrawal symptoms so soon after leaving the Palace of Westminster barely two months ago? . . . It seems perverse for a Welsh radical to give aid and comfort to the forces of England's right-wing establishment by joining their club.[8]

Gwerfyl Arthur recalled the impact of his decision to enter the House of Lords on her fellow Plaid Cymru members:

> There was disillusionment among his followers. When he wore his tweeds, he became someone different. He liked to do unexpected things. I remember going past Maes-y-Bryner [Dafydd's

Merioneth residence] on my way home. I had my cat Pero with me. Dafydd had been cooking woodcock for Sunday lunch, and Pero had the skeleton. He was quite the country gent by then.[9]

His close ally in the constituency, Dyfrig Siencyn, also reflected on his seemingly growing gentrification:

> The odd thing about Dafydd was that he had turned into some kind of country gentleman in Nannau, confusing people who had thought he was a Communist, and he seemed to have become a Tory-like High Churchman.[10]

His former school friend Selwyn Williams despaired of his elevation as 'anwerinol' – loosely translated as 'not of the people' – and believed that he had chosen his liking for good wine and smart menswear over continuing with the political struggle. His former colleagues and supporters in Plaid Cymru felt a sense of betrayal,[11] and his former wife Elen felt it was a desperate step to take, and 'I was very angry about that. There was no consistency. Was it because he was in "no man's land" in terms of employment?'[12]

Dafydd Elis stoutly defended his decision to join the House of Lords:

> I cannot see anything wrong in representing Plaid Cymru and Wales in the House of Lords for the Upper House has an important role when it comes to new legislation. My acceptance of the title does not necessarily mean that I agree with the principle of people being nominated rather than being elected to the Upper House, but one cannot escape the fact that the opportunity to serve there surely gives Plaid a new standing in British politics.[13]

On taking his seat in the Lords, he was sponsored by Lord Thomas of Gwydir (Peter Thomas, the former Conservative Secretary of State for Wales and former attendee at his father's church in Llanrwst), and Lord Emlyn Hooson. In discussion with the heraldic figure, the Garter King at Arms, who advises new members on their nomenclatures, Dafydd Elis insisted on not using his patronym, mistakenly believing there were too many Thomases in the Lords already. In fact, there were only two other Thomases – Peter Thomas and Martin Thomas, the former Liberal

Democrat politician from Wrexham. But he also decided to mischievously specify Nant Conwy as his territorial connection, not only because he had been raised in the Conwy valley and that he had represented the area as an MP, but also because the title deliberately invoked the most powerful of the Welsh princes, Llewelyn ab Iorwerth (c.1173–1240), and his resistance to the aggression of the English Marcher lords.[14] He therefore chose his baronetcy name as Baron Dafydd Elis Elis-Thomas of Nant Conwy in the county of Gwynedd,[15] changing his name from Thomas to Elis-Thomas by deed poll. He resolved to sit as a crossbench peer, because he maintained he would need to be non-political in his later role as chair of the Welsh Language Board, and only took the Plaid Cymru whip eventually in 2012, having being joined in the Lords by Dafydd Wigley.

Working with the Conservatives

Although taking the ermine robe to enter the Lords earned Dafydd Elis-Thomas considerable scorn, yet he had acted with clear purpose, and the role that Wyn Roberts had in mind for him in the House of Lords as the chair of the new Welsh Language Board, was due to be established in 1993 after the legislation had been passed in Parliament. He had particularly impressed the Minister and his civil servants in the Welsh Office with his earlier support for the Education Reform Act of 1988 which made the Welsh language a compulsory part of the curriculum in some areas of Wales. Roberts had played a key part in driving this reform through, despite the misgivings of the Prime Minister, Margaret Thatcher.

The legislation also allowed parents to opt out of local Welsh language schooling at local expense, which reduced the degree of conflict which had excited protests from both sides of the argument in the seventies, by anti-Welsh language groups such as Education First and the Language Freedom Movement.[16] Huw Onllwyn Jones, one of Wyn Roberts's private secretaries in the Welsh Office, recalls the dramatic showdown between Wyn Roberts and the Prime Minister over the Welsh language education policy included in the Bill:

> He was called in off his train from Cardiff. He had had two Stellas and a driver was waiting for him in Paddington, not to take him home as he thought, but to the Prime Minister's office in the House of Commons, where he had been summoned. There, he

was given a tumbler of whisky by the Private Secretary to the Prime Minister, Archie Hamilton, and asked by Thatcher to justify the inclusion of Welsh in the core national curriculum.[17]

That evening, Wyn Roberts made a note of their exchange with the Prime Minister in his diary. She started by stating that:

> You can do what you like in your Welsh-speaking schools but look here ... you define them as schools where the majority of subjects are taught through the medium of Welsh. Don't you see that your nationalists will exploit that definition, use a bit of Welsh in teaching all sorts of subjects and claim to be Welsh-speaking schools even though their pupils are monoglot English?

Wyn Roberts had to be on his mettle in reply:

> 'No chance, Prime Minister. Welsh medium schools are clearly identified.' We had been at each other hammer and tongs for an hour and forty minutes and I had not been worsted as far as I was aware. I knew it would be fatal to give in to her. My blood would be on the carpet and my brains on the curtains.[18]

He was aided in his attempt to take this controversial legislation through the House of Commons by Dafydd Elis who was also Plaid's education spokesman, and whose academic background and understanding of Welsh language issues gave him a valuable insight into the importance of establishing Welsh as part of the core school curriculum. His closeness to the Welsh Office Ministers arose mainly from his personal friendship with Wyn Roberts and individual Conservative members of the House of Commons, such as Peter Walker, MP for Worcester and Secretary of State for Wales (1987–90), a Cabinet left-wing so-called 'wet' with whom he had been paired and to whom he took a liking. His successor, David Hunt, the MP for Wirral West, another 'wet', had been the only Cabinet member to have supported Michael Heseltine when he stood unsuccessfully for the leadership against Margaret Thatcher.

Dafydd Elis and Wyn Roberts had known each other from Wyn's early career as a television executive in TWW in the 1960s, where he had produced current affairs programmes, with Dafydd contributing as a presenter or contributor. They became friends during the 1970 General Election when both stood in Conwy. The fathers of both were Nonconformist ministers, and both sets of parents knew each other well. Dafydd's mother and aunt lived in Wyn's constituency in Trefriw, and he was a fellow member in their local chapel.[19] In 1974, Dafydd's mother had written to Wyn to ask him to 'look after' the youthful Dafydd Elis, in Parliament. Their upbringing as sons of the manse gave them a common bond, and as Dafydd Elis explained, 'the manse was like a Welsh-medium public school – it taught you how to speak and behave in public'.[20]

In the 1980s and 1990s, Conservative policies unintentionally led to enhanced support for devolution. Economic decline and the run-down of coalmining and other heavy industries, created the impression that Thatcherism was also a form of English colonialism. Yet paradoxically, Conservative policy towards the Welsh language was progressive and interventionist. It included the setting up of S4C as the Welsh language television channel, the establishment of a statutory Welsh Language Board, the 1988 Education Reform Act, which led gradually to the Welsh language becoming a compulsory part of the school curriculum, and the passing of the Welsh Language Act in 1993, which placed an onus on the public sector to treat Welsh and English on an equal basis.[21]

In encouraging Elis-Thomas to agree to be nominated to the Lords, Wyn Roberts had made it clear to him that his membership of the Lords was also the precursor to being appointed as chair of the yet-to-be-created, Welsh Language Board, as Elis-Thomas recalled:

> One of the arguments that I was given about membership of the upper house was that there were lots of chairs of public bodies throughout England, Wales and Scotland, who were also involved in the second chamber and so that would give me the opportunity to influence legislation, but also to be able to talk on equal terms with other equalities' agencies and public bodies. It is part of the vision of the United Kingdom as a multicultural, multilingual, multinational state and I would use those words exactly when promoting the work of the Board with other agencies.[22]

The summer of 1992 was an important turning point in his personal and professional life. It marked the end of his 18-year career in the House of Commons, and his decision to join the House of Lords was momentous for him and his party. This gave him the opportunity to continue his political career, but in a different sphere and without the encumbrance of party affiliation. In that same summer, on the 4th of July, his relationship with Marjorie Thompson came to an end, ironically on the USA's anniversary of the Declaration of Independence.

The relationship had deteriorated over the past year. They quarrelled over Dafydd's reluctance to pay his full share of the mortgage on their London flat, and she insisted that he leave. As her leaking to *The Times* of the news about his elevation to the House of Lords suggests, the trust in their relationship had not only deteriorated but now broke down irretrievably.

He had been under financial pressure in the period between 1989 and 1992, of which his friends and family were aware. He paid maintenance for his three children, paid rent on his rural home of Maes-y-bryner, and also paid the mortgage on the family home in Dolgellau. He was also paying some of the mortgage on Marjorie's flat in London, persisting in buying fashionable clothes, and maintained a hectic lifestyle, travelling widely in his role as the party's president and MP, between Dolgellau and London, and throughout Wales.[23]

Partly in order to deal with his difficult financial position, from 1988 onwards, he undertook various freelance projects and rediscovered his delight in creative writing and broadcasting. He was commissioned by his old college friend, Cenwyn Edwards, then the director of factual programmes at HTV, to write the screenplay for a film based on the life of Islwyn, the Welsh language poet, and his poem *Y Storm*, which focussed on the death of his 20-year-old fiancée Ann Bowen, and its theme of expectation of reunion in heaven. Located in a bilingual secondary school, its curious mix of Grange Hill-like school intrigue and magical realism excited interest and controversy. In this period, his name was also linked with one of the unsuccessful bidders for the lucrative HTV franchise. He also presented a series of documentaries on Europe for BBC Wales, and was commissioned by his friend Geraint Stanley Jones, the chief executive of S4C, to write a substantial strategy document mapping out the future role of S4C. After the 1992 General Election, he returned to university lecturing, initially to Aberystwyth University to teach drama as maternity cover for Elan Closs Stephens, and 'they found out in Bangor, so I was asked to go to Bangor University. I did some stuff for the Department for Welsh Language and Literature in Cardiff. It regenerated me intellectually and emotionally'. He was also appointed as an unpaid member of the BBC's General Advisory Council, and as the paid chair of the Welsh Screen Council, responsible for the development of film in Wales.[24]

The Welsh Language Board

Both David Hunt, the Secretary of State for Wales, and Wyn Roberts, the Minister of State, had enthusiastically promoted Dafydd Elis's elevation to the House of Lords to the Prime Minister's office, who had the final decision. Their private view and expectation was that he would then become the chair of the proposed Welsh Language Board, to be set up the following year. Concerns about the Welsh language in the early 1980s had become more pronounced after the publication of the 1981 Census showing a decline in the number of Welsh speakers from 20.7 per cent of the population in 1971, to 18.9 per cent. There had been immediate demands for legislation to protect the language, with a new and more effective Welsh Language Act proposed, and with a statutory body to be created for oversight of language policy. The initial failed proposal for legislation came from Lord Gwilym Prys Davies in 1985, which was followed by a bill to amend the Welsh Language Act 1967 in order to give official status to the language, introduced by Dafydd Wigley in 1986, attracting cross-party support, including a number of Conservative MPs.[25]

As the Government's lead Minister on language policy, Wyn Roberts wished to ensure that moderate Welsh speakers, and influential elements within civil society, were not radicalised by the perception of government 'indifference'. He therefore set up an advisory body, the Welsh Language Council, with a committee of eight public figures under the chairmanship of John Elfed Jones, the head of Welsh Water.[26] But this committee's ambitions rapidly outgrew its original purpose and by its third meeting, demanded the creation of a language unit within the Welsh Office, and a permanent and funded commission to begin work on creating a framework for a new Welsh Language Act. Shortly afterwards, it was re-named the Welsh Language Board and given a statutory role. Wyn Roberts's private secretary, Huw Onllwyn Jones, recalls how his boss risked his own reputation to support this proposal:

> He was persuaded by the then non-statutory Board of the need for legislation. He hadn't cleared his agreement with David Hunt at the time, but I wrote a note immediately, circulated to the

Permanent Secretary and Secretary of State in the Welsh Office, telling of Wyn's commitment. David Hunt proved very supportive and essentially told the civil servants to 'get on with it'.[27]

The passing of the Welsh Language Act in 1993, for the first time provided the Welsh language with a defined statutory role in the public sector, and created the Welsh Language Board which was given the task of disseminating best practice through the creation of language schemes and promoting the use of the language.[28] However, language activists were disappointed by the Board's close relationship to Government, its lack of authority over the use of Welsh in the private sector, and the Government's refusal to give formal official status to the language, but it was hardly created as a pliant government quango. The majority of its Board were not political activists, but rather cultural nationalists. According to its chair, John Elfed Jones, he was asked by Hunt to continue as chair of the new Welsh Language Board, but partly due to the barrage of criticism he had suffered, often from those he had considered to have been personal friends, he declined, but would prove to be very supportive to his successor.[29]

The Welsh Language Bill had its second reading in the House of Lords on 19 January 1993. Much of the debate focussed on the fact that although Welsh was now to become an official language in Wales, there was no statement to that effect in the bill, primarily because the full, practical and legal implications of such a designation were not clear, and partly because the English language also did not have official legal status as such. The bill's requirements were confined to public sector bodies only because Government did not wish to burden private companies with linguistic demands and give them an excuse either to leave Wales or not establish there, because of the extra costs involved in offering Welsh language services. Roberts worried that the bill's passage through the House of Commons would not be as easy as its journey through the House of Lords, because the opposition were 'hell bent on mischief',[30] and confided his hope in his daily diary, that the Board would be able to remove the language issue from the political arena:

> The proposed new board will explore all the enthusiasts' aspirations for the language and deal with all the complaints too. It will promote and facilitate its use. That should be the end of the language issue politically and legally, but of course, it will only shift

the battle on to new ground – probably the financial resources available for its implementation. We shall spend £1 million and create a lot of vested interests but they will only ask for more.[31]

He reflected on the opposition to the bill from language activists, including Cymdeithas yr Iaith Gymraeg:

The Welsh Language Society is disappointed that it does not impose statutory bilingualism, which I abhor and so does Labour. The people would not tolerate such an imposition. Furthermore, it would kill the language rather than save it. Plaid Cymru is playing to the gallery of critics who would find fault with God if they had Him in the dock.[32]

The bill was first introduced in the House of Lords in January 1993, and the unamended bill was passed to the House of Commons on 25 February. Lord Elis-Thomas made his first contribution in the House of Lords during that debate on the bill and supported the Government. In a public rally in Bala, the following weekend, he was accused by his sister Elin, of having 'cotton wool in his ears' for not opposing the Welsh Language Bill.[33]

On the bill's second reading in the House of Commons, on 25 May, the Secretary of State for Wales, David Hunt, announced Lord Elis-Thomas's appointment as the new chair of the Board. Yet again in their lengthy relationship, Elis-Thomas's decision had caught Dafydd Wigley totally unaware, because he was only informed ten minutes before the beginning of the debate. The appointment was welcomed by all parts of the House, although Rhodri Morgan, the Labour Opposition spokesman, rather cynically, and misleadingly, suggested with no evidence, that the appointment was subject to a deal with Plaid Cymru to support the Government's controversial European Maastricht Treaty proposals.[34]

On the day of his appointment, Elis-Thomas was in Cardiff when he was summoned to be present in the gallery of the House of Commons for the announcement:

The funniest part of it was quite hair-raising, really. On the day of the announcement of my appointment, there came this message that I was required to be in the public gallery of the House of

Commons in four hours, because David Hunt, the Secretary of State for Wales, was making the announcement. John Elfed and I had got down to the train station and then he thought, 'No, this is not quick enough.' Instead of going all the way to Paddington, we went as far as Swindon and got a car, which he'd organised, and drove us to Westminster in good time for the announcement to be made that I was to be the chair of a new statutory Welsh language board, which hadn't been established as yet, and the legislation hadn't been passed.[35]

On the final vote on the bill, the four Plaid Cymru MPs opposed it, and together with a small number of Labour Members, forced a vote on whether the language should receive official status, but lost by 123 to 19 votes. Lord Elis-Thomas formally began his role on 15 July 1993, and Wyn Roberts wrote in his diary that his appointment may not have been 'universally popular but that his credentials were impeccable . . . [He] had cherished left-wing views at one stage but I had always found him more understanding and amenable than his colleagues on language issues. Like me, he did not treat the language as a political football.'[36]

In his new role, Elis-Thomas delighted in provoking his political foes. To the fury of his critics, even as he started on his duties, he contended that 'the battle for the language is over' and that the struggle now was to promote the use of Welsh in everyday life.[37] In his first appearance as the Board's chair on the National Eisteddfod field, in August 1993, he rebutted the critics of the new Act, and pointed to the language's resilience: 'Welsh has been an official language throughout its history. There have been attempts to reduce its functions but they have failed.' He warned against the language becoming a source of conflict, and challenged those who opposed the creation of the quango:

> We should encourage organisations to use both languages as a norm in their lives and provide a complete service, and in the future, I can't think of any public service which won't provide a Welsh language service . . . I totally fail to understand why so many believe that the wording of 'official language' is more important than having an official Board to promote the language, with wide constitutional and legal powers. As for that argument that as a statutory Board, that we are not, and won't be a democratic body,

the country of the Welsh non-departmental public bodies isn't a model of democracy in any way. To those who have a concern for democracy, campaign, as many of us did, for self-government for Wales. When an elected Senedd is created, Welsh will then be an official language, as it has always been. I don't have time to discuss linguistic negativism. The door is open for discussion.[38]

From its creation in 1993, the Language Board was targeted by Cymdeithas as an example of the iniquity of the quango system of governance, but they in turn were accused of 'running in the wrong direction' by the author of its original manifesto, the MP for Ceredigion, Cynog Dafis. The *Western Mail* reported a public meeting in the National Eisteddfod to discuss the new Welsh Language Act, pitting young Cymdeithas activists against the chair of the Language Board:

> During an Eisteddfod show-down between Cymdeithas chairman Alun Llwyd and Lord Elis-Thomas, chair-designate of the Welsh Language Board, Mr [Cynog] Dafis said that 'there would have been no development of the language over the past 20 years without the language society. But that doesn't mean they don't make mistakes – and I believe they are making a mistake now'. Mr Llwyd retorted 'Do we really believe John Redwood[39] is going to choose the people we want to see on the quango?' Speaking from the floor Dafis warned Cymdeithas that 'it would be dangerous causing people who hold the language dear to be afraid of taking up a post on the Welsh Language Board'. Although the debate had been called by Cymdeithas, roughly half the audience seemed to side with Dafydd Elis-Thomas and Plaid Cymru.[40]

The membership of the statutory Board was appointed in November 1993 and included thirteen individuals[41] who covered the spectrum of Welsh speaking Wales and beyond. The names were agreed between Roberts and Elis-Thomas, and John Walter Jones, a trusted civil servant who had served in Wyn Roberts's private office, was appointed chief executive.[42] In Elis-Thomas's first formal meeting with David Hunt after his appointment, the Secretary of State ventured playfully that 'we're taking a big risk with you. One minute you're in the Commons denouncing the Conservative Government. Then you get a peerage – and now you're working for a public body under a Conservative Government.' 'Yes, but circumstances change', Elis-Thomas replied.⁴³

When in September 1989, in the conversation with Wigley, Elis-Thomas, then Plaid Cymru President, had put forward the future strategy for the party of 'a march through the institutions' and moving from a 'quango state' to a democratically elected parliament, it had seemed an extremely gradualist and abstract proposal. His decision to chair one of the Government's most high-profile public bodies in Wales therefore seemed bold and extremely surprising. There was no doubt about the depth of influence of quangos in Wales. In 1991, the Secretary of State for Wales made 1,400 appointments to eighty quangos, a narrow definition that excluded bodies like the myriad training bodies, for example. A 1995 survey, based on a broader definition of quangos, such as the inclusion of health trusts, showed there were about 350 quangos in Wales.⁴⁴ Formal appointment processes lacked transparency and lay in the hands of individual Ministers. Tony Lewis (TL), an eminent former cricketer and also a Welsh Conservative, was appointed with little formal process to become chair of the Wales Tourist Board. He gave evidence about his appointment to the Select Committee on Welsh Affairs and its chair, Gareth Wardell (GW) MP:

> GW: You did not have an interview at all?
> TL: Nothing at all.
> GW: You had a letter just confirming your appointment as Chairman of the Board?
> TL: No, I had a telephone call to ask if I would accept tourism then I think I had the form and then I think the official letter came.
> GW: But in fact no interview, no situation where you were asked detailed questions by a panel of people, nothing like that?
> TL: No
> GW: Just a straightforward telephone call asking you whether you would like the job and then in fact a letter confirming your appointment?
> TL: Yes.⁴⁵

The Minister of State in the Welsh Office, Wyn Roberts, was the go-between for this undemanding selection process, as he was for hundreds of similar appointments throughout the 1980s and 1990s. It was of course difficult to find reliable Conservative members in a country where they were so weakly represented, with only six of the 36 Welsh MPs in 1992-7 being Conservative and almost extinct in local government, and where civil servants in London and Cardiff had only limited knowledge of individuals proposed for specific posts.[46] When the Thatcherite John Redwood, became Secretary of State for Wales in June 1993 he found both the Welsh Conservative party, and the Welsh policy process, a bitter disappointment. There were no Tory think-tanks, few Tory intellectuals, and little commitment to Thatcherite principles. Redwood saw the Conservative party in Wales as a 'decadent party' weakened by government largesse and dominated by 'quango crazy sycophants'.[47]

Even Wyn Roberts accepted, privately, that the days of the 'quango state' were numbered. In his diary entry, following a debate in the House of Commons on Public Accounts Committee proceedings on 25 October 1993, the arch-exponent of the appointment system admitted that:

> the scope for dishonesty is vast! The ultimate consequences for Wales are serious. Both the Welsh Development Agency and the Development Board for Rural Wales will be discredited and maybe the whole quango system. There will be a case for making them directly accountable to a Welsh elected body – it will be argued – or for abolishing them altogether.[48]

For the academic and Cymdeithas activist Richard Wyn Jones, the system of quango appointments were a sinister method of curbing dissent:

> There is a tendency among those sections of civil society which have to deal with agencies such as the Language Board to keep quiet and avoid rocking the boat. This is the self-censorship which ensures uniformity and quiescence within civil society . . . This is a deliberate and explicit attempt to 'de-politicise' the language question; or more correctly, an attempt to marginalise those discordant voices who deign to cast doubt on the political elite's vision of the future.

He criticised Elis-Thomas for attempting to suppress Cymdeithas's constant criticism of the Board, but also accepted that their view may have

1. (*above*) 'Popular and attractive'. Dafydd's parents' wedding in April 1944, in a photograph taken at the Cawdor Hotel, Newcastle Emlyn, after the service at Bethania Methodist chapel. From left to right, unknown, Revd Huw Llywelyn Williams (best man and W.E.'s cousin), W.E., Eirlys, her sister Gwenfil, her uncle Tom Davies; seated, W.E.'s sister Annie Thomas, and Eirlys's mother Mary James.

2. 'The golden child' with his favourite toy.

3. Dafydd and his sister Elin Mair, before the harp competition at the local Llanrwst Eisteddfod 1960. Note Dafydd's CND badge.

4. *(below)* Dafydd among the winners of the Urdd public speaking competition for Welsh grammar schools, at Llanrwst Grammar School, 1964. From left to right, G. O. Jones (Welsh teacher), Dafydd, Norma Lloyd Roberts, R. J. Parry (headmaster), and Rosemary Roberts.

5. *(above)* Leading Plaid Cymru students, at the centre of the protest against the opening of the Tryweryn dam, 21 October 1965. © Reach Plc.

Lone "rebellion" at UCNW graduation ceremony

Sit-down protest during anthem

A 20 years old honours graduate sat down in the front row at Monday's graduation ceremony at University College, Bangor, while the national anthem "God Save the Queen" was being played.

Mr. Dafydd Elis Thomas, of Frondeg, Llanrwst, who earlier received a first class honours degree in Welsh, told reporters: "I always do this when I am in Wales because I do not acknowledge the Queen of England as queen of my country."

Mr. Thomas, who is a member of Plaid Cymru and of the Welsh Language Society, added "I was also making a protest against the way in which no effort was made at the ceremony to speak Welsh correctly."

No attempt was made to pronounce Welsh phrases correctly, said Mr. Thomas. "This is typical of the attitude in this university college towards the Welsh language. It was as if an attempt was being made to make a joke of the language.

The incident took place after the playing of "Hen Wlad fy Nhadau."

GREETED IN WELSH

During the ceremony, at which 213 students received degrees, the Dean of the Faculty of Art, Professor C. W. K. Mundle, presented students to be admitted in Welsh. They were received on the stage by the acting vice-chancellor, Professor Paul Richards, who spoke in Welsh, and then greeted by the President of the University, Lord Kenyon, again in Welsh.

Of the 213 degrees awarded, 12 were with first class honours, 112 with second class honours, 10 with third class honours and 76 were ordinary BA degrees. Three students received honours B.Mus. degrees.

Mr. Dafydd Elis Thomas.

6. The lone protester at his own degree ceremony, July 1967.

7. His wedding to Elen at Ebeneser Wesleyan chapel, Dolgellau, July 1970. From left to right, best man Derec Llwyd Morgan, Dafydd's mother Eirlys, Dafydd, Elen, Margaret Williams, Dafydd's sister Elin Mair Thomas, and Elen's mother Mary Williams.

8. 'What just happened?' The announcement of Dafydd's victory, in the early hours of 1 March 1974. From left to right, Merioneth returning officer Ieuan Lloyd Jones, Elen (behind, the Conservative candidate Roy Owen), Dafydd, and the Plaid Cymru organiser in Merioneth Elfed Roberts.

9. The rise of Welsh nationalism? The jubilant scene outside Parliament, when Gwynfor Evans joined the two Dafydds in Parliament, October 1974. © Aled Betts.

10. The 'President's committee' held at Gwynfor Evans's home in Llangadog, 1975. Meetings were usually restricted to Evans's close allies, but now included other key Plaid figures. From left to right, Gwynfor Evans, Dafydd Elis Thomas, Phil Williams, Dafydd Wigley, party researcher Rob Griffiths, Eurfyl ap Gwilym, and party general secretary Dafydd Williams. © Plaid Cymru.

11. Street politics rather than parliamentary debate – the anti-apartheid campaign was one of Dafydd's numerous causes. He was a vice-president of the movement and led this protest march through Cardiff in 1982. From left to right, chair of Anti-Apartheid Wales Chris Short, Labour MP for Rhondda (1983–2001) Allan Rogers, Dafydd, and secretary of the UK Anti-Apartheid Movement Mike Terry.

12. Dafydd and Elen's three sons in their flat in Willesden Green, London, in 1981. From left to right, the eldest Rolant, the youngest Cai, and Meilyr.

13. 'Intoxicated with each other'. With Marjorie Thompson at his 'gentleman's residence' of Maes y Bryner. Their relationship lasted eight years until the summer of 1992.

14. Dafydd and Mair Parry-Jones on their wedding day, 29 December 1993. They were married at Conwy registry office, with only two witnesses present.

15. Leading the protest march in St Davids against the Ministry of Defence proposals to raise radar masts at RAF Brawdy in July 1990. From left to right, Osi Rhys Osmond (flag on shoulder), Syd Morgan, Gwerfyl Arthur, Dafydd Iwan, Jill Evans, Cynog Dafis, and Dafydd.

16. A production meeting in 1988 with his college friend Cenwyn Edwards, head of drama and factual programmes at HTV, to discuss the drama based on the poet Islwyn's doomed love affair – a 'curious mix of Grange Hill-like school intrigue and magical realism'. © ITV Wales.

17. Dafydd's last speech as Plaid Cymru President at the party's annual conference in Porthmadog, October 1991. He arrived an hour late for his own speech, after being delayed on his return from the Queen's opening of the Conwy tunnels.

18. The handover in 1992. The Plaid Cymru MPs welcoming Elfyn Llwyd as Dafydd's successor in Parliament. From left to right, Dafydd Wigley, Elfyn Llwyd, Dafydd Elis-Thomas, and Ieuan Wyn Jones. © Plaid Cymru.

19. As chairman of the Welsh language Board, Dafydd rarely missed the opportunity to bait language activists – here at the National Eisteddfod in 1994.

20. With the Hollywood actor Sir Anthony Hopkins, April 1998, at the launch of the successful National Trust appeal to buy a farm on the slopes of Eryri. Hopkins chaired the appeal and, donated a million pounds towards the target of three million. Dafydd was vice-president of the appeal.

21. Celebrating the devolution referendum victory in the early hours of 19 September 1997, at the Park Hotel, Cardiff. From left to right, MP for Cardiff West and later First Minister Rhodri Morgan, Dafydd, and Rhodri Morgan's researcher Kevin Brennan (who later succeeded Morgan as MP for Cardiff West).

22. The plan for the National Assembly building. Richard Rogers's model for the chamber was exhibited to Members, Dafydd accompanied here by Minister for Finance and Local Government Edwina Hart (2000–3). These two close colleagues were instrumental in ensuring the building of the new Assembly.

23. Not a football team, but the remarkable honorary doctorate graduates at Bangor University, June 2009. Left to right, back row, Lord Merfyn Davies of Abersoch, Lord Dafydd Elis-Thomas (University Chancellor), Sir Peter Davies, Professor Merfyn Jones (Vice-Chancellor), Dr Malcolm Jones, Professor Gareth Edwards-Jones, David Roberts (Registrar); front row, the recipients of honorary degrees, Rhodri Morgan (First Minister), Archbishop Desmond Tutu, Professor John Meurig Thomas, Sir David Attenborough. © Bangor University.

24. The opening of the National Assembly building by the Queen on St David's Day 2006. From left to right, Lord Lieutenant of South Glamorgan Sir Norman Lloyd-Edwards, Camilla Princess of Wales, Charles Prince of Wales, First Minister Rhodri Morgan, The Duke of Edinburgh, The Queen, and Lord Dafydd Elis-Thomas.

25. Their last conversation. King Charles and Dafydd during the ceremony to mark twenty-five years of Welsh devolution.

26. The last journey. The funeral procession before the Senedd, led by the former Archbishop of Wales, Rt. Revd Dr Barry Morgan, with the staff of the Senedd forming a guard of honour for Lord Dafydd Elis-Thomas, 14 March 2025. © Matthew Horwood.

27. The packed congregation at Llandaff Cathedral to celebrate and pay tribute to a life well lived, 14 March 2025. © Matthew Horwood.

been 'too simplistic . . . . Dafydd Elis's decision to migrate from the party-political world to "quangoland" was part of a specific and deliberate political strategy'.[49] Elis-Thomas's successor as chair of the Language Board, Rhodri Williams, recalled that Dafydd had been amongst those who opposed the Conservative Government's ideology, but also thought that ignoring it gave little advantage:

> We had a way of going forward. People like Cymdeithas yr Iaith Gymraeg were critical of him, and for someone who had been so prominent on the left, people struggled with what he had done, but the one thing about Dafydd was that he was exceptionally bright and always a couple of steps in front of other people in this period. People would later see the fruit of what he put in place.[50]

The first challenge for the Board was to introduce a new system of language schemes for the public sector, and voluntary schemes in the private and voluntary sectors. Elis-Thomas viewed the securing of Welsh as part of the national curriculum to be an important precursor for their work:

> We weren't starting from scratch, but from the national curriculum ... a similar idea of equality between two languages had already been established in law, so that was very helpful. We began by making the Welsh Office itself have the equivalent of a language scheme, and we expected other departments of the UK estate that were administrating Wales, including the administration of justice, to follow suit. I think the most difficult thing was explaining to people what the principle meant, and how it would work. The key thing I didn't want was disagreement. I didn't want public bodies saying that we can't do it because this is too difficult. I was very fortunate in the high quality of my chief executive and of the officials of the Board, people who'd been trained in the Welsh Office or in administration and education. We had people on the Board who were experienced in public life in Wales and who understood exactly what we were trying to do, which was to create consent for the language.
>
> The other thing that was important was making sure that Welsh local education authorities and all the agencies who had

to implement these schemes would not find it difficult and we made it clear that we weren't looking for consistency throughout Wales, either in the services that would be available or in the way the administration worked. What we wanted to do was show that we were generating demand as a result of the new legislation in a way that would work in the different parts of Wales.

People thought that we were going to try to force them to do something. I remember a meeting I had in Monmouthshire and I'd decided that the way to handle this was to understate pretty radically what we wanted them to do because people might object. We said the same to the eastern areas of Powys, for instance. Clwyd was different because there'd been a long history of secondary Welsh medium education in the county. It was quite funny really because after I'd had this initial discussion with Monmouthshire, they came back and said they wanted to do more than we had asked them to do.

It was an astounding success but that was mainly down to the quality of the officials and the way we did it and the support we got from Welsh local government and from people who themselves had indicated that they wanted to support the language and indeed in some cases, learned it, like the Blaenau Gwent council leader, Peter Law, an amazing person. It was amazing that counties and services were competing with each other in the implementation of this legislation. That was something very special but very creative and productive.

I was also keen to avoid this terrible thing that used to work across a lot of public appointments, that posts needed to be Welsh essential or Welsh desirable (well, Welsh is desirable everywhere). We were successful because we adopted an approach which was not intended to get people's backs up. The people who were most shocked at what we were trying to do were the people I met from the Irish Language Board and Catalonia and the Basque country, because they just couldn't understand how it was possible that the United Kingdom government, through its territorial department in Wales, was promoting the language. The approach was firmly based on what the Government wanted and what parliament had agreed and for that reason I felt that I was in a very strong position.[51]

He set out his philosophy of language renewal in his BBC lecture in January 1994, titled *A Life for the Language*, a conscious echo of Saunders Lewis's seminal radio lecture in 1962, *Tynged yr Iaith* (The Fate of the Language), which had called for a revolution in attitudes towards the language in public life. In his view, Lewis's lecture was now 'terribly old fashioned in style, in ideas and in content', and considered it to be 'redolent of its age . . . eschatological in the context of the threat of nuclear holocaust. The world, Wales and the Welsh language were seen to be under fateful pressure.' His contribution was an antidote to Saunders Lewis's doom-laden apocalyptic vision:

> The greatest challenge to the language is safeguarding Welsh as a community language, enhancing the opportunities for the increasing numbers of young people who speak the language and for the learners who are busily learning the language, and defending the language itself from being debased.

He gave the example of Menter Cwm Gwendraeth as a successful local enterprise run by local people, and emphasised the enhancement of the opportunities for speakers of the language as a vital part of its promotional work:

> The Act enhances the status of the language – we have already seen private companies' awareness of the Welsh language increasing daily. They have started to see the commercial advantages the language gives them. The Welsh Language Act and its implementation can help us. That is certain. But that is not the final salvation. Let everyone examine his own conscience. There is little point in relying on the dedication of the few. The greatest enemy to the Welsh language is the apathy of the majority, not the alleged deficiencies of legislation.

In a swipe at Cymdeithas yr Iaith, he warned against those carping voices whose 'endless unconstructive bickering and constant negative attitudes . . . will cause us to lose the battle', and called on them to work in harmony together:

> Instead of seeing the Welsh language constantly under threat from economic, social, demographic or political forces, we

should concentrate rather on its strength and on its revival as a means of translating those experiences, and by translating them, assimilating them. That is my vision of life for the language as part of a European and worldwide multi-lingual pattern for its next millennium.[52]

Cymdeithas yr Iaith attempted but ultimately failed to undermine the Board.[53] The constant refrain from the new statutory Board chair echoed Wyn Roberts's earlier wish to take the language out of the political arena. In the 1995-6 Welsh Language Board Report, Dafydd Elis stated that 'one of the most encouraging developments is seeing the Welsh language gradually rise above party politics. Today, all the main political parties in Wales have strong policies in relation to the Welsh language.'

In 1997, he wrote of his pleasure at the political consensus during the General Election in favour of the language, and noted the 'unequivocal commitment to the language in New Labour's manifesto for Wales'. In his last report, in 1998, after five and a half years as chair, he again welcomed 'the importance of consensus where Welsh is concerned, so that the language may rise above party politics ... I am confident that that will continue when the National Assembly for Wales begins its work.'[54]

Under his chairmanship, he attempted to re-distribute public spending on the Welsh language in order to increase its impact. He held independent reviews of the effectiveness of the National Eisteddfod, Urdd Gobaith Cymru (the Welsh League of Youth), and the Books Council of Wales. He made a significant cultural statement in his decision to cut the National Eisteddfod's grant by £100,000, challenging the venerable institution to improve its own fundraising efforts, and diverted the funding to local language ventures and targeted the youngest children through the Welsh Nursery Schools Movement. More funding was directed towards giving opportunities for young people to learn and use their Welsh, and a Board member at the time, Rhodri Williams, recalls difficult conversations with their more traditionally minded clients:

> Dafydd questioned why so much funding went to the National Eisteddfod and so little on the Welsh language nursery schools movement, Mudiad Ysgolion Meithrin. During his first year, he had a controversial meeting with representatives of the

National Eisteddfod Council in the board's offices in central Cardiff. These members of the Eisteddfod 'Sanhedrin' included heavyweight public figures such as Alwyn Roberts, a former National Governor of the BBC, Gwilym Humphreys, former director of education for Gwynedd, and the former chief executive of South Glamorgan council, Hugh Thomas. They had come to demand an increase in the money paid to the institution, and in the meeting room, they refused to be seated and demanded to know by what right Dafydd Elis-Thomas was taking away some of their funding and alleged that he was undermining the Festival.

Williams recalls that their response 'reflected the view of some entitled Welsh-speaking Welshmen that it was they who should decide how much money they should be granted'. The meeting became so acrimonious that Elis-Thomas walked out, quickly followed by his chief executive, and fellow Board member, Rhodri Williams. Following this meeting, and the review of the National Eisteddfod, he increased the grant given to the nursery school movement from £10,000 in 1995–6 to over half a million pounds in 1996–7, and the nascent local Welsh language consortia named 'Mentrau Iaith', which encouraged the use of the language at a local level, also benefited.[55]

For both the Board and Wyn Roberts, a mark of the success of Elis-Thomas's strategy was to draw the political sting out of the language issue, and secure cross-party support. Steve Eaves, a prominent Cymdeithas activist, reflected that before the 1993 Act, Labour had been perceived to have been against the Welsh language, Plaid for the Welsh language, and it had developed into a political football. What the legislation set in motion, under a Conservative Government, was 'the process of depoliticising the language . . . suddenly people saw there was nothing political about having bilingual signage at the hospital in Bangor. We all speak Welsh here.'[56]

Language activist and nationalist Sion Jobbins, pays tribute to his success:

Dafydd Elis-Thomas said, 'look, we're not going to make the language an issue now'. To some extent, after '93, people were tired. People had given a lot of time to the language; there's a natural inclination then for people to get on with their lives. I think by '97, the Welsh language had been depoliticised to some extent. Wyn Roberts had made Welsh compulsory in school. and I don't think a lot of people registered this ... Cymdeithas decided 'OK, we're taking time off', and they didn't make big demands.[57]

Elis-Thomas came to regret that as the chair of the Language Board, he could sometimes be carelessly acerbic in his criticisms of the language organisations that stood to gain most from the Board's support:

'Whingers' was what I called people who were complaining against what we were doing. I may have been impatient with some people who couldn't see what we were trying to do. The language organisations and many communities were all benefiting in one way or another through the support that they were getting from Government in different forms, from particular schemes. I was trying to create a development agency model, and ... it made it easier for people if they could see there was some benefit to them ... in working alongside the board.[58]

Dafydd Elis's legacy as chair was that he gave people a sense of security around the language, and ensured that the language wasn't perceived as a threat, according to Rhodri Williams:

He and the Board received a great deal of criticism but he thought through how to influence Government. They were criticised fiercely but were long-sighted enough to ensure that if their work was to succeed, they needed the support of the Government. By 1999 and the introduction of devolution, the Welsh language had moved on from being a controversial issue to being mainstreamed. When the Assembly was established, we had a national democratic institution, that would operate totally bilingually, and for that, Dafydd's role in the Board was crucial.[59]

As chair, Elis-Thomas altered the tone of the discussion around the future of the Welsh language, and over 350 Welsh language schemes were agreed with public bodies. His own valedictory verdict on his role as chair of the Language Board is unsurprisingly optimistic, but he considers that 'the Board's emphasis from the outset was consistently on developing partnerships, on undertaking our statutory duties under the Welsh Language Act and most important perhaps by ensuring that support for the language lay beyond party politics'.[60]

Quite consciously, he set out his stall for his next role, highlighting in his last report as chair, that the Board was already collaborating with the future National Assembly, the first bilingual parliamentary body in Britain, to provide a creative impetus for promoting bilingualism and linguistic understanding.[61] The 1993 Welsh Language Act had fallen short of the expectation of many who had campaigned for the legislation, but nevertheless it was a turning point in the promotion of the Welsh language. It transformed the role that the Welsh language played within public administration in Wales and created 'a discourse within institutions which had never previously been required to discuss the needs of Welsh speakers'.[62] He ensured that the Welsh Language Board became a promotion agency rather than a narrow regulatory body and created the first coherent example of minority language planning in the UK.

The 1997 devolution referendum campaign

The 1997 referendum campaign contrasted markedly with the 1979 campaign in its lack of vitriol over the language issue. Whereas in 1979 the language issue had been seized by opponents of devolution who described the Assembly as creating 'jobs for the boys', or accusations that the language 'would be forced down people's throats' by making it compulsory throughout Wales, it had lost its political piquancy by the 1997 devolution campaign.[63] Widespread political acceptance of the Welsh language had moved it from being an inflammatory and controversial subject to at least a tolerated part of Wales's national life. When the National Assembly was established, it operated fully bilingually from the very beginning, and the role of the Board in delivering that was all important.

By the time he stood down from the Board in March 1999, he had established a new tone for public discourse about the Welsh language, and both the UK Government and the parties campaigning for the nascent Assembly supported it and emphasised the promotion and facilitation of the language.

The chairmanship of the Welsh Language Board had been a part-time appointment for two days a week, but he also undertook an exhaustive myriad of public roles throughout the 1990s. Between 1992 and 1999, he was a board member of the Welsh Arts Council, the Ramblers' Association, the National Trust, and the BBC's General Consultative Council. He was Vice-President of Swansea's Year of Literature, President of the Hay on Wye Literary Festival, the Llangollen International Eisteddfod, Keep Wales Tidy and a member of the Wales Committee of the National Trust and the Prince of Wales's Trust. He was a paid director of an environmental company based in Bangor, a paid chairman of SGRIN, Wales's Film Agency, and a board member of cultural bodies including Oriel Mostyn in Llandudno, the National Botanical Gardens and MFM Marcher, the commercial radio station for north-east Wales and the Marches. He was also a trustee of the Big Issue Foundation, the theatre company *Theatr Bara Caws*, and, quixotically, the honorary president of the Welsh National Culinary Team, 'active in recording the quality of Welsh food'. In the House of Lords he was also a member of the environment and European committees.[64]

These numerous cultural and social commitments showed a remarkable appetite for public life as well as a need to supplement his income, and they coincided with a new relationship, with a distant cousin, Mair Parry-Jones. They had met in the summer of 1992, and Mair ran a translation company in Caernarfon. On 29 December 1993, on a bitterly cold day, Dafydd re-married discreetly at Conwy Registry Office, with only two witnesses present, and a photographer. Both their mothers were only informed on the morning of the wedding and were absolutely livid not to be invited. This private ceremony was followed by a blessing by a friendly priest in a local church. Their honeymoon was spent in a hotel in Dyffryn Ceiriog, which they had booked after seeing a special holiday deal advertised in the *Daily Post*, but which unfortunately, attracted a number of other romantic couples from the Caernarfon area, including a number of their acquaintances and friends, who had spotted the same tempting bargain, and were surprised by the well-known newly-weds' presence. They settled in the centre of Caernarfon, and from there, Dafydd commuted to the Welsh Language Board's headquarters in Cardiff or to London and the House of Lords. Their friends in the town tended to be university-educated middle-class nationalists, and the newly ennobled Lord was easily lampooned by his friends and neighbours. One of the most popular satires directed towards him was by one of Mair's co-translators, Geraint Løvgreen, whose song *Cân yr Arglwydd* (The Song of the Lord), written in 1999, is an exuberant invective that satirised his antipathy to traditional nationalism:

> Ein harweinydd ysbrydol yw'r hen Dafydd El (Our spiritual leader is Dafydd El)
> Come on now baby join the Party of Wales.
>
> CHORUS:
> Lord Elis-Thomas, dwi'n sôn am Arglwydd Elis-Thomas. (I'm talking about Lord Dafydd El)
> Fo ' di Llywydd y Blaid, Plaid Lewis Valentine a DJ a Saunders.
> (He's President of the Party, the party of Lewis Valentine, DJ and Saunders)
> Dio'm yn genedlaetholwr nac yn ffasgydd ychwaith
> Dio ddim yn licio bois Cymdeithas yr Iaith.
> (He's not a nationalist or a fascist either
> He doesn't like the boys of Cymdeithas yr Iaith)
>
> CHORUS:
> Os ti'n Sais gwrth-Gymraeg neu'n berchennog ty ha'
> Mi ffeindi di fod y Lord yn ddiawch o foi da.
> (if you're anti-Welsh English or a summer home owner
> You'll find that the Lord is a hell of a good guy.)
>
> CHORUS:
> Mae o'n lladd ar y Meibion[65] ond o blaid ANC,[66]
> Mae gwrthryfela'n iawn ond ddim yn gwlad ni.
> (He's against Meibion but in favour of the ANC,
> Rebelling is fine but not in our country.)
>
> CHORUS:
> If you're scared that the Welshies gonna burn your house down,
> You'll be OK as long as the Lord is around. [67]

This chorus of contempt from traditional Plaid Cymru supporters would follow him for the next twenty years, but he felt no loyalty to the traditional version of Welsh nationalism and railed furiously against those who either supported Meibion Glyndŵr's arson campaign, or remained silent.

As a cross-bencher in the House of Lords, and as chair of a Government sponsored quango, he had little direct engagement with Plaid Cymru between 1993 and 1998, but his role as chair of the Language Board gave him a high public profile. Plaid Cymru's view of his role in the Language Board was ambivalent, for he had positive relationships with many Plaid members who were active in language organisations, and he worked closely with local government leaders in all regions of Wales, so that he maintained and renewed a wide spectrum of political networks. Because of his formal role in the Language Board, he could not involve himself publicly in the campaign for the National Assembly for Wales during the 1997 Referendum.

However, less than a year before hand, in October 1996, Peter Hain, who would become the Welsh Office Minister responsible for organising the devolution campaign, was briefed, interestingly, by both Dafydd Wigley and Dafydd Elis-Thomas, about their party's stance on devolution, and made firmly aware of Plaid's doubts about Labour's ability to deliver:

> Elis-Thomas sharply warned Peter that he himself would not repeat the mistakes of 1979, with Plaid having to support Labour's campaign while Labour MPs campaigned actively against it. Peter understood that Plaid and the Liberal Democrats saw Labour's proposals as weak but argued that they could maintain their own integrity and their distinctive positions while acting alongside the all-party Yes campaign.[68]

Labour won a handsome majority in the May 1997 General Election and maintained their commitment to hold referenda on devolution in Scotland and Wales. Plaid Cymru activists were suspicious of repeating the experience of the 1979 referendum and of being the foot soldiers in an ultimately disappointing campaign. The party did not finally decide on its policy towards the vote until a special conference on 26 July 1997, held only eight weeks before the referendum. Wigley suggested that Plaid should oppose Labour's plans if no increase in devolved powers were offered, but Dafydd Elis indicated he would be prepared to compromise and back the plans as long as Labour campaigned for its own proposals. As a result, while Plaid continued to emphasise its campaign to achieve the same powers as Scotland, it desisted from criticising the Labour Government's proposals.[69] Importantly, as Wigley stated, 'there were lessons we learnt for the 1997 referendum from the 1979 referendum to make sure that we were welded into Ron Davies's thinking.'[70]

A group of Plaid activists argued that Plaid should take on a more radical position so that Yes for Wales should be seen as a more moderate campaign, but Elis-Thomas criticised this stance for creating confusion. He was also angrily dismissive of the pessimists within Plaid in the early days of the campaign:

> There are some people, fundamentalists in both religion and politics, people that I always find difficulty in talking to, they are about ... deifying or raising up the ideology over and above the practical programme and they're the people who lead people into the wilderness and make them suffer for forty years and they're no bloody use to anybody.[71]

The political parties and organisations on the left worked together through the Yes for Wales campaign, and in spite of his public position as a quango chair, he spoke at Yes rallies. Val Feld, the Labour activist, recalled that Elis-Thomas 'was there for Plaid ... The "Yes for Wales" activists watched transfixed at the spirit of inclusivity that was breaking out. I remember the moment when Dafydd Elis-Thomas kissed Anita Gale (the Labour party general secretary for Wales) and Hywel (Francis) and I, sort of standing back, and saying "we're making history here".'[72] The campaign brought together people of all parties, apart from the Conservatives, and re-united those who had worked together diligently during the miners' strike.

The outcome of the momentous referendum on devolution in Wales, held a week after the Scottish Referendum, on 18 September, was extremely close, with the Yes campaign for the Assembly side winning by only 6,721 votes. Elis-Thomas had been extremely nervous about the result:

> I wasn't confident at all really, and I spent most of my time making the most minimalist case possible, and denouncing people who talked about self-government and about other grandiose terms or worse, such as independence, and overstating the case.

What I always believe about Welsh politics is that it moves by gradual changes ... it's no use running ahead of opinion. My argument was that it was the question of accountability for decisions and that devolution was nothing new, that we'd had delegated government, we'd had forms of devolution but it had been administrative, not policy making, and we couldn't actually do things differently, properly, because we hadn't got the capacity or the institutions. Therefore the only way we can deal with it is by having an elected body which is sufficiently powerful to be able to influence things but it's got to be incremental ... The last thing I wanted in a devolution campaign was an appeal to old fashioned, cultural nationalism, because that's not what it was about.

He emphasised the importance of being able to appeal to the English incomers to mid-Wales, for instance, in the referendum campaign:

I think it's been very important over the years that we've been able to appeal to people who've come in to live to Wales from wherever, that there are things going on here that are worth supporting and being part of and that's not defined by nationalism. I was so surprised by the result that I made it my pin number – I remember it to this day.

I had a bit of fun, because I did the Radio Wales results programme with Vincent Kane and a few others, overnight. Because I'd just been doing the language schemes of Welsh local authorities, I'd been around a lot of them, I knew fairly well what the political tendencies were in a lot of these, so when results started coming through, in Wrexham or the old Glamorgan and Monmouth, I said, well this is very good because these are areas that I wouldn't have expected to have voted so substantially in the way they have and of course everybody else was predicting a No vote.

I got the result long before it was actually announced. I knew that the Yes vote would be big in Carmarthen because of its political history, so when it happened, I just felt that everything I'd done had been vindicated, that everything had been worth the trouble.[73]

In early 1998, Dafydd Elis-Thomas decided to stand for the new National Assembly for Wales in the Meirionnydd Nant Conwy constituency. He was encouraged by local Plaid members, and he had strong support from family and friends:

> It went back to what my father said, that when people asked you to do something, you don't think twice about it (well actually, you think about it for a few hours) and then you say, yes, because if they think you're good enough to do something, then it's not up to you to tell them, no, I'm not going to do it – that is arrogance. I had huge loyalty from people in the old Meirionnydd, and then Nant Conwy, because that's where I was brought up and have lived for most of my life . . . and I also felt I owed something to the community which has made me what I am.[74]

One of his most active supporters, Elwyn Vaughan, acted as his minder, 'watching my back and ensuring that I didn't antagonise people more than was absolutely necessary, if I was trying to do something new'. There were still those causes and communities that he had supported strongly as an MP, such as the Trawsfynydd nuclear power station, the slate communities of Blaenau Ffestiniog, Corris, Aberllefenni and Abergynolwyn, the farming community, and organisations such as the National Trust, one of the major landlords in the area: 'I didn't need much persuasion but on the other hand, it was gratifying to be asked to carry on doing the things I had been doing in the Westminster context.'[75]

He had retained his personal involvement in Meirionnydd Nant Conwy throughout his period as chair of the Welsh Language Board, and was passionately committed to Parc Cenedlaethol Eryri – the Snowdonia National Park – created in 1951, that included most of the constituency. He became vice-President to Sir Anthony Hopkins's Snowdonia Appeal for the National Trust, which bought part of Yr Wyddfa (Snowdon) – the Hafod y Llan farm, near Beddgelert, on the southern flank of the mountain.

His selection as the Assembly candidate for his old Parliamentary constituency was in little doubt. Dyfrig Siencyn, later the chair of his constituency party and leader of Gwynedd Council, was one of ten candidates who stood for the seat. He recalls approaching Dafydd in the National Eisteddfod in Bala in 1997 to ask if he would support him for the candidacy. His response was to advise him 'to stand in the queue'. At the hustings meeting in Dolgellau, Dafydd, according to Siencyn, 'wiped the floor' with the other candidates. His immediate rivals were Liz Saville Roberts and Dr Carl Clowes, but the vote in his favour was overwhelming. There was little concern about his views on language policy, for example, and there was a general acceptance that he would make controversial remarks from time to time.[76] In October 1998, Dafydd and Mair moved from Caernarfon to Penceunant, a smallholding that had belonged to Mair's family, near Swallow Falls, outside Betws-y-Coed, and located conveniently within the Meirionnydd Nant Conwy constituency:

> The changes in my personal life meant I still lived in the areas I represented, or just about, and so I was involved in social activity and in all that goes on in countryside life ... people were encouraging. In 1998, as the legislation for the creation of the National Assembly for Wales began to be discussed in the Houses of Parliament, it included the creation of the first Presiding Officer role. That was something which I'd never imagined that I would do but I realised, thinking about it in the cold light of day ... that I had experiences in Wales and in United Kingdom politics which meant that I had a network and experience that would be very useful. I had taken an interest from the beginning in parliamentary procedure, because I had done a lot of 'whip type work' in the Commons or I had sat on select committees and various other committees in both Houses, over the years, which meant that I not only understood parliamentary procedure, but could assist people in making more effective use of it.[77]

He resigned from the Welsh Language Board on 28 February 1999, on his adoption as a candidate. When asked at the time if he had his sights on becoming the National Assembly's first Presiding Officer, his response was both diplomatic and combative:

> That's for colleagues, isn't it? But it would be about campaigning for the body as a force in the UK and Europe, a champion for the new body. That role would certainly appeal to me. I don't want 'front-benchers' and 'back-benchers' in Cardiff. I don't want the silly mumbo-jumbo of the Hon. Member this and

Rt Hon. Member that, and Lord this and that, carrying maces and jumping about, state prayers and all that.[78]

He certainly would not wish to transfer Parliament's archaic practices to the new democratic institution of the first National Assembly for Wales. For those familiar with Lord Elis-Thomas's train of thought, his interest in the role of Presiding Officer suggested that he was already auditioning for the role.

6

The Birth of the National Assembly for Wales

Lord Dafydd Elis-Thomas's most politically significant legacy was his role as the first Presiding Officer of the National Assembly for the first twelve years of its existence, from May 1999 until May 2011. He and Rhodri Morgan, the second First Minister, between February 2000 and December 2009, laid the foundations of devolution, separating the parliamentary body from the Government, and to laying the foundations of the new institution as a law-making body.

Together with allies such as Edwina Hart, then the Minister for Local Government, and Sue Essex, the Minister for the Environment, Dafydd Elis-Thomas secured a home for Welsh national democracy in the building of the Senedd, in the teeth of widespread political opposition. His aspiration was to create a modern, bilingual democratic parliamentary institution that would be unrivalled in its transparency and openness. This, he believed, should be reflected in the maturing of its politics and be symbolised by the new Assembly building.

By the time of the devolution vote in 1997, the political landscape seemed very different to the context of the disastrous 1979 referendum. Labour's fresh faced leader Tony Blair, basking in public adulation, had led the party to its first General Election victory since October 1974. Change in Scotland, less so in Wales, was a key part of his manifesto for radical democratic reform. The trauma of Thatcherite radical economic surgery in the 1980s was a critical factor in persuading Labour party members in Wales to support devolution, and the impact of steel and coal closures, and the mounting economic and social dislocation wrought by Conservative Governments, caused a major re-consideration of Wales's place in British politics. The impact of the 1984–85 miners' strike and the creation of the multi-party Wales Congress in Support of Mining Communities were key events that taught the Labour Party that 'it was possible over a very specific issue to build bridges with parts of Wales which had long fallen into disrepair'.[1] The bridge building in turn served to ease some of the suspicions which characterised the devolution debate in 1979 and Dafydd Elis Thomas was one of those key politicians who built alliances across those political divides.

Rhodri Morgan attributed the change in attitudes towards devolution in 1997 to the mood of the Labour Party's grass roots and local government in particular, 'gnashing its teeth at what it could do to overcome its impotence'.[2] This pressure for constitutional change from the Labour groups on local councils was crucial given that they were some of the most significant opponents of devolution in 1979.

Uniting Welsh Labour

The most disunited of those internal groups was the Welsh group of Labour MPs. At a meeting in January 1990 in the House of Commons, only nine of the seventeen MPs spoke in favour of an elected Welsh Assembly, and Ron Davies was the only member to argue for a strong body with the powers of the Welsh Office.

But those who had opposed devolution in 1979, such as the party leader between 1983 and 1992, Neil Kinnock, were influenced by the shifting balance of opinion in his Shadow Cabinet, which now contained a number of senior Scottish figures who were pro-devolutionist: 'There was no point in having a big scrap with them . . . it wasn't worth a punch up'.[3] In April 1992, for the first time since October 1974, the Labour Party went into a General Election with a manifesto commitment to set up a Welsh Assembly. But if they had been elected the leadership would have insisted on another referendum, and while there had been a significant shift in the mood of the Party towards devolution for Wales since the referendum in 1979, the consensus for change was uncomplete.

The 1992 General Election result in Wales had Labour at 49.5 per cent of the vote, the Conservatives at 28.6 per cent, Liberal Democrats 12.4 per cent, and Plaid Cymru at 9 per cent.[4] In spite of Labour's impressive showing in Wales, the overall General Election result was won by John Major's Conservative party, with 42 per cent of the popular vote.

From November 1992, when he was appointed shadow Secretary of State for Wales, Ron Davies, the MP for Caerphilly, became the key figure within the Labour party in Wales in progressing devolution policy. His party leader, the staunchly pro-devolutionist Scottish MP, John Smith, had succeeded Kinnock as leader, and it was only as he offered Davies the post, that he realised he hadn't checked whether both agreed on the issue of devolution. Davies recalls that he said: 'I want you to make sure that you in Wales get a proper Parliament like the one we'll get in Scotland.' He hesitated. 'You are in favour of devolution?.'

Ron Davies had voted against devolution in 1979 but his Damascene moment had been Labour's failure to win the 1987 General Election in spite of the party gaining a majority in Wales:

> There was a very strong feeling that democracy was being undermined. A system of representation is contradicted when a country like Wales can vote one way and be delivered something completely different. Touring my constituency the day after the vote I came across graffiti on a railway bridge in Nelson – 'We voted Labour, we got Thatcher!'. That summed the whole thing up for me.[5]

Labour's revised stance on local government reform in 1989, to replace the unpopular two-tier structure of county and district councils with a single tier of multi-purpose authorities, gave a 'window of opportunity' for pro-devolutionists to advocate a 'regional, co-ordinating tier' in the form of a directly elected All-Wales body. But Davies calculated that if devolution was to capture the imagination of the Labour Party it had to be related to everyday concerns, and in his first major speech as shadow Welsh spokesman, in Treorchy in November 1992, he emphasised the Conservatives' illegitimacy in Wales, where they only had six seats:[6]

> The present regime is thoroughly undemocratic. It is the deepest affront to the people of Wales that those who have no mandate and who cannot be held accountable, are those who, in effect, govern Wales. The integrity of Wales as a national, cultural and political entity is beyond dispute. We have administrative devolution . . . the problem is that it is undemocratic government.[7]

Davies particularly attacked the proliferation of quangos, which he described as 'Government without ballot and power without scrutiny', giving the example of the former Welsh Office Minister Ian Grist, who having lost his Cardiff Central seat in the 1992 General Election, was appointed within weeks as chair of South Glamorgan Health Authority, where he controlled a budget of £232 million, and arguably wielded greater power than he did as a backbench MP.[8] The impotence of Welsh Opposition MPs was highlighted by the suspension of a House of Commons Standing Order, which entitled all Welsh MPs to sit on legislative Committees relating to Wales. Its suspension for the passage of three pieces of Wales-related legislation – the Cardiff Bay Barrage Bill, the Welsh Language Bill and the Welsh Local Government Bill – in as many years, allowed Conservative MPs sitting for English constituencies to be members of these Standing Committees, thus creating Conservative majorities, and strengthening perceptions of a 'democratic deficit'.[9]

The pro-devolutionists generated resentment against the succession of English Secretaries of State for Wales, namely Peter Walker (1987-90), David Hunt (1990-3), John Redwood (1993-5) and William Hague (1995-7), imposing their policies on the Welsh electorate. Whereas the advocates of a Welsh Assembly in the Labour Party at the time of the 1979 referendum had been criticised for concentrating on constitutional and emotionally arid arguments, Ron Davies now asserted that creating a Welsh Assembly was a necessary and inextricably linked element of Labour's approach to the transformation of society.

He was forced to take backward steps in accepting Blair's insistence on a referendum, even though fewer devolved powers were offered to Wales than for Scotland. But he was a combative street fighting politician who pushed Welsh devolution through his party and created the conditions for the success of the closely fought referendum campaign in September 1997. On the morning of his victory, he greeted the referendum result as one of the most important days in the history of Wales, stating that 'eighteen years ago the proposal for devolution was defeated by four to one. Tonight's Yes vote is a stunning turnaround'.[10]

The referendum vote in Wales was held a week later than in Scotland, in the hope that the greater enthusiasm for devolution there might rub off on the more sceptical Welsh. The beginning of the campaign was totally disrupted by the death of Diana, Princess of Wales, on 31 August 1997, and the following week became a period of mourning in which all political activity ceased. The referendum vote was held on 18 September, but in the short period available for campaigning, the Yes campaign had the support of all political parties apart from the Conservatives, while the No campaign was an amateur, virtually penniless outfit. The turnout of only half of the potential electorate and a winning margin of less than one per cent (only 6,721 votes), suggested that they shared Tony Blair's own lack of enthusiasm. He dutifully visited Cardiff on the morning of the count in order to publicly celebrate the result, but said privately to a relieved Ron Davies that 'this is a fine mess you've got us into', Blair's tone suggesting he was not entirely joking. He had been dragged by the coat-tails of his party's previous commitment to devolution, and those close to the Prime Minister were convinced that, rather than giving life to the Assembly by such a tentative margin, he would rather that the Welsh had throttled it at birth.[11] But the swing from the 1979 referendum of 30 per cent and its margin of four to one against devolution, reflected a marked sea change in attitude after a lengthy period of Conservative domination. Ron Davies's particular success in the referendum campaign was based on his ability to develop a coalition of support beyond Labour, from the Liberals and Plaid Cymru.

Throughout the nineties, he had kept in close touch with Plaid Cymru's leader Dafydd Wigley and the Liberal Democrats' leader, Richard Livsey in particular, offering an inclusive vision of the new Assembly, with a Cabinet of all the talents, not restricted to the biggest party, together with a system of proportional representation. Davies was not however blind to the inherent flaws of the new order, modelled as it was on the earlier constitutional proposals which were based on a local government structure, and which failed to separate the parliamentary and governmental functions of the National Assembly. *The Guardian*'s astute political commentator, Andrew Rawnsley, paid tribute to his diligent lobbying for Welsh devolution within Government after its landslide victory in May 1997:

> Wales was treated as Scotland's small and ugly sister. Interest in the less powerful assembly proposed for Cardiff was confined to the Welsh, and the idea did not enthuse many of them. Wales had rejected devolution by a margin of four to one on the last occasion it had been offered. His colleagues' indifference was exploited by the Secretary of State for Wales, Ron Davies. A barrel-shaped man with a face which appeared to have just

emerged from a rugby scrum, Davies was more devious than he looked. He would wait for the other ministers on the committee to exhaust themselves disputing Scotland and then get his proposals through on the tired nod.[12]

Dafydd Elis-Thomas – Political Re-entry

Throughout the 1990s, Dafydd Elis-Thomas's role as chair of the Language Board meant that his most crucial political relationship had been with the Conservative Ministers of the Welsh Office. His link with Ron Davies had been tenuous at best, dating back to their first meeting when the gruff Labour MP had not warmed to Lord Elis-Thomas's more urbane style. As the party's shadow agriculture spokesman at the time, Davies had campaigned to outlaw young calves locked in small crates and imported to Britain, and when they met, ostensibly to discuss Welsh language policy, Davies was singularly unimpressed:

> Dafydd asked me to go to the House of Lords to have a meal with him because I was Shadow spokesman. He was very courteous, almost like a vicar or undertaker. It was totally different from any other political relationship. In that sense I wouldn't have sworn at him, for example. I didn't have that sort of relationship. He was almost like a wine waiter with me, taking me through to the dining room. The idea of the lunch was to establish a relationship and I said to him – 'Is it Danish veal on the menu?' and Dafydd said, 'Oh yes! We have the very best here in the House of Lords!' His desire was to impress me.
>
> The next time I met him was after the 1997 election and I was invited to launch the Welsh language scheme in Torfaen. I said I realised these issues are sometimes difficult and I expect that you will be implementing not only the letter of the law, but the spirit of the Act.
>
> I remember Dafydd Elis sitting up when I made a comment about the forthcoming referendum and about everybody having a vote – including himself as a member of the House of Lords! The issue in my mind was the referendum and the issue of the language was important as I was trying to persuade people that we were serious about the language in this period, including

meetings with Cymdeithas yr Iaith, trying to persuade them to support an elected Assembly.[13]

Dafydd Elis-Thomas's contribution to the referendum campaign was inevitably low-key, given his public role as chair of the Welsh Language Board. His former researcher, Tim Williams was the most animated voice in the No campaign and was relieved that Elis-Thomas's public role as chair of the Language Board inhibited his ability to campaign, considering him 'a brilliant and charismatic communicator who would have been an asset to the Yes campaign if he had been more involved'.[14]

After the Referendum vote was won, Dafydd Elis-Thomas's main noteworthy intervention in the House of Lords during its debates on devolution in 1998 was his amendment to change the proposed name of the new institution from 'Welsh Assembly' to 'National Assembly for Wales'. The amendment was not immediately passed, but Ron Davies confirmed that the name would be changed.[15]

Davies now had the responsibility for guiding the legislation to set up the National Assembly for Wales and started to change the nature of the Welsh Office's approach to devolution.

He described his own managerial style as 'very command and control' but found an enthusiastic ally in the Welsh Office's Permanent Secretary, Rachel Lomax, who was 'very up for it . . . They were all very enthusiastic about it.' But even as a member of the Cabinet, he was not in the Prime Minister's inner circle.[16] According to Rawnsley, in his period as Secretary of State, the longest conversation he had with the Prime Minister since the General Election was little more than fifteen minutes. He was not regarded as a Blairite 'moderniser', and Scotland was more at 'the front of New Labour's mind, Wales was put right out of it'.[17]

In Wales, however, he was rather more highly regarded, and in September 1988, he was selected by party members as Labour's prospective First Secretary in Wales, over Rhodri Morgan. Credited as the architect of devolution, Davies won the overwhelming support of over 90 per cent of trade union and affiliated bodies, 60 per cent of MPs, MEPs and Assembly candidates, and 52 per cent of the local parties.[18]

Elis-Thomas was then approached by Lomax, on Ron Davies's behalf. She was a dynamic, high flying civil servant, who had already rejected an approach from the Chancellor of the Exchequer, Gordon Brown, to leave her post and join the Bank of England as Deputy Governor. She was dedicated to Welsh devolution and relished working for the dynamic Secretary of State for Wales. On a train journey between London and Cardiff, at Davies's request, she urged Dafydd Elis to put himself forward as Presiding Officer of the new Assembly. He had already been selected as the Plaid Cymru candidate for Meirionnydd Nant Conwy, and Elis-Thomas recalls that 'Ron had taken for granted that I would be the Presiding Officer – both he and his Permanent Secretary, the formidable Rachel Lomax, had made that clear'.[19]

It was Elis-Thomas's understanding of their agreement that the 1998 Government of Wales Act 1998 was the most minimal in order to be palatable to the Labour Government, but that as long as Ron Davies was leader, that they would move on quickly to further legislation to enhance the Assembly.[20] But within weeks, on 27 October 1998, Davies sensationally resigned, following his 'moment of madness' on Clapham Common, where he was mugged at knifepoint at a well-known gay meeting place. He later acknowledged that he was bisexual and was receiving treatment for a personality disorder which led him to seek out risky situations. Elis-Thomas referred to this as a 'tragedy of historic proportions' and Lomax reportedly commented at the time, that 'it was like walking along the edge of a cliff on devolution, where suddenly Ron fell off the end'.[21]

Paul Flynn, the acerbic Labour Member of Parliament for Newport West and an enthusiast for devolution, viewed Davies as:

> The cement that held together the control needs of New Labour in London and the Party Bosses in Wales with the aspirations of many Labour members here for more say over their own Party, and the desire of many people for a new politics. Now he has gone, the struggle between those asking for more democracy and those seeking to secure their own political future is out in the open. The outcome of this struggle will decide the fate of the Assembly and new Wales.[22]

Davies's departure ushered in the Blairite Alun Michael, Member of Parliament for Cardiff South and Penarth, to the role of Secretary of State for Wales. With Michael in post, Davies's trusted lieutenant, Rachel Lomax left the Welsh Office in March 1999, to take up the post of Permanent Secretary at the Department of Employment, although not until, in Ron Davies's words, she 'had done the most difficult part of the job'.[23] Her replacement as Permanent Secretary, Jon Shortridge, a town planner from Shrewsbury, brought a less enthusiastic commitment to his role in the establishing of the new devolved institution.

The 1999 May Assembly election proved extremely disappointing for Labour, in failing to gain its expected majority, and losing the iconic seats of the Rhondda and Islwyn, Neil Kinnock's former parliamentary constituency.[24] Tony Blair had made it abundantly clear that Alun Michael was his preferred candidate for the role of First Minister, but this proved to be a liability for Michael, making him appear to be the imposed Blairite candidate rather than the choice of Welsh Labour. While Rhodri Morgan had already been chosen for an Assembly seat, Alun Michael had to be shoehorned into the regional list of candidates for Mid and West Wales, and against local wishes. This proved an embarrassment throughout his leadership campaign and the Assembly election.

Labour's performance was overshadowed by Plaid's strong showing, gaining 17 seats and over 30 per cent of the vote, against Labour's 28 seats and 35.5 per cent.

Dafydd Elis-Thomas shared in Plaid's success in Meirionnydd Nant Conwy, and easily won the seat with the biggest share of the vote, compared with his previous elections, and a majority of 8,742 over the Labour candidate:

Dafydd Eis-Thomas Plaid Cymru	12,034	63.8 per cent
Denise Jones, Labour	3,292	17.4 per cent
O. J. Williams, Conservative	2,170	11.5 per cent
Graham Worley, Lib Dems	1,378	7.3 per cent
Majority	8,742[25]	

The deputy chairman of the party in Meirionnydd at the time, Dyfrig Siencyn, recalls the highly idiosyncratic nature of Elis-Thomas's local campaign:

> There were no leaflets, he went round personally, he was very minimalistic in his campaigning. Plaid's organisation in the constituency wasn't good. We had no canvassing returns at all. His style was to keep his head down, but he knew so many people. He didn't discuss politics, only personal matters. Politics didn't come into it. Everyone knew him.[26]

The first responsibility of the National Assembly for Wales was to select its Presiding Officer, who was expected to be chosen from the second largest party, and Plaid Cymru's leader, Dafydd Wigley, was enthusiastic, and magnanimous enough to nominate his former colleague, even though, as Ieuan Wyn Jones noted dryly, their relationship had 'not been at its best in the 1970s and 1980s'.[27] Wigley recalls that:

> Dafydd Elis was bursting his gut wanting the job, and I was totally sure in my mind that there wasn't anybody else within the Assembly with the experience, the ability and the personality to deal with the task. It was also important that the first Presiding Officer spoke Welsh. The only other eligible one, in my opinion, was Rhodri Morgan.[28]

Not everyone in the Plaid group was as supportive. Some could not forgive him for having joined the House of Lords, and others did not think it appropriate that a member of the House of Lords should preside over the Assembly. Wigley was warned that he would regret giving Dafydd Elis such recognition, but his support for him was unwavering:

> A Presiding Officer was needed who would be sufficiently strong to withstand pressure from the government of the day, whether in Cardiff or London. In spite of various differences of opinion between Dafydd and myself, I had no doubt at all in putting his name forward before the Assembly.[29]

Within days of the Assembly election, and before the selection of the Presiding Officer, Alun Michael, now the regional list member for Mid and West Wales and the imminent First Secretary, insisted on giving the prospective Presiding Officer a job interview, in his capacious office in Cathays Park. His biggest concern, as Dafydd Elis recalled, 'was to ensure that I did not pursue my own personal political agenda. I used my experience as the chair of the Welsh Language Board under a Conservative Government to illustrate my impartiality'.[30] He was subsequently elected unanimously on a motion of the Assembly, and also received a great deal of goodwill from across the parties. Many of the new Labour Members had campaigned with him during the miners' strike and in the CND and civil rights movements. The new Member for the Vale of Glamorgan, Jane Hutt, recalls that his Westminster experience had shown how well he could work with people from other parties, 'right from the word go, in the early days, we were always very respectful of each other – we got to know each other – and rekindled relationships on a political basis'.[31]

With such widespread political support, this new challenge excited Dafydd Elis-Thomas, who 'felt the sense of responsibility, as well as huge trepidation – because it was such a new institution and because I also knew there were still people inside the civil service that didn't want it to happen and didn't expect it to last'.[32] He was formally nominated by the Plaid leader, Dafydd Wigley, and seconded by the Labour group's business manager, Andrew Davies. Dafydd Elis recalled that:

> My strongest support came from Welsh Labour, which I think went back to the miners' strike, the fact that I'd been loyal to the Wilson government way back in 1974 onwards and I think all that activity made it clear that they could trust me, that was the key thing ... they were absolutely determined that they would nominate me. I also had the strong support of those people who became the officials of the institution because again, we'd worked together, and, as someone told me, we 'want somebody that when Her Majesty comes to open the Assembly, it's somebody that she knows and is content with them'. I had been an independent peer, so I was able to get cross-party support and clearly I had a very good relationship with Nick Bourne and the Welsh Conservatives which continued over the period I was Presiding Officer, so there was a consensus.[33]

Maintaining respectful relations with all the parties in the Assembly became a mantra for the new Presiding Officer, but he was helped by his long-standing friendships with a number of the Assembly's politicians. Nick Bourne recalls his first meeting with Dafydd Elis:

> Our first meeting was on the 125 train between Cardiff and London. There were a few convivial occasions like that over a couple of glasses of wine and a meal. There is very much that strand in Dafydd, of cultural conservatism regarding the Welsh language and Welsh culture, and he was very much in tune with

David Hunt and Wyn [Roberts] – there was very much that respect that endured between them. We had William Hague as leader of the party, who understood devolution, partly because of Ffion [Hague's Welsh-speaking wife], and he was very quick to pick up things on issues of devolution. All parties supported him for that role, for different reasons. We saw him as someone who would lend stability, dignity and gravitas, which were key in those early days. He spoke with authority – no-one else would have been as effective.

One of Bourne's challenges in the wake of the referendum was to ensure that the nine strong Conservative group in the Assembly, and its leader for the first year, Rod Richards, took a supportive approach to the new institution:

My role was to ensure that the party accepted the result ... Assembly members were pretty much of that view. People had to differentiate between the Assembly and Government. We had weekly meetings and sometimes he would give advice in the approach to the institution. I would sometimes disagree with his rulings, but I would say to my team that we don't disagree with the referee.[34]

Ron Davies had recovered from his personal disgrace sufficiently to be elected as the Assembly Member for Caerphilly in May 1999, and welcomed Dafydd Elis-Thomas's election to the Presiding Officer role as 'pretty benign because he had experience, he had gravitas, the support of Plaid, and fitted in with the constitutional requirements'.[35]

The National Assembly was opened by the Queen on 27 May 1999, to the accompaniment of flag-waving school children, gentle harp playing and a stirring solo from the 13-year old Charlotte Church, but also followed by a barn-storming open-air concert featuring Welsh singing greats performing before the royal family, including Tom Jones singing *The Green, Green Grass of Home*, Michael Ball, Bonnie Tyler and Shirley Bassey in a red dragon dress made of the Welsh flag. The only jarring note was the Manic Street Preachers band's refusal to perform in front of the Queen, protesting that the monarchy was 'outdated'.[36] The presence of the Queen, and a powerful speech by the

Prince of Wales, gave a royal stamp of approval to the new institution, and was a powerful affirmation of the legitimacy of the National Assembly. The Prince emphasised that the new Assembly would nourish Wales's continuing growth:

> In the Assembly, the voice of Wales will have its authentic and vigorous expression, in ways not possible before. Welsh minds will be directed to Welsh matters ... This is an historic day for Wales. To you, the sixty members of this Assembly, falls the honour of being pioneers. I would like to express to you my heartfelt good wishes as you take up this important responsibility.[37]

The sensitivity of the role of the royal family in the opening of the National Assembly was negotiated by Elis-Thomas, the 'reformed republican', who had to balance the views of vocal republicans with those more traditionally right-wing conservatives, who may not have been enamoured of the Assembly. He attempted to secure the commitment of the head of state, and the Prince of Wales, to the newest democratic institution in the United Kingdom. Beforehand, he visited Prince Charles at Highgrove in Gloucestershire, and later described how Charles had been keen to understand how the monarchy could support the new National Assembly:

> It was clearly inappropriate to describe either the head of state, or the future head of state, as supporters of devolution. But they were definitely supporters of the constitution. And definitely supporters of being part of a constitutional monarchy, and of believing in the importance of democratic accountability and the role that the Royal Family, the head of state and future head of state, could have in relation to helping political figures to make constitutional change acceptable to the population because of it being democratically agreed.[38]

The event was a 'royal' rather than a 'state' opening, but treated as a 'semi-state' opening, with the royal family in their day dress rather than ceremonial robes. The extravagance of the occasion was minimal and low-key compared to state occasions, in keeping with the temporary nature of the Assembly debating chamber, located in an old computer room in the former home of the Welsh Combined Health Services Authority in Crickhowell House, an office building in Cardiff Bay.³⁹

Confidence and Alun Michael

Alun Michael formed his first Cabinet in the wake of his party's poor election result, as Ron Davies recalls:

> It was a bit of a shambles. Plaid did very well, I don't know if things had been different if I'd been leader. Alun Michael was appallingly ill-suited in every sense. I can remember him reading a piece of the Bible in the religious service to celebrate the opening of the Assembly. He read, without a trace of irony, considering his treatment of his fellow Labour members, from the epistle of John, 'You did not choose me. I chose you'. He was extremely arrogant towards his fellow AMs. The general view in the Labour group of 28 was that 'he might be crap but he's our crap'. His core supporters in the group were no more than about five in all. Michael's refusal to enter into a coalition with Liberal Democrats and his reluctance to work with other parties, meant that the Government were unable to command a working majority for normal business. Michael's deficiencies were obvious to those who worked with him.⁴⁰

Edwina Hart, the Assembly's first Minister of Local Government, recalls Michael's behaviour towards his colleagues as 'terrible – he would shout at me – interrupt me in meetings – awful – he worked hard but couldn't show any outcomes. He read papers but not the right ones – he'd always listen to London.'⁴¹ Throughout his period as leader, Michael was never able to detach himself from the epithet of Tony Blair's poodle, and Labour's former deputy leader, Roy Hattersley, attacked the Prime Minister's inability to relinquish control of him:

> Blair dictates that, in principle democracy must be extended at every level. But, in practice, that means only as long as Tony Blair can be guaranteed the result which he wants . . . By its very nature, devolution means that sometimes Cardiff will disagree with London. If the Prime Minister is not prepared to risk the

leader of the Welsh Assembly arguing for Wales, he is denying the purpose of the Assembly's existence.[42]

As the Assembly's first Presiding Officer, Elis-Thomas's first priority was to ensure that it established itself as a modern and competent parliamentary body, and to promote the institution to the people of Wales, because the referendum result had been so close. He was aware that he should not do anything to 'frighten the horses', and to build trust in the institution:

> That had to be done within the framework which was absolutely effing appalling because it was not the proper constitutional structure. It was equally important for me that the institution would be established from the beginning as the most bilingual legislature in the United Kingdom and that wasn't difficult, but I don't think some officials who worked for the old Welsh Office thought it would be so radically different from what had happened before.
> The key thing was that the phraseology of the 1993 Welsh Language Act became part of the constitution of Wales, so that the principle about the languages being treated on the basis of equality was immediately accepted. The other thing was the introduction of digital technology. There was enough interpretation capacity available from people who had worked in county councils in different parts of Wales, so that achieving a bilingual organisation from day one was possible.[43]

One of the Assembly's greatest deficiencies was its nature as a 'corporate body', with no distinction between the opposition members in this parliamentary body, and those members who were part of the government:

> From the beginning I decided that I would operate on the principle of separation of powers, so I called the Welsh government the Government of Wales, as I thought nobody is going to argue with that because we were all part of the government of Wales. But the parliament of Wales – Cynulliad Cenedlaethol Cymru – translates as the *Assemblée Nationale de Pays De Galles*, and of course I was involved in all of the discussions getting it called

that, rather than the original intention of the legislation which had been to call it the Welsh Assembly. That is where I got strong support from the party leaders because they believed that they were working in an institution which should have more powers than were in the original legislation. We understand why that happened, so I understood it would be wrong to push for substantial change and development too soon and I always had to have regard to what was going on within the civil service, because there was no separate provision for a civil service for Wales. That is why I established this thing called OPO – the Office of the Presiding Officer.[44]

In the Government's eyes, the Presiding Officer's legal and procedural advice was to be provided by the Welsh Office's Permanent Secretary, Jon Shortridge, and the newly appointed Counsel General, Winston Roddick, a Queen's Counsel, who did little to enamour himself to the Presiding Officer. Both considered themselves to be the Presiding Officer's chief advisers, but given their first loyalty was to the governing administration, for Elis-Thomas this raised the probability that their constitutional advice would be partial.

He recalled that Jon Shortridge came to see him and told him that he was his senior adviser, 'I pointed to the sky and said, 'He is my adviser . . . Look, you can't try this one on me – I know the constitution of the United Kingdom inside out because I worked within it.'[45]

He was, however, provided with an experienced Westminster parliamentary clerk, John Lloyd, and they worked together effectively, and with the support of the other new democratic institutions of the Scottish Parliament and Northern Ireland Assembly. But Lloyd found himself sandwiched between the demands of the Presiding Officer and those of his line manager, the Permanent Secretary. In this period, Elis-Thomas was also made aware of Shortridge's pessimism about whether the institution would last. This led him to consult and obtain independent legal advice from a distinguished law professor, and a colleague on the Church in Wales's governing body, Professor David Lambert, whose later advice was crucial in dealing with the vote of no confidence in Alun Michael.

The first ten months of the National Assembly's existence was marked by a constant sense of crisis, with a minority Labour Government scrabbling for votes, an impending crisis over the failure to secure match funding for the European Commission's Objective One funding aimed at poorer areas of Wales, and Michael's tenuous grip on his own party. There was a steady build-up of political tension in the autumn of 1999 between Michael and the other political parties in the Assembly over the European Objective One funding issue. West Wales and the Valleys constituted almost two thirds of Wales and, from 1 January 2000, qualified for an extra £300 million a year of funding from the European Regional Development Fund for the next seven years. But that could not be accessed unless there was match-funding in the shape of extra funding from the Treasury, a concession that would be in addition to the normal Barnett formula for public expenditure that Wales received.[46] The Treasury did not wish to commit funding before the Public Expenditure Statement due in the summer of 2000. As Rhodri Morgan later commented, 'it remains a mystery why Tony Blair wasn't able to influence Gordon Brown [the Chancellor of the Exchequer] to release some kind of letter of comfort that would have defused the issue'.[47] However, Blair's press secretary Alastair Campbell had no doubt why he did not do so; Gordon Brown 'had told someone that he was not helping Alun Michael because he was a Blairite. Alun was facing a vote of confidence over the match-funding issue and our basic argument was there was no need to do the match-funding now.'[48]

But while a sense of crisis started to overwhelm the Assembly Ministers, this was not shared by the Presiding Officer:

> I didn't think of that for a minute because I knew if I started thinking like that, I'd become nervous about it all. We had no legislation to do in the early days, apart from secondary legislation, but I interpreted those widely, and it was very important to me that the National Assembly for Wales could debate anything. The fact that we couldn't do anything about it, was neither here nor there, because we were there also to express the gathered opinion of the people of Wales about whatever it may be and that was quite important ... I was very keen to make us look and feel like a parliament, although for five years, we were in a converted computer room in Cardiff Bay with no daylight, but it was important to build up the institution from the beginning.[49]

Alun Michael's style of leadership had, in the meantime, alienated many of the Labour group in the Assembly, and although the lack of an overall majority could well have led to talks about coalition or formal cooperation with other parties, many of his colleagues felt that Michael lacked the desire to work constructively with his political opponents. Within the party, he had the reputation of being overly controlling. The former leader of the Yes campaign in the 1997 Referendum, Kevin Morgan, reported that:

> People within the Cabinet have privately told us that Alun's obsession with control has some very, very debilitating consequences. He seems unwilling, or unable, to delegate authority, yet on the other hand he has a tendency to prevaricate. This makes a fatal combination and is not conducive to effective policy making. It stifles initiative.[50]

The parliamentary commentator, Andrew Rawnsley, reflected that Michael had adopted the template of Blairite command and control politics, and exaggerated it into 'a parody of control-freakism':

> His ministers were not even allowed to write their own replies to letters from MPs. Everything had to go across Michael's desk for approval. This did not live up to the promise of a more consensual style of politics. Michael was running the Welsh Assembly as though he had an impregnable majority, when he possessed no majority at all.[51]

In the autumn of 1999, Plaid Cymru made an increasingly major issue of the Treasury's refusal to provide the necessary match funding to attract European aid to deprived areas of Wales. Gordon Brown refused, for his own reasons, to indicate whether the money would be made available, and a no confidence motion in the Welsh First Minister was tabled for 9 February 2000.[52] Tony Blair's own private secretary, Jonathan Powell, recognised that Plaid had a strong case for extra match funding:

> The Plaid Cymru argument seems pretty good to me. The CSR (Comprehensive Spending Review) can take care of what happens from 1 April 2001 but not for what happens from 1 January

2000, when the EU money comes available. Under the EU rules Wales will lose the £180 million allotted for this year unless it is committed in this financial year.[53]

No. 10's civil servants grew increasingly concerned over Michael's inability to handle the crisis and warned that Michael 'could easily come a cropper over this':

> He has not helped matters by failing to depress expectations, but that is now where we are. The PM has already gone pretty far publicly with words to the effect that we will not let Wales down. A more skilful operator than Alun Michael would have been able to work with that quite comfortably.[54]

Blair's political secretary, Pat McFadden, failed to persuade Blair to get Gordon Brown to intervene:

> Welsh politicians do not have the weight/credibility to make this message carry so it must come from here, ideally from GB. TB should personally minute GB asking him to make clear, before Feb 15th, that Wigley is wrong, that there is no short-term crisis over this, no need for a decision in Feb and this will be negotiated through the CSR. As for the CSR itself, TB and GB will have to decide, though it looks to me like Welsh have strong case for more.[55]

With days to go before the no confidence vote against Alun Michael in the National Assembly, McFadden became even gloomier about Michael's fate:

> We suffer in Wales from lack of leadership and direction. The key to recovery of our position lies in taking on the Nationalists who are running the whole agenda in Wales. But this is not happening. We are far too defensive and reactive. There is no strategy to defeat Plaid ... Alun has very little support in the group, is obsessed with details and seems incapable of thinking about the big picture. He will not be able to develop a winning strategy. We need a big intervention on Monday. Otherwise, we're letting

the nationalist case win by default. The orthodoxy in the Welsh press is that the Nats' case on this is right. Suggest that GB brief the Welsh press ... we need to challenge.[56]

This sense of crisis was heightened by the result of a parliamentary by-election in Ceredigion on 3 February, six days before the no confidence vote, where the Objective One funding row was a 'decisive factor' in Plaid Cymru retaining the seat, with 10,716 votes, while Labour fell from second to fourth place with a swing of 9.9 per cent against the party.[57]

With central government seemingly not coming to Michael's rescue, there was a general acceptance that the vote would be lost. He stated privately that if he lost the vote of confidence, he would stand again and be re-elected, and that the Liberals would be asked to support Michael. This was most clearly expressed in a private note to the Prime Minister by Paul Murphy, the Secretary of State for Wales, sent on the Friday before the crucial vote:

> No reason to think that Alun will not lose the vote. An election for a new First Secretary should then be held on Thursday – assuming the Presiding Officer calls a plenary session for that day. Alun is likely to be the only candidate and so re-elected. We do not know whether the other parties will then table a further no-confidence motion. I am still pressing for all Alun's Cabinet to resign with him on the Wednesday. That would emphasise the solidarity and determination within the group. Unfortunately, it appears unlikely this will happen ... While members of the group continue to profess loyalty in public, it is important they are reminded they are expected to respect the Labour party's rules. At the same time channels have been opened to the Liberal Democrats at both Parliamentary and Assembly levels. Some progress has been made but clearly, the parliamentary leadership is keener on co-operation than the Assembly group.[58]

The evening before the no confidence vote, the Liberal Democrat UK leader, Charles Kennedy, was summoned to Number Ten, where Blair tried to persuade him to cajole his six Members in the Assembly to support Michael. Blair was reported as saying 'we simply can't have Rhodri. He'll be a disaster,' but Kennedy replied that he couldn't deliver the Liberal

Democrats in the Assembly.[59] The no confidence vote in Michael was an unprecedented challenge for the Presiding Officer, who had been taking his own soundings with the other parties and publicly predicted that they did not augur well for the First Minister. On Radio Wales the previous Sunday, he advised that 'if I were Alun Michael, I would go and pray'. *The Independent* suggested that 'divine intervention appeared to be the only hope left for Tony Blair's representative on earth'.[60]

The Presiding Officer rejected the formal advice on the conduct of the vote, given to him by Jon Shortridge and Winston Roddick, the Counsel General. Much to his annoyance, this advice was not delivered discretely to his office but presented as part of a collective view of the Executive, with both the Permanent Secretary and First Secretary involved in its formulation. He also discovered that this advice was filtering back to the Wales Labour Party executive, the office of the Secretary of State for Wales, the Prime Minister's office and Labour headquarters in Millbank. In fact, he had yet to consider fully what to do at that stage in the procedure for the vote.[61] His advice from Lambert and others stated that it was for him and him alone to establish a precedent for a vote of confidence, as he recalled:

> I do believe still, although Alun Michael wouldn't I think, agree with me, that the motion of no confidence in the First Minister (*sic*), that was tabled quite early on, was a serious milestone in the Assembly's history, showing clearly that it wanted to determine its own future as an elected body ... this was something which caused all sorts of consternation in the civil service at the highest level, amongst UK permanent secretaries, as well as in Wales. In those early days there'd be regular weekly meetings of Permanent Secretaries, in order to basically control devolution, to make sure it wouldn't get out of hand.
>
> I had the highest respect for Alun Michael as a Minister in the UK government as well as an MP, but I was also conscious that he was not someone who could lead as the First Minister (*sic*) of Wales in a devolution situation, and of course that was decided by the Assembly when it came to the motion of no confidence. He blamed me for that view. I had had a specific discussion about the procedure with the senior legal adviser that I respected from the days of the Welsh Office, David Lambert, along with

other respected constitutional lawyers. In fact, because of my connections in Westminster I made sure that we didn't do anything which was contrary to the Government of Wales Act. It was possible for the Assembly to entertain a motion of no confidence in the First Minister (*sic*), or at least a debate on the motion. I thought it was too soon [in the Assembly's life] to have that, but it was clear this is what the members wanted.

At the time, he believed there was a plot within the Labour group to ensure Michael would not be re-elected as leader but denied that there was ever a conspiracy to oust the First Secretary. However, he was informed beforehand by a number of Labour Assembly Members that he should not be concerned if the outcome was a motion of no confidence, and 'I was assured there would be an alternative – although Rhodri and I never discussed it formally until two nights before'.[62]

That evening, he and Rhodri Morgan had met to discuss the likely outcome of the vote against Alun Michael. Both lived in the village of Michaelston-le-Pit, set in rolling green fields but no more than two miles from Cardiff's city centre. Dafydd and Mair had rented a home within a quarter of a mile across fields from Rhodri and Julie's home. That evening, after Rhodri's dog had been taken for a walk, both couples discussed politics over curry leftovers in the Morgans' famously untidy kitchen, which had so appalled Tony Blair when he stayed there previously and featured as one of the Prime Minister's less convincing reasons for not promoting him after the 1997 General Election. They discussed whether, if Alun Michael lost the vote, it would be in order for him to stand again for the role of First Secretary. Rhodri recalled that Dafydd 'was adamant, that such a second motion would be clearly vexatious and that it would bring the Assembly into disrepute . . . he would rule the second motion out of order'.[63]

Elis-Thomas's clear view was therefore contrary to that of Michael's, and was that if a motion of no confidence was passed, the governance of Wales would have to continue nevertheless:

> It was nothing to do with a conspiracy. It was just for me to understand, that if the motion was passed that this would not bring about a political crisis. So, I knew then that Labour was making or had made a decision, but that was a matter for them

as a party, as a group. My concern of course was that a fragile, new institution, has got to have continuity. There can't be a constitutional crisis which lasts more than a day or an hour if you can manage it . . .

Nothing that we did then was anti-democratic, nothing was threatening to devolution. But it was clear to me that devolution and the National Assembly was only safe if we could make it a more powerful institution, with the consent of the members and the electorate.[64]

Before the vote, he coordinated closely with Labour's Chief Whip, Andrew Davies, who had the unenviable task of balancing Michael's need for political survival with the majority of the Labour group's antipathy towards him. Davies recalls how difficult this crisis was for both he and Dafydd Elis:

> We had a session – like a therapy session. There was no separation of powers then – the civil service was serving both the Government and Opposition – he was not sure where their loyalties lay. I could see how he would think their loyalties lay both ways and it was clear from the advice they gave him that they were trying to box him in. The civil service was weak, had a very controlling culture, was the biggest block on devolution. They were condescending and under pressure from the UK civil service – these were all tensions. It was clear Dafydd felt under massive pressure. We felt we had a shared mission.

Andrew Davies had a meeting with Ieuan Wyn Jones hours before the vote and made it clear to him that if Alun lost the vote, then an alternative Labour candidate would be put forward. Davies recalls that 'we all felt he had to go'. He also had a final conversation the day before the vote with Elis-Thomas, who made it clear that if Alun lost, he would not accept a further motion in his name. When Andrew Davies reported this back to Michael, he lost his temper and attempted to sack Davies, but was talked out of doing so by his Environment Minister, Sue Essex. Davies denied that he had conspired against Michael, stating that he had 'tried to play a straight bat'.[65]

On the afternoon of 9 February, in an 'emotional speech' in the Assembly chamber, Michael rejected the opposition's claims that he had failed to deliver for Wales. In a dramatic gesture, he submitted his letter of resignation, but failed to prevent the vote of no confidence, whilst insisting that it was up to Labour, not Plaid Cymru, to determine who should lead the Labour minority administration in Cardiff.[66]

His action in resigning in order to pre-empt the vote of no confidence was widely seen as ill-judged, not least amongst the majority of his own side. It also angered the Presiding Officer, who accused him of 'amateur dramatics'. Amid confusion in the Chamber, the Presiding Officer insisted, to the fury of many Labour members, in calling for a vote of confidence motion, which was carried by 31 to 27 with one abstention, Alison Halford, the Labour Member for Delyn.[67]

As journalists packed the Assembly's public milling area, hoping to hear him explain his decision to resign, Michael slipped out of the chamber by a side entrance. That evening, he announced his intention to stand down as leader of the Labour party in Wales. According to Andrew Davies, there was a half-hearted attempt afterwards to keep him in place. Two Labour members, Tom Middlehurst and Peter Law, indicated they wished to re-nominate Michael and to elect Andrew Davies as temporary leader. But barely an hour after the Assembly vote, in a hastily convened meeting of the Assembly Labour group, Andrew Davies nominated Rhodri Morgan, who was selected unanimously.[68]

As the no confidence vote was being held in the Assembly, in the House of Commons, the Prime Minister stoutly defended Alun Michael's record, saying 'I believe the Welsh FM is doing an excellent job.' Simultaneously, the Conservative MPs' pagers pulsated with the news that Michael had resigned. A floundering Blair endured his most humiliating moment at the dispatch box since becoming PM. That evening he accepted the inevitable by offering a glowing endorsement of the 'total loyalty' of the 'highly effective' Rhodri Morgan, the man he had described as a 'total disaster' the previous evening.[69]

The Guardian reported Michael's dismissal as 'a bombshell, then oblivion', and as the dust settled, Tony Blair found himself uttering words which nine months earlier he would have shuddered to state: 'Rhodri Morgan has impressed everyone with the total loyalty he has shown to Alun. His record in Government has also been highly effective. I welcome his nomination as First Secretary.'[70]

Dafydd Elis-Thomas was jubilant as he declared enthusiastically that 'this is the first day of devolution' and contended that the National Assembly had made clear in its vote of no confidence that 'we don't want this style of politics . . . and we expressed these views. This was the majority view of the Assembly. This is real democracy.'[71] This melodrama was a defining moment in the story of Welsh devolution and registered a fundamental shift in the underlying political culture of Wales, between the old order, as exemplified by the Welsh Office and the UK Government's power of patronage, to the new order and the first assertion of the Assembly's desire for institutional autonomy.[72]

Edwina Hart, then the Minister for Local Government and Regeneration, recalls the institution's earliest struggles and the Presiding Officer's attempts to deal with the early shortcomings of devolution:

> It was like a county council on sticks and the way the [Assembly's] committees worked, muffled devolution . . . Alun was straight out of Tony Blair's pocket – his heart and soul was not in it. Rhodri had a much better understanding. Alun didn't have a way with people – and not with enough of the other parties, or within the Labour group . . . He wasn't radical – we weren't going anywhere. If Dafydd hadn't played the straight bat, devolution could have collapsed under Alun, but Rhodri was more charismatic.[73]

Nick Bourne supported Elis-Thomas's management of this crisis and thought the outcome had been inevitable:

> Alun didn't do himself any favours. With hindsight, there was high drama. Dafydd was criticised by some Labour members who were Alun Michael loyalists, but I don't think he could have done it differently.'[74]

But within days of Michael's resignation, Dafydd Elis was attacked from an unexpected quarter. Marjorie Thompson, his former partner, had been infuriated by Dafydd Elis's accusation of misogyny against some of his fellow Assembly members for their attacks on the Agriculture Minister in the Assembly, Christine Gwyther. It had 'stuck in her craw' to read that, 'as Speaker of the Assembly, he denounces "macho politics" when opposition parties seek to censure the female Agriculture Minister, as happened last Christmas. He should not masquerade as a feminist.'[75]

In her article in the society magazine, *Harpers and Queen*, Marjorie Thompson portrayed the Dafydd Elis-Thomas of ten years earlier, as an indulgent dandy. She wrote that:

> After having shared the mortgage on our flat (I had the deposit) for four years, Dafydd then stopped contributing, although he was claiming a London living allowance as an MP and spending it on his wardrobe. For two years, I paid the mortgage on my own, as well as the bills, only to find Paul Smith, Giorgio Armani, Hugo Boss and Aquascutum shopping bags hidden under the bed. Dafydd's contribution was the rent (£130) on the constituency home where we spent frequent weekends. Occasionally he would splash out on expensive and unwanted gifts for me. 'You can buy these things when the bills have been paid', I would tell him. 'Don't be so bourgeois', he would tell me ... In the final year we were together, I endured the humiliation of answering the door of the constituency home, to his creditors: the Nannau Estate (we lived in half of an old hunting lodge), the gardener, or the people who leased Dafydd's car.
>
> When the car lease's debt-collector started coming to our north Kensington flat. I said Dafydd should find himself another place to live. I suggested, in fact, that he and I should cease our association together. This was met by incredulity and disbelief. How could I possibly give up such a good thing?[76]

In response, Dafydd Elis recognised that in the late 1980s, he had been under a lot of financial pressure due to separating from his first wife, that he had to keep three households going:

> Marjorie may have paid the mortgage on our London flat for a time, but I had paid for the place to be refurbished. It was one of those give and take things you get in relationships ... All my parliamentary allowances were properly passed by the fees office in the House of Commons. If I have a weakness for designer clothes, I always purchase these objects only at discounted prices. The fact is our relationship ended, like many do.

But he also pointed that the timing of the attack, in the wake of Michael's resignation was unlikely to be coincidental; 'The timing of this attack is so obvious to me'.[77] His former student friend, Emyr Price noted that his interest in smart clothes had always been the source of comment and satire, recalling that 'he never stopped being the embodiment of Hardy Amies through all his changes of fashion, from the 1960s to the present (2009), where he is now investing in the most recent clothes of *Country Life* and *Esquire*'.[78] Pat Hannan, the political commentator, recorded his acerbic impression of Dafydd Elis-Thomas in this period:

> Dafydd El tends to glide ... [and] gives of an air of 'calculation and guile'. Dafydd El pays serious attention to the quality of things like food and drink. He's fastidious about his appearance. When a former girlfriend gave a revenge interview to a glossy magazine she claimed that, even in times of severe financial pressure, he would still buy designer clothes, although sometimes they had to be hidden under the bed. His comment was that, yes, he did buy designer clothes, but only in the sales.
>
> This matter of appearance, the studied care he takes, go further than just modish personal taste. In his years as the Assembly's Presiding Officer, he has emerged rather more than a little presidential. On the weekend, you might come across him in something green and tweedy, as though he was just back from shooting a bit of wildlife. Or perhaps he'll be sporting a pair of startlingly yellow corduroy trousers or, in summer, a rakishly-worn straw hat; or again he might be in the sober outfit suitable for Sunday morning service at Llandaff Cathedral, where he is a regular attender. This is all the more fun because of the fact that such display drives the many class warriors who remain in Plaid Cymru mad with disapproval. They see it as a deadly combination of affectation and betrayal. And they hate it even more because he is, as Lord Elis-Thomas of Nant Conwy in the County of Gwynedd, a member of the House of Lords. Worse than that, he clearly enjoys being so.[79]

The incoming First Secretary, Rhodri Morgan, was less of a style guru – he often wore a rugby shirt and jeans and the former Oxford and

Harvard graduate underplayed his formidable intellectual abilities, but as Edwina Hart suggested, he was really 'a middle class intellectual, a member of the Welsh-speaking "crachach"'.[80] As the First Secretary, he quickly brought in his own team of special advisers, including the future First Minister, Mark Drakeford, who recalled the period immediately after Alun Michael's departure as 'perilous':

> We were an administration – it wasn't a government in those days – without a majority. We were an administration that couldn't pass a budget. We had an institution built on the most unstable foundations of what was called a corporate body with no distinction between those in the parliament and those in the government ... I came to work in the Assembly in the spring of 2000 ... and I did think to myself this was an institution that may not survive – that it was an institution on the edge, and that people who worked in it were on the edge. And maybe that great experiment that so many of us had worked so hard to bring about was about to fail in front of us.[81]

In the aftermath of Alun Michael's overthrow, Dafydd Elis-Thomas took the first step towards appointing an independent group of officials to serve the Assembly, when on 29 February he announced the formal appointment of David Lambert as his independent legal adviser. Two days later he made a speech to the Wales Governance Centre, summarising his concerns about the contemporary devolution settlement:

> The 1998 Government of Wales Act which had established the Assembly did not represent a new constitutional settlement. It was too close to the Wales Act 1978 for that. Rather, it was merely the best that could be achieved in the circumstance of the time. It is not based on a clear legislative principle. It could be said to have elevated piecemeal development to an art form ... We are not at the beginning of a new constitution for Wales. We are at the beginning of the end of the old constitution. We have the least that could be established at the time. We shouldn't say that a political fix is a national constitution.

He advocated that the parties should come together in conference under his chairmanship and produce a draft Parliamentary Bill granting full legislative powers for the Assembly, to be presented in the year leading up to the 2003 Assembly elections.[82]

Dafydd Elis-Thomas's readiness to act radically to improve Wales's constitutional settlement was matched by Rhodri Morgan's 'personal authority, political skill and deep determination'. Within a few months, he had formed a working partnership with the Liberal Democrats, a budget had been agreed which gave the Assembly an increase in its funding of ten per cent a year in its first four years, and he and Dafydd Elis-Thomas resolved to achieve the greatest possible separation between the legislature and executive.[83]

As the tempestuous first year of the Assembly drew to a close, its members could look back on a stormy journey. Rhodri Morgan optimistically boasted that the new body was now becoming established in the public mind, and that it had 'blazed a trail for democracy and open government. The devolved body had now found its feet after a turbulent first year of life', he said, and 'although the Assembly had often hit the news for the wrong reasons, behind the strident headlines lay a story of quiet success, of a body knuckling down to business'.[84]

But it was from the autumn of 2000 that the Assembly's public legitimacy became established, when its Government was confronted by two major crises, the petrol tanker dispute, in which it had to deal with protests over the price of DERV in September 2000, followed by serious rail disruption after the Hatfield rail crash after which a maximum speed limit of 30 mph was imposed on all rail travel. And then the foot-and-mouth epidemic amongst cattle and sheep from February 2001. For the first time, the Assembly's government came to be thought of as an effective organisation.[85] Floods in north-east Wales tested the emergency services, and Corus's announcement that the company intended to close the heavy end of the Llanwern plant, together with the threatened closure of the Cardiff site of the Allied Steel and Wire plant (which was eventually saved), all made the Assembly more relatable to everyday issues.[86] Within the Assembly, Edwina Hart considered that Dafydd's influence 'was extremely practical':

> He wanted to see it work. If you had to compromise, so be it. He knew the end game was to get more powers, to turn it from an Assembly to a Parliament. I think that's what he did from day

one and I don't think people realised it. He understood the end game, and we got there with enhanced powers.[87]

Challenging the civil service

Elis-Thomas worked hard to change the nature of the civil service in Wales from its traditional mindset as part of the Welsh Office, a territorial Whitehall department only established in 1964 and integrated into the British civil service, to be accountable to the National Assembly for Wales rather than the Welsh Office and part of the Home civil service. Between May 1999 and the end of 2001, he issued a battery of complaints against the Assembly government's civil service, and in particular, its Permanent Secretary in Wales, Jon Shortridge, whose diligence within the Welsh Office was admired, but who found difficulty in adjusting to the new power dynamic of a parliamentary body keen to gain its independence from the government's administration.

Crucially, the partnership agreement to form a coalition government between the Liberals and Labour in October 2000, committed to securing the independence of the office of the Presiding Officer and those civil servants who worked directly for him. The change was expressly recognised when the Assembly agreed to establish a House Committee to advise the Presiding Officer and £24.3 million was allocated for his office for the running of the Assembly. But no means had yet been found of spending the money without recourse to the executive, which still controlled every aspect of procurement, the Assembly's compliance with the Government of Wales Act 1998, and its finance and personnel function.[88]

In this formative period, Elis-Thomas challenged the authority of Shortridge and his civil service incessantly in a series of major clashes. The most crucial disagreement arose over the procedures surrounding the vote of no confidence in First Secretary Alun Michael in February 2000, but as early as November 1999, they argued whether Members should even have the right to question the Secretary of State for Wales after the first of his formal addresses to the Assembly, given to outline the Westminster Government's forthcoming legislative programme. When the Presiding Officer ruled that he should take questions, the governing administration attempted to have the ruling withdrawn. In early 2000, Shortridge attempted to veto which Assembly Members could meet with visiting dignitaries. Elis-Thomas considered that this was his responsibility, and overruled Shortridge's objection. And lastly, a dispute in July 2000 over those resolutions, approved by a majority in the Assembly, that had not been acted upon or ignored by the Administration.[89]

He rebuked Shortridge's attempt to admonish an Assembly member, the Conservative William Graham, insisting that dealing with complaints made against Assembly members was a matter for him, and in another row, fell out over the allocation of civil servants, sparked by a minor amendment to an Assembly resolution on sustainable development, which proposed to relocate the civil service's Sustainable Development unit from the Agricultural department to the Central Policy Unit. The Permanent Secretary objected partly because of cost, but more fundamentally because he felt it should be for himself rather than politicians to make operational decisions on how the Assembly's civil servants should carry out their duties.[90]

This series of confrontations came to a head during a meeting of the party leaders in the Assembly at which both Lord Elis-Thomas and Jon Shortridge were present. There were ill-tempered exchanges between the two men, which caused Elis-Thomas to write a strongly worded letter to Shortridge the following day, defending his right to uphold Assembly decisions and attacking the civil servant for seeking to circumvent them.[91] The letter was widely copied and leaked to the press by the unrepentant Presiding Officer:

> It represents a challenge by an official to the authority of the democratic process and seeks to undermine the powers of the Assembly. As PO I consider I have a duty to defend these. I am also concerned that your actions in seeking to question my authority and the decisions which I take as the person elected by the Assembly to make the necessary judgements in such matters constitutes a serious impropriety; it is not the place of an official to seek to question my decisions, which I take on behalf of the Assembly.

This was copied to the party leaders, and the head of the Home Civil Service, Sir Richard Wilson. It is understood that Wilson offered to Shortridge that he could request the PM to speak with Lord Elis-Thomas in an effort to smooth things over, but he declined.[92]

The Presiding Officer sought to defend decisions made by the Assembly, the position of backbench Members, and the integrity of his own office. Underpinning these disputes were different perceptions of the Assembly's role and the way it should develop. From Elis-Thomas's point of view, the higher echelons of the executive were trying to operate as if the old Welsh Office was still in existence with the Assembly acting as a mere advisory body. From the executive's point of view, the PO sought to push the remit of the Assembly beyond what was laid down or envisaged in the 1998 Government of Wales Act. The result was to push the Assembly in the direction of a parliamentary body with aspirations for even wider powers.

This row was reported to No. 10, and in a letter to the Prime Minister, Rhodri Morgan stepped in to defend the civil service:

> I thought I should update you on the 'spat' involving Lord ET and Jon Shortridge, the Permanent Secretary, although Sir Richard Wilson has no doubt informed you about most of the recent developments. The PO has represented the issues as the Perm Sec questioning the validity of motions passed by the Assembly, or worse, refusing to implement them.
>
> This was not the case. I chaired the meeting, an informal meeting between the four party leaders, PO and Perm Sec. At no time did JS say anything that could remotely justify Dafydd's interpretation of events. Jon did not question the lawfulness of the motion on sustainable development passed on 14 September. I made this absolutely clear during the Assembly's plenary session yesterday. I also put it on the record that it is reprehensible to attack public servants in the media either by way of leaks or interviews when they are constrained from defending themselves. I hope we can draw a line under this unseemly episode.

But in defending Shortridge, Morgan also brought attention to the fundamental quandary at the heart of the Assembly and its creation as a corporate body, and accepted Elis-Thomas's thrust of argument:

> There is an underlying problem here. The Assembly is technically a corporate body, but we have been moving steadily to a *de facto* separation of the Administration on the one hand, and the Presiding Office and the body of the kirk of the Assembly on

the other. Some parties may still seek to direct the Administration on the detail of its work, rather than to hold it to account in the classical Parliamentary manner. There are technical reasons why such motions can't be ruled out of order. Of course, where such motions have a bearing on efficient management of staff, you can see the Perm Sec's problem ... The difficulty we now have is in judging whether the attacks on the PS by the Presiding Officer will now cease. I don't want to attack the PO since you can imagine the press 'field day' that would create. On the other hand, it would create problems, leaving aside the personal unfairness on Jon, if there are further attempts to undermine his function as PS and Accounting Officer.[93]

The Presiding Office had already been recognised as independent of Government, had its own budget, and its clerk had been delegated powers over his staff and resources. A note to the Prime Minister from one of his advisers suggested a suitable reply to Rhodri Morgan's letter:

Lord ET's allegations about JS re part of a wider political problem in Wales, and his comments are as much an attack on Jon Shortridge's role as on him personally. The timing of ET's attack is particularly unpleasant because Jon has been seriously ill for several weeks. . . . I would find it helpful if you replied to Rhodri Morgan along the lines of the attached draft, signalling your belief that it is not acceptable to attack public servants in the media in this way. Underlying some of this seems to be the wish for an independent Welsh Civil Service, as indicated both in the Partnership Agreement between the Labour Party and the Liberal Democrats in Wales and in Lord ET's comments. I do not suggest that you raise this with Rhodri Morgan, but you should be aware that the issue is around.[94]

In Government, Rhodri Morgan's Cabinet Secretary, Lawrence Conway, advised him on which officials were keen on making devolution a success and which were much happier in the old Welsh Office:

With our system, the Perm Sec [Shortridge] was the head of the civil service. Indeed, he still attended the weekly prayer meetings of all the permanent secretaries in London, chaired by the (Whitehall) Cabinet Secretary . . . A complication for Sir Jon was that he was also head of those civil servants who had applied for jobs serving the Assembly Members' side of things down Cardiff Bay . . . it did mean a difficult relationship for Sir Jon with Dafydd Elis-Thomas, the PO, in which I had to intervene from time to time in order to keep the peace.[95]

Morgan had his own issues with Shortridge, and 'the main bone of contention' was that 'he thought I was trying to politicise the civil service. I thought he was being a stick in the mud.' But Morgan continued 'stretching the elastic' of the Government of Wales Act and standing orders without actually breaking them. Five years later the Government of Wales Act 2006 came into force but in the meantime, they were seeing how far we could stretch the separation.[96]

In the summer of 2000, Dafydd Elis-Thomas and Rhodri Morgan had agreed to initiate a review of procedure within the corporate body of the Assembly with a view to further separate the executive and the parliamentary body. As a result of its coalition agreement with the Liberals, the Government had also agreed to start a review of the Assembly's powers, and requested Ivor Richard, from Aberdare, the former European Commissioner and former Labour Leader in the House of Lords, to consider future options for the powers and structure of the Assembly. His committee started its work in 2002 and reported in March 2004.[97]

The Presiding Officer's spats with civil servants highlighted a major structural defect in the devolution settlement, which was understood, if not entirely appreciated, in Whitehall. In a memo to David Miliband, the head of the Government's policy unit, one of his staff prophetically pointed to the likely need for further legislation:

> There is a complicated corporate structure in Wales, to Westminster eyes muddling the legislature and the executive. The key initiative is the review of the Assembly's internal workings cooked up between Rhodri Morgan and Dafydd Elis-Thomas. I would expect one outcome of that to be more separation between executive and legislature which could enable a better definition of respective remits to enable the first to develop confidence as

Ministers. Stability in the Lab-Lib Dem pact is also an opportunity for Ministers to develop authority and confidence. But, beyond a certain point, the corporate structure will require new legislation to unscramble.[98]

In March 2001, after the retirement of John Lloyd, Elis-Thomas appointed a new chief clerk, Paul Silk, who had been a respected parliamentary clerk in the House of Commons:

> I was determined to have a traditional parliamentary clerk, because that is something we had never really had, and I found out that Paul Silk was willing to do it . . . What was important to me was that somebody was there, who I had known from working together in parliament and also that his name would be taken seriously in Scotland, Ireland and especially in both Houses of the UK parliament . . . What Paul did in the particular engaging way that he has was to bring people along in the institution (and there were increasing numbers of people in the old Welsh Office), who really wanted to be proper parliamentary clerks and he was able to bring that attitude. Because of his style and background, he did transform the institution. In my view it was essential as a signal for the National Assembly of Wales that we had a chief executive who was a proper parliamentarian.[99]

The Richard Commission's report in 2004 recommended full legislative powers for the National Assembly and sparked a vigorous debate within the Welsh Labour party. Most MPs at Westminster wished for a referendum before any more powers were granted, although Rhodri Morgan declared one would not be necessary. While there was agreement for more powers for the Assembly, there was less consensus for Richard's recommendation to increase the number of Assembly members from 60 to 80, and for them to be elected more proportionally by the Single Transferable Vote system.[100]

The Commission did not recommend a referendum, but its key achievement was to secure cross-party unity, including the Conservatives, in favour of legislative powers, and crucially, the Labour party's manifesto for the 2005 General Election committed the party to enacting most of the Richard Commission's report.

But as Elis-Thomas applied himself to the creation of this new democracy, his sister Elin died extraordinarily suddenly of cancer, in April 2002, at the age of 51. Six years younger than Dafydd, they had become increasingly estranged. His decision to take his place in the House of Lords had angered her, and his chairmanship of the Language Board convinced her that her brother had lost his political compass. They also disagreed over what she considered to be his lack of concern for his mother, who had moved in the late 1980s to live in sheltered accommodation in nearby Bala, and who she visited regularly, in spite of their difficult relationship. Elin died only two days after she was diagnosed with the condition, on Friday 8 April 2002. She had lived in Llanuwchllyn, where her father's family originally came from, throughout her married life. A pillar of the community, she and her husband, with their three children, owned the local garage, and she was the chapel organist, an accomplished harpist and choral accompanist, active in the Sunday School, a keen public debater and perceptive literary reviewer in print and the media, and presenter of Radio Cymru's weekly arts programme. The minister, Revd W. J. Edwards, described her as 'a livewire', a 'big soul in a small body, on fire for everything of value'.[101] She trained generations of young people to recite and sing, as well as producing the local drama company: 'she was held in very high regard by so many people as a very talented person who was always prepared to contribute to community life, being a person who loved being involved with people'.[102]

Her mother was profoundly affected by Elin's passing. At the age of 88, she had not been in the best of health for a number of years and her former minister from Trefriw, Revd Dafydd Andrew Jones, recalls visiting her at the time, 'the death was a terrible shock. She was a broken woman already after her husband's death – she had had problems with her blood and she had existed on the equivalent of baby food for years. Before, she had been queen of her home and chapel, but that broke down overnight.'[103] At Elin's death, she told her minister that 'they've taken the only thing that I had from me'.[104] Dafydd's mother died two years later, on 21 July 2004, in a nursing home in Pentrefoelas.

Building the Senedd

The Senedd building in Cardiff is the physical legacy of Dafydd Elis-Thomas's contribution to Welsh devolution. The eight-year-old saga of deciding on the site of this new home of Welsh democracy, the commissioning of its design, and its building, reflected the lack of confidence that the Welsh administration not only had in its own identity, calling itself the oxymoronic Assembly Government, but its lack of confidence in the permanence of devolution. The delays in its building is explained by the nervousness of the Assembly's political leadership and a wish not to create a hostage to fortune by building an expensive edifice that would be hung like an albatross around the necks of proponents of devolution.

Elis-Thomas did not believe that 'a proper parliament in Wales' could function in an old Welsh Office building such as Crickhowell House, named after the Conservative former Secretary of State for Wales, Nick Edwards, ennobled as Lord Crickhowell:[105]

> It was a pretty dysfunctional office block. But I also knew that we should not be building new office accommodation for the new parliament – that would not be appropriate, but we had to have space that would have daylight and fresh air; where the public could feel that this building was theirs. Crickhowell House was okay as a back-office because we had no alternative, but it could never be anything but a short-term option. There was always a budget, albeit never enough, for a building. I had huge support and advice from the Royal Society of Architects in Wales. Even before I became Presiding Officer, I went to see Dewi-Prys Thomas, founder of the Welsh School of Architecture,[106] and I would have regular discussions with those who were Dewi's successors at the School and they were inspirational.[107]

In 1998, when the design competition for the new building was launched, the proposed site for the building had been a business park on the water's edge of Cardiff Bay. The Assembly's office block, Crickhowell House, was renamed unilaterally as Tŷ Hywel by Dafydd Elis-Thomas in 2008, after Hywel Dda, the law-giving prince of Deheubarth in the tenth century. These served as the Assembly's offices and also included the inadequate Assembly Chamber, which had been installed in a former computer room. An empty space at the back of the building was eventually earmarked for the new Assembly

Chamber, and it was hoped that its design would exemplify the virtues of Welsh democracy.

In 1995, Zaha Hadid's ground-breaking design for the opera house, to be housed adjacent to Crickhowell House, had been discarded by a combination of architectural conservative parochialism and fear of its innovative design. Rhodri Morgan, a local MP at the time, joked that the design was based on Mecca and might incite a fatwa. His philistinism was echoed by the city fathers who opposed her design even after she won the competition to build the new Opera House, and the final rejection came from the project's main funder, the Millennium Commission, who granted money for such projects from the National Lottery. They were accused of wishing to avoid controversy and to fund more popular projects such as Cardiff's Millennium Stadium.[108]

Percy Thomas Architects, a local Cardiff firm, was chosen to create a revised opera house, now named the Millennium Centre, but this controversy gained Cardiff a poor reputation in the architectural world. However, crucially for the design, the chair of the jury created to judge the design of the proposed Assembly building, Lord Callaghan of Cardiff, the former Prime Minister and longstanding Member of Parliament for the Cardiff docklands area between 1945 and 1987, wrote an inspiring brief for the project, specifying that it should reflect the needs of a small and newly democratic country in the next millennium, and should 'not be overly adversarial in shape or argument'.[109]

Due to Cardiff's recent history of commissioning iconic buildings, the design team at the Richard Rogers Partnership (RRP) were not optimistic when they put forward their design bid for the new Assembly. Rogers's project manager, Ivan Harbour, recalls that their high ambition 'induced an unbelievable pressure even before we started ... To be relevant, it would have to look forward to appeal to young people – the politicians of the future.'[110] Elis-Thomas was a huge supporter of Rogers's work:

> I first came across Richard Rogers's work when I saw some photographs of the Pompidou centre in Paris, and I went to see it and I was delighted with it. I had always had an interest in architecture but no personal expertise, so I decided if, and when we come to build a parliamentary building in Wales, it has got to be as good as the Pompidou Centre. Edwina [Hart] and I shared this view that we had to have quality.[111]

Rogers succeeded in winning this international architectural design competition, and it was agreed that the debating chamber would be on the new site, adjacent to Tŷ Hywel, at Capital Waterside in Cardiff Bay. Ron Davies, having failed to ensure his first choice of City Hall in Cathays Park, enthusiastically supported the project. Even after his resignation as Secretary of State for Wales in October 1998, he championed Rogers's design and, as an Assembly member, privately helped Rogers's team to navigate its political cross-currents with civil servants.[112] The existing Assembly chamber, a dingy ill-lit room was hot, uncomfortable and unhygienic, as one of the new Members, Dafydd Wigley, recalled:

> The ceiling is low and the pillars block Members from seeing each other. The room is inappropriate for visitors, who have a restricted view of the Assembly. Worse than that, the room becomes hot and the air is unhealthy to breathe. After sitting uninterruptedly in the Chamber for three hours, I have a splitting headache. It isn't acceptable for the National Assembly of Wales to meet in such a room which is so inappropriate.[113]

The chamber was lampooned mercilessly by visiting parliamentary sketch writers, when Tony Blair visited the Assembly on 30 October 2001. *The Times*'s Matthew Parris compared the chamber of the Assembly to 'the passenger lounge on a Sealink ferry, circa 1985. The surroundings were wrong: a makeshift Assembly in a half-finished docklands development.'[114] Simon Hoggart of *The Guardian* thought that the chamber 'resembles a function room in a provincial hotel',[115] and Quentin Letts in the *Daily Mail* was no less scathing: 'The National Assembly's current digs in Cardiff, on a windswept industrial estate, are small and pokey. The claims department of a provincial insurance company might have proved a more inspirational arena in which to discuss great matters of state.'[116]

In keeping with his profound scepticism about new building projects, Rhodri Morgan halted the Assembly's build immediately on his accession as First Secretary on 22 March 2000, in order to carry out a complete review. He had been vehemently opposed to building a new edifice and had wished for the Assembly to take over the City Hall in the centre of Cardiff's civic centre in Cathays Park. He compared Rogers's design to a 'Tesco hypermarket' and thought it made no allowances for the microclimate of Cardiff Bay 'with its occasionally ferocious south-westerlies whipping in from Penarth Head' and its three miles distance from the civil service's headquarters in Cathays Park. He tried to revive the purchase of City Hall but, to his lasting regret, was foiled by the financial demands made by the devolution-sceptic, Labour leader of Cardiff Council, Russell Goodway.[117]

An understandable reason for his concern was the spiralling cost of the project, which by March 2000 had risen from the original estimate of £17 million to £32 million. In a move to support the Rogers proposal, the worried members of the Royal Society of Architects in Wales twinned all 60 AMs with an architect in their constituency to argue the case for the use of modern architecture in the project.[118] In the process of the detailed design of the building, Morgan suggested to Rogers that the Assembly building would be overshadowed by the new Millennium Centre, the replacement for Zaha Hadid's beautiful design for an opera house, and Rogers was required to draw sketches for him to demonstrate how its scale could work. Both Liberal Democrat and Plaid were fiercely supportive of the Rogers plan, whilst the Labour group was split, and the Conservatives were opposed.

At one stage, Morgan proposed that a small debating chamber in an adjoining car park would be preferable, but even the Conservative sceptic Glyn Davies, the member for Montgomeryshire, pointed out that Morgan's suggestion of a 'mini-conservatory' would be the worst of all options.[119] Morgan quickly abandoned his alternative proposal.

Harbour recalls that when he first displayed the design for the new building, it 'went down a storm. Edwina was in tears. It was in Crickhowell House, we did a presentation, and we then unveiled the model. People said "Oh my God" – that was the moment.'[120] But on 17 July 2001, the concerns over cost over-runs forced the Assembly Government to cancel its contract with the Richard Rogers Partnership [RRP]. Edwina Hart, the Finance Minister, publicly blamed RRP for the project's cost over-runs, which Rogers refuted and alleged that they were 'being made a political scapegoat for a catastrophic failure properly to manage the project. RRP's advice was consistently ignored. It is plainly untrue for the Finance Minister to assert that RRP underestimated the costs.'

Rogers claimed that the original costing for the building of between £13 and £14 million still applied, but only to the shell of the building. He said his firm had been kept in the dark about the remainder of the costs, which had initially risen to £26 million and now by a further £15 million by July 2021. These costs were for the contents of the Chamber, its fittings, communications systems and offices, for which the administration was entirely responsible. These points remained uncontested and unanswered.[121]

Behind the scenes, Hart felt she had been manoeuvred into her difficult position by the lack of political support from her party colleagues, and from Rhodri Morgan in particular, who had been bolstered by the advice given to him by the chartered surveyors for the building project, the Idwal Symonds Partnership. The Rogers partnership took the Assembly to the court over the cancelled contract, and won the legal wrangle, leaving the Government to pay disputed invoices of £796,000 in costs. Rogers's architect, Ivan Harbour, recalled that 'we saw it going awry, and that we needed to stop the works and rethink the design. But we were then sacked. The Assembly's advisers wanted to sue us. We counter-claimed, went to arbitration and we won costs. Only then did they sack Symonds, the consultants.' Harbour recalls speaking to Hart who told him afterwards that 'I didn't feel right sacking you. The problem was that I didn't get any political support for my position. They basically said it was my decision. In those circumstances, I was obliged to follow their expert advice.'[122]

The Presiding Officer and Edwina Hart were agreed that they needed a new, prestigious building of good quality, but as Hart recalls:

> It became mired in controversy – it became a political football. It was an impossible task. Dafydd and I stuck with it – together we were solid and believed that we could get it for the agreed price and we had to remain strong. Rhodri described it as a 'carbuncle' in his memoirs, the Tories were barking away, but Dafydd was very supportive of me, even when I stopped Richard Rogers. I had to battle for the building through the Labour group and Cabinet. Rhodri was very difficult.[123]

This dispute led to a further hiatus of eighteen months on the project. Throughout the first three years of the Assembly, an annual vote had been held in order to agree for the further work to be developed and funded. Before the third vote, in July 2003, the Presiding Officer's commitment to the project was on display as he stood outside the Assembly chamber next to a small model of the new building, exhorting members to vote in favour of funding its completion. He recalls standing in front of the chamber, 'the only way for members to come in . . . I had been able to get from Rogers Partnership a very detailed model of building. I said "Look, this is what you get, and if you don't vote for it today, you won't get anything else and you will be here for the rest of your time as Assembly members."'[124]

The second fixed price contract for the project, for £50 million, was eventually agreed following the Assembly's vote by 46 votes to 12 to proceed with the project. This was opposed by the Conservative group whose spokesman branded it 'an incredible waste of money', and who were joined by a single Labour AM, the Blaenau Gwent Member Peter Law, who described the project as a 'bauble of self-indulgence and narcissistic extravagance'.[125] The contract was granted to Taylor Woodrow, but the Richard Rogers Partnership, as the project architects was still considered *persona non grata* by the Assembly government. Elis-Thomas recalled that on the day of the awarding of the contract, Hart urged him to persuade Rogers to return to the project:

> Edwina insisted I go to see Lord Rogers immediately in the House of Lords; she said 'You must go today, you must explain what has happened and tell him there are those of us, including you, that want him to continue to be our architect, because otherwise, we will not get the building of quality which we need.'[126]

Continuity was achieved by Taylor Woodrow's retention of Lord Rogers as the scheme's architect, and he worked closely with the Assembly and Dafydd Elis-Thomas to maintain the project's architectural integrity. Crucially, a new steering group was formed, chaired by an experienced Assembly project manager, Richard Wilson, which was enabled to take financial decisions, and had sufficient budget to cover the construction costs.

Harbour recalls that, in theory, they could not speak to the project team but did so anyway: 'we had been blacklisted in theory – but that position was impossible. By the second time round, Richard Wilson, who was very experienced and at the end of his career, made sure we could go through him as the chair of the project board.'[127]

The cost was now nearly six times over the original 2000 budget, due partly to the unforeseen consequences of the security measures required after the 11 September attacks, which added approximately 15 per cent to the cost,[128] and because the Assembly administration had not maintained independent cost appraisals of the scheme over the three years since December 2000. Construction of the building was finally completed in February 2006.

Dafydd Elis-Thomas's love and regard for Rogers's design and building was unquestionable:

> When we invited guests from other devolved parliaments, they were blown away by it. It is such a distinctive building. It could only be something that looks like a centre of power and a centre of accessibility. The thing I most enjoyed was when demonstrators came there and commented on what a nice place it was to demonstrate, because they could stand in the rain under the overhanging roof![129]

Edwina Hart credited Dafydd Elis-Thomas for 'how he chaired and got it through – it's very modern and the juxtaposition with the Pierhead building is wonderful. I think it is beautiful.'[130] The building was modernist in its design, and incorporated the highest environmental standards, with the use of renewable technologies and energy efficiency integrated into its design and use of Welsh materials such as slate and Welsh oak in its construction. The timber ceiling and centre funnel were made of Canadian cedar, but the slate came from Elis-Thomas's constituency in Cwt y Bugail, Blaenau Ffestiniog. The building was designed to use an earth heat exchange system for heating, rainwater was collected from the roof for flushing toilets and cleaning windows, and the roof features a wind cowl which funnels natural light and air into the debating chamber below. The building was awarded an 'excellent' certification by the Building Research Establishment Environmental Assessment Method (BREEAM), the highest ever awarded in Wales, and was nominated for the 2006 Stirling Prize.[131] Harbour recalled Elis-Thomas's passion for the project:

> I remember sharing a journey with him up to London and I remember him talking about what it should be called. There was something annoying about the fact that it was two languages – you don't want just 'the Welsh Assembly' – it's not a very

emotional name. He was worrying about it. I said if you asked people they would be bound to say no. The only people who would respond would be those who would object. The best way of going through these things would be just to do it. On another trip, he'd mulled over it, and he came up with all these names – old Welsh, old English and looked for words that he felt belonged – and connected both languages. He had a list of names – we went through them and I said – just do it. This policy became realised in the names of the parts of the building – the *Cwrt, Neuadd, Oriel, Siambr* and of course the name of the building itself, the *Senedd*.

Dafydd Elis-Thomas's unilateral naming of the building as the *Senedd* was controversial. He recalled Harbour telling him '"Why don't you just call it *Senedd* and be done with it?" I asked, "Can we do that?" "Of course you can!"' Dafydd Elis recalls that:

> That was the moment I realised it was an easy word to pronounce in any language. What I wasn't sure about was would it would be used in the English language both as the name of the building and the institution. A few members did go berserk about it, but we had to have a name for the building, which was not necessarily of the institution. I did know that that would happen, as every parliament building is usually called something in one of the languages of the country in which it is located, and that applies as the description of the building. It was an executive decision basically.[132]

The Labour member for the Rhondda, Leighton Andrews, was the most vocal protestor against the choice of a Welsh language name for the new building, asserting that 'no-one has agreed this. There has never been a vote in the Assembly on it. The Welsh Assembly Government doesn't use the term . . . We appear to be tiptoeing into a situation where the monolingual Welsh name *Senedd* is forced upon us by the Welsh establishment.'[133]

The issue then came to even greater prominence when a prior leak of the Queen's speech at the opening of the new building, revealed she intended to call the building the *Senedd*. Following Andrews's complaint, the name did not appear in the final draft of her speech, but the building continued to be called the *Senedd* in the Assembly's official information. For the Presiding Officer, the name of the building was a key element of the identity of the devolved parliamentary institution, '"the meaning is the use" is one of my favourite expressions in linguistics, that when people begin to use a name, it begins to mean something to them and therefore the name becomes the use'. His interest in semiotics and language led him throughout his career in the Assembly to use the term Government of Wales when there was formally no Welsh Government, and to use the term National Assembly for Wales rather than Welsh Assembly.[134]

The new building was finally opened by the Queen, with most of the Royal Family in attendance, on St David's Day, 1 March 2006. The new building had cost £70 million, which included £50 million in construction costs, and Ivan Harbour believes that the project would not have been completed at all but for Lord Elis-Thomas's support. Accompanying the Queen were Prince Philip, the Duke of Edinburgh, Prince Charles and his wife Camilla in her first official royal duty. The Queen paid tribute to 'this remarkable example of modern architecture', which, she said, 'shows pride and confidence – in the future of Wales, in the future of democracy, and in the central role of the National Assembly in the life of the nation'.[135]

While this confidence did not extend to christening the new building the *Senedd*, its blessing by the Royal family gave the institution greater legitimacy in the eyes of those who may not have been rabid republicans. Many noted how comfortable the Presiding Officer was in the company of the Royal family. The Queen had already opened the Assembly twice, in 1999 and 2003, and Dafydd Elis had a good relationship with Prince Charles, whom he had first met in 1969. Dafydd recalled one of his friends noting at the time:

> 'The trouble with you is – we've got to welcome the Queen, she's the head of state – but why do you have to look like you're enjoying yourself so much' and I thought, well, I am enjoying it . . . One of the things I had to do, for example, with the new building, was to decide on the size of the tablet to commemorate the opening . . . This plaque has got to be big enough so that people can see it when they come into the building, but it mustn't be too big, otherwise people will think we're just a bunch of royalists and it mustn't be too small, otherwise people will think that this is not a serious building. In the end, we got it right and we put

it up there. So, when she unveiled it and stood in front of it, she turned to me, she said, 'I really like this', and I thought, 'oh, we've done something right then!'[136]

Ivan Harbour is one of the most experienced and highly regarded architects in the UK and counts the creation of the *Senedd* building as one of the highlights of his career. He considers the building to be 'an evolution of how to deal with space. It is still forward thinking today, especially when it deals with the environment and its approach to material – it is a landmark.'[137]

The Government of Wales Bill 2006 – 'Crossing the Rubicon'

The publication of the June 2005 Government White Paper, *Better Governance for Wales*, was a major surprise for commentators. It committed the UK Government to legislate immediately for the transfer of primary legislative powers to the National Assembly for Wales, although those powers could only be unlocked after an affirmative vote in a national referendum to be held at some unspecified point in the future. The Secretary of State for Wales, Peter Hain, had crossed the political rubicon and given real hope that the Assembly could be turned into a legislative body. He succeeded in persuading devolution-sceptical Labour MPs that the threat of a referendum could block the granting of legislative powers.

The White Paper also went even further than the proposals of the Richard Commission, and by permitting the Assembly to create Measures, conferred primary legislative powers on the National Assembly even without a referendum being held.[138] Hain's success in working with Rhodri Morgan to steer the legislation proposals through the Labour party's various policy filters was a substantial achievement. The Act formally established the National Assembly for Wales and the Welsh Assembly Government as separate entities, and created a process in which Welsh legislation could be taken through the Assembly as well as Westminster. It committed to devolution of primary powers to the Assembly subject to a referendum, and also, most controversially, barred candidates from standing both in constituencies and list seats.[139]

This legislation created a halfway house to granting the Assembly legislative powers, in the form of Legislative Competence Orders (LCOs), that would prove practically difficult to implement.[140] The process of the Act was delayed during its passage through the House of Lords by Members' opposition to the proposal to stop Assembly members from being able to stand both on the regional list of candidates, and in the constituency. This opposition had excited Labour's ire, who drew attention to the most recent Assembly election in 2003 in Clwyd West, where the Labour AM Alun Pugh won, but bizarrely, all three defeated candidates were also elected as regional AMs.[141] By June 2006, Dafydd Elis-Thomas had lost none of his capacity to surprise his own party, and he opposed his own party's policy in calling on his fellow members of the Lords to end their opposition to the Bill on the issue of 'dual candidacy', arguing that carrying on the fight would only delay new powers being devolved to the Assembly and that 'the important thing ... is to get the Bill on the statute book, to get the next stage of devolution properly set up. There will be slippage if there is last minute ping pong.'[142] He understood the significance of the ban on dual candidacy for Peter Hain in winning over Members of his own party in Parliament, and in distracting them from the Bill's ground-breaking powers in making the Assembly a legislative body for the first time.[143]

This legislation received Royal Assent on 25 July 2006, preparing the way for the next stage of devolution. Elis-Thomas was already limbering up for the next steps in the growth of the Assembly, and in May 2006, created controversy when he questioned the Assembly's committee structure and claimed that AMs were not loved by the public because they did not offer value for money. Calling on Members of the Assembly to show greater commitment to their task, he said:

> We've got a wonderful chamber, the public come to look at us, we've had 110,000 visitors and yet it is difficult to point out anything (of value) that has happened recently. I think regional committees are a complete waste of time. The way committees are structured does not allow us to question ministers. We sit in plenary for two and a half-days a week and often finish early. I find that absolutely exasperating.[144]

In a BBC interview, he vented his frustration at the Assembly's 'horrendous time wasting', and also stated his readiness to abandon the Assembly's child-friendly hours: 'After all, it would mean after 6 o'clock only two nights a week and I think the people of Wales would expect us to do that – not every night but some nights.'[145]

The Conservative leader of the Assembly, Nick Bourne, worried that with the new legislation, Elis-Thomas was now of the opinion that it should not only mean enhanced powers for the institution but should also mean enhanced powers for himself:

> There would be occasions when I would disagree with him, as would other party leaders and other committee chairs. There were some confrontations. Let's be honest, he could be incredibly charming and coax the birds from the trees, but he could also be cantankerous. I do remember one occasion, to do with the chairing of the business committee which was to review the standing orders for the 2007 Assembly. Dafydd had wanted to do it – Ieuan [Wyn Jones] and Mike [German] and I went to meet him at our behest. We knew Dafydd wanted to chair the committee and we wanted Jenny Randerson,[146] and we proceeded to tell him. It didn't go down well to say the very least. We were treated to an extraordinary display of Dafydd saying he'd never been so badly treated in his entire life.
>
> I thought the crescendo was that we were going to be thrown out of his office. At a key moment Mike said he had to go to the lavatory, and this led to a release of tension. As Mike strode off, Ieuan said, 'I remember the dying days of Thatcher but I've never seen anything like this!'. Dafydd could feel strongly about things. He then flounced off but calmed down incredibly quickly. He didn't get his way, and Jenny Randerson became the chair.[147]

In meeting the challenge of implementing the Act, and separating the Assembly from Government, Elis-Thomas was handicapped by his lack of operational control over the staff and resources of the Assembly. That was in the hands of the Assembly's House Committee, chaired by the redoubtable independent Assembly member for Wrexham, and Deputy Presiding Officer, John Marek. Dafydd Elis was only an ex-officio member of that committee and lacked the authority to allocate money in preparation for the separation of the Assembly and Government. The House Committee worked independently of the Presiding Office, and while it initiated a number of key projects, such as the creation of a separate translation and reporting service for the Assembly, its pace in addressing change was slow.

He therefore decided to bypass the House Committee and what he considered Marek's obstructionism. In Spring 2006, a Welsh Government civil servant, Caroline Turner, was seconded by Jon Shortridge to take forward the work of setting up a Shadow Commission to separate the parliamentary body from Government. Reporting directly to the Presiding Officer, she recalls that there 'were lots of tensions – it took time for people in the Assembly to accept her role. It took time to earn that trust, and within the Assembly between politicians and civil servants.' Her challenge was to ensure the cooperation of senior civil servants in the Assembly to prepare for the separation with Government, due in May 2007. Even after a cross-party Shadow Commission had been set up to prepare, Turner recalls that 'we weren't permitted to see internal working papers by the Assembly's civil servants', and it was only gradually that she was able to gain the confidence of senior staff in the Assembly, who had worked through Marek's House Committee.[148]

By the summer of 2006, Elis-Thomas was concerned that the Assembly was still in no fit state to meet the challenge of becoming a separate Parliamentary institution with its own staff. He did not feel there was the impetus or will to make the necessary change amongst the senior managers, and in his view, even the Assembly's chief clerk, Paul Silk, was not totally aware of what needed to be done to meet the new challenge. An unassuming and key figure in the development of the Assembly in its first six years, he had an excellent understanding of parliamentary procedure and convention. But his 'hands-off' style of management frustrated Dafydd Elis, who felt that he was failing to grasp the need to respond swiftly to quickening constitutional change. That concern was shared by the Permanent Secretary, Jon Shortridge, who was also anxious about the lack of progress on Assembly reform, and the timetable for separation, to be achieved by the election in May 2007 was tight for such a huge constitutional and cultural change.

This concern led to a crisis meeting in the summer of 2006, between Jon Shortridge, Rhodri Morgan, Dafydd Elis-Thomas and Paul Silk, in which he was encouraged to work more quickly to meet this challenging deadline. But this meeting failed to generate greater urgency, and on the first of September 2006, it was announced Paul Silk was leaving his post to return to the House of Commons, stating that it was clear to him that 'someone with a different skill set from mine' was being sought to undertake the new post.¹⁴⁹ Silk was replaced by Claire Clancy, a career civil servant, who had been chief executive at Companies House, and whose title of chief executive, as well as clerk, more accurately reflected the Presiding Officer's trenchant view of the organisational needs of the Assembly:

> We couldn't mess about any more – we were becoming a proper government, a proper parliament and therefore we should recognise that. I never wanted to push too hard, but I realised this was what Rhodri wanted, and it was the best relationship in my life with any other politician, no question. We both knew what the other was up to, and there was no need to discuss things. We very rarely had formal meetings, because we didn't need to ... But also, I admired that he had developed his career and had bided his time and knew when it was time to strike and make things happen. I don't think that the Welsh Government would have come into existence without Rhodri quite frankly ... it was key to have his support, and he was such a brilliant leader for Welsh Labour.¹⁵⁰

After Silk's departure was announced, Elis-Thomas became embroiled in a bitter dispute with his Deputy Presiding Officer, John Marek. Feelings ran high about the perceived ousting of Silk, and one anonymous AM alleged that 'Dafydd Elis-Thomas has lost the support of his own group and now he has alienated a lot of AMs in other parties who have previously backed him ... I can't see him being re-elected as PO next year.' Marek sent an extraordinary email to Dafydd Elis, copied to every AM and staff member, protesting about the forcing out of Paul Silk, and complaining that the Assembly would need his services when primary legislation would come through the various procedures in the Assembly:

> A chief executive appointment, probably from local government, will put us on a level with county councils. I would like to think that you do not wish that to happen. We won't succeed in replacing Paul Silk with anyone who has his particular expertise and diligence exactly in the area where we are to have the new duties!¹⁵¹

Dafydd Elis rejected the view that the head of the Assembly Commission necessarily needed to be an experienced parliamentary clerk:

> The most important thing we have to do in 2007 is to make our proceedings intelligible to the public, as well as open and effective. That means much improvement in our scrutiny activity, and a much clearer way of operating in plenary without being hidebound by very rigid standing orders, as we have been so far. We don't need any of this clerking mumbo-jumbo.[152]

Within days, Marek resigned as chair of the House Committee, 'in an angry exchange of views' at a meeting of the committee in which Elis-Thomas challenged his authority to deal with the setting of the Assembly's budget.[153] But the feud with Marek rumbled on for months, and involved one excruciating stand-up row, in a plenary session of the Assembly, when he cut off Marek's microphone as he attempted to protest at Silk's departure. On another occasion, when the opposition parties challenged the Assembly budget for the following financial year (2007–8), Elis-Thomas emailed his deputy suggesting that he should chair the Budget debate. If that had happened, Marek could not have voted, and being an independent member, Labour's budget would have passed. In the event, this farcical situation was avoided when Elis-Thomas backed down and agreed to chair the Budget debate himself, and consequently, Labour lost by one vote.[154]

But Dafydd Elis-Thomas had won the battle against what he saw as the inertia of the senior leadership of the Assembly civil service, so that the Assembly was prepared for the next stage of its development as a legislative body and parliamentary body separate from Welsh Government. In the last week of the May 2007 election campaign, the *Western Mail* marked the Assembly members for their performance during the previous term; 'Top marks went to Dafydd Elis Thomas; has done a superb job as Presiding Officer. Has quietly achieved an immense amount in driving forward devolution.'[155]

In the May 2007 Assembly election, he was re-elected in the re-created seat of Dwyfor Meirionnydd, with 60 per cent of the vote and a massive majority of 8,868 over the Conservative candidate. The re-drawn boundaries of the seat now incorporated much of the former Caernarfon seat, including the Llŷn peninsula.

Dwyfor Meirionnydd National Assembly seat

Party	Candidate	Votes	% vote
Plaid Cymru	Dafydd Elis-Thomas	13,201	59.7
Conservative	Mike Wood	4,333	19.6
Labour	David Phillips	2,749	12.4
Lib Dems	Stephen Churchman	1,839	8.3[156]

Plaid Cymru won 15 seats, and with Labour only on 26, it was inevitable that there would have to be a coalition or agreement to form the next Welsh Government. The first action of the new Assembly was to appoint a Presiding Officer, and Lord Elis-Thomas had fully expected to be re-nominated for the third time, and was fully supported by Plaid's party leader, Ieuan Wyn Jones. On the morning immediately after the election, in the first meeting of Plaid Cymru's Assembly group, Plaid AMs discussed whether they should pursue a coalition with either Labour or a 'rainbow coalition'. They then discussed the Presiding Officer's appointment. Helen Mary Jones, the member for Llanelli, opposed his nomination, feeling that in his time as Presiding Officer, he hadn't done Plaid members 'any favours'.

This led to a heated discussion for a few minutes and the opposition to his nomination gained momentum. It was eventually cut short by the party's head of communications, Alun Shurmer, who warned the group that it had been a successful election campaign for Plaid Cymru, and there was an opportunity to form the Government, 'but if we didn't support Dafydd, it would overshadow the party's success by giving the impression that the party was arguing internally and imploding'. Helen Mary's response was to archly insist that 'I will not be dictated to by an unelected official'. However, the meeting calmed and eventually agreed to support Dafydd Elis's nomination, who was subsequently elected unanimously by Assembly Members.[157]

Presiding over Coalition and Moving towards Legislative Powers

Agreeing on the shape of the next Government proved much more difficult. Labour had failed to win an overall majority, with only 26 seats of the 60, with the Conservatives with 12 seats, the Liberals with 6, and

Plaid with 15. Labour initially attempted to form a 'rainbow coalition' with the Liberal Democrats, which only failed due to the disagreement of the Welsh Liberal Democrat executive and the casting vote of the executive committee chair for Wales, Rob Humphreys. In this period, Elis-Thomas was ostensibly neutral, but eighteen months before the election, he had predicted that there would be a Labour-Plaid coalition, and in the immediate period after the election, advised Ieuan Wyn Jones discreetly. Two months after the election, Plaid Cymru entered into coalition with Labour, and were given four Cabinet posts, with its leader Ieuan Wyn Jones as Deputy First Minister and the Minister for Economic Development, Elin Jones as Minister for Agriculture, Rhodri Glyn Thomas as Minister for Culture, and Jocelyn Davies as Deputy Minister for Housing. Before nominating his members of the Cabinet, Ieuan Wyn Jones had already asked Elis-Thomas privately whether he wished to be considered for a Ministerial role if the opportunity arose. To Jones's surprise, he refused, stating that his role as Presiding Officer was of greater significance, a decision that Jones believes, he later regretted.[158]

In implementing the 2006 Government of Wales Act, Elis-Thomas's practical concern was that the new law-making system created under the Act should work efficiently. This attempt to create the Assembly's primary legislation for the first time was based on 'Legislative Competence Orders' (LCOs) that allowed the Assembly to legislate but only with the consent of the House of Commons through the Select Committee on Welsh Affairs. For the Assembly to move on to a fully functioning legislative model, a referendum would have to be held in the future, so that the Welsh electorate would need to agree to the proposal. A condition of the new coalition between Plaid Cymru and Labour, agreed in the summer of 2007, was that a referendum for full law-making powers would be held 'as soon as practicable, at or before the end of the Assembly term'.[159] An all-Wales Convention was set up in 2007 under the chairmanship of Sir Emyr Jones Parry to study the issue of increasing the powers of the Assembly to a full legislative parliament.

For Plaid Cymru Ministers, these LCOs proved difficult and frustrating to implement. Plaid Cymru's special adviser at the time, Rhuanedd Richards, recalls that they were nicknamed 'Hellcos' because 'they were bonkers, and were hell on earth to make work'.[160]

Many, including Rhodri Morgan and Dafydd Elis-Thomas, had expected the measure-making system to work in a relatively straightforward manner, but by late 2009, with the LCOs being drafted in an increasingly restrictive fashion on the insistence of Whitehall and Westminster, it was clear that this system was becoming too complex and unworkable, and the seemingly interminable delays associated with the whole process had become obvious to all.[161]

Both Plaid and Labour Welsh Ministers became profoundly disillusioned with the process. For instance, an LCO presented by the Minister, Jane Davidson on the subject of environmental protection and waste management, was deemed to have been drawn too widely for the House of Commons. In an interview at the time, Elis-Thomas said that he had hoped:

> That there would be an understanding of the new settlement as being one that would allow the maximum devolution within the Act when a clear request came from the Welsh Government to the UK Government and that was supported by the majority of AMs – which I'm sure it would be in this case, because climate change was a main issue in the manifestos of all parties in Wales. Therefore, if it appears in any sense that the Welsh Government which emerged as a result of the election is being frustrated in its attempts to legislate on its manifesto commitments, that is a serious constitutional issue and goes to the heart of devolution.[162]

After the first three LCOs had been laid, a new protocol was issued under which the Assembly Government agreed not to lay draft LCOs before the Assembly until they had been agreed by Westminster. This further slowed the already snail's pace of new legislation, which was highlighted by Sir Emyr Jones Parry's All-Wales Convention, which recommended that the Assembly should progress to becoming a Parliament with full legislative powers.

On 9 April 2008, the Assembly was granted the power to legislate for the first time, in the field of special educational needs. As Rhodri Morgan pointed out, it was the first time in more than 500 years that Wales had been able to make its own laws. But even this non-contentious matter, amounting to five paragraphs, took ten months to process through two legislatures. In comparison with other proposals for LCOs, this was speedy progress indeed.[163] On the day the order was signed by the Queen, the chair of Tomorrow's Wales (the campaign set up to argue for further powers), Barry Morgan, the Archbishop of Wales, described the LCO system in his evidence to the All Wales Convention 'as a mess' and deficient in principle and in practice.[164]

Perhaps surprisingly, Elis-Thomas's response to the Archbishop stoutly defended the LCO system:

> It is no greater or lesser mess than the constitution of the Church in Wales, with which of course I am familiar. My suggestion to my spiritual leader and lifelong friend is he might consider appointing a new constitutional adviser. The constitution of Wales is a developing narrative.[165]

This was a less than convincing argument, and he continued to defend the increasingly discredited LCO system, but when the House of Commons's Welsh Affairs Select Committee claimed that the number of LCOs risked swamping the system, he attacked the committee, disputing its claim, and suggesting that 'these objections are coming not from MPs who are concerned about the volume of LCOs, but from those who would prefer for the Welsh Labour MPs on the committee to complain about the volume of work caused by a system they had insisted was introduced'. It was indeed rich for the Welsh Labour MPs on the committee to complain about the comparatively small volume of work caused by a flawed LCO system they themselves had introduced.[166]

In 2007, Dafydd Elis-Thomas had predicted that a mark of the success of the Assembly's legislative programme would be the number of measures passed each year. He suggested there should be a minimum of eighteen measures annually – six from Assembly committees, six from the Government, and six from individual Assembly members, but by 2009, only four uncontroversial LCOs had gone through in two years with the most controversial stalled, and in the case of an Affordable Housing measure, withdrawn.[167] This byzantine and opaque system infuriated not only ordinary Members of the Assembly, but Labour Ministers too. Gwenda Thomas,[168] the Deputy Minister for Social Services, entered the complexity of the LCO system in 2007 and voiced her disillusionment with the process:

> When Rhodri was First Minister and we had the first set of powers, I think there was real frustration because we were having

to take policy decisions, having to catch the train to Westminster, and just sit there giving evidence to a committee up there, asking please can we do this, is it all right with you if we do that? And I did that on various things and I think that kind of 'begging bowl' attitude towards Wales was completely intolerable . . . devolution had to move on because something had to give. Those legislative powers, the LCO system, couldn't sustain a nation that was to grow more independently in its power to serve the people.[169]

Plaid Cymru had made the holding of a referendum on direct law-making powers one of the fundamental conditions for the formation of the One Wales coalition agreement. Elis-Thomas had been fearful of a referendum, but by mid-2009, he had changed his mind and argued in favour of holding one. The key crisis point in the coalition was reached on 24 November 2009 when Plaid Cymru threatened to bring down the Government unless a referendum was scheduled before the end of the Assembly term, and Rhodri Morgan capitulated. One of the new measures agreed by the 'One Wales' Government was legislation to establish a Welsh language Commissioner, and to give official status to the Welsh language. However, the restrictions of the LCO process were not what optimists like Dafydd Elis had wished for, which was for Westminster's role in the process to be restricted to checking whether a proposed LCO was constitutionally compatible with the Assembly's powers. The legislation that created the role of Language Commissioner came into being in February 2011, and the Commissioner's role was to address the long-standing weaknesses of statutory compliance in relation to the provision of Welsh language services to the public, a development that had been strongly advocated by Welsh language supporters. But this legislation, much to Dafydd Elis's chagrin, had also attempted initially to include the Assembly amongst the organisations regulated by the new Commissioner. That attempt failed but the Welsh Language Board, which he had help create and develop, and to which he felt loyalty, was abolished.

Both Rhodri Morgan and Dafydd Elis-Thomas were of the previous generation of politicians bruised by the experience of losing the 1979 devolution referendum. They were grateful for the powers given to the Assembly by the 2006 Government of Wales Act, and both had felt it unwise to risk this in a referendum. But Rhodri's replacement as party leader in 2009, Carwyn Jones, had the greater confidence of a younger generation of politicians. Elis-Thomas only changed his mind in mid-2009 in the face of the failure of the LCO system, but according to Rhuanedd Richards, even until the day of the referendum, on 3 March 2011, Rhodri Morgan thought that it may not be won, in spite of the positive polling data. Her and Carwyn Jones's younger generation were much more confident of the outcome.

In the event, the Yes side had the support of Labour, Plaid Cymru, the Liberal Democrats, the Conservative Assembly group, and almost every civil society organisation in Wales. The referendum was won by a handsome majority of 63.5 per cent in favour, to 36.5 per cent against, albeit with a relatively low turnout of 35.6 per cent.[170] For Dafydd Elis-Thomas, this result delivered his ambition since his first involvement with Plaid Cymru in the early 1960s, to create a legislative parliamentary body for Wales.

The period between the passing of the 2006 Government of Wales Act and the Referendum had been difficult in that the LCO process had needed to be shown to be a failure before the campaign for a legislative Assembly could move on to the referendum. Rhuanedd Richards recalls Elis-Thomas as having been awkward and sometimes obstructive in his attitude in dealing with the LCO system in his role as Presiding Officer:

> It was an odd period. Dafydd had been very frustrating (to Plaid) because of the LCOs. Dafydd was saying it was a really important step, but it was hell on earth to operate as a process. Our generation felt very differently, and our view was that 'we're better than this. We'd passed the stage of being handed down permission to legislate. We demanded more. The younger generation was more confident. We thought – 'get over it' – we're a confident nation.[171]

However, the following 2011 Assembly election proved a great disappointment to Plaid Cymru. It failed to capitalise on its sole period in government, and the party was, as Richards recognised, 'in a mess' by the summer of 2011.[172] Labour increased its number of seats from 26 to 30, and Plaid Cymru lost four seats, from 15 to 11. Labour increased its vote by 10.1 per cent in its constituency vote and 7.3 per cent in its regional vote, while Plaid Cymru had a decrease of 3.1 per cent in its overall vote.

In Dafydd Elis-Thomas's constituency of Dwyfor Meirionnydd, he gained 47 per cent of the vote, with a majority of 5,000 over his Conservative opponent. He had already agreed with his Deputy Presiding Officer, Rosemary Butler, that, after three terms as Presiding Officer, on his return to the Assembly, he would step down in her favour:

> I did three full terms of four years between 1999 and 2011. That was more than enough. I thought it would be good for the institution, therefore, to have a change. I was certain that there would be experienced people that would be prepared to stand for the position. I decided that I wouldn't seek a fourth term. It would be inappropriate. I had no intention at that stage of having a serious disagreement with my party group, because I still found it very valuable to work in my constituency.
>
> Remember I had four boundary changes during my period as AM, so therefore, I was working in new areas, I was working in the old Meirionnydd, then my home patch of Nant Conwy, then in Dwyfor, so that it was always important to me to make sure that I did my constituency weekends and recess weeks and so on properly, and had a very good relationship with the local councillors and officials, so we could get things done in the area. I was a high-profile representative.[173]

But his friend Edwina Hart judges that he was mistaken to have stood down as Presiding Officer:

> I think he got a bit fed up. There was talk about him standing down before. People were complaining about him ... and there was general discontent towards him in the Plaid group. But on the other hand, I think he would have won. I think he simply woke up one morning and decided to stand down.[174]

Lord Dafydd Elis-Thomas's role as Presiding Officer of the National Assembly for Wales for the first eleven years of its existence, was crucial for the development of the institution. In spite of the constitutional disarray that he and his fellow Assembly members had inherited from the 1998 Government of Wales Act, he fought to place the mechanism in place for the separation of powers between the parliamentary institution and the Government and did so with the support of the First Minister, Rhodri Morgan, in particular. Moreover, with the support of his friend and colleague, Edwina Hart, he drove the Assembly building project in the teeth of the Government's scepticism and Rhodri Morgan's reluctance to support the creation of the democratic home of a Welsh Parliament. Finally, he established stability in the last Assembly term as Presiding Officer, so that the Assembly was ready to meet the challenge of becoming a legislative Assembly. Together with Rhodri Morgan, he was arguably one of the two most important and influential public personalities in the development of Welsh devolution in its first eleven years.

Tim Williams, one of the leaders of the 1997 anti-devolution campaign, and a friend, considers that as the Presiding Officer:

> He gave his office a sense of authority in a high-level national role. He thought that the Assembly was where the nation would be created. He took procedure very seriously. How lucky was it for the national idea that Dafydd Elis-Thomas was there at this time? I can disagree with him, but I was impressed by him. Gwynfor couldn't have done it – Wigley couldn't have done it.[175]

He had made numerous enemies in his period as Presiding Officer. A number of Labour Assembly Members and their advisers thought he could be maverick and inconsistent. Many Plaid Assembly Members regarded him as insufficiently partisan towards the party, and that he could be too much of a *bon viveur* on social occasions around the Members' tea rooms and receptions. But he was compassionate and understanding of Members' needs and mindful of the rights of the less senior Members of the Assembly. He was vocal in his defence of the institution, and always prepared to honestly criticise its worst elements, whether in the conduct of its members and its time wasting, its bizarre structure of regional committees or in the dilatory response to the dire need for a building worthy of its ambition. He had been the only Presiding Officer of the Assembly for the eleven years of its existence, but by May 2011, at the age of 65, he had resigned himself to standing down from his role as Presiding Officer, and his challenge was now to adapt to his unfamiliar new role as a Plaid Cymru back-bencher.

7

Dissent, Departure and Ministerial Office

The new back-bencher

After the May 2011 Assembly election, it became increasingly evident to his own staff that Dafydd Elis-Thomas found difficulty in adjusting to becoming an ordinary Assembly Member for the first time. His research assistant, Elin Llŷr, recalls that 'he was like a new member after the 2011 Election, because he had been the Presiding Officer for the whole period of the Assembly. He now had too much time on his hands.'[1]

Plaid failed to capitalise on its part in coalition government in 2007–11, and its performance in the 2011 Election was a great disappointment, with its number of seats reduced from fifteen to eleven and relegated to third place in the Assembly. A week after the election, its leader Ieuan Wyn Jones announced that he would stand down during the first half of the Assembly term. He stayed on as leader until June 2013, and in that time attempted to re-organise the party, and brought in a new chief executive, Rhuanedd Richards, previously his special adviser, to prepare Plaid Cymru for the next election.

She was initially welcomed by Elis-Thomas and found him 'very supportive and lovely and he said he'd be with me all the way. It was hard to square that with what he did afterwards – I didn't get that support from him.'[2] Ieuan Wyn Jones had been Dafydd Elis's main ally within the Plaid group. They knew and respected each other and had worked closely together as Members of Parliament between 1987 and 1992. Elis-Thomas had supported him as candidate for the leadership to replace Wigley in 2000 and remained one of his main allies after his second election as leader in 2003, when he fought off an attempt to unseat him.

Ieuan Wyn Jones's announcement that he would stand down as the party's leader within the year, in March 2012, was not unexpected. But more surprising to Dafydd Elis-Thomas's wife Mair, and to his staff, was the former Presiding Officer's decision to bid for the leadership. He had not indicated his intention beforehand, and subsequently claimed that members of his local party had encouraged him to put his name forward.[3] His stated motivation was to initiate an open discussion about Plaid's political direction, and he had unhelpfully criticised the party's political strategy during the 2011 election campaign, in which he believed they had mistakenly disowned the value of their coalition with Labour:

> There appeared to be a determination to be as negative as possible towards our previous partners in government and I don't think the position of the party was sufficiently clearly explained . . . It's very clear that the Welsh people have decided that they trust the leadership of Carwyn Jones as First Minister.[4]

Elin Llŷr was taken aback at his decision to stand, and even more surprised at his request for her to organise his campaign:

> I had never imagined that I would be leading Dafydd's leadership campaign. When Sioned, his office manager in Porthmadog was told, she initially laughed. His aim was to split the vote. I don't think he thought he would win but he was there to mix it up, and he certainly did that. He opened up a lot of conversations about the future of the party, about nuclear power, and independence. He created a discussion throughout Wales and made it interesting. Many thought he was bonkers to put his name forward. A lot of the 'old stagers', Plaid veterans, supported him, as the younger generation supported Leanne Wood.[5]

What surprised Rhuanedd Richards was that during the 2007–11 period of the Assembly, Dafydd in party meetings would often introduce one of his rivals for the leadership, Elin Jones, as his 'favourite and the next leader of Plaid Cymru'. She was surprised that he didn't back Jones, because 'she was so popular amongst members in rural areas like Meirionnydd. It was a surprise, and it was inconsistent'. She believed that he had little chance of winning the leadership race and that he had already become a statesman-like figure: 'why did he want to do it? ... I think he saw it as a way of becoming Minister or First Minister in the future.'[6] Elin Llŷr did not think that Dafydd expected to win:

> He is very sure of his own ability and clear about the need to educate people in the party. I'm not sure whether he wanted simply to affect the result or thought he could win. Sometimes, I felt that Dafydd wasn't sure either of his intention and didn't seem sure about which version of him would appear today.[7]

Significantly, of the eleven Plaid members in the Assembly group, Dafydd Elis-Thomas could only count on his own vote, while six backed Elin Jones, the member for Ceredigion, and three supported the left-wing republican Leanne Wood. Simon Thomas, a regional member for west Wales, initially declared he would stand, but withdrew in favour of Elin Jones, on the basis of what Elis-Thomas termed publicly as a 'secret deal', in which Simon Thomas would be made her deputy leader. Ieuan Wyn Jones abstained as the retiring leader, and was disappointed at Dafydd's decision to stand, believing 'it was a mistake for him ... because people were looking to go in a different direction. He didn't ask me for advice. He knew what I would have said.'[8] On the other hand Elis-Thomas did gain the support of a range of the party's local government leaders such as Dyfed Edwards, leader of Gwynedd council, Cardiff councillor Delme Bowen, and Peter Hughes Griffiths and Emlyn Dole, both prominent Plaid councillors on Carmarthenshire Council.

Leanne Wood's supporters were more broadly-based, and included the former Member of Parliament, Adam Price, Jonathan Edwards MP, the Assembly Member Bethan Jenkins, and perhaps surprisingly, Lord Dafydd Wigley, who was persuaded by her enthusiasm and the possibility of re-focusing the party's message to target the valleys seats of south Wales. Dafydd Elis-Thomas's performances in the hustings debates varied wildly, from disengagement to ill-disguised contempt for his fellow candidates, in which he alienated more traditional Plaid members. Elis-Thomas surprisingly, urged his supporters to give their second vote to the young upstart contender, Leanne Wood, rather than to the experienced Elin Jones.

His advice may have given comfort to those Plaid members who had thought of Leanne Wood as too radical and overly fixated on her Rhondda base, rather than Plaid's rural heartlands. Whilst the younger rebellious

Elis-Thomas may have been drawn to the radicalism of Leanne Wood, they had already confronted each other in the Assembly. He had expelled Wood from the chamber for a day in 2004 for referring to the Queen as 'Mrs Windsor' during a debate in response to the Queen's Speech. She boycotted every official opening of the Assembly, together with the opening of the new Assembly building in March 2006, citing that her conscience would not allow her to attend the ceremony: 'As a republican, I just wouldn't feel right attending an Assembly meeting presided over by an unelected head of state.'[9]

As Presiding Officer for eleven years, he had been inured to the need to ingratiate himself to the party. His public interventions had been from his perspective as Presiding Officer rather than as a back bench Plaid Cymru Assembly Member. Not unexpectedly, Dafydd Elis-Thomas was the first candidate to be knocked out in the first round of the election, having gained 1,278 votes, 21.1 per cent of the total. Leanne Wood gained 2,879 votes (47.4 per cent) and Elin Jones 1,884 votes (31.2 per cent).

In the second round, Leanne Wood comfortably defeated Elin Jones with 3,326 votes and 57.1 per cent of the vote cast.[10] Leanne Wood had won because she excited the younger members of the party, was the only candidate to engage effectively through social media, and gained the influential support of hundreds of Cymdeithas yr Iaith members after she had campaigned to gain formal official status for the language in the 2011 Welsh Language Act.

Ironically, given his intellectual interests, Dafydd Elis thought his rival candidates dwelt too much on theory: 'A party is not somewhere to discuss political philosophy. People asked me to stand. I wanted to kick ass, to show that I was still around! But I didn't think I would win.'[11] However, he was bruised and personally disappointed at his rejection and became swiftly dissatisfied with Leanne Wood. Elin Llŷr recalls that his long-standing support for Trawsfynydd nuclear power station led to disagreements with Wood on energy policy, and he found her strident politicking to be very different to his low-key style: 'he felt bitter – he had such detailed policy knowledge of the environment, for instance. He is a politician of the old school and could have been very supportive, but he struggled with such a new approach – he hadn't expected her to win.'[12]

He had underestimated Leanne Wood and had not given her due regard as a serious politician. Rhuanedd Richards, the party's chief executive, recalls how dismayed he was at her victory:

While he was fond of her ... Dafydd's disappointment was obvious. He had lost the support he thought he had within Plaid ... It didn't mean that people had lost respect for him – they hadn't – he was still an important figure, but he hadn't dealt with Plaid internally for many years.[13]

As Elin Llŷr recalls, the only Plaid Assembly Member who had any influence on Elis-Thomas at this time was Ieuan Wyn Jones, who could 'keep the peace' with him, but when he left the Assembly in 2013, Dafydd lost an ally: 'He had no other friends in the group, but he knew other members in the other political groups well. It was also how gossip was told and retold, and Dafydd was blamed for that.'[14] But although many were surprised at Wood's victory, she herself attempted from the outset to mollify her critics. She delighted and surprised Elis-Thomas by using her power of patronage as leader to install him as the chair of the Assembly's Environment committee, and was made Plaid Cymru's spokesperson for Environment, Energy and Planning. He was then moved as party spokesman to Rural Affairs, Fisheries and Food in 2012, and later to transport in 2013. But he found it difficult to adjust to life beyond the Presiding Office, and also felt out of tune with most of the Plaid Cymru group:

> I didn't foresee that there would be conflicts, but obviously, there were undercurrents. I was made transport spokesperson. The proposal for integrated, public-sector supported public transport in Wales was something I always thought was important and I hoped would happen. There was a view among other parts of the leadership of the group that spokespeople should pursue a line which was determined by the party, not pursue a line which the spokesperson might feel was the best approach in terms of public policy. Whereas, I'm afraid I couldn't agree with that as an approach. I thought it was essential that spokespersons should work with those people operating in the policy area. The making of policy options should not be just left to the party conference, the party national council, or another policy-making body in the party, but there should be an active involvement by any spokesperson with those who are operating in the policy field.[15]

His freedom from the party's discipline that he had enjoyed as a Presiding Officer did not extend to his new role as a comparatively minor member of the Plaid Cymru group, and its new leader now demanded greater loyalty to the party's policies. His more freewheeling approach to party discipline would create inevitable conflict with the party's leadership.

Rebellion

Elis-Thomas was appointed as Chancellor of his former *alma mater*, Bangor University in the summer of 2000, and this cherished role required him to be present at the University's annual degree ceremonies. As Presiding Officer, he had ensured that he was available to attend to his university duties, but this resulted in his first major row with Leanne Wood. She called for a vote of no confidence in the Labour Health Minister, Lesley Griffiths, because of a proposed re-configuration of health services throughout Wales, on Wednesday 12 July 2012, precisely when Elis-Thomas was due to discharge his duties of granting degrees in Bangor University. He was unsympathetic to Wood's view on health services reform and disagreed with the party's opposition to the Minister's proposals for his constituency, which would have led to facilities in Blaenau Ffestiniog closing and being transferred to Porthmadog, ten miles away.

When he pointedly declined to return to Cardiff for the vote, the party's Chief Whip, Jocelyn Davies wrote to the party's group chair, Alun Ffred Jones, demanding disciplinary proceedings against him, alleging that he had not only disobeyed the party whip but had made derogatory comments publicly about the vote of no confidence:

> He replied that he had responsibility for the graduation of 400 students. I urged him again, pointing out that I wouldn't ask him if it wasn't important ... On Wednesday morning I discovered that Dafydd had contacted the media on Tuesday evening to let them know he would not be changing his plans. As a result, the media asked us to comment and this placed us in a very difficult position publicly. I also discovered that he had telephoned the BBC on Wednesday morning. I am aware that Leanne Wood then rang him and during their conversation he confirmed that he would not be coming to Cardiff. I later

became aware that he undertook television and radio interviews confirming that he wouldn't be attending the Assembly because he fundamentally disagreed with our stance on reconfiguration of the Health Service and he also made derogatory remarks about the Party and the Group.[16]

Rhuanedd Richards now threatened to issue a press release contrasting Leanne Wood's commitment to scrutinising the government's record on health, with Elis-Thomas's commitment to Bangor University.[17] Locally, Plaid activists also tried to press him to toe the party line, and in this period, a constituency meeting witnessed two party officers, Ioan Roberts who worked for the Caernarfon AM Alun Ffred Jones, and Mabon ap Gwynfor who worked for the north Wales regional AM, Llŷr Gruffydd, unusually attend a meeting in order to pressurise him to change his mind, and 'tried to stir the party locally from the Dwyfor area'.[18]

This serious breach of party discipline only briefly led to the withdrawal of the party whip. He was unapologetic in opposing the no-confidence vote on health policy, and publicly challenged Wood's assertion that he opposed protecting core health services at community level:

> That is wrong ... what I don't believe is appropriate is where you have facilities built that are not properly commissioned. I represent two hospitals within ten miles of each other, both of whom are not properly staffed. The job of an Assembly Member is to be a champion of quality services. And when the time comes for a change in public service, then that should be supported, provided it delivers better quality. And that is what the health board is doing in the north.[19]

Rhuanedd Richards interpreted Dafydd's attitude at the time as being coloured by his personal disappointment in not winning the leadership:

> Contradicting Plaid policy – we had agreed that we would never do that. Members were upset. I remember in the Royal Welsh Show a few weeks later, talking to him, telling him we were trying to work as a team. Dafydd was upset and angry and said, 'well it's my business, it's not for you'. He was still talking really about the leadership. A number of the group were pressing to

remove Dafydd at that time. The worst thing was that Leanne didn't deal with it and get rid of Dafydd, but it would have been a big deal. The relationship between Leanne and Dafydd was awful. I tried to make them reconcile, but Dafydd couldn't see past his personal disappointment.[20]

From the summer of 2012, Plaid Cymru employed a consultant, Claire Howell, whose organisation, Really Effective Development Company (RedCo) specialised in personal development and organisational psychology. She had worked on the Democrats' Presidential campaign for Barack Obama in the USA and had also advised on the transformation of the Scottish National Party's fortunes for the past eight years, before being asked to help to improve the electoral fortunes of Plaid Cymru. RedCo had worked extensively with Alex Salmond to transform the SNP in Scotland, and Claire Howell was credited as having softened Salmond's image and made him appear less confrontational during TV interviews. She helped to move the SNP from a party of protest and grievance to a party of government, and eventually to the 2014 Scottish referendum on independence. After the 2011 election, Plaid's chief executive, Rhuanedd Richards, met the SNP's general secretary, Peter Murrell, who recommended Claire Howell as 'the catalyst for their success'. Howell recalled:

> Rhuanedd got me involved – I met Dafydd Wigley, Rhuanedd and Leanne. It was to help Leanne but it then obviously spread and I ran a lot of sessions for Plaid across the country, much around applied psychology, and how to get your message across. Plaid had got themselves into the same space as the SNP had been – it was a party of complaint, a party of grievance, and unless you're in power, that's useless. The sessions were around getting people to vote for you, using applied psychology techniques. They bang on about independence, Plaid, but what's the point? I showed them how to capitalise, not to complain, and I got change – especially with Leanne and Rhuanedd. I thought she (Leanne) was very brave. I helped to shape Leanne, who was unconfident when she took over. Looking back at the TV debates during the 2015 General Election, for instance, it takes inner steel to stand up against (David) Cameron and others.[21]

Howell organised a training weekend for the Plaid leadership team at Gregynog Hall, the University of Wales's residential centre near Newtown in Montgomeryshire. The group included Leanne Wood, together with her fellow Plaid AMs, their three MPs, its MEP Jill Evans, and life peer Lord Wigley. Activities included a great deal of team building exercises. Howell has fond memories of the course: 'I have huge "hiraeth" for it; a lot of fun. It is an extraordinary place – we had community singing at the end of the day.' One of the rules she imposed was a prohibition on discussion of contentious policy differences such as nuclear power or wind farms:

> You need to use the techniques and tools first before fighting over policy, to change the party's thinking process so that they become more successful. We had two days, with loads of applied psychology. I fined them a penny if they were in any way talking negatively or putting down either themselves or anybody else. We really bonded – it was fabulous.[22]

But on her drive home, she received a call from Rhuanedd Richards apologising that the journalist Martin Shipton was writing a story about the weekend: 'it was in the *Western Mail* the next day. Why tell people what you're doing in a competitive environment?' Dafydd Elis was suspected of being the source of the leak. At Gregynog, Howell thought he had 'behaved perfectly, he did everything he was asked to do, contributed to the discussion. He was fascinated. I would say he was that because of self-interest, but he wouldn't learn.'[23]

The *Western Mail* described, based on a conversation with Elis-Thomas, how this event was seen to have contributed to his rehabilitation in the party: 'Dafydd Elis-Thomas . . . has been brought back into the fold and that was cemented during the sessions at Gregynog. It was all quite "touchy feely" and the watchword in future is positive.'[24]

Leanne Wood however, recalls that the whole leadership team had agreed on the need for party unity, in order to win the 2016 Assembly election. The Gregynog weekend facilitated honest discussion between the elected members present and emphasised that members should not attack other members of the party in public:

> It was great, and we were all signed up to that, and it didn't take long at all for the whole thing to be undermined by Dafydd.

He was doing it quite openly. I was limited in the tools I could use for discipline, and removing the committee chair was one of the tools I had . . . He was in agreement and didn't speak out against anything, but not really engaged either. In this period, he was a wrecker, a spoiler . . . whatever we were trying to achieve, he was trying to undermine it.

Leanne Wood recalls that prior to 2012 she had enjoyed a warm relationship with Dafydd. Together with a number of other young women members, she had decided not to stand as a candidate in 1999 in protest against Plaid's lack of action on ensuring a gender balance in the selection of candidates:

> Dafydd was very encouraging of me to stand for the Assembly in 2003. His warm words were a factor in me standing. I saw him as someone to respect, and he encouraged me to stand. Our relationship was very positive up until 2004, when I had referred to the monarch as 'Mrs Windsor'. The Member for the Rhondda, Leighton Andrews, complained, Dafydd supported him and had me ejected from the chamber. That was another disappointment (with him). We got on together up until the leadership election in 2012. We got on well throughout that election but after the result, things changed dramatically. It was such a big change – he didn't want anything to do with me, and it became an obstacle to what we were trying to do.
>
> I didn't understand his change in attitude. I put it down to some sort of misogyny, not being able to accept that a younger woman had defeated this well-established, well-known politician and he seemed to be irked by it. But I never understood it, and we never discussed it.[25]

From the summer of 2012 onwards, Plaid's central office retained a list of Dafydd Elis-Thomas's perceived misdemeanours, noting occasions when he either spoke out against party policy or made controversial comments that raised the ire of Plaid Cymru supporters.

In October 2012, he suggested that he would support the Labour candidate, Tal Michael, for the role of Police and Crime Commissioner in North Wales. In a plenary session in the Assembly, on 24 October, he disagreed publicly with his party's spokesman, Simon Thomas, over the issue of University mergers in south-east Wales. In the Assembly chamber, he 'visibly disagreed' with Elin Jones when she questioned the Health Minister. In December 2012, he expressed his support for 'his friend, the Prince of Wales' on a Radio Wales programme, while in another programme he also warned against taking too pessimistic a view of the relative decline in the number of Welsh speakers. He was found to be re-tweeting Labour party messages constantly and stated his support for a reduction in the number of local councils in Wales, which was against Plaid policy.

Most bizarrely, in May 2013, when he tweeted 'thanks to Ieuan Wyn Jones for his leadership legacy in local government as he took us into Welsh Government', he was criticised for contradicting the party's strategy of linking Leanne Wood with Plaid's success in council elections in Ynys Môn. In June 2013, in response to a speech made by him in the House of Lords, the central office report noted that it 'illustrated once more why he is at odds with many in present day Plaid Cymru'. In it he declared himself an out and out federalist, and gave his view on independence for Wales, the official policy of the party: 'the principality of Wales is not a creation of Norman military ascendancy. It is the creation of Welsh leaders themselves and that project was already federal in nature.' In February 2014, he was thought to have undermined party policy during a Plaid Cymru sponsored debate on European agricultural policy.[26]

At the end of a long day, in May 2013, the Assembly's environment committee, on a visit to Brussels for meetings on the European Union's Agriculture and Fisheries policy, held a private dinner in an upstairs room at a local restaurant. As usual, the members gossiped about politics, during which its chair, Elis-Thomas criticised Wood's leadership, expressing concern at her republicanism and her past decisions to boycott official openings of the Assembly by the Queen. He was reported to have referred to comments made by a prominent Plaid Cymru councillor in Caerphilly, who said Ms Wood's anti-royalist stance, and particularly her refusal to meet the Queen, had gone down badly on the doorstep during the recent local election campaign, and had contributed to Plaid's heavy defeat in Caerphilly.

One of the Labour members recalls the dinner:

> We were in a private room, in a mixed group that included a

couple of Labour members, a couple of Tory members, and two Plaid members. Everyone had a nice meal around a table seating about nine or ten. It was very convivial. It was lateish. There was a bit of banter and a bit of commenting on politics and Dafydd said that 'my party is now in the hands of the hard left'. That was it . . . but everybody were complaining about their own parties and it was pretty innocuous. Dafydd had had a couple of glasses by then so his tongue was loosened a bit, so it was one of those comments that can be made, and we were all doing a bit of soul searching.[27]

His fellow Plaid AM, Llŷr Gruffydd reported back to his chief whip what had been said. The *Western Mail* reported a source close to Plaid Cymru defending Elis-Thomas:

Dafydd made these comments at a private dinner where Chatham House rules are expected to apply. The only other Plaid Cymru AM present, Llŷr Huws Gruffydd, a regional AM in north Wales, reported the comments back to the Plaid group, and there has been talk of getting Dafydd to apologise or disciplining him. This has been raised in the last two Plaid group meetings. If they keep putting pressure on Dafydd, there is a possibility that he could leave Plaid and join Labour. Is that what they want?

The article also quoted an un-named Assembly Member who was on the trip to Brussels but did not wish to be identified, who said 'I am very surprised that Dafydd's comments on this occasion were reported back to the Plaid group. It's very unhelpful and smacks of control freakery.'[28] A Labour member present at the dinner said that the reaction to this disciplinary process was that 'it was a pretty poor thing to do':

Someone gives his life to a political movement and deserves a bit of respect, and it isn't a way to treat people. Leanne was a strange fish. She was very self-conscious of her 'vanguardist' status . . . but within a mature politics, and with respect and recognition, what's the big deal? Why would anyone want to report that in a Stasi manner. I thought it incredibly disrespectful of Dafydd. I'm sure it felt the same for him.[29]

This incident sparked an even steeper decline in the relationship between Leanne Wood and Elis-Thomas. Elin Llŷr, his research assistant, tried to bridge the political divide between Elis-Thomas and Leanne's office, and Plaid Cymru generally, but without success. However any formal disciplinary action was held off until another incident, on the eve of Plaid Cymru's 2014 Spring conference in Cardiff. In a press briefing, Wood had referred to UKIP as 'un-Welsh', and Dafydd Elis-Thomas now openly criticised her:

> I don't know what the word 'un-Welsh' means, because sitting in this Assembly we emphasise equality, we emphasise this place belongs to all the people of Wales. And therefore, you don't start calling your fellow citizens, your colleagues in Wales, names even if they are in a party with which you disagree.[30]

In her subsequent conference speech, Leanne Wood doubled down on her comments, and criticised UKIP for its values which, she considered, not to be 'the values of Wales. A vote for UKIP is a vote against Wales – a vote against the Welsh national interest. We cannot and will not let their ugly politics divide us.'[31] Afterwards, Elis-Thomas brazenly retorted to journalists that 'it is facile and assumes a kind of superiority that we decide who is Welsh and who is not Welsh ... It [UKIP] clearly represents a point of view in Wales.'[32]

Wood's response was that 'we fundamentally and sincerely believe that their [UKIP] politics and policies are not in the best interests of the people of our communities. Dafydd Elis-Thomas decided to publicly oppose this position without raising any concerns in advance.'[33] Wood was absolutely furious at his intervention:

> We were trying to change the narrative on UKIP and demonstrate its British nationalism and anti-Welshness. He [Dafydd Elis-Thomas] gave an interview the night before the conference, in which he undermined the argument. And I remember someone seeing him when he was giving the interview, he made this stirring the pot motion, showing he was trying to stir things up. I remember mostly our staff being upset, especially the communications staff, and those who worked hard organising the conference on the theme of unity, and this being undermined by one person.[34]

After a further week's consideration, Wood met with him on Wednesday evening, 12 March, and then sent a formal letter, strangely in English only, dismissing him as chair of the Assembly's environment committee and as Plaid Cymru's transport spokesman. In response, he claimed that AMs were now 'more gagged and have less of a democratic scrutiny' than Westminster.[35]

The party's chair, Dafydd Trystan, justified his sacking at the time, since 'the party needed to be disciplined in order to present a 'progressive, positive agenda'. He argued that appointing committee chair-people in the Assembly was a matter for parties and their leaders, adding that it was 'entirely appropriate when matters of discipline arise that the party leader uses every means at her disposal'. Looking forward to the next Assembly elections in 2016, Trystan said, rather optimistically, that he had 'no doubt that Dafydd Elis will play a positive and constructive role in fighting his seat in Dwyfor Meirionnydd and making a broader contribution.'[36]

But Elis-Thomas challenged Wood over her action in sacking him as the chair of the Environment Committee, stating that the current system where committee chairs are nominated by the political parties undermines members' independence.[37] Subsequently, the rules of the Assembly were changed, making it impossible for individual party leaders to appoint or dismiss a chair of an Assembly committee. In an interview with ITV Wales, Elis-Thomas rejected the suggestion that he hadn't become reconciled to Leanne's leadership, saying 'it's not a matter of who the leader is; it's where the leadership is taking us', and said that the party's direction 'should be focused on improving devolution . . . rather than making negative attacks on other parties'.

At the time, Claire Howell pressed for him to be thrown out of the party, but Leanne Wood felt constrained:

> I wish I had taken that action earlier but it's quite difficult to take action against people who are elected. I could see that he was basically telling us that he wasn't going to hang around in Plaid Cymru beyond the 2016 election. Yet his local party wanted to carry on with him as the candidate, regardless of what had happened. By then he had stopped participating in the group, coming occasionally but didn't contribute really. In this period, I don't remember him being problematic in the group but he probably he wasn't there very often. I should have been more ready to discipline earlier.

I was too liberal and I let things slide. But these problems were new to us because we hadn't had those sort of problems often.[38]

Without status or responsibility within the Plaid Cymru group, he increasingly become more disengaged and spent more time in the House of Lords. During the General Election in June 2015, he criticised his party's demand that Wales should be treated in the same way as Scotland, and said the campaign had not focused sufficiently on Wales's future. He also contended that the argument that electors should vote Plaid 'because we're more Welsh' was 'arrogant' and 'a bit sectarian'.[39] He publicly disagreed with his party's policy of opposing the holding of the European referendum on the same day as the Assembly election in 2016, arguing that having them on the same day would boost turn-out, but this put him at odds again with Leanne Wood, as well as the Labour First Minister.[40] By early July, matters were coming to a head with the party centrally, and not surprisingly, there was speculation that Plaid Cymru might remove Elis-Thomas as its candidate for Dwyfor-Meirionnydd.[41]

Elis-Thomas and Wood's recollection of their relationship between the summers of 2012 and 2016 was, not surprisingly, very different:

> There was no intentional falling out, but if I was asked, I would voice my views. I had support in the constituency. The problem with her was that she didn't understand the job – she had no interest in anywhere beyond the south Wales valleys. Plaid wasn't very successful under her leadership.[42]

While Dafydd Elis-Thomas had hardly been the most loyal of members in the Plaid Assembly group, in Elin Llŷr's view, Plaid also bore some of the responsibility for the break-down in the relationship, 'and did not handle things very well. They could have used his experience'. By January 2016, she believed he would leave the party:

> He would go to the Plaid group, but I felt that both sides had lost their way. They said that Dafydd Elis-Thomas losing the committee chairmanship was the worst thing they could do to him, but in my opinion it gave him too much time on his hands and it was the worst thing they could have done. He did not have enough to do – he needed to be kept busy. There was one

thing after another. He went to the House of Lords more often in 2014, to speak on the Wales Bill. That kept him busy, but in this period he wasn't sufficiently appreciated. He is remembered in this period as a troublemaker, but Plaid was not mature enough to manage him more subtly.

She felt that while Dafydd's conduct made her job more difficult, the relationship with her fellow Plaid staff members deteriorated so badly that she did not even feel able to join them in the daily lunch queue in the Assembly canteen:

> He had no interest in the party after his sacking as committee chair – he lost his enjoyment for being there, and he noticeably socialised more with Labour members. Things had broken down totally with Plaid ... perhaps the turning point had come in 2013, when Ieuan Wyn Jones stood down from the Assembly. He had been the only Plaid member able to talk sense into Dafydd.[43]

Claire Howell believed that Leanne had been too tolerant of Dafydd Elis, and that he should have been tackled sooner. In May 2015, she helped prepare Leanne for the General Election:

> I'd go over to Cardiff weekly, and helped with rehearsing speeches and the television debates, in which she impressed against David Cameron, Nigel Farage and Ed Miliband. It was terrifying ... Just before she went on in the first debate, she sat down and said to me, 'I can't do it; I can't go on'. She didn't have the confidence to do it. She said, 'I can't go on- I'm going to be sick'. I grabbed her and I took her into a room and said you've got two choices – to go on or she couldn't do it. She went on and I always remember when they came back from the stage, Cameron turning to me and saying 'Your girl did really well'.[44]

Leanne Wood was then at the height of her popularity, displaying a strong image as a radical feminist leader. But Dafydd Elis continued to disparage her leadership and during the 2015 General Election, attacked the party's election strategy. The *Western Mail* reported the party's intention to act against him:

The party's leader confirmed talks were under way about how to respond to criticism he made of Plaid's general election campaign that the party spent too much talking about comparisons with Scotland and failed to convince voters to switch from Labour. Ms Wood stressed the need to present an 'united front as a successful government in waiting ahead of next year's election'. Asked whether Dafydd Elis would be de-selected, she said that 'I am not judge and jury and executioner. I'm the party leader and these matters are for the party'.

The *Western Mail* reported that it was 'no secret' that she and Lord Dafydd Elis-Thomas had disagreed, and that he had angered some in his party with his comments.[45]

In Claire Howell's view, he should have been sacked earlier, 'without question':

> He did build a hugely loyal team in his constituency, and they adored him. But it became about him and not the party. You always get what you've always done if you don't change. He systemically undermined Leanne throughout the period 2013 to 2016. He was bomb-proof because of his service – he had large support in the party. But the party warmed to Leanne – she won the [leadership] election – but you can't have someone carrying a poison chalice such as Dafydd saying stuff all the time and leaking stuff to the press ... That's ego, just ego. And he wasn't short of that. No week would go by without that – he was always doing something- so Plaid would say 'it's Dafydd El again'. Dafydd Elis-Thomas was always charming. Certainly, I had conversations with Leanne and Rhuanedd about him going. With Dafydd, I don't think the national executive helped. I think there was a belief that he was bomb-proof and the fallout would have been so great ... They had grave doubts, but he is a canny operator and his constituency was four square behind him.[46]

The party's hierarchy insisted that the local constituency party should meet to discuss whether Elis-Thomas should be re-nominated as the party's candidate. Matters came to a head in a meeting in the Ganolfan

Community Centre, Porthmadog on a sunny evening on Tuesday, 28 July 2015, where representatives of Plaid's national executive met over a hundred members of the Dwyfor Meirionnydd constituency party to discuss the conduct of their local Assembly member, who was facing internal disciplinary action for publicly questioning Plaid's election priorities. Representing the national executive were the party's chief executive Rhuanedd Richards, the chair, Dafydd Trystan, and Alun Ffred Jones, chair of the Plaid Assembly group. Trystan found the meeting 'hideous':

> Some on the party's national executive argued that he should have been sacked, but this would have made him a martyr and would have destroyed the party in Dwyfor Meirionnydd. It was also likely that he would have been re-elected as an independent member of the Assembly. The aim was to jointly agree the way forward, between the constituency, the party nationally, and Lord Dafydd Elis-Thomas himself.[47]

Alun Ffred Jones, the party chair, opened the meeting by stating that the National Executive had a number of issues with Dafydd Elis, and that a commitment was required from him not to speak out against party policy. Dafydd Elis's response then was essentially to appeal to members' loyalty, to remind them of his record, and ask the membership to 'stick with him'.

The high emotion of the event was heightened by the first contribution from the packed audience, from Hotel Portmeirion's owner and crowned poet, Robin Llywelyn, who quoted the emotive poem *Y Gwrthodedig* (The Outcast) by Robert Williams Parry, drawing comparison between Elis-Thomas and the dismissal of one of the party's founders, Saunders Lewis, from his post as a college lecturer after his imprisonment for an arson attack on a proposed RAF aerodrome on the Llŷn peninsula. The poem sarcastically criticised the 'dear country' that could afford to dispense with the most learned amongst its ranks:

> Hoff wlad os gelli hepgor dysg
> Y dysgedicaf yn ein mysg,
> Mae'n rhaid dy fod o bob rhyw wlad
> Y fwyaf dedwydd ei hystad.

(Dear country, if you can discard the learning
Of the most learned amongst us,
You must be, of all countries,
The happiest its estate.)[48]

This scornful and contemptuous dismissal of the party's concerns indicated the fraught tone of the meeting and the passion of Elis-Thomas's supporters. Robin Llywelyn recalled his address:

Why should these people belittle and denigrate him when he had been an inspiration to a generation of people to fight for language rights, bilingualism and for Welsh language radio and television. I quoted Williams Parry and then sat down. I said 'he's a hero, an inspiration to my generation – do you seriously want to get rid of someone who is a hero? For what? Who have you got in his place?'[49]

Elis-Thomas quickly agreed to leave the hall and the discussion between the national officers and constituency members took place in his absence. A BBC reporter, Aled ap Dafydd, was stood outside, and asked Elis-Thomas as he left, 'whether it was a stormy night?', referring to the meeting. Walking away, Dafydd Elis replied that the Cnicht (the local mountain whose cloudy or sunny appearance foretold the local weather) 'was clear', a measure of his optimism that evening.[50] Dafydd's constituency secretary, Sioned Roberts, who remained in the hall, describes the dreadfulness of the occasion:

The whole way how the process had been held – whatever the disagreement, people ran him down … it went out of control … people were nasty. The person who saved him was Liz Pugh, chair of the constituency party at the time, who won the day for Dafydd – she was sober and serious and urged him to hold on. People, including a clutch of councillors from Dwyfor and Blaenau Ffestiniog said that he hadn't shown respect to the party, although the MP, Liz Saville Roberts was even-handed, and he was also supported by other councillors such as the veteran Selwyn Griffiths, Porthmadog. The majority of those who spoke opposed him, but the final vote was 80 to 20 in his favour, and as members poured out of the hall, many declared Dafydd the winner.[51]

The meeting affirmed the support of the constituency party members for the sitting Member, and Councillor Dyfrig Siencyn, the chair of the meeting, was instrumental in brokering an agreement that was, for the time being, acceptable to both sides. This committed Elis-Thomas to securing the consent beforehand of the constituency party before making any 'national' public statements, and that any controversial matters in the statement would be discussed with national officers beforehand. In addition, there would be discussions between him and the National Executive in order to improve their relationship. This agreement was doomed to failure, sacrificing as it did, his accustomed freedom of action to say what he liked, whenever he liked. This bruising meeting however further poisoned the relationship between him and the party centrally and Dafydd Trystan believed even at the time, that the underlying issues had not been resolved. The party's national executive consequently decided not to deselect him, but in the autumn, rumours soon started to circulate that he was considering standing as an independent candidate in the 2016 Assembly election. The former Member of Parliament for the seat, Elfyn Llwyd, let it be known that if he was to do so, then he would stand himself as Plaid Cymru's candidate in Dwyfor Meirionnydd.

Lord Dafydd Elis-Thomas returned to the National Assembly that autumn with greater confidence in his position, but took even less interest in the workings of the Plaid Cymru group in the Assembly. He was now secure of his support in the constituency, and the party centrally did not wish to challenge him again before the election, as Dafydd Trystan recalls:

> This was a strange period. There was a contrast between Leanne's method of running the party and Dafydd's wish to constantly attract attention to himself. He felt that the [Plaid] group in the Assembly was beneath him. Dafydd had gained from a store of goodwill – many liked and admired him – but if Leanne had really tackled him, then Plaid Cymru in Dwyfor Meirionnydd would have come to an end. Plaid has never tackled anybody at any time – and on the whole, Dafydd behaved well after the July meeting, although he could still be pretty independent in his views.[52]

After the Porthmadog meeting, Elin Llŷr, his researcher and office manager in the Assembly, found the tension between Elis-Thomas and the party difficult for her personally:

> I was also part of a team and it was difficult when Dafydd pulled against the party. After the meeting, things gradually broke down in the constituency and became more difficult. Some people in the constituency weren't happy with him. Liz Saville Roberts wasn't supportive, although the chair Dyfrig Siencyn was, but he had lost support amongst a number of members in the Bala area, and in Dwyfor.

In January 2016, she left her role with Dafydd Elis-Thomas for a post in Deryn, the political lobbying company, believing that he would inevitably leave Plaid in the near future, 'I didn't want things to sour while I was there. I had a history lesson every day with Dafydd. I learnt a lot. But a lot of my job by the end was to keep the peace. Dafydd didn't care what he said . . . I feel sad that this is what people remember of him in this period.'[53]

Following the Porthmadog meeting, Dafydd Elis's nomination as Plaid Cymru's candidate for the Dwyfor Meirionnydd constituency for the May 2016 Senedd election was endorsed unanimously by the local party but had to be confirmed by the party centrally. The chief executive, Rhuanedd Richards recalls receiving his nomination paper for the election in April 2016:

> I was supposed to sign the candidates' forms for the May 2016 Assembly election, and I signed every one's apart from Dafydd. I pinned it up on the wall in the office for a week and did not sign it. I couldn't help feeling that this was not going to work out, and that by the time the election was over, he would have left the party. But there was another part of me that said he would stay. It wasn't my place to stop him from standing but I thought – there's something going to happen here.[54]

Rhuanedd Richards signed his form, and his election campaign went well in Dwyfor Meirionnydd. He won handsomely in the May 2016 Assembly election, with 47 per cent of the vote:

Plaid Cymru	Dafydd Elis-Thomas	9,566	47.1 per cent
Conservative	Neil Fairlamb	3,160	15.6 per cent
Labour	Ian Macintyre	2,443	12.1 per cent
UKIP	Frank Wykes	2,149	10.6 per cent[55]

The internal party tensions clearly had not impacted in the least on his local standing. He had achieved one of the party's best results, only surpassed by Leanne Wood's stunning win in the Rhondda, where she beat the incumbent Labour member and ex-Minister, Leighton Andrews. But Dafydd Elis-Thomas hardly acknowledged his party in his campaigning for the seat. The BBC journalist Aled ap Dafydd noted that 'on his own Twitter page he describes himself as a 'independent environmentalist' with no mention of Plaid Cymru.'[56]

Departure

Plaid Cymru had invested a great deal in the National Assembly elections in May 2016. The highpoint of its campaign was Leanne Wood's crushing win in the Rhondda, and she had gained a UK wide profile after appearing in the 2015 General Election leaders' debates. Many of the party's activists had convinced themselves they would become the largest party, and Clare Howell had forecast that Leanne Wood would become First Minister, but Labour managed to hang on to 29 of the 30 seats it had previously held, fending off challenges from the Conservatives in all Labour/Conservative marginals. The overall result, with Plaid on 11 seats, the Conservatives also on 11, UKIP on 7 and the Liberal Democrats reduced from 5 seats to 1, failed to vindicate Plaid's pre-election optimism.

During the election campaign, Dafydd Elis-Thomas again disagreed publicly with his party, and suggested he intended to give one of his two votes to the Labour party. Days before the election for the Police and Crime Commissioner role in north Wales, on the same day as the National Assembly election, Elis-Thomas provoked his party by announcing that he was supporting the Labour candidate, David Taylor, who responded that he was 'deeply honoured' to have received his backing, adding that 'although we are from different parties, he is one of Wales's leading statesmen and someone I respect a great deal'. The Plaid Cymru candidate, Arfon Jones won that election,[57] but as if this was not enough to raise the party's ire, he criticised Plaid Cymru's main election demand that Wales should be treated in the same way as Scotland, and again put his future within the party at risk. At weekly press conferences during the election, senior Plaid Assembly candidates had wriggled uncomfortably in their seats when asked to support him, 'his supporters say he is a constitutional visionary, a politically uniting figure rather than a tribal politician. He has in the past been able to fall back on local support to get him out of internal party scrapes.'[58]

The final act that persuaded Dafydd Elis-Thomas to leave Plaid Cymru, was the decision by Leanne Wood, encouraged by Adam Price amongst others, to put herself forward as the First Minister, even though she did not have a majority of the seats in the Assembly.

Before the 2016 election, there had been 'light-hearted banter' between the Labour leader, Carwyn Jones, and Elis-Thomas about him leaving Plaid. Jones knew that he wasn't happy in Plaid:

> I started talking to him before the 2016 Election, in a light-hearted way – not too seriously – saying that we could work together. I didn't think he would leave Plaid then because he was still a candidate, and I didn't expect he'd join Labour. I told him that if he left Plaid, there would be a place for him in Government, but there was no question of agreeing anything before the election.[59]

The first decision of the new National Assembly was to elect a new Presiding Officer. The vote on 11 May 2016 was preceded by a totally unexpected phone call to Elis-Thomas by Adam Price, at Leanne Wood's request. Price persuaded him to put his name forward for the role of Presiding Officer, probably calculating that if he succeeded, he would not wish to defect from the party, and also conceivably to block Elin Jones, the Plaid Cymru member for Ceredigion, who had also been nominated for the role of Presiding Officer. Whatever the motivation, making him Presiding Officer would have dealt with Wood's most troublesome rebel, but this stratagem failed. In the contest between Elin Jones and Elis-Thomas, he was defeated by 25 to 34 votes. Many of the Labour members opposed him, not wishing to alleviate Wood's problems, and supported the Plaid member Elin Jones as the new Presiding Officer.

After the election of the Presiding Officer, Leanne Wood then attempted to seize the initiative from Labour by putting herself forward for the role of First Minister. This was supported by the Conservatives and UKIP, but crucially she did not have the vote of the sole Liberal Democrat, Kirsty Williams, who ruled it out stating that the idea of running a Government with such a small number of Plaid AMs was unworkable. The eventual vote was tied at 29 each, and after a week's frantic negotiation with Plaid Cymru, it was agreed that Labour would form a minority Government, and they were joined by Kirsty Williams who was appointed Education Minister.[60]

Carwyn Jones had initially asked Dafydd whether he would leave Plaid Cymru for the Labour party before the First Minister vote, but Dafydd refused, on the basis that while he was a member of the party, he would have to follow the party's whip. When the crucial tied vote for First Minister was held, he felt he had to vote for Leanne Wood, even though he profoundly disagreed with her candidacy:

> Such a person has to be able to command a majority in the Assembly, and to establish a stable government. It requires inter-party discussion and cooperation. That doesn't involve putting up a rival person for the post of a First Minister. You can't be both the head of the Government and not signed up to a notion of consensus if you're operating in a multi-party democracy. That's why I thought it was a constitutional nonsense, really, to put a name forward in that situation.

He recalled that there was no attempt at consensus before the vote to nominate Leanne Wood as First Minister, and, as a member of the group, he 'was on a three-line whip, therefore, I had to vote alongside the rest of the group. When this happened, I was obviously very concerned that the stability of Welsh government was being threatened. That was my concern. It was a constitutional one.'[61]

Mark Drakeford, the Cabinet Secretary for Finance in June 2016, believes that for Dafydd at this time, it was difficult to stomach not only putting forward Plaid Cymru's leader as First Minister, but having to depend on the seven UKIP members for their support:

> There was something pretty fundamentally distasteful in finding yourself in casting a vote in the first session of a new Assembly with a group of people you have nothing in common with, so I

can see why he thought that way. I was aware of conversations with Carwyn . . . my politics are quite close to his really. The real fault lines in the Assembly are the Conservatives on one side, and the other three parties on the other. There are always overlaps between sensible people within those parties – Labour, Plaid and Liberal Democrats – that police the fault line and don't attack each other unnecessarily. The enemy's over there and we are in different ways closer to one another than to them.[62]

Carwyn Jones, the Labour nominee, was eventually confirmed as First Minister, in a second vote of the Assembly, on 18 May.[63] Wood's failed attempt to become First Minister proved the last straw for Dafydd Elis and his loyalty to the party. Although he had been required to vote in Leanne's unsuccessful attempt to unseat Labour, he had already started discussing with Carwyn Jones the possibility of leaving Plaid Cymru and becoming an independent member, rather than joining the Labour party:

> They asked if I would break the whip if they put the motion down again. I said, 'No, I can't do that, because I'm committed to the whip already. If I vote against the party on a three-line whip, I would be expelled', and I wasn't prepared to go down that route. Then, we had a further meeting with Mark Drakeford present, but I didn't mention any of this to the constituency party at the time. What we discussed was that if I was able to sit as an independent and cease to be a member of the Plaid group for an unspecified period, that Carwyn was prepared to offer me a substantial role in Government. That was the understanding we came to.[64]

Carwyn Jones recalled that once his election as First Minister was confirmed, he told Elis-Thomas that there was a place for him in the Government, although he couldn't say at the time when the opportunity would arise, 'I wasn't sure when we could have our new reshuffle, but he didn't push. I was trying to tempt him over – of course I was – it was a political opportunity.'[65]

On 14 October 2016, on a cold and rainy Friday night at the Plaid Cymru office in Porthmadog, about a dozen members of the executive committee of his constituency party had congregated for their monthly meeting. There, in addition to Dafydd Elis-Thomas, were the local Member of Parliament, Liz Saville Roberts, Dyfrig Siencyn, the deputy leader of Gwynedd Council at the time, the constituency secretary Gwerfyl Arthur, a number of councillors, including the town councillor Simon Brooks, and Dafydd Elis-Thomas's secretary, Sioned Roberts. After Elis-Thomas detailed his report of his activities as an Assembly Member, and the most recent progress of the Government's 2017 Wales Bill, which allowed the Assembly to change its electoral arrangements and to change its name to Senedd, he expressed his disappointment at the refusal of Plaid Cymru's group in the Assembly to cooperate with the Labour Party in securing a stronger government for Wales. He then said that he had no other choice but to resign not only from the group in the Assembly, but from Plaid Cymru, and intended to continue as the independent Assembly Member for Dwyfor Meirionnydd.

He stated that he would not take questions. The members were totally stunned, although a number attempted to respond. Simon Brooks asked whether he would remain in the party, even though he was leaving the Plaid group in the Assembly, and he replied that the split was total. A short discussion was held and he then left the meeting.[66] After forty-four years as Plaid Cymru's representative for the constituency, either in the National Assembly or as its Member of Parliament, he walked out of Plaid Cymru for the last time, and drove the short distance to attend a pre-arranged small dinner to celebrate his forthcoming seventieth birthday, at the smart Portmeirion Hotel. Dafydd Elis recalled this traumatic meeting:

> I still have, and had, a very close friendship with the chair of the constituency (Dyfrig Siencyn), the leading Plaid person in local government in Gwynedd, and there were other colleagues who had been aware of the difficulties that I was having. We ensured that none of this had become public . . . I had decided that it was no longer possible for me to remain within Plaid, and therefore would become independent. It came as a bit of a shock to them. It was not an easy meeting, so I didn't stay there very long.[67]

For those left in the room, the impact was profound. Liz Saville Roberts's reaction was one of anger and bitter disappointment. Attacking him personally, she accused him of having betrayed the national movement. Dyfrig Siencyn's response, on the other hand, while mildly critical, was one of 'great

DISSENT, DEPARTURE AND MINISTERIAL OFFICE

sadness.'[68] Sioned Roberts, Dafydd Elis's office manager in the Porthmadog office, then politely informed the gathering that they were now meeting in the premises of an independent member of the Assembly, and that the room needed to be vacated. All those present spilled on to the pavement and made their way to the nearby Sportsman pub, where they booked a private room to consider their response. The secretary, Gwerfyl Arthur, a friend of Dafydd for over forty years, was asked to inform the party leader, Leanne Wood, and its chair, Dafydd Trystan, that he had resigned from the party. Liz Saville Roberts had already texted Leanne Wood with the news, and the re-convened constituency committee formulated a press release stating their sadness at his resignation and thanked him for his service over the past 45 years. But the short press statement also asked him to 'search his conscience and we ask him to stand down and to create a by-election and call a meeting soon, in order to discuss the situation further'.[69]

Liz Saville Roberts's immediate response was to demand a by-election in Dwyfor Meirionnydd, a call that was greeted with rather less enthusiasm by those party's local supporters who wished to avoid a schism within the party locally. Leanne Wood recalled that she was 'disappointed that he left. He was a capable guy, but just had the ability to disappoint at every turn. I don't have any ill feelings towards him. I'm just sad that his legacy in Plaid Cymru has been overshadowed by how it ended, and it's a shame.'[70] The response of Gwerfyl Arthur, a long-standing friend and political ally, was typical of many Plaid members in Meirionnydd:

> I felt he had betrayed me. He had betrayed his people – they would have gone through fire and water for him, but he didn't think about them at all. I think he was treated badly by Leanne, but he should have gone when he finished as Presiding Officer. He would have kept his dignity. He had accomplished much. I recall him at the election count in Dolgellau in May 2016 – he was in a terrible mood. I think he knew that evening what he intended to do. We had fought for him in the campaign, paid for the campaign and the election – but he'd gone within a few weeks, and it wasn't the Meirionnydd Plaid members who got rid of him. I thought we were friends. In the end, we weren't.[71]

His election agent, Dyfrig Siencyn, was disappointed that there had been no prior indication of his intention to leave the party, 'I had given him a lot of support. I'd worked very hard to save his skin and to get him out of a [political] hole.'⁷² On the other hand, Dafydd's close friend, Robin Llywelyn, who hosted his seventieth birthday dinner at the Portmeirion Hotel on the evening of his resignation, supported his decision to leave the party, because it had 'degraded' him. But he also pleaded with him that evening not to stand again at the next election, 'he had been put in a corner . . . I asked him please not to stand as an independent. You would split the vote. Very honestly, I was glad he was nearing retirement age!'⁷³

Simon Brooks remembers that in the months immediately following his announcement, Dafydd Elis was less visible in the constituency, with little coverage of him in the local press. The constituency party was torn in its response to his announcement, with one faction, led by Liz Saville Roberts, pressing for him to stand down immediately, which would have led to a by-election, while another faction, led by Dyfrig Siencyn, wished him to remain until the 2021 Assembly election, and thus avoid internal conflict. As a member of the executive committee of the constituency, Brooks recalled the varied responses of the local party towards his resignation:

> I applied for the Plaid Cymru nomination to follow Dafydd, and I visited every Plaid member in the constituency. There was real hatred towards Dafydd, but there was also real love towards him too. It is difficult to say what would have happened if he had stood again as an independent candidate, but you couldn't dismiss the possibility that he would have won. He had a personal vote in Penllyn and throughout Meirionnydd, and he would have supporters amongst Labour and the Conservatives, who may have voted tactically in order to keep Plaid out. That could have raised his vote to over 34 per cent. He was wise to step down, because if he had stood, he would have caused bitterness. He definitely had support. Why did people hate him? There was a history of disagreement between him and the more hard-line nationalist elements over a period of decades. His position had been undermined by his quarrels with the language movement dating back to the late 1980s, the hard left faction hated him for his undermining of Leanne Wood, and the influence of social media also played a part.

DISSENT, DEPARTURE AND MINISTERIAL OFFICE

Brooks considers that to some extent, the opposition to Dafydd came from people outside the constituency who understood little of his work:

> These were people who had no understanding of his contribution locally and to Wales. They could be unpleasant towards him. Within the constituency, Liz Saville Roberts, the local MP, didn't like him – that was made obvious and she could be prickly with people she didn't like. She believed that Dafydd was undermining the discipline of the party, and that it needed to be more disciplined, like the SNP. But Plaid is a different type of party locally. Plaid Cymru represents the whole of society in rural Gwynedd – it is different to the SNP which is more of a political sect. He was a bit like the prodigal son. Many of his constituency party had grown up with him as their representative over a period of over forty years, but the support for him was increasingly isolated.[74]

From her vantage point as the party's chief executive, Rhuanedd Richards noted that the general response of Plaid members throughout Wales was one of disappointment, but that 'there was very little hatred – there was too much respect for him for that'.[75] Dafydd Elis's response to his critics was sober and unemotional, and in becoming an independent member of the Assembly, Dafydd Elis saw similarities with his experience in the House of Lords:

> In terms of arithmetic, the government had an extra vote. It was nothing new for me because that's how I'd operated in Westminster all my life. I didn't think of it as a case of voting with Labour, but as a case of representing what my constituents would want me to do, who elected me to make judgements on their behalf. It cannot be that public representatives should betray their own consciences. Otherwise, what have you got? . . . Had I been talking about a fight in the playground in primary school, I would have said that I didn't start it.[76]

He explained that his decision to leave Plaid Cymru resulted from the party's agreement with UKIP to support Leanne Wood as First Minister in May 2016, and believed that his view of the role of an elected member was at odds with Plaid's view:

Plaid's approach to UKIP was an indication that the strategy of opposition was more important for the Plaid group than contributing to the governance of Wales. I have a very simple view of politics and that is that my job is to ensure Wales has good governance. The argument then is who runs the government of Wales and I do not believe that relying on the support of Welsh Conservatives and UKIP was an appropriate strategic position. It made me think of fundamentalist approaches in religion and faith communities, and how exclusion comes about . . . I believe that in the history of Plaid, there is a deep love of being an opposition, a deep affection for the argument that somehow we'd been badly treated and badly done by, and that Wales is oppressed, and that our job is to set Wales free. I found . . . in my days in Plaid . . . that the citizens of Wales generally don't feel themselves to be oppressed people. Plaid is for representing the people of Wales, but it mustn't believe itself to be the only party that delivers constitutional development, social and economic justice, or linguistic equality. The trouble with me, of course, is that I went off and did things that were to do with Government, but I didn't do them as a member of Plaid. I did them as an independent, as soon as I became a crossbench member of the Lords and chair of the Welsh Language Board. The approach for Plaid should be to deliver that, and that must mean partnership and adopting policies which do not include an ill-defined or undefined notion of independence.[77]

Freed from his party constraints, he started a debate about the role of the National Parks in Wales and proposed the creation of a US-style National Parks and Wildlife Service. This controversial idea led to him being asked by Welsh Government to lead the Future Landscapes Review, which reported in 2017, and led to the establishment of the Tirweddau Cymru – Landscapes Wales organisation in 2020, creating a partnership of the protected areas in Wales, namely the three national parks – Eryri, Bannau Brycheiniog and Pembrokeshire, and the 'national landscapes' of the Anglesey coast, the Clwydian mountain range, the Gower and Llŷn coastline and the Wye Valley.

The Welsh Government Minister for Culture, Sport and Tourism

It was not until the autumn of 2016 that the First Minister Carwyn Jones, started discussions with Dafydd Elis-Thomas about the details of a role as a Minister in the Welsh Government, but it seems he was less than discreet in his negotiations. Jones recalled that 'reshuffle rumours increased in intensity in line with the number of conversations I enjoyed with Dafydd', but he admired him as 'a true statesman, with the sort of political heft, intellect and hinterland who deserved a shot at government'.[78]

In his earliest discussions with both Carwyn Jones and the Finance Secretary Mark Drakeford, Elis-Thomas agreed to take the Labour whip and provide the Government with a valuable extra vote. Becoming an independent member was a necessary precursor to being offered a ministerial post:

> I made it clear that I didn't think it would be appropriate for me to be involved in language policy because I'd been there before and I knew it had been controversial, and I also thought that bilingual language policies generally shouldn't be linked in with a particular portfolio, but it should be part of government more generally. The final offer, and the final discussion, was responsibility for culture, sport and tourism. I felt for the first time in my life, I would be actually responsible for things I knew something about because I'd been there and done things in those areas, and they were part of my continuing interests.[79]

However, Carwyn Jones did not have the opportunity to hold a reshuffle until a year later, on 3 November 2017, when Elis-Thomas was appointed Minister for Culture, Sport and Tourism. His ministerial brief also gave him responsibility for creative industries, and with his deep interest and experience of the arts and heritage, and his long experience of dealing with tourism, he was admirably suited to the role.[80] A cultural polymath, he had a keen appreciation of arts and literature, had a close interest in tourism through his lengthy experience representing a constituency where hospitality was a key part of the local economy, and had a keen passion for heritage. Huw Thomas, BBC Wales's former culture correspondent, describes him as 'the best-informed culture minister of any Welsh government, a fact which instilled varying levels of fear and admiration in the state-sponsored organisations that depended on him for their funding.'[81]

However, his role as deputy Minister was a comparatively junior one in Government, and arguably, given the value of his support for Carwyn Jones, he could have well bargained for a more senior role. Not to do so reflected his passion for the arts and culture rather than a thirst for a more senior Ministerial position. He relished his new role and nourished his relationship with his staff and stakeholders. One of his senior civil servants recalls that he 'was a bit of a rascal' in his ability to tailor his message to different audiences. But people warmed to him, and he could make everyone one feel they were 'special. His long experience in politics meant that he not only knew everybody but knew their parents too.'[82] He had clear ideas for his role as a Minister and he delighted in undertaking the tourism brief in particular:

> My first meeting as a minister was with some tourism bodies. I was very well served by officials and had a very well-managed private office. It helped that my office was located very close to the First Minister, so there was a sense that I was joining an organisation where I felt professionally and personally comfortable for the first time in my life. It had been difficult when I was at the Welsh Language Board, where the perception was that I was working for a Conservative Welsh Office.[83]

Terry Stevens, a specialist in tourism policy, viewed him as:

> The ideal minister for tourism – exceptionally good for Wales and of Wales. He was willing to listen to professional advice on tourism investment. He always showed empathy and willingness to be guided in decisions. He was someone who was considerate and rounded, and he could articulate a rationale or strategy for a decision. Even the way he could speak bilingually made people comfortable, and the enunciation of a decision was clear.

Elis-Thomas had made no demands of Carwyn Jones when appointed deputy Minister, but one policy he opposed strongly, albeit discretely, was the imposition of a tourist tax, or visitor levy, on Welsh hoteliers.

He had previously made a personal commitment to the tourism industry in north Wales to passionately oppose it, and as the responsible Minister, he refused to develop this controversial policy. Stevens explains that the Government's concept of a tourist tax hadn't 'been thought through very well. It hadn't taken notice of international expertise, it is a contentious issue, it was wrongly timed, wrongly articulated, and created wildfires. All Dafydd Elis could do was to pour cold water on the wildfires.' In his period as deputy minister, the policy was left in abeyance.[84]

He rejected a report commissioned by a previous Minister, from the consultants Price Waterhouse Cooper, which had recommended out-sourcing CADW, one of the most significant heritage bodies, and he shifted its priorities from its celebration of English-built castles such as Caernarfon, to focus on conserving and celebrating Welsh castles, investing in rundown castles such as Ruthin, and supporting local authorities to take over about half a dozen castles previously in private hands such as Tretower Court and Castle near Brecon. His friendship with Prince Charles led them to work together to celebrate those castles built by the Welsh princes, and Tretower, whilst credited as being built by the Normans, had in fact been home to an early Prince of Powys.[85] He supported the National Museum in resisting being merged with other heritage organisations, and crucially approved the initial funding for the modernisation of the National Museum's Llanberis slate museum in 2019–20, which laid the foundations for the successful bid, led by Lord Wigley, to secure UNESCO world heritage site status for the slate areas of north Wales in the following year. This earmarked the area as a truly important cultural landscape and joined the Blaenavon World Heritage Site and the Pontcysyllte Aqueduct in recognition of Wales's outstanding contribution to the Industrial Revolution, and joined the castles and town walls of King Edward in Gwynedd as the county's second World Heritage site.

One of his achievements as Minister was the setting up of Creative Wales in 2020 as a Welsh Government agency, in order to provide support for the creative industries sector, to provide training opportunities and to advise on funding. But the least productive relationship he had with any of the public bodies he was responsible for was the National Library of Wales. He had little patience with its leadership over the Library's failure to market itself, and he disagreed with its Board over its insistence on advertising its chief executive role as one in which the Welsh language was essential, fearing that they were unnecessarily limiting the range of expert candidates. Because of his doubts about the National Library of Wales's ability to deliver on its public commitments, for a year, he postponed funding a joint project with the BBC to make its sound and vision Wales archive available to the public. He eventually capitulated to pressure from the National Library's chief executive, Pedr ap Llwyd, one of his former critics in Plaid Cymru, and the Library's President and chair, Rhodri Glyn Thomas, one of his former Plaid colleagues in the Assembly.

In sport, he prioritised moving funding to women's sports in order to redress the imbalance in resources with men's organisations, but it was the arts section of his portfolio that proved the most challenging of his brief. The chair of the Welsh Arts Council was Phil George, a former television producer, the third in a succession of ex-BBC former senior managers, and the second to be closely aligned with the Labour party.[86] His assessment of Dafydd Elis-Thomas's contribution was mixed. While regarding 'Dafydd El as a very enjoyable Minister who loved the arts and enjoyed the role', he considered that while 'he believed passionately in the arm's length principle and allowed us to get on with it, I didn't always feel that he was active enough around the table in our cause'. George felt that he could have been more influential in his role and could have pressed harder for more funding for the arts:

> I think he would accept the argument about the tightness of funding but not make sufficient argument about the social and economic benefit of the arts. When I became chair of the Arts Council I was very keen to continue arts in education, but I felt that we needed to do something similar in health. I don't think Dafydd did. He understood the issue ... the arts' relevance to placemaking and the environment. It was something where he needed to be more on the front foot. But he didn't drive the cultural agenda enough, and at this stage of his life, he was wanting to be supportive and protecting but not change the scene. He didn't move the story on. He was a benign older politician, which went hand and hand with his academic scholarship, but he viewed it as theoretical rather than shifting resources.[87]

The greatest challenge to him as a Minister was to deal with the Covid-19 pandemic, and its profound effect on the arts, in the period between February 2020 and the end of his term as Minister in May 2021.

George believed he dealt with the Covid crisis in exemplary fashion, ensured that individual freelancers were financially supported, and that the 'portfolio' companies, the main arts organisations in Wales, maintained their funding. He did so, even before the UK Government and the Department of Digital, Culture, Media and Sport announced the creation of the Cultural Recovery Fund in July 2020. This sustained arts organisations, and forwarded around £90 million for arts and culture in Wales, succeeding in sustaining the whole sector throughout the pandemic.[88] Elis-Thomas's support was also critical for sustaining the cultural element of the Welsh Government's programme for Government, ensuring the renovation and re-designing of Theatr Clwyd with over £27 million of Government funding, and encouraging local authorities to renew the funding of music in schools, which was made a priority.[89]

His former political colleague Edwina Hart, while recognising his ambition to end his career as a minister, suggested that he was too modest in his initial agreement with Carwyn Jones, and he should have put himself forward as a full Cabinet Minister. The sole Liberal Democrat member in the Assembly, Kirsty Williams, for instance, joined the Labour Cabinet as the Education Secretary in May 2016. He declined to claim such a high prize, and was content to accept his role as a Deputy Minister, reporting to the Cabinet initially through the Minister for the Economy, Ken Skates. In Government, Hart felt that he wasn't allowed to do what he wanted to do; 'I think they tried to clip his wings. He enjoyed what he wanted to do. He knew higher education very well and would have sorted the universities out. I was always surprised that he could have had something more. He was more than capable.'[90]

But for the first time in his lengthy political career, he relished the opportunity to wield power in Government office:

> The key instrument of a departmental minister responsible for different functions is the way in which officials can know the mind of a minister and understand what the minister is likely to support and what he's not likely to support. When it came to signing submissions off, these were always extremely well researched, well-developed, and the proposal for the funding very clearly set out. I did not find it easy because obviously there's a lot of reading and studying to do to make sure you get it right, and some people would say, 'Oh, we applied to the government,

but we didn't get what we wanted,' but then we got substantial funding which was available to Wales, because of the competitive funding available to the nations. What I found most enjoyable and useful as a minister was my strong relationships with colleagues in other departments, in the UK where I had the responsibility of working with the Department of Digital, Culture, Media and Sport, and it was always delightful to work with SNP colleagues and with colleagues in the North of Ireland, and of course in areas like tourism, with the whole of Ireland. That was very positive. We established a very close relationship, especially with the Cabinet in Dublin, as well as in the North of Ireland.[91]

On a personal level, Rhuanedd Richards was pleased for him, that he had the opportunity to be in Government but she believed he paid a high price for his rejection of Plaid Cymru: 'I'm not sure what he got out of it – turning his back on his political heritage, turning his back on decades of belonging to something that had supported him for so long. Was the prize worth it? Has it given him lifelong friends? Does he feel that he succeeded?'[92] But for Elis-Thomas, this fulfilled a life-long ambition:

> This was an opportunity to do something in a role I'd never thought I'd be in. Some would always argue that the role of Plaid is to share in the governance of the country it represents. I felt that I was doing it as an individual, and that wasn't down to me. It was the situation I got into because I just couldn't persuade party colleagues at the time that we should all take a more positive attitude towards Welsh Labour in government.[93]

The response of former Plaid colleagues in the Assembly to his role as a Minister was more positive than he had feared. He found them suddenly very interested in what financial support might be available for their constituencies from his department, 'I can't recollect any situation, whether privately in conversation or certainly in the Assembly chamber, where I had anything but a positive reaction from colleagues on all sides. That was very, very helpful.'[94]

The last two years of his term as a Deputy Minister was dominated by the blight of Covid. Its advent in February 2020 caused much of Government business to be conducted remotely by Zoom or Teams, and he was one of four Welsh Government Ministers over 70, who were required to self-isolate throughout the Covid pandemic. Even before the onset of Covid, his office manager in the constituency, Sioned Roberts, detected the extra pressure that the new role entailed, 'it was more of a job than he thought. I saw a strain in him. It was a bigger job than he'd expected perhaps.'[95] The pandemic led to a crisis in the viability of the arts sector, the rapid decline of tourism and the financial challenges to the major cultural institutions, including the National Museum, the National Library of Wales, and CADW. Mark Drakeford took over as First Minister in December 2018, and paid tribute to Dafydd Elis's Ministerial contribution:

> We were hugely lucky to have him. His portfolio suited him down to the ground. He was a huge enthusiast – he put all the hours in – and although not the portfolio that has the most decisions to make, it is one with the heaviest demands in terms of its time. He gave it everything – he was a round peg in a round hole. He had no difficulty in being in a Labour-run Government . . . he did not seem to feel any political strain to being in the same room with the people he hadn't been in the room with before – as his Cabinet colleagues. He brought such a depth of his own history, his own political hinterland, his immersion in Welsh culture and his contribution in discussion . . . he had a view on things that nobody else in that room could have brought. I thought that was wonderful. This was something that we would miss. We talked about second homes a lot during Covid – he would give you the inside story, the much longer history over the past 50 years – he would tap into those strands that were not available to other people around that table. He was a hard worker, he never missed a meeting. He was always in our [remote] nine o'clock meetings every morning during Covid. He was very keen. Because a number were all over seventy – Dafydd was shielding, as was Jane Hutt and Julie Morgan. It concerned me at the beginning, but they never felt not part of it. Dafydd was always the first to join the meeting – you'd see his name coming up in the corner. No arguments – he had a very well-developed understanding of 'collective responsibility'. I never felt anxiety that he was out there.[96]

Dafydd Elis-Thomas's assessment of his own ministerial legacy was that he met his biggest challenge, which was the threat of Covid to public services, and which dominated his time as Deputy Minister:

> I think it was making sure that the decisions of government reflected the aspirations, especially, of the businesses that wanted government support. We did this particularly in the area of tourism, where we had weekly meetings online throughout the whole period.
>
> In tourism, I thought it was very important that all areas of Wales should be represented, and I recognised mid-Wales as a very important area, although it didn't quite tally with what was going on in the rest of the government sometimes. By building on my experience . . . it was about making government accessible to business and to users of services. I was able to invest public money in areas of policy where you know that it will have a positive effect . . . I know there's this argument now that there's too much tourism, that it's overheating in some areas. I don't necessarily agree with that argument. I think it's a case of marketing other areas to bring them up to the level of interest that people have in certain hotspots (such as Yr Wyddfa) and so on, but that's a policy issue. Making those daily decisions based on ministerial advice was the most important thing that I did.[97]

A Nation-builder – the legacy

On Sunday 12 April 2020, on BBC Radio Cymru's flagship Sunday morning current affairs programme, presented by the veteran broadcaster Dewi Llwyd, Dafydd Elis-Thomas announced his intention to retire as the Senedd member for the constituency of Dwyfor Meirionnydd at the following election in May 2021. The presenter was taken aback by this unexpected revelation and recalls that even Dafydd Elis himself seemed surprised by what he had just said.[98] There had been no warning of his intention to his staff or family. If he had stood again, he may well have won the Dwyfor-Meirionnydd seat as an independent candidate, but he would have caused a major rupture within Plaid Cymru locally, and it would have taken him through to the next scheduled Senedd election in 2026, when he would have been almost eighty.

In his interview, he ruminated on the impact of Covid and reflected that 'selfishness would be the worst thing that anybody could turn to while developing public policy. We needed a sense of community, society and cooperation and mutual understanding in the public framework.'

He asserted that his principles had been constant for his fifty years in public life, from his election as the youngest MP in the House of Commons at the age of 27. In his period of forty years as an elected representative, and seven years as President of the party, he argued that his greatest contribution to Plaid Cymru was to make it a more credible political force, and to encourage collaboration with progressive political alliances in Wales, eventually paving the way to the creation of a legislative parliament for Wales.[99]

Dafydd Elis-Thomas had little doubt about his most important legacy, that his work in creating the National Left, and his role as President of Plaid Cymru, 'made it possible to have Welsh devolution and then finally, to make it work with a better relationship between Plaid and Labour':

> I just thought it was absolutely terrible that the progressive forces should be divided. Politics is not about preaching to the converted or the unconverted ... it's about ... what do we do next? If we are elected, we have a responsibility. It's not authority. It's responsibility to do what is appropriate. That's where I was coming from.[100]

In his role as the first Presiding Officer of the National Assembly for Wales, he used his undoubted political skills to help develop the institution as a fully functioning representative body and separate from the functions of the Welsh Government. With his appreciation of the way Westminster worked, he was insistent that the new institution should not emulate that arcane culture. Instead he strove to give the National Assembly a more distinctive character and, together with Rhodri Morgan, ensured that the institution gained its separation from government.

The success of the 2011 referendum on greater legislative powers for the Assembly was a particular revelation to him, because of the large size of the majority in favour and 'because that meant that it worked. We'd shown that Welsh democracy was possible, that it delivered. That things actually happen.'

His objection to Plaid Cymru's stated aim of independence remained fundamental, and his opposition to nationalism had been consistent since 1974, when he revealed his secret revulsion to his party's fundamental aim, to his friend Gwynn Matthews:

> Independence, to me, basically is a post-colonial concept. You can't argue that a Wales which produced, still in my view, the strongest political state of development of England and Wales in the Tudor revolution and its consequences in Wales, particularly on the Welsh language and the Elizabethan Settlement... we wouldn't be speaking Welsh in Wales now if it wasn't for what the geniuses of the Elizabethan period managed to achieve with the support of the governing class at the time. It's something which former colonies have achieved, but it's clear worldwide that the only way to work is not by independence, but by co-dependence... I find it quite amusing, but dangerous, the extent of nationalist rhetoric coming from the centre-right in England.[101]

His rejection of independence, coming from a senior elected representative of the party and its President for seven years, frustrated and confused many Plaid Cymru members. He shared the view that many of the intellectual founders of the party were crudely, 'a bunch of ultra-reactionary fascists'.[102] His role as Presiding Officer gave him a remarkable opportunity to become the formative influence on the culture and nature of the new Assembly. He viewed himself as being unencumbered by his allegiance to Plaid Cymru, and felt duty bound to serve Welsh democracy rather than his party. Ieuan Wyn Jones believed him to have been one of the Welsh political figures of most significance in the past fifty years, and to have been:

> Part of the party that broke through in Parliament and emphasised extending Plaid beyond its traditional base. As Presiding Officer, his contribution was to turn the pathetic Assembly in 1999 into a powerful Senedd by 2011. Looking back, I don't think anyone else could have done that. Rhodri Morgan was a successful and excellent First Minister, but he could not have done what Dafydd succeeded in doing.[103]

As one of the Labour's most experienced Ministers, having held the Finance, Health and Economy portfolios, Edwina Hart considered his role as Presiding Officer as his main contribution to Welsh politics, and that his personal flamboyance led him to be underestimated:

> He never forgot he wanted to represent people irrespective of their politics – he had a readiness to work with others, was open to ideas and friendships, and working with the trades union movement, for example. With the Yes campaign in 1997, it was won on a narrow vote – he saw past that and took the opportunities when he became Presiding Officer, of building alliances, taking forward the agenda of more powers, creating coalition governments, pushing forward. His pressing for the end game of more powers was quite significant. He never lost a sense of where we needed to be as a nation and that is the greatest compliment I can pay him. But for him there would not be an Assembly building, he gave stability for the institution and took a new parliamentary body forward through its paces and ensuring it didn't collapse within the first four years.

For Edwina Hart, Dafydd was a 'renaissance man' and in her view, people often didn't wish that in politics, preferring 'someone down the line, like Alun Michael, or someone with a bit of life, like Rhodri Morgan, but a bit boring, like Carwyn Jones, and they like competence, like Mark Drakeford'. Dafydd's love of the arts and wider interests enamoured him to many who otherwise had little time for politicians. In comparing his contribution with that of Rhodri Morgan, she considered both 'to be on a par':

> In the first Assembly term, Dafydd was first class – Rhodri woke up the nation in a very different way. Dafydd knew what the end game was, while Rhodri was feeling his way – Rhodri wasn't as radical as people thought – he had a brilliant brain, but I was not certain if Rhodri always knew where he wanted to go. He gave people their heads – I see Rhodri as the spirit of the nation because he embodied devolution. I see Dafydd at the core of ensuring that devolution survived. Both were equally significant in their different ways.[104]

Mark Drakeford became First Minister in December 2018, and has a high opinion of Elis-Thomas's political skills:

> His contribution is huge and multi-faceted. That's what makes him stand out. Others have made significant contributions over fifty years of Welsh life. But would you find anyone else who has made so many different contributions of such a high order? Presiding over a Parliament, being a Minister, leading a groundbreaking arm's-length organisation, being a Member of Parliament with a very distinctive reputation, doing things that others did not have the courage to do. How many other people can you think of who have done that range of things, and all at the top of his tree.

Drakeford worked closely with Rhodri Morgan as his special adviser before replacing him as member of the Assembly for Cardiff West, and later as First Minister, and was well placed to compare their respective contributions:

> They had some similarities. He and Rhodri agreed that in Welsh his title would be 'Prif Weinidog' [Prime Minister]. There were lots of shared things. I would say that Rhodri did not have the breadth of experience that Dafydd had in his career but in the end Rhodri was the most fundamentally serious politician. If I have a criticism of what Dafydd did, he never stuck to anything. Rhodri was single-mindedly determined to do everything he could to establish that new institution in the minds and the lives of people in Wales so there could be no going back on it. It was a very narrow referendum result in 1997 – then came the resounding referendum result in 2011, Rhodri said to me 'my work is done'. We'd gone from a 6,000 vote majority to 21 out of 22 council areas voting in favour of legislative powers. It shows how Rhodri had taken the Assembly through his single-handed dedication to a single purpose. Rhodri had it. Maybe the more eclectic career of Dafydd didn't have it.[105]

Certainly, Dafydd Elis did not share the single-mindedness of his fellow Plaid Cymru Politicians, such as Gwynfor Evans and Dafydd Wigley, and his political journey suggests an element of the maverick. Carwyn Jones had known him since the beginning of the Assembly:

> Dafydd El's contribution was all important. He had been so young starting in politics, and he had vast experience inside and outside politics. He gained great respect as Presiding Officer. If I had told the young Dafydd El in 1974 that by 2017, we would have a Senedd with legislative and tax-raising powers, nobody would have believed me, and he has been an important part of that journey.
>
> He and Rhodri Morgan are the two significant figures on this journey. As a Presiding Officer, you had to have someone with political experience, and experience of Westminster. You had to have someone strong and somebody who was ready to ensure, insisting on order and not too partisan, someone who wanted to see the institution grow. If anybody in that position had shown bias, that would have caused great problems. The fact that he was seen as neutral was all important.[106]

Dafydd Elis-Thomas was a member of Plaid Cymru for 56 years, until he left the party in October 2016. The party's members had a wide range of views about Dafydd El's contribution to the party. His colleague and rival, Dafydd Wigley, active in the House of Lords as one of the two Plaid Cymru peers, believed that Elis-Thomas should have stood down from the Assembly after the 2011 election, when he would have received the 'full fanfare', instead of being embroiled in the 2012 leadership campaign, and alienating many within the party.[107] The leader of Gwynedd council for seven years, Dyfrig Siencyn, the councillor for Dolgellau, was a close personal friend, as well as an often-frustrated chair of his constituency party. He did more than anyone to save him from being expelled from the party before the 2016 Assembly election, 'politically both of us have lived and represented the Welsh language linguistic conservatism that is also at the heart of the support for Plaid Cymru'. He felt that Elis-Thomas tried to be more broad-minded and less defensive than his fellow members:

> In a Plaid meeting in 2021, we had a meeting on policy, and I referred to Dafydd Elis. I said that one thing I learnt from Dafydd Elis-Thomas was that being in opposition was good for nothing.

I'm sure he was dreadful in a group – but he gave leadership and raised the standard of political discussion.[108]

Siencyn's predecessor as Gwynedd's council leader, Dyfed Edwards, had no doubt of his significance:

> For me, in the last forty years, he is the one national figure who has moved Welsh democracy to where it is today. In my view, Welsh democracy was born in 1979 with the Referendum defeat, and throughout the following years, we gradually built the conditions for a Welsh democracy. He was the one person, without exception, who built modern Welsh democracy, if we look at his contribution since 1979. There was some 'wandering in the desert' in the 1990s, and that's not all bad, but he was the one who had the vision to look forward, to drag people along with him, and was creatively restless. Rhodri was of course, an important figure – a man of real presence, but constitutionally there is no question that Dafydd is the outstanding figure. Rhodri was excellent in placing himself on the left of the Labour party in London, and that was a help constitutionally as well.

In assessing the contributions of Elis-Thomas and Wigley respectively, Dyfed Edwards compared them to football players with their own styles of play:

> In managing a football team, you can either say the team should be working harder, or to say – hold on – we need to think of the game differently – we need to get new players and try new formations. In this analogy, Dafydd Wigley is the dedicated midfielder who has given his life to the team. But Dafydd El has always been the more strategic free-running attacking midfielder, who while often frustrating his teammates, is visionary in his forward play.[109]

Dafydd Elis-Thomas's *bête noire* in Plaid Cymru, Leanne Wood, had little to say in his favour:

> I only remember the grief he caused the party. In the early days he made a very positive contribution in the positioning of Plaid

Cymru especially after the 1979 Referendum disaster result. He did a lot of good work on where Plaid stood on the key questions of the day such as the miners' strike. Unfortunately, a lot of that work has been undone by his undermining of Plaid Cymru for no good reason other than a personal sense of grievance after the 2012 leadership election. Also, sometimes people have felt he has trolled the party, winding people up on purpose, putting things out there knowing that members would be angry, especially for his support for the royal family, and why? To what end? I genuinely don't understand, don't know where he's coming from, is it for fun? As for joining the Government, why did he do that? What did he achieve?[110]

One of his persistent adversaries in the party, Dafydd Iwan, characterised him as an 'intellectual acrobat and political chameleon' and considered that his political weaknesses outweighed his strengths, especially as a party leader. Iwan believed in the party's left-ward shift during the miners' strike, but that Elis-Thomas's 'tendency to go in so many directions made him an ineffectual leader'. Iwan regarded the long running ideological disputes between Wigley and Elis-Thomas as not so much an argument between left and right, but whether Elis-Thomas was a weaker nationalist than Wigley.[111]

Rhuanedd Richards believed that in 2007, Dafydd may have regretted not taking the opportunity to gain Ministerial office in the Plaid-Labour coalition, but recognised the substance of his political legacy:

> His biggest contribution is that he succeeded in expanding the appeal of the party in the 1980s. He got more people to discuss the constitutional question, and he bridged between rural Wales and the industrial coalfield in south Wales especially. His legacy is that the two parties – Plaid and Labour – became nearer and he reduced the poison between them. He gave authority and status to the new Assembly. My sadness is that it could have been a greater legacy. If he had worked better within the party process – any party – he would have been more effective. He's not a team player and he can't obey other people's rules. A lot of people miss him. People . . . only declared disappointment – not

hatred, or even anger, at his departure from the party. I still have the utmost respect towards him.¹¹²

The chair of Plaid Cymru during the period of Dafydd Elis's departure from the party, Dafydd Trystan, considered that he has been one of the most significant Welsh politicians since the 1960s:

> His work in positioning Plaid Cymru was substantial, and as chairman of the Language Board, he created a new method of developing the Board to become an organisation that made strides for the language, and as Presiding Officer of the Assembly a combination of his experience and ability took the devolution project onwards and made a notable contribution to Welsh public life. He and Rhodri Morgan were the key figures in developing the new institution after its unpromising beginnings, and without him, the construction of the Assembly building might not have happened.¹¹³

For one of his former supporters in the constituency, the Welsh language academic Simon Brooks, Dafydd Elis was in the lineage of Welsh intellectuals that have created national institutions, and then won power within them:

> He is a man who believes that a nation needs to create institutions, and he is a devolutionist, who does not believe in independence. To some extent, he has been too large a figure in too small a pool. It is easy to imagine him as a Cabinet member, but perhaps too maverick to be the Prime Minister. He created the space for the Left within Plaid Cymru to win greater influence and power. However ironically, although he created the National Left in the eighties, it was because of the left wing within Plaid that were also so intolerant of him that Dafydd felt he had to leave the party.
>
> He hasn't believed in independence, he has believed in self-government, and he sees this as connected with the royal family. Wales's view of itself has been of a self-governing Wales within a united Britain – that has been Wales's point of view for the last 500 years. This is rather different to the SNP's view of

independence, and for Dafydd this led to tension with his fellow members of Plaid.

Brooks believes that Elis-Thomas's disagreement with Welsh nationalism's emphasis on independence was based on his identification with the traditional Liberal politics of the cultured Welsh language heartland of Merionnydd, and his regard for his predecessor as MP, Tom Ellis:

> He is a creature of the rural, rustic, cultured Liberal Welsh language heartland ... He seems like an old Liberal, in Tom Ellis's tradition of Penllyn patriotic Liberalism, in the tradition of Michael D. Jones and Lloyd George. Dafydd is the son of the manse, in the Welsh language liberal and Nonconformist tradition of rural Gwynedd that accepts it is part of Britain, but that wishes to be respected and given freedom within the British state. That is his political standpoint and has been Wales's constitutional position over the centuries. Dafydd's view is a traditional one. The essential question is whether Plaid Cymru has any relevance in this argument. It could be argued that it is the Labour party that holds the key to greater recognition for Wales. Dafydd's contribution has been massive. He has extended Plaid's political horizons, sometimes uncomfortably. I have the greatest of respect for him, which is not a popular view amongst Plaid members. Their majority view is that he has turned his back on the party and that he is a traitor. But in spite of this, and I have disagreed with him, and had trouble to vote for him sometimes, I have a very high opinion of him.[114]

It is ironic that on 18 August 2023, in an interview with ITV Wales's political editor Adrian Masters, Dafydd Elis-Thomas announced his intention to re-join Plaid Cymru, because of what he considered to be the more mature leadership given by Rhun ap Iorwerth,[115] its newly elected leader:

> The most important thing that's happened is that Plaid Cymru's leadership has changed, and trying to extend the reach of the party beyond its traditional appeal means that I am very happy to support him. The important thing is that we develop an

understanding across the centre-left in Wales, and I'm sure that is Rhun's view. He has emphasised the need to communicate with people. I declare my support.

He said he had requested to re-join the party, and that he had spoken with the party leader:

> I don't want to die (I'm healthy at present!), but I want to feel that I belong to something that's worth belonging to, and that's true of religion, and that also includes politics. He admitted to only missing the party recently since Rhun ap Iorwerth's leadership; 'I think we are in a situation to extend Plaid's reach further, and that means I can re-join with my friend Lord Wigley.'

However, when pressed whether he would retain any allegiance to Labour, his reply would not have consoled Plaid members: 'I accept the Labour whip from Debbie Wilcox [the Labour party's Welsh whip in the House of Lords]. That shouldn't change. After all, my relationship with Welsh Labour has been very close.' But when asked, theoretically, who he would vote for in an election in Cardiff West, the diplomatic reply is that 'if Plaid Cymru had a chance of getting in, then I would support them.'[116]

Far from welcoming the prodigal son's return, the party's response was to set up a hostile internal panel to consider his application, comprised of the chair, Alun Cox, a member of Plaid's national executive, and two Gwynedd councillors, Cai Larsen and Beca Brown. They wrote to Elis-Thomas on 12 October 2023, stating that it had met to 'consider the concerns that have been raised about your application for membership, and it was agreed that there was a case to answer on the basis of the party's rules, under "3.iii Actions or statements which harm, or possibly harm, the good name of Plaid Cymru".' Specifically, the panel raised two issues dating back to 2016:

> Following your election as Assembly Member for Plaid Cymru, you left the Plaid Cymru group and joined the Labour Government, thereby depriving Plaid Cymru of the Official Status of Opposition and causing harm to the good name of the party. During elections for the Police Commissioner for north

Wales, you encouraged supporters to support the Labour candidate, thereby undermining Plaid Cymru's campaign.[117]

On receiving this less than encouraging email, Elis-Thomas decided not to engage with the panel and its disciplinary process, and to attend what seemed to him be a kangaroo court held on a remote video link. While these questions may have been legitimate, the panel failed to balance them with his record of service as the party's representative for Meirionnydd for eighteen years as a Member of Parliament, twenty-two years as a member of the National Assembly and Senedd, and his service as the party's president for seven years.

Lord Dafydd Elis-Thomas remained outside the party that he led and to which he gave so much over the past 55 years, but that he also provoked, baited and challenged. His achievements, while made possible by his political base within Plaid Cymru, are greater than the limitations imposed by party affiliation. He brought together elements of the left in the 1980s in a way that made it possible for devolution to be delivered in the 1997 referendum, through the collaboration of many elements within Welsh civic society and the political left, for whom he gave imaginative and creative leadership. Arguably, it was through his vision and tenacity that Wales has a Senedd building to be proud of, and in collaboration with Rhodri Morgan, he played a crucial part in growing devolution from the disastrous beginnings of the National Assembly in 1999, into the parliamentary and law-making institution of the Senedd. That is a proud legacy.

Postscript

The Right Honourable Lord Dafydd Elis-Thomas of Nant Conwy, known to most as Dafydd El – effectively withdrew from public life following his retirement from Senedd politics in May 2021. The need to isolate himself against the experience of the Covid pandemic radically curtailed his social life, and he restricted himself to very occasional walks from his home in Cardiff's Pontcanna area. He ceased to attend the House of Lords, and in 2024, showed early signs of becoming frail.

At the end of 2024, he found it increasingly difficult to swallow his food, and changed his diet in the hope that his condition would improve. His GP had referred him for urgent tests, but before they were completed, he died on 7 February 2025.

His unexpected passing was marked by generous tributes from political foes and friends. His successor, Elin Jones, the Senedd's Presiding officer stated that 'this Senedd today is what it is because, to a very great extent, of Dafydd Elis-Thomas and certainly all of us in this wonderful Senedd building and this wonderful *Siambr* are here because of Dafydd's vision and perseverance'.[1]

Eluned Morgan, the First Minister, stated that 'Dafydd's story was interwoven into the fabric of our nation':

> For those who knew him well, he was far more than a lengthy list of his achievements ... He was an incredible character, a political giant with a mischievous side. He was a master at building bridges, and he succeeded in doing that while appearing to be entirely effortless, always principled, always constructive ... He encapsulated the best of the Welsh intellectual tradition – learned, but always ready with a sparky response in one language or the other. His example in terms of how to serve with passion and humour, with principle and friendliness, will continue to be an inspiration for all of us who had the privilege of knowing him.[2]

The Plaid leader, Rhun ap Iorwerth, emphasised his decades of service to Plaid Cymru, 'its leader for eight years, and part of its DNA for way over 50 years'. His former Plaid colleagues were also gracious in their tributes. His successor as the Member of the Senedd for the Dwyfor Meirionnydd constituency, Gwynfor Evans's grandson, Mabon ap Gwynfor, described him as a 'giant' and an 'unconventional and enigmatic politician' who was always courteous and supportive to him personally.

His successor in the Meirionnydd Westminster seat, Liz Saville Roberts, chose to recall Dafydd El's earliest contributions as a Plaid MP, and how his politics had inspired so many to support the party in Meirionnydd:

> His tireless work and his commitment to Wales, its people and to democracy leaves a massive gap in our history. He gained respect from colleagues across the political spectrum for his ability to build bridges across political differences and his deep passion for Welsh culture and identity. Dafydd El was a colourful politician and never boring.[3]

The Conservatives' leader in the Senedd, Darren Millar, described him as 'a titan of Welsh politics', and as 'a man of great intellect, wit and conviction, never afraid to challenge the status quo, yet always open to evolution of his own thoughts.'[4]

Following Dafydd's death, his widow Mair received over four hundred messages of sympathy covering the whole range of the political spectrum. Both the Labour and Conservative party groupings in the Senedd sent their condolences, the Labour Group expressing gratitude for 'his unstinting commitment, hard work and dedication as our very first *Llywydd*. His sense of vision made the Senedd what it is today – a strong, confident, outward looking and modern Parliament.'[5]

Many individual present and former Members recalled his kindnesses towards them. The Labour Minister of Health, Jeremy Miles, said that although Dafydd had not been a member of the Labour party, 'in a number of ways Dafydd had been an inspiration – and his contribution to Wales immeasurable.'[6] The former Conservative regional Member for Mid and West Wales, Lisa Francis, recalled his care for all Assembly Members:

Definitely, he was the father who established the Senedd – he cared passionately for the place and its Members – he saw no difference between regional and constituency members and treated everybody equally, when many didn't. I always admired him for not paying attention to bigots, tribalists and those who were parochial.

As a former Conservative candidate standing against 'Dafydd El' in Dwyfor Meirionnydd, she recalled that:

> in his constituency he was a 'legend' and he would joke with me how he would harvest the votes of Conservatives in Aberdyfi! I'm sure that's totally right. I enjoyed his company. He was charming, warm and witty, and sometimes he could be a bit acerbic and inconsiderate if he didn't agree with you – but that was part of his marvellous charisma.[7]

His former Plaid Cymru colleague, Elfyn Llwyd, mentored by Dafydd Elis to succeed him as the Member of Parliament for Meirionnydd Nant Conwy, paid warm tribute to 'a man of remarkable substance, bravery and vision', whose 'tireless work to create structures to change the Assembly into a Senedd would be remembered for years to come':

> He, more than anyone, was the main architect of today's Senedd, and he succeeded in doing so almost on his own, and in the face of numerous difficulties placed in his way by other less ambitious politicians. I'm sure, from knowing him well, that such problems stimulated him to go further and to work harder to reach his goal on those constitutional matters in which he was such an expert.[8]

The letters of sympathy were not restricted to politicians, but included prominent members of the Church of Wales including the Bishop of St Asaph, Lords Lieutenants and High Sheriffs, and members of the public especially from Meirionnydd and north-west Wales, where he had served as an elected representative for forty years. The former chief executive of Swansea City Council and chair of the Welsh Consumer Council, Vivienne Sugar, recalled his engaging character:

I met Dafydd El on many occasions and found him to be a man who listened and acted on his promises. He was highly esteemed and respected by people across Wales and from all walks of life. His service to the Welsh Language Board, to the people of Dwyfor Meirionnydd as their representative, becoming our first Presiding officer and holding Ministerial office all demonstrated a belief and commitment to whatever was in the best interests of Wales.

He was of course very independently minded. He could be indiscreet about his political colleagues and no meeting would pass without an anecdote or two – but told with warmth and a twinkle in his eye rather than from any malice.[9]

The Arts Council of Wales's chair, Maggie Russell, paid tribute to him as a 'cultural giant', and how he gave a sense of leadership to the arts sector:

During his period as a bold and visionary Minister for Culture, Sport and Tourism in Wales, and indeed throughout his long political career, he was a consistent source of inspiration, his passion encouraging us to take risks for the good of the arts, and claim the place of Welsh culture in the World.[10]

A remarkable tribute was paid to him by Gerry Adams, the former President of Sinn Féin, who had criticised him in the past:

I am saddened to hear of the death of Dafydd. He was a champion of the rights of the people of Wales. His contribution to Welsh politics and society was enormous. Dafydd was also prepared to stand up for the rights of others. Following the death of Bobby Sands MP on hunger strike in 1981 he moved the writ for the by-election in Fermanagh/South Tyrone. That election as won by Owen Carron. Please accept my solidarity and thanks at this sad time in the life of your family. Dafydd is very fondly remembered in Ireland.[11]

A similarly warm letter was received from King Charles, a friend to Dafydd for over fifty years, who expressed his deepest sympathy to Mair at his passing:

POSTSCRIPT

I was so terribly sorry to hear the very sad news about your husband and particularly wanted to write and send you my deepest possible sympathy . . . I cannot believe it is now more than fifty years since we were both at Aberystwyth University at the same time. So much has changed since those memorable days, and what a great part your husband played in those changes over the years. Wales has indeed, been fortunate to have had such devoted service through such crucial times.

To all things, your husband brought an independence of mind and a generosity of spirit, not to mention a wit, that I always found immensely impressive. Our public life will be so very much the poorer without his thoughtful and stimulating presence.

There can be few people who have contributed so much to the lives of their nation, in so many fields, for so long. I hope it will be of at least some small comfort to you, in your loss, to know the enormous respect in which your husband was held by so many people from all walks of life.[12]

Dafydd Elis's bilingual funeral was conducted in Cardiff's Llandaff Cathedral, where he had been a committed steward and lay canon. In keeping with his deeply serious religiosity, he had insisted on a traditional eucharistic service, which was conducted by his friend, the former Archbishop of Wales, Barry Morgan, and featured readings by the First Minister, Eluned Morgan, the poet Robin Llywelyn, who read a poem by Waldo Williams, and the eulogy by Aled Eirug. The packed congregation of over a thousand people were joined by those following the live stream of the service. The seating arrangements reflected his private and public life, with the front row on the right side including Mair, her nephew and niece Gwion and Heini, Dafydd's three sons, and four grandchildren. The front row on the left hand side included the First Minister, the Lord Lieutenant for South Glamorgan Morfudd Meredith, the leader of Plaid Cymru Rhun ap Iorwerth, the leader of the party in the House of Commons Liz Saville Roberts, the Presiding Officer of the Senedd Elin Jones, and Lord Wigley representing the King and his wife Lady Elinor Wigley.

In tribute to Dafydd Elis-Thomas's lifetime achievement, the funeral cortege drove in front of the Senedd, where the security guards and catering staff formed a line of honour. It then proceeded to a smaller and simpler private service at Wenvoe crematorium, led by a family friend, and his former Congregationalist minister in Dolgellau, Hywel Wyn Richards. It ended emotionally with a taped rendition of 'Cymru, Lloegr a Llanrwst'[13] by the punk rock band Y Cyrff, a song celebrating the independence of Dafydd's home town, to usher the mourners out. In accordance with his wishes, his remains are buried in Capel Garmon churchyard, overlooking the Conwy Valley.

His obituaries in the quality press recalled his mercurial character, and *The Guardian*'s Julia Langdon recalled a pragmatic politician, 'who was never afraid to speak his mind or to test the boundaries of what might be politically acceptable'. She paid tribute to his 'intellectual agility' that kept him 'ahead of the game' and he became 'one of the most influential Welsh politicians of his generation, who made an outstanding impact on the life of Wales'.[14] *The Times* charted the career of the 'softly spoken Welsh nationalist' from 'socialist firebrand to accepting a seat in the House of Lords'.[15] In addition to also labelling him as 'mercurial', the rather less generous *Daily Telegraph* described him as 'slight, blond-haired, impulsive and a self-proclaimed Marxist' but also referred to his political pragmatism, 'concerned with the realities of power rather than Celtic romanticism'.[16]

Dafydd was mischievous, challenging, entertaining and provoking, but also a profoundly serious man – throughout his life, he retained his interest in the semiotics of language, philosophy and the arts; and in religion, he remained a committee Christian, while moving gradually from the ascetic Calvinism of the Presbyterian church, through the liberalism of Congregationalism, to the Church of Wales.

While even his friends thought that Dafydd could sometimes be inconsistent in his political judgement, he would argue that he was simply adapting to the political realities of the time. He was perceptive, lively, hugely charming, courteous and inspirational, and was true to his fundamental belief in that whatever he did, he did wholly for the benefit of Wales.

His public roles were many but they came at a price. His personal life was often sacrificed to the needs of his party, parliaments and Senedd, and the public. One of his sons shared that Dafydd's method of coping was 'never to look in the rear view mirror', but always to look forward. His legacy, however, as a founding father of devolution and the Senedd, as a Welsh political giant and nation-builder, will surely stand the test of time.

POSTSCRIPT

Following the funeral, the poet Menna Elfyn, who had been a friend to Dafydd for over fifty years, wrote a remarkable poem in tribute to the passing of Lord Dafydd Elis-Thomas, a creator of modern Wales[17]:

Gwladweinydd
Er cof am Dafydd Elis-Thomas

i
O'r chwith i'r dde y daethom
i'r arwyl i gofio herarwr –
hyd yr eiliau awn i'n seddau
heb yngan gair – angau'n
pwyso'n drwm ar bob genau;
Yna, mud ydym wrth ymadael

ii
O Landâf i'r brifddinas,
O lecyn hedd ei Senedd-dy,
O'r llechi i'r muriau'n lloches
pob Plwy iddo'n rhan o'r Plas:
y Dalar hon fe'i daliodd hi
yn ei Law yn gyfewin Lywydd.

iii
A'n dyled olaf nawr. De a Chwith
a'r Canol llonydd, mor chwithig
yw datod un fu'n gyffröwr
yn rhyddhau cyffion ein gwlad.
Tynged yr Iaith?
Onid iaith ei afiaith a roddodd
inni'n waddol o'i ruddin?

iv
'Arglwydd i Gymru' ydoedd –
Gymrawd da i'w chamre hi,
ond rhy fyr yw edau bywyd
rhy frau yw i fesur ei hud:

v
Mae amser i'r llwyfan a'r lleferydd,
amser prin i'r Gair distaw main
estyn ei gywair i Gadeirlan –
a'r dwyfol yn iro'r dyfalwch.
Yn ddyn o ddeall, isel o aruchel
tad ein treftadaeth ydoedd,
o'r Chwith i'r Dde fel daw'r Canol
Aflonydd i seinio'n bedwar llais.

vi
Onid adnabod yw gwybod hefyd:
am y gŵr gwâr dros Blaid y Byd:
Un fydd ynom oll o hyd.*

Menna Elfyn   * *Vedas, Sansgrit*

Statesman
In memory of Lord Dafydd Elis-Thomas

i
From left and right we convene
at the funeral, lay an icon to rest.
We file along aisles, seek out a seat
and I think of him, living, where death
creeps in. It's weighty, a slab on all tongues.
It leaves us speechless, silenced at our parting.

ii
From the place of his spirit,
soul's centre point, Senedd,
his house is home. Foundations
to slate, his peace, all parishes
part of one dwelling and held
in the safe acre of his presiding palm.

POSTSCRIPT

iii
From leftfield, how left and right
and latent centre come together
to pay their debt. This stillness
of an agitator who shook our country's
shackles, its language, his rapture
bequeathed, cast in the form of his mettle.

iv
From 'Lord of Wales', friend
of her consciousness, to filament
too fragile to quantify
her enchantments.

v
From cathedral-song of service,
a time for the rostrum's rouse
to hush in the nook of each ear,
to pour its patient, sacred balm.
He, man of understanding, humble
and sublime, father of our lineage,
left and right or the restless centre, raising
one voice, in four soaring harmonies.

vi
To know him is to know
civilisation, a human affinity –
forever, one for all.

Menna Elfyn
translated from the Welsh by Emma Baines

Notes

Chapter 1

1. Interview with Dafydd Elis-Thomas (DET), 27 September 2021.
2. C. L. Sutherland and S. Bryson, *Report on an Inquiry into the occurrence of Disease of the Lungs from Dust Inhalation* (Mines Department, HMSO, 1930), p. 2
3. *Y Dydd*, 9 January 1874
4. Robert Griffiths, *S. O. Davies – A Socialist Faith* (Gomer Press, 1983), p. 34.
5. Griffiths, *S.O. Davies*, p. 34.
6. Eirug, Aled, *Opposition to the Great War in Wales, 1914–1918* (University of Wales Press, 2018), p. 192.
7. Edward Rees, *Cofiant T. Rowland Hughes* (Gwasg Gomer, 1968), p. 34.
8. Rees, *Cofiant T. Rowland Hughes*, p. 34.
9. Rees, *Cofiant T. Rowland Hughes*, pp. 36, 56.
10. Rees, *Cofiant T. Rowland Hughes*, p. 57
11. Translated as 'losing a leg, losing heart'.
12. Meirionnydd Archives, Oakeley quarry papers, DAF 45, injuries book.
13. *Y Rhedegydd*, 24 May, 7 June, 14 June 1928.
14. W. D. Williams, *Adlais Odlau* (Gwasg Gee, 1939).
15. Meirionnydd Archives, W. D. Williams Papers, Z/DDF/2/7/139 (1939).
16. *Cambrian News*, 21 April 1944; *Y Rhedegydd*, 20 April 1944.
17. Interview with DET, 27 September 2021.
18. Interview with DET, 27 September 2021.
19. Interview with DET, 27 September 2021.
20. Interview with Ann Ffrancon, 9 September 2022.
21. Interview with Ann Ffrancon, 9 September 2022.
22. *Ffrwyth y Coed* (Coed y Bryn Children's Committee, 2002), p. 85.
23. The three satellite branches were Cae Person, Tafarn y Fedw and Tanlan.
24. Interview with Dafydd Andrew Jones, 26 August 2022.
25. Note from Myrddin ap Dafydd to the author, November 2023. The names of the publishers were Hughes & Son, Gomer Press and the Brython Press.
26. Interview with Elen Tomos, 1 March 2022.
27. Interview with Nesta Wyn Ellis, 9 July 2022.
28. Interview with Elen Tomos, 1 March 2022.
29. Interview with Ann Ffrancon, 9 September 2022.
30. Interview with Gareth Tilsley, 1 March 2022.
31. *Marxism Today*, January 1989.
32. Interview with DET, 27 September 2021.
33. Interview with Ann Ffrancon, 9 September 2022.

34. Interview with Elen Tomos, 1 March 2022.
35. Interview with DET, 27 September 2021.
36. Interview with Selwyn Griffiths, 21 April 2023.
37. Interview with Elfyn Llwyd, 11 June 2022.
38. *The Grustensian*, 1963.
39. *The Grustensian*, 1964.
40. Interview with DET, 27 September 2021.
41. Interview with DET, 27 September 2021.
42. Interview with DET, 27 September 2021.
43. O. M. Roberts, *Oddeutu'r Tân* ((Gwasg Gwynedd, 1994).
44. Interview with DET, 27 September 2021.
45. Interview with Derec Llwyd Morgan, 27 April 2022.
46. Interview with DET, 27 September 2021.
47. Interview with DET, 27 September 2021.

Chapter 2

1. Martin Johnes, *Wales since 1939* (Manchester University Press, 2012), p. 226.
2. *Bangoriad* alumni magazine, 1994, pp. 14, 15.
3. Interview with Gwynn Matthews, 4 March 2022.
4. Interview with Mair Price, 27 April 2002.
5. Interview with Gwynn Matthews, 4 March 2022.
6. Emyr Price, *Fy Hanner Canrif i* (Y Lolfa, 2002), p. 80.
7. Interview with Emlyn Davies, 14 March 2022.
8. Price, *Fy Hanner Canrif i*, p. 80.
9. Price, *Fy Hanner Canrif i*, p. 75.
10. Interview with Gwynn Matthews, March 2022.
11. David Roberts, *Bangor University 1824–1909* (University of Wales Press, 2009), p. 76.
12. Saunders Lewis, *Tynged yr Iaith*, trans. E. Edwards (*Planet*, 4, 1971), pp. 13–27.
13. Johnes, *Wales since 1939*, p. 226.
14. Roberts, *Bangor University 1884–2009*, pp. 76, 77.
15. Interview with DET, 28 September 2021.
16. Interview with Dafydd Iwan, 22 September 2023.
17. Interview with Cenwyn Edwards, 9 February 2022.
18. Chris Rees (1931–2001), prominent Welsh nationalist, pioneer of the Ulpan method of teaching Welsh to adults; Harri Webb (1920–94), prominent satirical poet and militant nationalist.
19. Interview with DET, 28 September 2021.
20. Price, *Fy Hanner Canrif i*, p. 73.
21. Interview with DET, 28 September 2021; Bangor University student file for DET.
22. Interview with Elen Thomas, 1 March 2022.
23. Wyn Thomas, *Tryweryn: A New Dawn?* (Lolfa, 2023), p. 280.
24. Thomas, *Tryweryn: A New Dawn?*, p. 303.
25. Interview with DET, 28 September 2021.

26. Price, *Fy Hanner Canrif* i, p. 80.
27. *Y Dyfodol*, March 1966.
28. *Y Dyfodol*, October 1966.
29. Price, *Fy Hanner Canrif* i, p. 80.
30. Price, *Fy Hanner Canrif* i, p. 81.
31. *Y Cymro*, 20 October 1966.
32. Roberts, *Bangor University*, p. 79.
33. *Y Dyfodol*, November 1967.
34. *Ffenics*, 1/8, Spring 1967.
35. *Ffenics*, 1/9, Spring 1968.
36. *Ffenics*, 1/7, Spring 1966.
37. *Y Dyfodol*, October 1966.
38. Interview with Cenwyn Edwards, 9 February 2022.
39. Price. *Fy Hanner Canrif* i, p. 86.
40. Price, *Fy Hanner Canrif* i, p. 86.
41. Roberts, *Bangor University*, p.78.
42. *Forecast*, 12 May 1966, p. 8.
43. Price, *Fy Hanner Canrif* i, p. 86.
44. Interview with Gwynn Matthews, 4 March 2022.
45. *North Wales Weekly News*, 27 July 1967.
46. Interview with DET, 28 September 2021.
47. Interview with DET, 28 September 2021.
48. Interview with Derec Llwyd Morgan, 27 April 2022.
49. Interview with DET, 28 September 2021.
50. Johnes, *Wales since 1939*, p. 223.
51. Johnes, *Wales since 1939*, p. 225.
52. Interview with DET, 28 September 2021.
53. Interview with Wyn Thomas, 26 July 2022.
54. Interview with Gwynn Matthews, 4 March 2022.
55. Interview with DET, 28 September 2021.
56. The Conway constituency was re-named Conwy in 1983.
57. Interview with DET, 28 September 2021.
58. *Y Ddraig Goch*, November 1969
59. Interview with DET, 28 September 2021.
60. Johnes, *Wales since 1939*, p. 235.
61. Johnes, *Wales since 1939*, p. 235.
62. *I'r Gad*, 1, Spring 1968 (ed. Heini Gruffudd).
63. Interview with DET, 28 September 2021.
64. Interview with DET, 28 September 2021.
65. *North Wales Weekly News*, 5 June 1969.
66. *North Wales Weekly News*, 5 June 1969.
67. Interview with DET, 28 September 2021.
68. Interview with Dafydd Andrew Jones, 26 August 2022.
69. Interview with Ann Ffrancon, 9 September 2022.
70. Interview with Dafydd Andrew Jones, 26 August 2022.

71. Interview with Cenwyn Edwards, 9 February 2022.
72. Beti Jones, *Parliamentary Elections in Wales 1900–1975* (Y Lolfa, 1977), p. 151.
73. Jones, *Parliamentary Elections*, p. 151.
74. Jones, *Parliamentary Elections*, p. 150
75. Johnes, *Wales since 1939*, p. 239.
76. Interview with DET, 28 September 2021.
77. Peter Stead, *Coleg Harlech: The First Fifty Years* (University of Wales Press, 1977), p. 127.
78. Interview with DET, 28 September 2021.
79. *Daily Post*, 29 May 1972.
80. Interview with DET, 28 September 2021.
81. *Daily Post*, 29 May 1972.
82. Interview with Dafydd Wigley, 25 March 2022.
83. *Daily Post*, 19 July 1971.
84. Interview with Dafydd Wigley, 25 March 2022.
85. Interview with DET, 28 September 2021.
86. Interview with Dafydd Wigley, 25 March 2022.
87. Interview with DET, 28 September 2021.
88. Interview with DET, 28 September 2021.
89. Simon Thirsk, *Not Quite White* (Gomer Press, 2010), foreword, p. 9.
90. National Library of Wales, Plaid Cymru Archive, file A6, minutes of the National Council, 18 April 1970: Andrew Edwards, *Labour's Crisis: Plaid Cymru, the Conservatives, and the Decline of the Labour Party in North-West Wales, 1960–74* (University of Wales Press, 2011), p. 219.
91. Interview with Meirion Edwards, 14 July 2023.
92. Interview with Meirion Edwards, 14 July 2023.

Chapter 3

1. Andrew Edwards, *Labour's Crisis* (University of Wales Press, 2011), pp. 120–1, quoting Phil Williams, *Voice from the Valleys* (Plaid Cymru 1981), p. 71.
2. Edwards, *Labour's Crisis*, p. 123.
3. Edwards, *Labour's Crisis*, interview with Owen Edwards, secretary, Blaenau Ffestiniog Labour Party, p. 121.
4. *Y Ddraig Goch*, July 1970.
5. Edwards, *Labour's Crisis*, p. 215.
6. Edwards, *Labour's Crisis*, p. 121.
7. Beti Jones, *Parliamentary Elections in Wales* (Y Lolfa, 1975), pp. 113, 117.
8. Interview with DET, 29 September 2021.
9. Interview with Eleri Edwards, October 2023.
10. Meirionnydd Archives, Correspondence between Wil Edwards and John Cooke, TGWU officer, file Z/DEB/6/1/7, 30 November 1973.
11. Draft Correspondence between Wil Edwards and John Cooke, TGWU officer, Meirionnydd Archives, file Z/DEB/6/1/7.
12. Interview with Eleri Edwards, October 2023.
13. *Y Cymro*, 26 February 1974.

14. *Y Cymro*, 1 October 1974.
15. Interview with Ieuan Wyn Jones, 24 January 2024.
16. Interview with DET, 29 September 2021.
17. *North Wales Weekly News*, 24 January 1974.
18. Interview with Revd Dafydd Andrew Jones, 26 August 2022.
19. Interview with Revd Dafydd Andrew Jones, 26 August 2022.
20. *North Wales Weekly News*, 24 January 1974.
21. Interview with Elen Thomas, 1 March 2022.
22. Interview with DET, 29 September 2021.
23. Jones, *Parliamentary Elections in Wales*, p. 159.
24. Interview with DET, 29 September. 2021; George Thomas, the MP for Cardiff West, had been the Secretary of State for Wales, 1968–70, and would become Speaker of the House of Commons, 1976–83.
25. Interview with Elen Thomas, 1 March 2022.
26. Interview with DET, 29 September 2021.
27. Interview with Elen Thomas, 1 March 2022.
28. Interview with DET, 29 September 2021.
29. Gary Wilson, Constitutional reform in the UK: A note on the Legacy of the Kilbrandon Commission, *Liverpool Law Review*, vol. 38, pp. 339–54.
30. Hansard, House of Commons Debates, 14 March 1974, vol. 870, cc. 371–511.
31. Interview with DET, 29 September 2021.
32. Plaid Cymru, *Power for Wales: Plaid Cymru Election Manifesto* (Plaid Cymru, October 1974).
33. *Y Cymro*, 1 October 1974.
34. Edwards, *Labour's Crisis*, p. 227.
35. *Western Mail*, 4 October 1974.
36. *The Guardian*, 20 September 1974.
37. *The Guardian*, Obituary of Will Edwards, 5 September 2007.
38. Interview with DET, 29 September 2021.
39. Edwards, *Labour's Crisis*, p. 228.
40. Interview with DET, 29 September 2021.
41. Jones, *Parliamentary Elections in Wales*, p. 166.
42. Interview with Dafydd Wigley, 25 March 2022.
43. Interview with Dafydd Wigley, 25 March 2022.
44. Rhys Evans, *Gwynfor* (Y Lolfa, 2005), p. 358.
45. Pat Hannan, *When Arthur Met Maggie* (Seren 2006), p. 149.
46. D. Ben Rees, *Cofiant Cledwyn Hughes* (NLW, Cledwyn Hughes collection, letter 4 August, 1979), pp. 156–7.
47. Interview with Dafydd Wigley, 25 March 2022.
48. Interview with DET, 28 September 2021.
49. Interview with Dafydd Wigley, 25 March 2023.
50. Interview with Robert Griffiths, 18 March 2022.
51. Interview with Dafydd Wigley, 25 March 2022.
52. *Y Ddraig Goch*, December 1974–January 1975.
53. *Y Saeth*, 1, Spring 1976.

54. *Welsh Nation*, 18–24 October 1974.
55. Interview with Gwynn Matthews, 4 March 2022.
56. *Welsh Nation*, 27 June–3 July 1975.
57. *White Paper on Democracy and Devolution: proposals for Scotland and Wales* (Command paper 5732), September 1974.
58. *Wales and Devolution*, House of Commons Research Paper 97/60, 19 May 1997.
59. Interview with DET, 29 September 2021.
60. Interview with DET, 29 September 2021.
61. *Western Mail*, 2 June 1975.
62. Interview with DET, 29 September 2021.
63. Interview with Ieuan Wyn Jones, 24 January 2024.
64. *Daily Post*, 7 June 1975.
65. Rhys Evans, *Gwynfor* (Y Lolfa, 2005), p. 364.
66. *Western Mail*, 6 August, 30 October 1975.
67. *Daily Post*, 3 November 1975.
68. Dafydd Wigley, *Dal Ati* (Gwasg Gwynedd, 1993), p. 21.
69. Phil Williams, *Voice from the Valleys* (Plaid Cymru, 1981), pp. 94–5.
70. *Western Mail*, 1 July 1976; Evans, *Gwynfor*, p. 374.
71. *Western Mail*, 9 July 1976.
72. *The Guardian*, 17 December 1976.
73. Lord Morris of Aberavon, *Fifty Years in Politics and the Law* (University of Wales Press, 2011), p. 122.
74. NLW, Plaid Cymru Papers, APC A 73, 12 March 1977.
75. *Daily Post*, 22 March 1977.
76. NLW, Cledwyn Hughes diaries, A1, 21 March 1977.
77. *Y Saeth*, March 1977.
78. Evans, *Gwynfor*, p. 383.
79. *Daily Post*, 28 October 1977.
80. The SNP Member of Parliament for East Dunbartonshire, 1974–9; MP for Moray, 1987–2001; Scottish Parliament member 1999–2006.
81. Interview with Dafydd Wigley, 25 March 2023.
82. *Western Mail*, 3 March 1978; Rees, *Cofiant Cledwyn Hughes*, pp. 151–2; Robert Harris, *The Making of Neil Kinnock* (Faber and Faber 1984), p. 105; Martin Westlake, *Kinnock: The Biography* (Little, Brown and Co, 2001), p. 127.
83. Interview with DET, 29 September 2021.
84. House of Commons Debate, 2 March 1978, col. 696.
85. House of Commons Debate, 9 March 1978.
86. Interview with Dafydd Wigley, 25 March 2022.
87. David Foulkes, 'An Analysis of the Wales Act 1978', in David Foulkes, J. Barry Jones and R. A. Wilford (eds), *The Welsh Veto: The Wales Act 1978 and the Referendum* (University of Wales Press, 1983), p. 94,
88. Evans, *Gwynfor*, p. 391.
89. *Western Mail*, 17 August 1978.
90. K. O. Morgan, *Callaghan* (Oxford University Press, 1997), pp. 627–38.

91. Account based on interviews with Dafydd Wigley, 25 March 2022 and DET, 29 September 2021.
92. Interviews with DET, 29 September 2021, and Dafydd Wigley, 25 March 2022.
93. *Financial Times*, 2 November 1978.
94. *Welsh Nation*, December 1978.
95. Martin Johnes, *Wales since 1939* (Manchester University Press, 2012), p. 297.
96. Andrew Edwards and Duncan Tanner, 'Defining or Dividing the Nation? Opinion Polls, Welsh Identity and Devolution, 1966–1979', *Contemporary Wales*, vol. 18, 2006, pp. 54–71, 66–7.
97. Evans, *Gwynfor*, p. 196.
98. Leighton Andrews, *Wales Says Yes* (Seren, 1999), p. 29.
99. John Davies, *Hanes Cymru* (Allen Lane, 1990), p. 652.
100. Davies, *Hanes Cymru*, p. 652.
101. Gwyn A. Williams, *When Was Wales?* (Penguin, 1985), p. 295.
102. *Y Faner*, 3 March 1979.
103. Morris, *Fifty Years*, p. 124.
104. Interview with DET, 29 September 2021.
105. Huw Williams, *Atgofion Oes Elystan* (Y Lolfa, 2012), p. 262.
106. Interview with DET, 29 September 2021.
107. *Western Mail*, 22 March 1979.
108. Interview with Dafydd Wigley, 25 March 2022; Evans, *Gwynfor*, p. 405.
109. Interview with DET, 29 September 2021.
110. Interview with Dafydd Wigley, 25 March 2022.
111. *Politicsresources.net* official website.
112. *Politicsresources.net* official website.
113. Interview with DET, 29 September 2021.

Chapter 4

1. *Plaid Cymru Report of the Commission of Inquiry* (Plaid Cymru, 1981). Its terms of reference were to: 'consider a report back on the position of Plaid Cymru following the referendum and elections of 1979, and on the steps that need to be taken to facilitate the attainment of Plaid's Cymru goals of securing self-government for Wales and securing for Wales the right to become a member of the United Nations'.
2. Robert Griffiths and Gareth Meils, *Sosialaeth i'r Cymry/Socialism for the Welsh* (Y Faner Goch, 1979).
3. Rhys Evans, *Gwynfor* (Y Lolfa, 2005), p. 414.
4. *Y Faner*, 7 August 1979.
5. Griffiths and Meils, *Socialism for the Welsh*, pp. 1, 2.
6. Interview with Robert Griffiths, 18 March 2022.
7. Interview with Elen Thomas, 1 March 2022.
8. Leader of the Greater London Council, 1981–6, when the council was abolished, then MP for Brent East (1987–2001), Mayor of London (2000–8).
9. Interview with DET, 4 October 2021.
10. Interview with DET, 4 October 2021..

11. BBC News, *Saving Labour? The secretive plot to oust Jeremy Corbyn* (retrieved 8 September 2016)
12. Interview with DET, 4 October 2021.
13. Labour MP for Lewisham West (February 1974–83),
14. Interview with DET, 4 October 2021.
15. Nicholas Crickhowell, *Westminster, Wales and Water* (University of Wales Press, 1999), p. 18.
16. *Western Mail*, 23 June 1979.
17. *Liverpool Daily Post*, 21 July 1979.
18. Evans, *Gwynfor*, pp. 416–17, 525.
19. NA, PRO BD 25/327, R. H. Jones letter to P. J. Hosegood, 16 July 1979.
20. NA, PRO BD 325/37, Nicholas Edwards letter to William Whitelaw.
21. *Western Mail*, 23 July 1979.
22. *Western Mail*, 14, 15 September 1979.
23. *Y Cymro*, 23 October 1979.
24. *Y Cymro*, 6 November 1979.
25. *Western Mail*, 21 October 1979.
26. *The Guardian*, 17 December 1979.
27. Llafur, the Welsh people's history society, influential in developing a school of labour historians, bringing together academics, trade unionists and political activists.
28. Interview with Kim Howells, 12 December 2023.
29. Bleddyn Penny, *Steel Voices; A History of the Port Talbot Steelworkers* (WordPress, January 2015), based on his PhD, Swansea University, 2016.
30. Wales TUC, *Wales at the Abyss* (Cardiff, 1981).
31. Martin Johnes, *Wales since 1939* (Manchester University Press, 2012), pp. 385–7.
32. *The Times*, 17 September 1981.
33. John Davies, Lord John Gifford and Tony Richards, *Political Policing in Wales* (Welsh Campaign for Civil and Political Liberties, 1984), p. 19; Phil Thomas, *Operation Fire* (Cardiff, 1980); Richard King, *Brittle with Relics* (Faber, 2022), p. 209.
34. Wyn Roberts, *Right from the Start: The Memoirs of Sir Wyn Roberts* (University of Wales Press, 2006), p. 129.
35. Evans, *Gwynfor*, p. 433.
36. Evans, *Gwynfor*, p. 434.
37. Interview with DET, 4 October 2021.
38. Alwyn Roberts, 'Some Political Implications of S4C' (*Transactions of the Cymmrodorion*, 1989, pp. 211–19.
39. NLW, DET interview with Rhys Evans, *Welsh Political Archives*.
40. NA, BD 25/331, memo from Trevor Hughes to Nicholas Edwards, 9 September 1980
41. Evans, *Gwynfor*, 'Notes on the meeting held at the Home Office, 10 September 1980', p. 447.
42. Evans, *Gwynfor*, 'Welsh Office papers on Welsh language broadcasting', p. 447.
43. Evans, *Gwynfor*, p. 448.

44. Evans, *Gwynfor*, citing *An Phoblacht*, 19 October 2000.
45. David Beresford, *Ten Men Dead* (HarperCollins, re-published paperback version, 1992), p. 35.
46. Interview with DET, 4 October 2021.
47. Interview with DET, 4 October 2021.
48. *Y Ddraig Goch*, October/November 1980.
49. Evans, *Gwynfor*, p. 137.
50. Evans, *Gwynfor*, p. 391.
51. Evans, *Gwynfor*, p. 413.
52. *Y Ddraig Goch*, December 1980.
53. Plaid Cymru, *Report of the Plaid Cymru Commission of Inquiry* (1981), p. iii, 14.
54. Emyr Wynn Williams, and Dafydd Elis Thomas, 'Commissioning National Liberation', *Bulletin of Scottish Politics*, 2 (1981), pp. 135–55.
55. Evans, *Gwynfor*, p. 451.
56. NLW, Gwynfor Evans Papers, File W, Dafydd Wigley letter to Gwynfor Evans, 15 April 1981.
57. Interview with Danny Morrison, 29 February 2024.
58. Interview with DET, 4 October 2021.
59. Interview with DET, 4 October 2021.
60. Tony Benn MP stood as the standard bearer of the left, for the deputy leadership of the Labour party against Denis Healey, in September 1981. He lost by a margin of 0.8 per cent.
61. *Western Mail*, 28 June 1981.
62. Interview with DET, 4 October 2021.
63. Laura McAllister, *Plaid Cymru: The Emergence of a Political Party* (Seren, 2001), pp. 56, 57.
64. Evans, *Gwynfor*, p. 454.
65. Emyr Wynn Williams and Dafydd Elis Thomas, 'Commissioning National liberation', p. 154.
66. Dafydd Wigley, *Dal Ati* (Gwasg Gwynedd, 1993), p. 142.
67. *Rebecca*, October 1981.
68. Wigley, *Dal Ati*, pp. 55, 145.
69. Phil Williams, *A Voice from the Valleys* (Plaid Cymru, 1981), p. 99.
70. Salzburg University, Leopold Kohr Papers, letter by Gwynfor Evans to Kohr, 8 November 1981.
71. The Hydro Group, a small right-wing faction established to combat the National Left's growing influence. It was disbanded in 1987; McAllister, *Plaid Cymru*, pp. 173, 177.
72. Interview with Ieuan Wyn Jones, 24 January 2024.
73. Interview with Alun Davies, 4 July 2023.
74. Interview with Alun Davies, 4 July 2023.
75. Results of by-elections in the 1979–83 Parliament, *http://by-elections.co.uk/gower1982*.
76. *Western Mail*, 20 October 1982.
77. McAllister, *Plaid Cymru*, p. 116.

78. Professor Gwyn Alf Williams (1925–95), Welsh historian, author and television presenter, a republican, socialist and member of Plaid Cymru and the National Left.
79. *Radical Wales*, October 1983.
80. *The Times*, 'Poll setback as SNP rifts widen', 8 June 1982, p. 2.
81. Evans, *Gwynfor*, p. 462.
82. Richard Wyn Jones, 'From Community Socialism to Quango Wales', *Planet*, 118 (1996), p. 59.
83. Jones, 'From Community Socialism to Quango Wales', p. 60.
84. John Osmond, *Police Conspiracy?* (Y Lolfa, 1984), p. 28.
85. Jones, 'From Community Socialism to Quango Wales', p. 62.
86. Review of D. Hywel Davies, *The Welsh Nationalist Party 1925–45*, *Radical Wales* (Winter 1983).
87. Review of D. Hywel Davies, *The Welsh Nationalist Party 1925–45*.
88. Wigley, *Dal Ati*, p. 195; *O Ddifri*, chapters nine and ten.
89. Interview with Ieuan Wyn Jones, 24 January 2024.
90. Victor Jara, Chilean folk singer and radical, murdered by the Pinochet regime in Chile in September 1973 after its coup against President Salvador Allende.
91. Interview with Dafydd Iwan, 22 September 2023.
92. Interview with Alun Davies, 4 July 2023.
93. *Daily Post*, 29 October 1984.
94. *Western Mail*, 29 October 1984.
95. *Western Mail*, 28, 29 October 1984.
96. Interview with Adam Price, 27 October 2022.
97. Hywel Francis, *History on our Side: Wales and the 1984/5 Miners' Strike* (Lawrence and Wishart, 2009).
98. Interview with Kim Howells, 12 December 2023.
99. Interview with Kim Howells, 12 December 2023.
100. Francis, *History on Our Side*, p. 69.
101. Interview with Elen Thomas, 1 March 2022.
102. Interview with Adam Price, 27 October 2022.
103. *Radical Wales*, August 1984.
104. Interview with DET, 4 October 2021.
105. Interview with Alun Davies, 4 July 2023.
106. *Marxism Today*, February 1985.
107. Francis, *History on our Side*, p. 50.
108. NLW, Gwynfor Evans Papers, file T (1994), letter to DET from Evans.
109. NLW, Gwynfor Evans Papers, file T (1994), letter from DET to Evans.
110. *Western Mail*, 25 September 1984.
111. Interview with Dafydd Elis Thomas, *Penderyn*, September 1984.
112. Interview with Dafydd Elis Thomas, *Penderyn*, September 1984.
113. *Western Mail*, 11 January 1985.
114. *Y Ddraig Goch*, February/March 1985.
115. NLW, Gwynfor Evans Papers, letter from DET to Evans, 15 February 1985.
116. *New Statesman*, 21 June 1985.

117. *Western Mail*, 15 January 1985.
118. David Reynolds and Dafydd Elis Thomas, 'Four years on', *Radical Wales*, 9 (Winter 1985), pp. 18–19.
119. *Radical Wales* (Winter 1988), p. 19.
120. Undated local newspaper cutting included in the pamphlet published to commemorate the Blaenau dispute, *Safwn gyda'n Gilydd/We Stand Together, Blaenau Ffestiniog 1985–1986: Saith mis ar y Llechen/Seven Months on the Slate*.
121. Interview with Tim Williams, 11 September 2022.
122. *The Guardian*, 6 February 1991
123. Interview with Marjorie Thompson, 12 July 2022.
124. Interview with Tim Williams, 11 September 2022.
125. *Nannau.wales*, Maes-y-bryner House details accessed 21 May 2024.
126. Ann Clwyd, *Rebel with a Cause* (Biteback Publishing, 2017), p. 140.
127. Interview with Marjorie Thompson, 12 July 2022.
128. *News of the World*, 30 October 1988.
129. Interview with Marjorie Thompson, 12 July 2022.
130. *Radical Wales* (Winter 1985).
131. *The Guardian*, March 3 1986.
132. Wigley, *Dal Ati*, p. 239.
133. *Barn*, November 2010, p. 30.
134. Interview with Emyr Williams, 27 May 2022.
135. *Western Mail*, 12 July 1985.
136. *Western Mail*, 27 October 1986.
137. *The Guardian*, 3 March 1986.
138. Interview with Emyr Williams, 27 May 2022.
139. NLW, Gwynfor Evans Papers, 1994, file E, letter Meredydd Evans to Gwynfor; *Western Mail* 5, 11 August 1986.
140. NLW, Dafydd Elis Thomas Papers, A3/41, letter from Gwynfor Evans to Dafydd Elis Thomas, 7 December 1987.
141. Interview with DET, 4 October 2021.
142. *Daily Post*, 28 January 1987.
143. *The Guardian*, 28 January 1987.
144. Interview with Ieuan Wyn Jones, 28 January 2024.
145. Carwyn Jones, First Minister of Wales, 2009–18.
146. Interview with Carwyn Jones, 1 November 2022.
147. Matthew Parris, *Great Parliamentary Scandals: Four Centuries of Calumny, Smear and Innuendo* (London, Robson Books), p. 277.
148. *Western Mail*, 6 July 1988. Interview with Ieuan Wyn Jones, 24 January 2024.
149. Plaid Cymru, *The Welsh Senate and the Regeneration of Wales* (Plaid Cymru, 1987).
150. Electoral Calculus website, Election Data 1987, accessed 20 May 2024.
151. Gwerfyl Arthur, worked as administrative secretary in the Plaid Cymru office, and became secretary of the Meirionnydd Nant Conwy constituency from 1993.
152. Interview with DET, 4 October 2021.

153. Bangor University Registry, Dafydd Elis Thomas student file, Report by Professor J. E. Caerwyn Williams, PhD, external examiner, 1987.
154. Interview with Emyr Williams, 27 May 2022.
155. NLW, Emyr Humphreys collection, letter Gwynfor Evans to Emyr Humphreys, AI/459, 4 March 1989.
156. NLW, Gwynfor Evans Papers (2002), Dafydd Wigley letter to Gwynfor, 6 November 1989.
157. *The Guardian*, 28 May 1988.
158. *Western Mail*, 6 July 1988.
159. *Western Mail*, 19 September 1988.
160. *Daily Post*, 5 October 1988.
161. *Western Mail*, 30 October 1988.
162. Interview with Karl Davies, 18 February 2023; McAllister, *Plaid Cymru*, p. 80.
163. Interview with Emyr Williams, 27 May 2022.
164. Interview with Tim Williams, 11 September 2022.
165. Interview with Ieuan Wyn Jones, 24 January 2024.
166. Interview with Karl Davies, 18 February 2023.
167. Interview with Marjorie Thompson, 12 July 2022.
168. Interview with Ieuan Wyn Jones, 24 January 2024.
169. Wikipedia, United Kingdom European Parliamentary Election results, 1979–99, accessed 31 May 2024.
170. Wigley, *Dal Ati*, pp. 306–7.
171. Wigley, *Dal Ati*, pp. 307–8.
172. Wigley, *Dal Ati*, p. 310.
173. Robin Blackburn, 'Raymond Williams and the Politics of the New Left', *New Left Review*, I/168 (March/April 1988), pp. 12–22.
174. Richard Wyn Jones, *Putting Wales First* (University of Wales Press, 2024), p. 287.
175. NLW, Dafydd Elis Thomas papers, C37, letter from Pedr ap Llwyd to Dafydd Elis Thomas, 9 November 1989.
176. NLW, Dafydd Elis Thomas Papers, C37, 8 November 1989, letter from Derfel Gruffydd to Dafydd Elis Thomas.
177. NLW, Dafydd Elis Thomas Papers, C37, letter to Derfel Gruffydd, 5 December 1989.
178. Interview with DET, 4 October 2021
179. Dafydd Elis Thomas private papers.
180. Interview with Ieuan Wyn Jones, 24 January 2024.
181. *The Guardian*, 6 February 1991.
182. *Wales on Sunday*, 17 June 1990.
183. S4C, *Y Byd ar Bedwar*, 7 January 1991.
184. Wigley, *Dal Ati*, p. 329.
185. Interview with Ieuan Wyn Jones, 24 January 2024.
186. *The Times*, 13 January 1991.
187. *Western Mail*, 4 February 1991.
188. *Western Mail*, 9 September 1991.
189. O. M. Roberts, *Oddeutu'r Tân*, Gwasg Gwynedd, 1994, p. 159

190. Interview with DET, 4 October 2021.
191. Politics Resources, Election 1992, 9 April 1992, retrieved 23 May 2024.
192. Bishopsgate Institute, Andrew Roth Parliamentary Profiles Archives, File 5/34, Dafydd Elis Thomas cuttings file.
193. *Daily Post*, 6 June 1992.
194. McAllister, *Plaid Cymru*, p. 83.
195. Interview with DET, 4 October 2021.

Chapter 5

1. Interview with DET, 6 October 2021.
2. *The Times*, 21 April 1992.
3. Interview with DET, 6 October 2021.
4. Dafydd Wigley, *Be Nesa!* (Gwasg Gwynedd, 2013), p. 130.
5. *Daily Post*, 6 June 1992.
6. Ieuan Wyn Jones, *O'r Cyrion i'r Canol* (Y Lolfa, 2021), pp. 66–7.
7. *The Times*, 28 May 1992.
8. *Western Mail*, 8 June 1992.
9. Interview with Gwerfyl Arthur, 17 March 2023.
10. Interview with Dyfrig Siencyn, 27 February 2022.
11. Interview with Selwyn Gruffudd, 21 April 2023.
12. Interview with Elen Tomos, 1 March 2022.
13. *Daily Post*, 6 June 1992.
14. J. Beverley Smith, *Llywelyn ap Gruffudd: Prince of Wales* (University of Wales Press, 2014).
15. *The London Gazette*, 23 September 1992, p. 15921.
16. Andrew Edwards, Duncan Tanner, Patrick Carlin, 'The Conservative Governments and the development of Welsh language Policy in the 1980s and 1990s', *Historical Journal*, 54/2 (2011), 545, https://doi.org/10.1017/S0018246X11000112.
17. Interview with Huw Onllwyn Jones, 6 March 2023.
18. Wyn Roberts, *Right from the Start* (University of Wales Press, 2006), pp. 220–1.
19. Interview with DET, 6 October 2021.
20. Interview with DET, 6 October 2021.
21. Edwards, Tanner, Carlin, 'The Conservative Governments and the development of Welsh language Policy in the 1980s and 1990s', *Historical Journal*, 54/2 (2011), 529–551, https://doi.org/10.1017/S0018246X11000112.
22. Interview with DET, 6 October 2021.
23. Interview with Marjorie Thompson, 12 July 2022.
24. Interview with DET, 6 October 2021.
25. Edwards, Tanner, Carlin, 'The Conservative Governments and the development of Welsh language Policy', p. 541.
26. Roberts, *Right from the Start*, pp. 235, 257; the members were Ron Jones, television executive, Eddie Rea, company director; Elan Closs Stephens, drama lecturer in University College, Aberystwyth; Peter Law, leader Blaenau Gwent council; the barrister Winston Roddick; Wynford Evans, chairman of the South

Wales Electricity Board; the broadcaster Euryn Ogwen Williams, and John Walter Jones, the civil servant who supported the Board.
27. Interview with Huw Onllwyn Jones, 6 March 2023.
28. Edwards, Tanner, Carlin, 'The Conservative Governments and the development of Welsh language Policy', p. 547.
29. John Elfed Jones, *Dyfroedd Dyfnion* (Y Lolfa, 2013), p. 142.
30. Roberts, *Right from the Start*, p. 270.
31. Roberts, *Right from the Start*, pp. 272–3
32. Roberts, *Right from the Start*, p. 273, diary entry 1 July 1993.
33. *Daily Post*, 1 March 1993.
34. Dafydd Wigley, *Dal Ati* (Gwasg Gwynedd, 1993), p. 389.
35. Interview with DET, 6 October 2021.
36. Roberts, *Right from the Start*, p. 273.
37. *Western Mail*, 2 August 1993.
38. *Western Mail*, Eisteddfod edition, August 1993.
39. John Redwood, Secretary of State for Wales, May 1993–June 1995, known as a right-wing Thatcherite,
40. *Western Mail*, 6 August 1993.
41. Welsh Language Board Annual Report, 1993–4; Gareth Roberts, author, Normal College Bangor; Meri Huws, lecturer, Caerleon College, Gwent; Gwerfyl Pierce Jones, Welsh Books Council; Geraint Thomas, deputy secretary Welsh Local Government Association; Medwin Hughes, lecturer, Trinity College Carmarthen; Gwilym Owen, director, Midland Bank; Gwyn Griffiths, solicitor, from Buckley, Flint; Eddie Rea, businessman and chair of the Institute of Directors; Ron Jones, owner of Agenda, the media company; Elan Closs Stephens, lecturer at Aberystwyth University; and four Welsh language learners, Patrick Thomas, rector of Brechfa, Godfrey Williams, managing director of Marcher Sound, Neil Caldwell, director of the Campaign for the Protection of Rural Wales, and Peter Law, Blaenau Gwent Council.
42. Roberts, *Right from the Start*, p. 288.
43. Interview with DET, 6 October 2021.
44. Kevin Morgan and Ellis Roberts, *The Democratic Deficit, A Guide to Quangoland* (University of Wales College, 1993).
45. Kevin Morgan and Geoff Mungham, *Redesigning Democracy* (Seren, 2000), p. 58.
46. Edwards, Tanner, Carlin, 'The Conservative Governments and the development of Welsh language Policy', p. 549.
47. Hywel Williams, *Guilty Men: Conservative Government 1992–97* (Aurum Press, 1998), p. 51.
48. Roberts, *Right from the Start*, p. 288.
49. Richard Wyn Jones, 'From Community Socialism to Quango Wales', *Planet*, 118 (1996), p. 67.
50. Interview with Rhodri Williams, 25 January 2023.
51. Interview with DET, 6 October 2021.
52. Lord Dafydd Elis-Thomas, *A Life for the Language* (BBC, 1994).

53. *Western Mail*, 5 August 1983.
54. Welsh Language Board Annual Report, 1998–9, p. 1.
55. Interview with Rhodri Williams, 25 January 2023.
56. Richard King, *Brittle with Relics: A History of Wales 1962–1997* (Faber, 2022), p. 427.
57. King, *Brittle with Relics*, p. 428.
58. Interview with DET, 6 October 2024.
59. Interview with Rhodri Williams, 25 January 2023.
60. Interview with DET, 6 October 2021.
61. Welsh Language Board Annual Report 1998–9 (Cardiff, 1999), p. 1.
62. Colin H. Williams, 'Cultural Rights and Democratisation: Legislative Devolution and the Enactment of the Official Status of Welsh in Wales', in I. Urrutia, J. P. Massia and X. Irujo (eds), *Cultural Rights and Democratisation* (Clermont-Ferrand: Institut Universitaire Varenne, 2015), p. 185
63. Leighton Andrews, *Wales Says Yes* (Seren 1999), p. 207.
64. *Wales on Sunday*, 13 February 2000; *Daily Post*, 20 July 1998.
65. Meibion Glyndŵr, who claimed responsibility for the arson campaign against second homes.
66. African National Congress.
67. Geraint Lovgreen a'r Enw Da, *Cân yr Arglwydd*, 1999.
68. Andrews, *Wales Says Yes*, p. 21.
69. Andrews, *Wales Says Yes*, p. 28.
70. Interview with Dafydd Wigley, 25 March 2022.
71. Andrews, *Wales Says Yes*, p. 204.
72. Andrews, *Wales Says Yes*, p. 99.
73. Interview with DET, 6 October 2021.
74. Interview with DET, 6 October 2021.
75. Interview with DET, 6 October 2021.
76. Interview with Dyfrig Siencyn, 27 February 2022.
77. Interview with DET, 6 October 2021.
78. *Daily Post*, 20 July 1998.

Chapter 6

1. Interview with Kim Howells, 12 December 2023.
2. Lee Waters, *The dog that wouldn't die: the fall and rise of devolution in the Wales Labour Party: 1979–1995* (Aberystwyth University dissertation, 1998).
3. Waters, *The dog that wouldn't die*, p. 2.
4. House of Commons Library, Research Paper 97/60, Wales and Devolution. May 1997, p. 37, 1995
5. Interview with Ron Davies, 18 August 2023.
6. *UK Election Statistics: 1918–2022, A Long Century of Elections*, House of Commons Library, p. 22. The 1992 General Election in Wales had Labour on 27 seats, Conservatives on 6, Plaid Cymru on 4, and the Liberal Democrats on 1.
7. Ron Davies, *Regeneration of the Valleys*, reproduced in Parliament for Wales Campaign (1994); 'Empowering the People: Response to the Labour Party's

Consultation Paper', *Sharing the Vision: The Powers and Structure of the Welsh Assembly* (Cardiff, PWC), p. 10.

8. Kevin Morgan and Geoff Mungham, *Redesigning Democracy* (Seren, 2000), p. 58.
9. Waters, *The dog that wouldn't die*, p. 39.
10. *Western Mail*, 20 September 1997.
11. Andrew Rawnsley, *Servants of the People; The Inside Story of New Labour* (Penguin, 2001), p. 239.
12. Rawnsley, *Servants of the People*, pp. 238–9.
13. Interview with Ron Davies, 18 August 2023.
14. Interview with Tim Williams, 11 September 2022.
15. Interview with DET, 12 October 2021.
16. Interview with Ron Davies, 18 August 2023.
17. Rawnsley, *Servants of the People*, p. 243.
18. Morgan and Mungham, *Redesigning Democracy*, p. 126.
19. Interview with DET, 12 October 2021.
20. Interview with DET, 12 October 2021.
21. Morgan and Mungham, *Redesigning Democracy*, p. 128; Paul Flynn, *Dragons led by Poodles: The Inside Story of a New Labour Stitch-up* (Politico's, 1999), pp. 29–31.
22. Flynn, *Dragons led by Poodles*, p. 31.
23. Interview with Ron Davies, 18 August 2023.
24. Martin Johnes, *Wales Since 1939* (Manchester University Press, 2012), pp. 417–18.
25. Electoral Commission, *National Assembly for Wales elections* (November 2003), pp. 110–15.
26. Interview with Dyfrig Siencyn, 27 February 2022.
27. Interview with Ieuan Wyn Jones, 24 January 2024.
28. Dafydd Wigley, *Maen i'r Wal* (Gwasg Gwynedd, 2001), p. 152.
29. Wigley *Maen i'r Wal*, p. 152.
30. Interview with DET, 12 October 2021.
31. Interview with Jane Hutt, 12 January 2024.
32. Interview with DET, 12 October 2021.
33. Interview with DET, 12 October 2021.
34. Interview with Nick Bourne, 5 September 2022.
35. Interview with Ron Davies, 18 August 2023.
36. BBC News, *UK Politics Stars Come Out for Wales*, 27 May 1999.
37. A speech by HRH The Prince of Wales at the opening of the National Assembly for Wales, Cardiff, 28 May 1999, royal.uk.
38. Huw Thomas, *Charles The King and Wales* (Parthian Books, 2023), pp. 237–8.
39. Thomas, *Charles The King and Wales*, p. 239.
40. Interview with Ron Davies, 18 August 2022.
41. Interview with Edwina Hart, 7 March 2022.

42. J. Barry Jones, 'Labour Pains', in J. Barry Jones and Denis Balsom, *The Road to the National Assembly for Wales* (Cardiff, University of Wales Press, 2000), p. 210, quoting Roy Hattersley.
43. Interview with DET, 12 October 2021.
44. Interview with DET, 12 October 2021.
45. Interview with DET, 12 October 2021.
46. The Barnett formula, named after Joel Barnett, Chief Secretary to the Treasury (1974–9), which calculates the yearly change to the block grant allocated to the devolved administrations.
47. Rhodri Morgan, *Rhodri* (University of Wales Press, 2017), p. 171.
48. Alastair Campbell, *Power and Responsibility 1999–2001*, vol. 3 (Arrow Books), p. 239.
49. Interview with DET, 12 October 2021.
50. John Osmond, *Devolution Monitoring*, July–Dec 1999 (Institute of Welsh Affairs, 1999).
51. Rawnsley, *Servants of the People*, p. 359.
52. Rawnsley, *Servants of the People*, p. 359.
53. National Archives (NA), PREM/49/1688 note from Jonathan Powell to Owen Barder, copied to Pat McFadden (political secretary) and Jeremy Heywood (Principal Private Secretary to the Prime Minister).
54. NA, PREM 49/1688, memo from Jim Gallagher to Jeremy Heywood and Owen Barder, copied to Pat McFadden – 18.35, 26 January 2000.
55. NA, PREM49/1688, memo *Objective One and Wales*, from Pat McFadden to Jim Gallagher, Jeremy Heywood, Owen Barder, 27 January 2000.
56. NA, PREM49/1688, Pat MacFadden to Jim Gallagher, Jeremy Haywood, Owen Barder, (27 January 2000).
57. Campbell, *Power and responsibility 1999–2001*, p. 239.
58. NA, PREM49/1688, Note from Paul Murphy to the Prime Minister, 4 February 2000.
59. Rawnsley, *Servants of the People*, p. 360.
60. *The Independent*, 9 February 2000.
61. *Western Mail*, 11 February 2000.
62. Interview with DET, 12 October 2021.
63. Morgan, *Rhodri*, p. 176,
64. Interview with DET, 12 October 2021.
65. Interview with Andrew Davies, 24 March 2022.
66. *The Guardian*, 10 February 2000.
67. National Assembly, Record of the Assembly, 9 February 2000.
68. Interview with Andrew Davies, 24 March 2022.
69. Rawnsley, *Servants of the People*, p. 360.
70. *The Guardian*, 10 February 2000.
71. *Western Mail*, 10 February 2000.
72. John Osmond, Devolution Relaunched, *Monitoring Devolution* (December 1999–March 2000), p. 2.
73. Interview with Edwina Hart, 7 March 2022.

74. Interview with Nick Bourne, 5 September 2022.
75. Interview with Marjorie Thompson, 12 July 2022.
76. *Harpers and Queen*, March 2000.
77. *Wales on Sunday*, 13 February 2000.
78. Emyr Price, *Fy Hanner Canrif I* (Y Lolfa, 2002), p. 80.
79. Pat Hannan, *When Arthur Met Maggie* (Seren, 2006), pp. 146, 147.
80. Interview with Edwina Hart, 7 March 2022.
81. Martin Shipton, Mark Drakeford feared Welsh Devolution would collapse, *Nation Cymru*, 14 September 2024.
82. Osmond, *Devolution Relaunched*, p. 24.
83. Martin Shipton, Mark Drakeford feared Welsh Devolution would collapse.
84. *Daily Post*, 6 May 2000.
85. Morgan, *Rhodri*, p. 212.
86. Morgan, *Rhodri*, p. 214.
87. Interview with Edwina Hart, 7 March 2022.
88. John Osmond, *Monitoring the National Assembly* (September–December 2000), pp. 14, 24.
89. John Osmond, 'Devolution Looks Ahead', *Monitoring the National Assembly* (May–August 2000), pp. 18–20.
90. Osmond, 'Devolution Looks Ahead', p. 15.
91. Osmond, 'Devolution Looks Ahead', p. 8.
92. Osmond, 'Devolution Looks Ahead', p. 16.
93. NA, PREM14/68, letter from Rhodri Morgan to Tony Blair, 16 November 2000.
94. NA, PREM14/68, note from Richard Eilspon to PM re Lord Elis-Thomas's accusations against Jon Shortridge, 20 November 2000.
95. Morgan, *Rhodri*, p. 194.
96. Morgan, *Rhodri*, p. 196.
97. John Osmond, A Period of de-Stabilisation, *Devolution Monitoring* (May–August 2001).
98. NA, PREM49/1689, Memo from Jonathan Tross to David Miliband, 10 October 2000.
99. Interview with DET, 12 October 2021.
100. John Osmond, 'Richard Commission Sets Agenda', *Devolution Monitoring* (March–June 2004), p. 1.
101. *Y Cyfnod*, 17 May 2002.
102. *Daily Post*, 10 April 2002.
103. Interview with Dafydd Andrew Jones, 26 August 2022.
104. Interview with Dafydd Andrew Jones, 26 August 2022
105. Lord Crickhowell, previously Nicholas Edwards, MP for Pembrokeshire, Secretary of State for Wales (1979–87), and director of Associated British Ports.
106. Dewi Prys Thomas (1916–85) was the first professor of architecture at the University of Wales, and the head of the Welsh School of Architecture, and had a profound influence on architecture and town planning in Wales.
107. Interview with DET, 12 October 2021.
108. *The Guardian*, 9 March 2008.

109. Trevor Fishlock, *Senedd* (Graffeg, 2010), p. 4.
110. Interview with Ivan Harbour, 27 June 2023.
111. Interview with DET, 12 October 2021.
112. Interview with Ivan Harbour, 23 June 2023.
113. Wigley, *Maen i'r Wal*, p. 207.
114. *The Times*, 30 October 2001.
115. *The Guardian*, 30 October 2001.
116. *Daily Mail*, 30 October 2001.
117. Morgan, *Rhodri*, p. 189.
118. Interview with DET, 12 October 2021.
119. *Western Mail*, 23 May 2001.
120. Interview with Ivan Harbour, 27 June 2023.
121. John Osmond, 'A Period of de-Stabilisation', *Monitoring the National Assembly Devolution* (May–August 2001), p. 12.
122. Interview with Ivan Harbour, 27 June 2023.
123. Interview with Edwina Hart, 7 March 2022.
124. Interview with DET, 12 October 2021.
125. Record of Assembly Proceedings, 1 July 2003.
126. Interview with DET, 12 October 2021.
127. Interview with Ivan Harbour, 27 June 2023.
128. Morgan, *Rhodri*, p. 241.
129. Interview with DET, 12 October, 2021.
130. Interview with Edwina Hart, 7 March 2022.
131. Fishlock, *Senedd*.
132. Interview with DET, 12 October 2021.
133. Leighton Andrews, http://Leightonandrews.typepad.com/Leightonandrewsam/2006/02/index.html.
134. Interview with DET, 12 October 2021.
135. 'An address by the Queen to the National Assembly for Wales' (March 2006), the Royal family website, https://www.royal.uk/opening-welsh-assembly-cardiff-1-march-2006 (accessed 8 July 2025).
136. Interview with DET, 12 October 2021.
137. Interview with Ivan Harbour, 27 June 2023.
138. Richard Wyn Jones and Roger Scully, *Wales says Yes Devolution and the 2011 Welsh Referendum* (University of Wales Press, 2012), p. 48.
139. John Osmond, *Monitoring Devolution – Consensus Politics born of Convenience* (Spring–December 2005).
140. Morgan, *Rhodri*, p. 275.
141. Betsan Powys, BBC Wales Politics, *Answering the Clwyd West Question*, 12 March 2013; *The National Assembly for Wales Elections 2003*, Electoral Commission, November 2003, pp. 110–15.
142. BBC News, 23 June 2006; Osmond, *Restructuring Devolution*, January–March 2006, p. 5.
143. Jones and Scully, *Wales Says Yes*, p. 51.
144. *South Wales Echo*, 22 May 2006.

145. BBC Wales News, *Attack on Assembly 'time-wasting'*, 22 May 2022.
146. Liberal Democrat Member of the Assembly for Cardiff Central, 1999–2011, Minister for Culture, Sport and the Welsh language (2000–3), Member of the House of Lords (2011–25).
147. Interview with Nick Bourne, 5 September 2022.
148. Interview with Caroline Turner, 11 December 2023.
149. BBC Wales News, *Elis-Thomas denies ousting clerk*, 4 September 2006; *Mystery over Marek 'resignation'*, 28 September 2006.
150. Interview with DET, 12 October 2021.
151. BBC Wales News, *Elis-Thomas denies ousting clerk*, 4 September 2006.
152. Martin Shipton, *Poor Man's Parliament* (Seren, 2011), p. 185.
153. BBC Wales Politics, *Marek steps down from committee*, 9 November 2006.
154. Shipton, *Poor Man's Parliament*, p. 185.
155. Shipton, *Poor Man's Parliament*, p. 198.
156. National Assembly for Wales, *2007 National Assembly Election Results* (July 2007), p. 78 of PDF.
157. Confidential source.
158. Interviews with DET 12 October 2021, and Ieuan Wyn Jones, 24 January 2024.
159. *One Wales: A progressive agenda for the government of Wales* (Welsh Assembly Government. 2007), p. 6.
160. Interview with Rhuanedd Richards, 6 May 2022.
161. Jones and Scully, *Wales Says Yes*, p. 82–3.
162. Shipton, *Poor Man's Parliament*, p. 208.
163. Shipton, *Poor Man's Parliament*, p. 220.
164. Shipton, *Poor Man's Parliament*, p. 229.
165. Shipton, *Poor Man's Parliament*, p. 221.
166. Shipton, *Poor Man's Parliament*, p. 228.
167. Shipton, *Poor Man's Parliament*, p. 256.
168. Gwenda Thomas, Assembly Member for Neath (1999–2016), Deputy Minister for Social Services (2007–11), Deputy Minister for Children and Social Services (2011–16).
169. Aled Eirug and Jane Williams, *The Impact of Devolution in Wales* (University of Wales Press, 2022), p. 15.
170. Jones and Scully, *Wales Says Yes*, p. 110.
171. Interview with Rhuanedd Richards, 6 May 2022.
172. Interview with Rhuanedd Richards, 6 May 2022.
173. Interview with DET, 13 October 2011.
174. Interview with Edwina Hart, 7 March 2022.
175. Interview with Tim Williams, 11 September 2022.

Chapter 7

1. Interview with Elin Llŷr, 15 December 2022.
2. Interview with Rhuanedd Richards, 6 May 2022.
3. BBC Wales News, *Ieuan Wyn Jones to stand down as Plaid Cymru leader*, 13 May 2011.

4. BBC Wales News, *Elis-Thomas calls Plaid's election strategy 'negative'*, 9 May 2011.
5. Interview with Elin Llŷr, 15 December 2022.
6. Interview with Rhuanedd Richards, 6 May 2022.
7. Interview with Elin Llŷr, 15 December 2022.
8. Interview with Ieuan Wyn Jones, 24 January 2024.
9. *Western Mail*, 22 February 2006.
10. Vaughan Roderick, *Pen ar y Bloc* (Y Lolfa, 2017), p. 270
11. Interview with DET, 13 October 2021.
12. Interview with Elin Llŷr, 15 December 2022.
13. Interview with Rhuanedd Richards, 6 May 2022.
14. Interview with Elin Llŷr, 15 December 2022.
15. Interview with DET, 13 October 2021.
16. Letter by Jocelyn Davies to Alun Ffred Jones, 18 July 2012.
17. Interview with DET, 13 October 2021.
18. Interview with Gwerfyl Arthur, 17 March 2023.
19. ITV Wales news, 26 July 2012.
20. Interview with Rhuanedd Richards, 6 May 2022.
21. Interview with Claire Howell, 12 July 2023.
22. Interview with Claire Howell, 12 July 2023.
23. Interview with Claire Howell, 12 July 2023.
24. *Western Mail*, 29 September 2012.
25. Interview with Leanne Wood, 11 July 2022.
26. Plaid Cymru document listing Dafydd Elis-Thomas's transgressions, in private hands.
27. Anonymous interview with an Assembly Member of the committee.
28. *Western Mail*, 2 June 2013.
29. Interview with anonymous Labour member of the committee, 13 September 2023.
30. BBC News Wales Politics, 13 March 2014.
31. *Western Mail*, 8 March 2014.
32. BBC News Wales Politics, 8 March 2014.
33. BBC News Wales Politics, *Dafydd Elis-Thomas fired from Plaid Cymru roles*, 13 Marcg 2914.
34. Interview with Leanne Wood, 11 July 2022.
35. BBC News, Wales Politics, *Dafydd Elis-Thomas fired from Plaid Cymru roles*, 13 March 2014.
36. BBC News Wales Politics, *Dafydd Elis-Thomas's sacking 'entirely appropriate'*, 16 March 2014.
37. *Western Mail*, 14 March 2014.
38. Interview with Leanne Wood, 11 July 2022.
39. *Western Mail*, 25 June 2015.
40. *Western Mail*, 7 June 2015.
41. *Western Mail*, 25 June 2015.
42. Interview with DET, 13 October 2021.
43. Interview with Elin Llŷr, 17 June 2022.

44. Interview with Claire Howell, 12 July 2023.
45. *Western Mail*, 25 June 2015.
46. Interview with Claire Howell, 12 July 2023.
47. Interview with Dafydd Trystan, 13 May 2022.
48. Robert Williams Parry, 'Y Gwrthodedig', *Cerddi'r Gaeaf* (Gwasg Gee, 1953; second edn), p. 50; trans. Bedwyr Lewis Jones, in R. Williams Parry, *Writers of Wales* (University of Wales Press, 1972), p. 72.
49. Interview with Robin Llywelyn, 28 April 2022.
50. Interview with Aled ap Dafydd, May 2023.
51. Interview with Sioned Roberts, 18 May 2022.
52. Interview with Dafydd Trystan, 13 May 2022.
53. Interview with Elin Llŷr, 15 December 2022.
54. Interview with Rhuanedd Richards, 6 May 2022.
55. Results and turnout at the 2016 National Assembly elections (Electoral Commission, 2016).
56. Interview with Aled ap Dafydd, May 2023.
57. BBC News Wales Politics, *Plaid's Lord Elis-Thomas endorses Labour PCC candidate*, 22 April 2016.
58. *Western Mail*.
59. Interview with Carwyn Jones, 1 November 2022.
60. Roderick, *Pen ar y Bloc*, p. 381.
61. Interview with DET, 13 October 2021.
62. Interview with Mark Drakeford, 17 July 2023.
63. Record of Proceedings, National Assembly for Wales, 18 May 2016.
64. Interview with DET, 13 October 2021.
65. Interview with Carwyn Jones, 1 November 2022.
66. This account is based on the recollections of Lord Dafydd Elis-Thomas, the minutes of this constituency meeting, and the account of a number of those present.
67. Interview with DET, 13 October 2021.
68. Interview with Dyfrig Siencyn, 27 February 2022.
69. BBC News, *Plaid Cymru AM Lord Dafydd Elis-Thomas quits party*, 14 October 2016.
70. Interview with Leanne Wood, 11 July 2022.
71. Interview with Gwerfyl Arthur, 17 March 2023.
72. Interview with Dyfrig Siencyn, 27 February 2022.
73. Interview with Robin Llywelyn, 28 April 2022.
74. Interview with Simon Brooks, 28 April 2022.
75. Interview with Rhuanedd Richards, 6 May 2022.
76. Interview with DET, 12 October 2021.
77. Interview with DET, 12 October 2021.
78. Interview with Carwyn Jones, 1 November 2022.
79. Interview with DET, 12 October 2021.
80. BBC News Wales politics, *Ex-Plaid leader Lord Elis-Thomas gets Labour Welsh Government job*, 3 November 2017.

81. Huw Thomas, *Charles The King and Wales* (Parthian, 2023), p. 254.
82. Interview with senior civil servant, 17 June 2022.
83. Interview with DET, 12 October 2021.
84. Interview with Terry Stevens, 11 May 2023.
85. Thomas, *Charles*, p. 255.
86. Geraint Talfan Davies, former Controller of BBC Wales, chair of the Arts Council of Wales 2003–6; Dai Smith, former head of programmes (English-language programmes), BBC Wales, chair of the Arts Council of Wales 2007–16; Phil George, former head of factual programming BBC Wales, chair of the Arts Council of Wales 2016–23.
87. Interview with Phil George, 27 July 2022.
88. Welsh Government, *Evaluation of the Wales Cultural Recovery Fund, 2020 to 2021* (June 2022).
89. Interview with Phil George, 27 July 2022.
90. Interview with DET, 12 October 2021.
91. Interview with DET, 12 October 2021.
92. Interview with Rhuanedd Richards, 6 May 2022.
93. Interview with DET, 12 October 2021.
94. Interview with DET, 12 October 2021.
95. Interview with Sioned Roberts, 18 May 2022.
96. Interview with Mark Drakeford, 17 July 2023.
97. Interview with DET, 12 October 2021.
98. BBC News Wales Politics, *Lord Dafydd Elis-Thomas vows not to stand in 2021 election*, 12 April 2020; BBC Radio Cymru, *Dewi Llwyd ar Fore Sul*, 12 April 2020.
99. BBC Radio Cymru, *Dewi Llwyd ar Fore Sul*, 12 April 2020.
100. Interview with DET, 13 October 2021.
101. Interview with DET, 13 October 2021.
102. *Radical Wales*, Winter 1983.
103. Interview with Ieuan Wyn Jones, 24 January 2024.
104. Interview with Edwina Hart, 7 March 2022.
105. Interview with Mark Drakeford, 17 July 2023.
106. Interview with Carwyn Jones, 1 November 2022.
107. Interview with Dafydd Wigley, 25 March 2022.
108. Interview with Dyfrig Siencyn, 27 February 2022.
109. Interview with Dyfed Edwards, 7 October 2023.
110. Interview with Leanne Wood, 11 July 2022.
111. Interview with Dafydd Iwan, 22 September 2022.
112. Interview with Rhuanedd Richards, 6 May 2022.
113. Interview with Dafydd Trystan, 13 May 2022.
114. Interview with Simon Brooks, 28 April 2022.
115. Rhun ap Iorwerth, Senedd Member for Ynys Môn (2013–), leader of Plaid Cymru (2023–).
116. ITV Wales News, *Ex-Senedd Presiding Officer Dafydd Elis-Thomas rejoins Plaid Cymru nearly seven years after quitting*, 18 August 2023.
117. The Plaid Cymru disciplinary panel's letter is in possession of the estate of DET.

Postscript

1. *Western Mail*, Senedd pays tribute to its 'founding father', 12 February 2025, p. 5.
2. *Western Mail*, Senedd pays tribute to its 'founding father', 12 February 2025, p. 5.
3. *Llygad y Dydd*, February 2025.
4. *Western Mail*, Senedd pays tribute to its 'founding father', 12 February 2025, p. 5.
5. Letter from Buffy Williams, chair of the Senedd Labour group, to Lady Mair Elis-Thomas, 13 February 2025.
6. Letter from Jeremy Miles to Lady Mair Elis-Thomas, undated.
7. Letter from Lisa Francis to Lady Mair Elis-Thomas, 7 March 2025.
8. Letter from Elfyn Llwyd to Lady Mair Elis-Thomas, 18 February 2025.
9. Letter from Vivienne Sugar to Lady Mair Elis-Thomas, 9 March 2025.
10. Press statement by the Arts Council of Wales, 7 February 2025.
11. Letter from Gerry Adams to Lady Mair Elis-Thomas, 18 February 2025.
12. Letter from King Charles to Lady Mair Elis-Thomas, 12 February 2025.
13. BBC Wales Online, 28 April 2006. The song is based on the seizure of the town from the diocese of St Asaph, by Llywelyn ap Gruffudd, the Prince of Wales, in 1276. It remained independent and controlled by Cistercian monks and consequently has its own coat of arms and flag.
14. *The Guardian*, Lord Dafydd Elis-Thomas obituary, 13 February 2025.
15. *The Times*, Lord Elis-Thomas obituary, 15 February 2025.
16. *Daily Telegraph*, Obituary of Lord Elis-Thomas, 12 February 2025.
17. Menna Elfyn poem, sent to the author, 3 April 2025.

Index

'04.05 ac ati' 33
79 Group SNP 112, 118

A
Aberfan 33
Aberystwyth 19, 27, 87
Aberystwyth students 25, 28
Aberystwyth University 32
Abse, Leo 77, 83, 86, 96
Adams, Gerry 139, 306
All-Wales Convention 246
Allaun, Frank 111
Anderson, Donald 77, 83
Andrews, Leighton 236, 262, 274
Annual Inter-college Eisteddfod 36
ap Dafydd, Aled 271, 274
ap Dafydd, Myrddin 12
ap Gwilym, Eurfyl 109, 150
ap Gwynfor, Mabon 259, 304
ap Iorwerth, Rhun 299, 300, 304, 307
ap Llwyd, Pedr 150-1, 286
Arfon 46-7, 50
arson campaign against second homes 102, 138
Arthur, Gwerfyl 142, 164, 278-9, 386, 388
Arts Council of Wales 184, 286, 306
AUEW (Amalgamated Engineering Union) 101

B
BBC 2, 7, 9, 14, 17, 20, 24, 33, 58, 98, 104, 169-70, 181, 184, 286, 290
BBC Annual lecture, *A Life for the Language* 179

Bailey, Christopher 76
Bain, Maggie 79
Bala 49, 64, 157, 172, 189, 228
Bala Presbyterian College 7
Bangor 9
Bangor University 4, 5, 19, 21-56, 169, 258-9
Bebb, Ambrose 121
Benn, Tony 88, 96, 321
Bennett, Elinor 121
Bennite left 113, 117
Best, Keith 141
Bethel Presbyterian chapel, Newcastle Emlyn 1, 8, 10
Betts, Clive 136
Big Issue Foundation 184
Blaen-Nant 126
Blaenau Ffestiniog 3, 4, 6, 9, 15, 48-9, 53, 55-7, 62, 70, 88, 90, 125-6, 130, 189, 235, 258, 271
Blaenplwyf television transmitter 82
Blair, Tony 89, 193, 196-7, 201, 206, 209-14, 216-17, 231
Board of Celtic Studies 37
Bowen, Delme 255
Bowen, Euros 21, 59
Bristol Channel Ship Repairs 76
British Steel Corporation 100
BSC Shotton steelworks 100
BSC Llanwern 100
BSC Port Talbot 100
Brown, Beca 300
Brown, Gordon 199, 209-11
Bush, Keith 123
Brookes, Beata 145, 149
Brooks, Simon 386-7, 389, 390, 413, 414

Butler, Rosemary 250
Butler, Steve 113

C
CADW 285, 289
Caernarfon 7, 41–2, 45, 47, 53, 58–9, 66, 89–90, 92, 115, 163, 184, 243, 259
Caernarfon 1979 General Election result 90
Caerphilly 38, 41, 60, 71, 90, 195, 204, 263
Callaghan, James 76, 78, 82–3, 86–7, 89, 230
Cambrian Coast railway 47, 54, 64
Cameron, David 260, 268
Campbell, Alastair 209
Carmarthen 1–3, 8, 38, 45, 59–60, 66, 81–2, 89, 110, 136, 188, 255
Carmarthen Plaid Cymru conference (1981) 112–16
Carrog 2, 7–8
Carron, Owen 110–11, 300
Campaign for Nuclear Disarmament 19, 92, 121, 132, 135, 153
Celtic Congress 111
Central Students Representative Council, University of Wales 35
CEWC (Council for Education and World Citizenship) 20
Charles, Prince of Wales 41–2, 205, 212, 237, 285, 306
Clark University, Massachusetts 153
Clowes, Carl 190
Clwyd 145, 148–9, 153, 178, 238, 246, 287
Clwyd, Ann 134
Coed-y-bryn primary school 2, 10
Coleg Harlech 20, 45, 48
Collet's bookshop 143
Colwyn Bay 16, 19, 40, 42, 114
Conservative party 56, 59, 62, 78, 84–5, 87, 89–90, 92, 96, 98, 118–19, 127, 140–1, 144, 147–8, 155, 161–2, 167–8, 175–7, 193–4, 196, 198, 203, 232, 248, 274, 280, 304

Conway 39–40, 44–5, 63, 68, 225
Conway, Lawrence 225
Cooke, John 48, 54–5
Cooke, Phil 113
Covenanters (Cyfamodwyr) 138, 144
Covid-19 pandemic 286–91, 303
Cox, Alun 300
Creative Wales 285
Crickhowell House 205, 229, 232
Crossbencher 47
Crymych 106
Culture Recovery Fund 287
Cunningham, George 79–80
Cwm Hermon 46
Cwt y Bugail slate quarry 235
Cymdeithas Meirionnydd 48–9
Cymdeithas Tai Gwynedd 68
Cymdeithas yr Iaith Gymraeg (Welsh Language Society) 19, 25–7, 76, 81–2, 100, 119, 139–40, 172, 174, 177, 179–82, 185, 198, 256
Cymric, Y 4–5, 24, 34
Cymru Fydd 56
Cymru, Lloegr a Llanrwst 308
'Cywyddwyr' 37

D
Dafis, Cynog 108, 174
Dan Sylw 33
Daniel, Sir Goronwy 105
Daniel, J. E. 121
Davidson, Jane 245
Davies, Alun 116–17, 122, 127
Davies, Sir Alun Talfan 98, 100
Davies, Ednyfed Hudson 41, 44, 68
Davies, Emlyn 24, 29
Davies, Geraint Talfan 100
Davies, Lord Gwilym Prys 170
Davies, Hywel 120
Davies, Ifor 77, 83
Davies, Jocelyn 245, 258, 333
Davies, John 85
Davies, Karl 146, 148
Davies, Ron 187, 194–200, 204, 230

INDEX

Davies, S. O. 4
Denbigh 19, 39, 44, 141, 148
Denbigh North Wales hospital 44, 57
Denmark 62
Department of Culture, Media and Sport 287-8
Devolution Bills 77
Devolution referendum campaign (1979) 83-7
Devolution referendum campaign (1997) 183, 186-8
Devolution referendum campaign (2011) 248-9
Diana, Princess of Wales 196
Dole, Emlyn 255
Dolgarrog Aluminium Works 7, 41
Doll's House (Henrik Ibsen) 6
Dolgellau 26, 28, 39, 45, 48-9, 55, 58, 65-6, 75, 94, 126, 151-2, 157, 162-3, 169, 190, 279, 295
Drakeford, Mark 219, 276-7, 283, 289, 293-4
Dwyfor Meirionnydd National Assembly election (2007) 243
Dwyfor Meirionnydd National Assembly election (2011) 249
Dwyfor Meirionnydd constituency party 250, 259, 266-7, 270-3, 278-9, 290
Dydd, Y 33
Dyfodol, Y 24, 29, 32-5

E

Eames, Marion 57
Eaves, Steve 181
Education First 166
Education Reform Act (1988) 168
Edwards, Brian Morgan 47, 68
Edwards, Cenwyn 27, 29, 31, 33, 35-6, 44, 169
Edwards Dyfed 255, 296
Edwards, Eleri 54, 56
Edwards, Jonathan, MP 255
Edwards, Meirion 51
Edwards, Nicholas (Secretary of State for Wales, Lord Crickhowell) 96, 103-5, 133, 136-7, 229
Edwards, Owen (BBC) 229
Edwards, Owen (Merioneth Labour secretary) 54
Edwards, W. J. 228
Edwards, William, MP 54-6, 58, 61, 142
Elfyn, Menna 309

Elis-Thomas, Lord Dafydd (also Dafydd Ellis Thomas (1946-64), Dafydd Elis Thomas (1964-92)
academic record 28
adopting nomenclature as Lord Elis-Thomas of Nant Conwy 165-6
announcement of retirement from the Senedd 290-1
appointment as chancellor, Bangor University 258-9
appointment of Paul Silk 226-7, 241-3
applying to Bangor University 21-2
appointment as chair of the Welsh Language Board 172-3
Assembly back-bencher 254-8
attitude towards:
 devolution 72-3, 77-8, 187-8
 devolution referendum (1979) 85-7
 European referendum (1975) 74-5
 gay rights 151
 independence 292
 Investiture 42
 National Left 156-7
 nationalism 71, 135, 157
 peace 122
 Plaid Cymru 111-12, 159
 role as Minister 284, 287-90
 role of Presiding Officer 202-4, 207-9
 second home arson campaign 189, 196, 139, 140

Elis-Thomas, Lord Dafydd (contd.)
attitude towards:
  Sinn Féin 190
  socialism 70, 92–4, 135
  Tryweryn 28–9, 49, 50
  Welsh language policy 182–3
Bangor University lecturer post 51
birth 1
Brussels dinner 263–4
building of the Senedd 228–38
Cân yr Arglwydd 185
chair of Plaid Cymru youth wing 41
change of mind about 2011 referendum 248–9
change of name from 'Ellis' to 'Elis' 26
children (Rolant, Meilyr and Cai) 57, 60, 94
commuting to London 60, 66
Conway election result 44
Covid-19 226–7, 241–2
criticism of Assembly members 239
criticism of Gwynfor Evans 107
criticism of Plaid Cymru early leaders 120–1
criticism of Archbishop Barry Morgan 246
criticism of R. S. Thomas 138, 144
death of Dafydd Elis-Thomas 303
death of W. E. Thomas 42–3
death of aunt Annie 44, 57
devolution referendum (1997) 183–91
divorce of Elen and Dafydd 151–2
doctoral research 36, 37, 142–3
early life 1, 2, 8, 10, 11
English in-migration 137–8
entering Parliament 82
explanation for leaving Plaid Cymru 278
family move to London 94; return to Dolgellau 126
Fermanagh and South Tyrone by-election 110–11
Ffestiniog slate dispute 131

Financial pressures 169, 170, 218
First engagement with politics 18, 19
Funeral service of Dafydd Elis-Thomas 307–8
his assessment of his Plaid Presidency 159
his assessment of his legacy 291
interview with Alun Michael 202
job applications (Clark University and Lampeter University) 153
joining CND 19
joining Coleg Harlech 45
joining Cymdeithas yr Iaith 37
joining the House of Lords 161–6
joining Plaid Cymru 19
Labour MP friendships 85, 86
leak of Gregynog event 261
LCOs (Legislative Competence Orders) 244–9
London Left 95
Llanrwst grammar school 15–18, 20
Maiden speech 61–3
marriage to Elen Thomas 45
marriage to Mair Parry-Jones 184
meeting with Rhodri Morgan before Michael no confidence vote 214–15
Minister for Culture, Tourism and Sport 283–90
Merioneth campaign (October 1974) 64–6
Merioneth political tradition 77
miners' strike (1984–5) 123–8, 130–1
Minister for Culture, Sport and Tourism 283–90
naming the Senedd 235–6
nomination as candidate for 2016 election 273
National Assembly House Committee 240–2
National Left 112–9
Newcastle Emlyn 14–15
no confidence vote in Alun Michael 206–17

INDEX

North Wales European election (1989) 144–9
obituaries for Elis-Thomas 306
opposing dual candidacy in the Government of Wales Bill (2006) 239
parents' wedding 8
Plaid Cymru candidate for Conway 39–41
Plaid Cymru central office list of his 'misdemeanours' 262
Plaid Cymru Assembly group's view on nomination for Presiding Officer (2007) 244
Plaid Cymru President leadership contest (1981) 112–15
Plaid Cymru President leadership contest (1984) 121–2
Plaid Cymru, resignation from 277–9, 281–2
Porthmadog Dwyfor-Meirionnydd constituency meeting (July 2015) 269–72
public roles held (1992–9) 184
public speaking skills 17, 19, 24
relationships with:
    Cledwyn Hughes 67, 78, 83
    Cymdeithas yr Iaith 81–2
    Dafydd Wigley *see* Wigley, Dafydd
    Gwynfor Evans 100, 104–5, 107
    John Morris 105
    Marjorie Thompson 133–5, 169
    Neil Kinnock 80–1
    Wyn Roberts 167–8
    Raymond Williams 113–14
    Will Edwards 54–6
    Conservatives 166–7
redistribution of Welsh language funding 180–1, 249–50
reflections on being a minister 290
refusal of Ministerial role 245
refusal to return for vote of no confidence 258–60
religious beliefs 151–2
renaming Crickhowell House 229
renting accommodation in London 68–9
resignation as Conway candidate 45
resignation from Plaid Cymru 277–80
right-wing capture of Plaid 143–4
Royal family 204–5, 236–7, 263, 297–8
role of Caroline Turner 240–1
row with party leaders 239–40
sacked from chairmanship of Assembly environment committee 266
selection as candidate for Merioneth Assembly election 189–91
selection as Merioneth candidate (1974) 46–8
sit-down protest at his degree ceremony 35
standing down as Presiding Officer 251, 253
standing down as candidate in Conway 45, 46
standing down as MP for Merioneth 154
standing down as President 155
standing for Plaid Cymru leadership (2012) 254–6
standing for Presiding officer role (2016) 275
standing for the National Assembly (1999) 189–91
student journalism 29–32
student politician 24, 33–5
talks with Carwyn Jones to join Labour Government 275–7
Talybont speech 136
trial of Welsh Socialist Republicans 119–20
tributes to him as MP 155–6, 158
tributes to him as Minister 289
TV early appearances 33
views of 1979 referendum campaign 115–17

Elis-Thomas, Lord Dafydd (contd.)
  Welsh Language Board 162, 166, 168–83
  Welsh language television channel campaign 136–48
  Will Edwards 74–6, 87, 193
  Welsh Office civil service 222–8
  wish to rejoin Plaid Cymru 299, 300–1
  'Yes for Wales' campaign (1997) 183, 186–8

Ellis, Nesta Wyn 11
Ellis, Tom Edward 56, 62, 73, 86, 299
Eryri (Snowdonia) National Park 189, 261, 282
European Economic Community/Common Market 74–5
European Objective One funding 208–9, 212
European referendum (2016) 267
Evans, Principal Charles 28
Evans, Fred 83
Evans, Garner, MP 19
Evans, Gwynfor 73–9, 81–4, 86–7, 89, 91–3, 100–10, 114–16, 118–19, 123, 127–9, 137–8, 144, 150, 294, 304
Evans, Ioan 83
Evans, Jill 261
Evans, Meredydd 138
Ewing, Winnie 60

F

Falklands war 132
Feld, Val 187
Fermanagh and South Tyrone byelection 110–11, 306
Festival of Britain 9
Ffenics 24, 32
Ffestiniog slate company dispute 131
Ffrancon, Ann 9, 10, 12–15, 44
First Minister 193, 219, 244, 247, 250, 254, 275–7, 283, 289, 292, 294, 307

First Secretary 210, 212–14, 216, 219
Flynn, Paul 200
Foot, Michael 63, 73, 74, 76–9, 82, 87, 89
Forecast 34
Francis, Hywel 124, 127, 187
Francis, Lisa 336
Free Wales Army 28
Future Landscapes Review 282

G

Gale, Anita 187
General and Municipal Union 112
General Election 1970, Conway constituency 44
Merioneth General Election result (February 1974) 58
Merioneth General Election result (October 1974) 65
George, Lloyd 299
George, Lady Megan Lloyd 18
George, Phil 286
German, Mike 240
Glanypwll crossing, Blaenau Ffestiniog 6
Goleuad, Y 3
Goodway, Russell 231
Government of Wales Bill (2006) 238, 245, 248–9
Graham, William 222
Great Mountain colliery 3, 4
Greater London Council 95, 117, 120, 127
Green movement 95, 149, 158
Greenham Common 121, 132, 134
Gregynog 261
Griffith, Moses 4
Griffiths, James 38
Griffiths, Lesley 258
Griffiths, Peter Hughes 82, 103
Griffiths, Robert 69, 93
Grist, Ian 196
Gruffydd, Derfel 151
Gruffydd, Geraint 5, 36

INDEX

Gruffydd, Llyr 259, 264
Grustensian, The 17
Gwaun-cae-Gurwen 126
Gwynedd Council 149, 162, 181, 255, 278, 295–6, 300
Gwyntoedd Croesion (J. O. Francis) 6
Gwyther, Christine 217

H

HTV 33, 44–5, 98–100, 169
Hadid, Zaha 229, 232
Hague, William 196, 204
Hain, Peter 186, 238–9
Halford, Alison 216
Hamilton, Archie 167
Harbour, Ivan 230, 232–7
Harlech, Lord 98
Hannan, Pat 219
Harrison, Walter 63, 66, 68, 73
Hart, Edwina 193, 206, 217, 219, 221, 230, 232–5, 230, 287, 293
Harvey, Robert 89
Hattersley, Roy 206
Hay on Wye Literary Festival 184
Heath, Edward 56, 85
Heath, Tony 130, 137
Heseltine, Michael 167
Hodges, Nick 120
Hoggart, Simon 231
Holland, Stuart, MP 96
Holyhead 6, 141, 147
Home Office 99, 103
Hooson, Lord Emlyn 161–2, 165
Hopkins Sir Anthony 189
House Committee of the National Assembly 240, 242
House of Commons accommodation 142
House of Commons Select Committee on Welsh Affairs 96, 175, 247
House of Lords 198–9, 202, 219, 227, 234, 263, 267–8, 281, 295, 300, 303, 308
Howard de Walden, Lord 6

Howell, Claire 260–1, 266, 268–9, 274
Howells, Geraint, MP 63, 148
Howells, Kim 100–1, 124–5, 127, 146
Hughes, Cledwyn, MP 19, 63, 67, 75, 78, 83, 105, 141
Hughes, David 117
Hughes, Glyn Tegai 19
Hughes, Gwenfron 58
Humphreys, Emyr 51
Humphreys, Rob 244
Hughes, Gwilym 29
Humphreys, Iwan 34
Hunt, David 162, 167, 170–4, 196, 203
Hurd, Douglas 139
Huws, Dafydd 137, 143
Huxley, Llew 47
'Hydro' group 116, 123

I

ICI works, Penrhyndeudraeth 65
Independent Broadcasting Authority 98, 104
Independent Labour Party 3, 4
Investiture of the Prince of Wales 27, 41, 43, 138
I'r Gad 41
Irish Republican prisoners' hunger strikes 106, 110–11, 119
Iwan, Dafydd 26–7, 33, 121–2, 139, 145–6, 148, 297

J

James, David Richard 1, 2
James, Mary Jane 1
James, Mary Gwenfil 1, 10, 14, 63
James, Hannah Ellen (Nel) 2
James, Tom 2, 8
James, Sarah Ann 2
James, Wynfford 82
Jenkins, Bethan 255
Jenkins, David 102
Jenkins, Emyr 105
Jobbins, Sion 181

Jones, A. E. (Cynan) 36
Jones, Alun Ffred 258, 270
Jones, Arfon 274
Jones, Bedwyr Lewis 57
Jones, Bob 99, 104
Jones, Carwyn 140, 248, 254, 275–7, 283–4, 287, 293, 295
Jones, Dafydd Andrew 11, 43–4, 228
Jones, David 20
Jones, Eifion Lloyd 146
Jones, Elin 244, 255–6, 263, 275, 303, 307
Jones, Geraint Stanley 169
Jones, Gwilym O. 16
Jones, Gwynoro 117
Jones, H. R. 48
Jones, Helen Mary 244
Jones, Huw 27
Jones, Huw Onllwyn 166, 170
Jones, Revd Idwal 9
Jones, Ieuan Wyn 56, 74, 116, 121, 140–2, 144, 147–8, 153–4, 202, 215, 240, 244–5, 253–5, 257, 263, 268, 292
Jones, J. E. 18, 27
Jones, John Elfed 170–1, 173
Jones, John Gwilym 5
Jones, John Walter 174
Jones, J. R. 152
Jones, Revd J. R. 2
Jones, Michael D. 108, 299
Jones, Richard Wyn 119, 120, 150, 176
Jones, Robert 12, 42
Jones, Tom 49, 50
Jones Parry, Sir Emyr 245–6
Joseph, Sir Keith 97

K
Kane, Vincent 188
Keep Wales Tidy 184
Kennedy, Charles 212
King Charles 306–7
Kohr, Leopold 115

Kilbrandon Commission on the Constitution 61, 79
Kinnock, Neil 74, 77, 80, 83, 137, 161, 194–5, 201
Komisarjevsky, Theodore 1

L
Labour Coordinating Committee 96
Lambert, David 208, 213, 220
Language Freedom Movement 166
Larsen, Cai 300
Law, Peter 216, 233
Le Pen, Jean-Marie 144
League of Nations Union 1
'Legislative Competence Orders' 238, 245–9
Letts, Quentin 231
Lewis, Robyn 47
Lewis, Saunders 25, 121, 179, 185, 270
Lewis, Tony 175
Liberals/Liberal Democrats 1, 19, 59, 82, 97, 118, 143–4, 197, 212, 222, 226, 244
'Lit and Deb' 14, 24
Livingstone, Ken 95, 111, 117, 127
Livsey, Richard 135, 197
Llafur 101
Llanarth 45
Llanbadarn Fynydd 2
Llanbedr, Royal Aircraft Establishment 65
Llanberis 29, 88, 285
Llandaff Cathedral 219, 307
Llanfachreth parish church 152
Llangefni 126
Llangollen International Eisteddfod 184
Llanrhian (Pembrokeshire) 102
Llanrwst 1, 6, 8–21, 39–40, 43, 103, 118, 165, 308
Llanuwchllyn 2, 48–9, 157, 228
Lloyd, David 96
Lloyd, Sir J. E. 5
Lloyd, John 208, 226

Llwyd, Alun 174
Llwyd, Dewi 290
Llwyd, Elfyn 16, 157-8, 163, 272, 305
Llyn Ffridd-y-Bwlch reservoir 3
Llŷr, Elin 253-7, 265, 267, 273
Llywelyn, Robin 270-1, 280, 307
Lol 27, 33
Lomax, Rachel 199, 200
Lord Lieutenant for South Glamorgan 307
Løvgreen, Geraint 185

M

MFM Marcher 184
Maastricht Treaty 172
McFadden, Pat 211
McShane, Frank 97
Maelor, Lord (T. W. Jones) 63
Maes y Bryner, Llanfachreth 133, 152, 164, 169
Maesteg 1
Maguire, Frank, MP 110
Mainwaring, Lynn 113
Major, John 164
Marek, John 240-3
Marxism Today 137
Maerdy 131
Masters, Adrian 299
Matthews, Gwyn 23-5, 31, 34-5, 39, 41, 44, 71
Mears, Cledan (Bishop of Bangor) 102
Meibion Glyndŵr 138, 152, 185
Meirionnydd Nant Conwy constituency 118, 150, 189, 190, 200-1, 249
Meirionnydd Nant Conwy constituency result (1987) 142
Meirionnydd Nant Conwy National Assembly election result (2007) 243
Mellish, Bob 63, 68, 73
Menai Vaults 36
MENCAP 149
Menter Cwm Gwendraeth 179
Mentrau Iaith 181

Meredith, David 100
Merioneth constituency 2, 7, 44, 46-8, 50, 53, 54-6, 58, 61, 64-5, 90, 118, 149, 165
Merioneth General Election results
  1974, February 58
  1974, October 66
  1979, March 89
Merioneth county council 54-6
Merioneth Labour party 54-6
Merthyr Tydfil 4, 33
Merthyr Vale lodge 125
Meyer, Sir Anthony 148
Michael, Alun 200-2, 204, 206, 208-20, 222, 293
Michael, Tal 262
Michaelston-le-Pit 214
Middlehurst, Tom 216
Miles, Gareth 92
Miles, Jeremy 304
Miliband, David 226
Millar, Darren 304
Millward, Tedi 42
Miners' strike (1984-5) 123-31
Monmouthshire 178
Morgan, Barry (former Archbishop of Wales) 246, 307
Morgan, Derec Llwyd 21, 33, 37
Morgan, Eluned 303, 307
Morgan, Elystan 33, 84, 86
Morgan, Geraint 19, 141, 148
Morgan, Kevin 210
Morgan, Rhodri 172, 193-4, 199, 201-2, 209, 212, 214, 216-17, 219, 220-1, 224-7, 229, 231-3, 238, 241-2, 244-5, 248, 250, 291-6, 298, 301
Morgan, Syd 123, 146
Morning Star 96
Morris, John, Secretary of State for Wales (1974-9) 77, 82, 85
Morris-Jones, Sir John 5
Morrison, Danny 111
Murphy, Paul 212
Murrell, Peter 260

N

National Assembly Environment committee 257, 263, 266
National Assembly Labour group 304
National Botanical Gardens 184
National Eisteddfod 9, 19, 20, 48, 82, 105, 138, 173-4, 180, 189
National Eisteddfod deputation 181
National Left 112-13, 115-18, 121, 123, 130, 136-7, 143, 146-7, 156, 291, 298
National Library of Wales 37, 45, 286, 289
National Museum 285, 289
National Trust 184, 189
National Union of Mineworkers (NUM) 88, 100-1, 123-6, 129, 130
National Union of Students 33-5
Neale, Gwyn 17
Nefyn 102
Newcastle Emlyn 1, 2, 8, 10-11, 24
Newtown 2, 261
North Wales European election result 149

O

Oakeley slate quarry 2, 3, 6
Ogwen, Euryn 33
Operation Fire 102
O'r Gazelle i'r Bel Fiw 31
Oriel Mostyn 184
Orwig, Dafydd 39, 40
Osmond, John 164
otter hunting 11
Outward Bound (Sutton Vane) 6
Owain Cyfeiliog Society 59
Owen, Emrys Bennett 46
Owen, Gerallt Llwyd 56
Owen, Gwilym 100

P

Pant y Bwlch, Newcastle Emlyn 1
Pantycelyn Hall, Aberystwyth 87, 140
Parliament for Wales campaign 18

Parliamentary Byelections
  Brecon and Radnor (1985) 135-6
  Caerphilly (1968) 38, 41, 60, 71
  Ceredigion (2000) 212
  Glasgow Govan (1968) 61, 146
  Glasgow Govan (1988) 146
  Gower (1982) 117-18
  Hamilton (1967) 60
  Pontypridd (1989) 146
  Rhondda West (1967) 38, 41, 60, 71
Parliamentary select committees 96-8
Parris, Matthew 231
Parry, Barbara 80
Parry, R. J. 20
Parry, Robert Williams 5, 21, 270
Parry-Jones, Mair 184
Patagonia 108
Penceunant, Betws y Coed 190
Penderyn 128
Penrhyn Quarry 41
Perkins, Max 100
Phillips, Dewi Z. 152
Pierhead building 235
Pinaclau Pop 41
Plaid Cymru annual conferences
  Bedwas (1987) 143
  Carmarthen (1981) 112-16
  Lampeter (1984) 121
  Porthmadog (1991) 156
Plaid Cymru Assembly group 257-8, 264, 266-7
Plaid Cymru Commission of Inquiry 108
Plaid Cymru Parliamentary group 117, 163
Plaid Cymru 'President's committee' 108
Plas Rhianfa 36
Plowden, Lady 98
pneumoconiosis compensation scheme 87-8
Pompidou Centre 230
Pontyberem 126
Porthmadog 156, 254, 258, 269, 271, 273, 277, 279

INDEX

Post Office 29, 30
Powell, Jonathan 210
Powell, Ray 129
Presbyterian church 2–4, 11–12, 42, 152
Presbyterian College, Aberystwyth 6
Presiding Officer 190-1, 193, 200–4, 207–9, 212–13, 216–17, 219, 222–6, 229, 233, 236–7, 240–1, 243–5, 249–53, 256, 275, 291–5, 298, 303, 306
Price, Adam 123, 126, 255, 275
Price, Chris, MP, chair Select Committee on Education 97
Price, Emyr 24, 27–9, 31, 33, 35–6, 70
Price Waterhouse Cooper 285
Prince of Wales, Charles 27, 41–3, 205, 237, 263
Prince of Wales Trust 184
Pugh, Alun 238
Pugh, Liz 271

Q

Quangos 150, 155, 175, 195
Queen Elizabeth II 41, 204, 236–7, 246, 256, 263
Queen's Speech 72, 83, 125
Question Time 153

R

Race, Reg, MP 96
Radical Wales 118, 135
Radio Bronco 29
Radnor Walk chapel 152
Ramblers' Association 184
Randerson, Jenny 240
Rawnsley, Andrew 197, 210
Real Effective Development Company 260
Redwood, John 174, 176, 196
Rees, Chris 26
Rees, Dewi 16
Rees, Gareth 113
Rees, George 101
Rees, Ioan Bowen 162
Reichel, Sir Harry 5
Reichel Hall of residence 21, 23, 29, 32, 34, 36
Reynolds, David 135
Richard, Ivor 226
Richard Commission Report 227
Richards, Hywel Wyn 308
Richards, Melville 34
Richards, Rhuanedd 245, 248–9, 253–4, 256, 259, 260–1, 269–70, 273, 281, 288, 297
Richards, Rod 204
Roberts, Alwyn 181, 320
Roberts, Elfed 47, 94, 143, 150–1
Roberts, Elwyn (Plaid general secretary) 20, 28–9, 38–9, 47
Roberts, Elwyn (Chief Constable of Merioneth) 28–9
Roberts, Emrys 92
Roberts, Enid Pierce 23
Roberts, Ernie 111
Roberts, Goronwy 20, 69
Roberts, Gwilym 16
Roberts, Michael 96
Roberts, O. M. 20, 156
Roberts, Owen 33
Roberts, Sioned Wyn 254, 271, 278–9, 289
Roberts, Wmffra 47
Roberts, Wyn 41, 44, 63, 92, 94, 96, 99, 104, 107, 161–2, 166–8, 170–1, 173–4, 176, 180–2, 203
Roddick, Winston 208, 213
Roderick, Caerwyn 63, 82
Rogers, John 47
Rogers, Richard (Partnership) 230–4
Rose, David 83
Rosser, David 77, 83
Rosser, Phylip 112
Roth, Andrew 158
Roundwood Park 110
Royal College of Nursing 92, 132, 135
Royal Society of Architects (Wales) 229, 231

RTZ 46
Ruddock, Joan 133
Russell, Bertrand 19
Russell, Maggie 306

S
Sain 68
Salmond, Alex 260
Sands, Bobby 110–11, 306
Saville Roberts, Liz 190, 279–81, 304, 307
Scargill, Arthur 123
Schiavone, Toni 140
Shurmer, Alun 244
Scotland Bill (1978) 79, 89
Scottish National Party 59, 60, 63, 67, 72–3, 75–6, 78–80, 87, 112, 118, 146, 260, 281, 288
Seion chapel, Llanrwst 1, 8–9, 11, 12, 14–15, 42
Senedd 42, 174, 193, 228, 235–7, 273, 301, 303–5, 307–9
SGRIN (Welsh film council) 184
Shipton, Martin 261
Short, Ted 75
Shortridge, Jon 200, 208, 213, 222–6, 240–1
Siencyn, Dyfrig 165, 189, 201, 272–3, 278–80, 295–6
Silk, Paul 226–7, 241–3
Sinn Féin 110–11, 139, 306
Sirs, Bill (general secretary of the Iron and Steel Trades Confederation) 101
Skates, Ken 287
Slate communities (Merioneth) 3, 9, 55, 88, 90, 131, 189
Smith, John 195
Social Democratic Party 111, 117
Socialism for the Welsh pamphlet 92–3
SOS Galw Gari Tryfan 9
South Glamorgan Health Authority 196

South Wales Police 120
St Mary's Church, Dolgellau 152
Steel, David 135
Stephens, Elan Closs 169
Stevens, Terry 284–5
Stone, Adrian 120
Suez crisis 1
Sugar, Vivienne 305
Swansea 2, 305
Swansea Teacher Training College 1
Swansea Year of Literature 184
Symonds, Idwal (Partnership) 232–3

T
Talfan, 2
Tal-y-bont (Conwy valley) 7, 8
Talybont (Ceredigion) 136
Talyweunydd 3
Taylor, David 274
Taylor Woodrow 234
Telynores Dwyryd 15
Thatcher, Denis 102
Thatcher, Margaret 89, 90, 96, 100, 106, 117, 120, 127, 148, 166–8, 176, 193, 195, 240
The Pretenders (Henrik Ibsen) 6
The Times 102
Theology Today 16
Theatr Bara Caws 184
Theatr Clwyd 287
Thomas, Cai 94
Thomas, Dewi-Prys 229
Thomas, Elen (née Williams) 12, 28, 45, 48, 50, 57–60, 92, 94, 126, 133, 135, 151–2
Thomas, Dyfrig 39
Thomas, Elin Mair 1, 8, 10, 13–16, 42, 44, 57, 172, 227–8
Thomas, George 58, 63
Thomas, Gwenda 247
Thomas, Huw 283
Thomas, Annie Thomas 1–3, 6–8, 10, 43–4, 57
Thomas, Ellis 2, 3, 4, 6

Thomas, Ellen and her children Ellen, Mary, Elizabeth and Peter 3, 4, 6
Thomas, Hannah Eirlys 1, 7, 8, 10, 11, 13–14, 43, 67
Thomas, Professor John Meurig 21
Thomas, Lord Martin 165
Thomas, Meilyr 94
Thomas, Owen John 92
Thomas, Percy (Architects) 230
Thomas, Lord Peter of Gwydir 165
Thomas, R. S. 138, 144
Thomas, Rhodri Glyn 244, 286
Thomas, Dr Roger 89
Thomas, Rolant Elis 57, 60, 94
Thomas, Simon 255, 263
Thomas, Terry 129
Thomas, Revd William Ellis 1, 2, 4–8, 10–12, 14, 16–18, 42–4
Thomas, Wyn 38
Thompson, George 63
Thompson, Marjorie 92, 132–5, 148, 151, 153, 163–4, 169, 217–18
Tilsley, Gareth 14
Tilsley, Revd Gwilym 9
Tomorrow's Wales 246
Torfaen 198
TGWU (Transport and General Workers' Union) 48, 54–6
Trawsfynydd nuclear power station 55, 65, 125–6, 189, 256
Trefriw 21, 43–4, 168, 228
Tretower Court 285
Trystan, Dafydd 266, 270, 272, 279, 298
Tryweryn (Capel Celyn) 25, 27–8, 49, 50, 100
TUC Wales 84, 100–2
Tumble 2–4
Turner, Caroline 240–1
Twrgwyn Calvinist Methodist chapel 32
TWW 29, 30, 167
Tŷ Hywel 229, 230
Tynged yr Iaith 25

U
UCAC (Welsh language teachers' union) 92
Ulster Unionists 67, 82
Ulysses (James Joyce) 16
University of Wales, Lampeter 153
University of London, Institute of Education 94
Urdd Gobaith Cymru 11, 13, 17, 110, 180
Urdd Eisteddfod, Colwyn Bay (1974) 57

V
Vaughan, Elwyn 189

W
Wales Bill 76, 80
Wales Congress in Support of Mining Communities 127–8, 130, 193
Wales Governance Centre 220
Wales Tourist Board 175
Wales Trades Union Congress 74
Walker, Harold 88
Walker, Peter, MP 147, 167
Wardell, Gareth 175, 177
Webb, Harri 27
Welsh Combined Health Services Authority 205
Welsh Council of Churches 124
Welsh Culinary Team 184
Welsh Development Agency 76, 83, 149, 176
Welsh Grand Committee 105
Welsh Language Bill and Act (1993) 161, 166, 168, 171–3
Welsh Language Board 163, 166, 168, 170–84, 186, 189, 190, 198, 202, 227, 248, 282, 284, 298, 306
Welsh language Commissioner 248
Welsh Language Council 170
Welsh language television channel 76, 82, 83, 98–107

Welsh Local Government Bill 196
Welsh Nation 128
Welsh Office 60, 78, 99, 105, 145, 147, 162, 166–7, 171, 176–7, 186, 196, 199, 200, 207, 213, 222, 229
Welsh Socialist Republican Movement 92–3, 102–3, 119, 120
Western Mail 64, 77, 83, 117, 122, 136, 145, 155, 174, 261, 264, 268–9
Whitelaw, William 98–100, 104–6
Wigley, Dafydd
  arson campaign 139
  Caernarfon 53–4, 59, 66, 89, 90
  House of Commons 60, 63, 67–8, 75–6, 79, 81–2, 85, 88, 105
  House of Lords 162–4, 166, 300
  leadership contest 113–18, 122
  Merioneth 44, 46–7
  National Assembly 202–3, 211, 230, 251, 253, 255, 260–1, 285, 294–5,
  Plaid Cymru 92, 100, 103, 128
  relationship with Elis-Thomas 69, 71, 73, 83, 87, 110–1, 127, 149, 150, 153–4, 170, 172, 175, 296–7
  Ron Davies 186–7, 197
  SDP 135–6, 141, 144
Wigley, Lady Elinor 121, 307
Willesden, London 94, 110
Williams, Arthur Vaughan 11, 14
Williams, Brynmor 20
Williams, Dafydd 103, 129, 136, 164
Williams, Emlyn 123, 126
Williams, Emyr (Gari) 14
Williams, Emyr Wynn 109, 113, 137, 143, 146
Williams, Archbishop G. O. 105
Williams, Glyn 29

Williams, Gwyn A. 85, 118, 127, 141
Williams, Gwynn 34
Williams, Professor Ifor 5
Williams, Professor J. E. Caerwyn 142
Williams, Kirsty 276, 286
Williams, Meurwyn 151
Williams, Norman 41
Williams, Phil 41, 71, 75, 79, 85, 92, 108, 115, 137, 155
Williams, Raymond 113, 150, 157
Williams, Rhodri 82, 177, 180–2
Williams, Selwyn 16, 165
Williams, Tim 132–3, 147, 250
Williams, Tom Nefyn 4
Williams, Revd Thomas (Gwalchmai) 2
Williams, W. D. 2, 5, 7, 8
Williams, Waldo 307
Williams, William 3, 7
Williams, William Mathews 11
Wilson, Harold 17, 61, 203
Wilson, Joe 148–9
Wilson, Richard (Assembly project manager) 234
Wilson, Sir Richard 223–4
Winter Gardens Llandudno 13
Wood, Leanne 254–6, 258–69, 272, 274–7, 279–81, 296
Workers Education Association 48
Wylfa power station 125

Y

Y Ddraenen Wen (R. G. Berry) 6
Y Gwrthodedig 270
Y Saeth 70
Ynys Môn 80, 136, 141, 263

Dafydd Elis-Thomas, Lord Elis-Thomas of Nant Conwy, was one of the outstanding Welsh public figures of the last fifty years. His political career spanned from first election to Westminster in 1974 as a Plaid Cymru MP, to his retirement in 2021 from the Senedd in Cardiff, having served as a minister in the Welsh Government. He was the first Presiding Officer of the National Assembly for Wales, stabilising the new institution and embedding devolution during its first tentative decade, and following his death in 2025 he was described as a 'true giant' and the 'founding father' of Welsh devolution. Elis-Thomas was also a controversial and magnetic character, whose life and work is captured in this approved biography – branded a 'maverick', an 'intellectual acrobat' and a 'political chameleon', he was labelled a 'terrorist' for his interventions in Northern Ireland, and a 'traitor' for oppositional stances adopted towards nationalism. Despite a career often marked by controversy and fearless passion, his unique vision and perseverance was central to the creation of Wales's first legislative parliament.